The Next American Essay

LIBRARY

ANTIOCH UNIVERSITY
LOS ANGELES

Also by John D'Agata

Halls of Fame

THE
Next
American
Essay

Edited and Introduced by

JOHN D'AGATA

Graywolf Press
SAINT PAUL, MINNESOTA

"To the Reader," selection, and headnotes copyright © 2003 by John D'Agata

Publication of this volume is made possible in part by a grant provided by the Minnesota State Arts Board, through an appropriation by the Minnesota State Legislature, a grant from the Wells Fargo Foundation Minnesota, and a grant from the National Endowment for the Arts. Significant support has also been provided by the Bush Foundation; Marshall Field's Project Imagine with support from the Target Foundation; the McKnight Foundation; and other generous contributions from foundations, corporations, and individuals. To these organizations and individuals we offer our heartfelt thanks.

Published by Graywolf Press
2402 University Avenue, Suite 203
Saint Paul, Minnesota 55114
All rights reserved.

www.graywolfpress.org

Published in the United States of America

Printed in Canada

ISBN 978-1-55597-375-9

6 8 9 7 5

Library of Congress Control Number: 2002102977

Cover design: Christa Schoenbrodt, Studio Haus

Contents

These are the facts, my friends, and I have much faith in them.
Cicero

▼▲▼

What do I know?

MONTAIGNE

▼▲▼

So I shall essay myself to be.

EMERSON

▼▲▼

To the Reader

For your records: there are 19 men in here, 13 women. Twenty-nine are Americans; 1 is a Mexican; 1 is Canadian. There's a Native American, a Korean American, an African American, a Thai American. I'll bet you there are probably some gay people, too. There's someone who's 25, another who's 90. I know for a fact there are poor people included, as well as a few others who are relatively rich. Four are dead. I do not know how many are smokers, although some of them surely are. I do not know how many are drinkers, although some of them surely are. They have children, cancer, Pulitzers, fans, families in crisis, careers on the rise, homes in Idaho, Vermont, Kentucky, New York, California, Oaxaca, Key West; they have something in common beyond North America, besides the late twentieth century; they have debt, nerve, good hair, nightmares, cars that smell like McDonald's sometimes; they have first books, no books, 40 books, e-books—348 books in all, 4 of which are memoirs. I'm telling you this now, at the start of our journey, because I know you are expecting such facts from nonfiction. But henceforth please do not consider these "nonfictions." I want you preoccupied with art in this book, not with facts for the sake of facts. A fact comes from the Latin word *factum*—literally, "a thing done"—a neuter past participle construction that suggests a fact is merely something upon which action has happened. It's not even a word that can do its own work. From the same Latin root for fact we get the words "artifice," "counterfeit," "deficient,"

1

"façade," "infect," "misfeasance," and "superficial." "There are no facts," Emerson once wrote, "only art." Let's call this a collection of essays, then—a book about human wondering. It begins in 1974, an arbitrary date as far as dates go because it does not mark the start of the essay. It marks, instead, the start of my own wondering—the only story I have any authority to tell. According to the story my mother likes to tell, in 1974 she purchased something called "a baby phone." She would hook up its wide blue funnel to her belly, lift up a little pink handset to her face, and read . . . but not Mother Goose, not Shakespeare, not Greek myths, not Dickens, not Grimm tales or Chaucer or Hans Christian Andersen. Because this year is 1974, and my mother has just graduated from college, and her husband is not yet back from a war, the first thing she reads to me in the womb is news. There is Richard Nixon resigning and Patty Hearst revolting and Charles Lindbergh dying and *People* magazine debuting. There is a certain urgency, therefore, in the literature she reads me. I get Emerson, Cicero, *Ms.* magazine, Montaigne. I get now why I feel some essays in my blood. Or, I should say: I understand why Mom's story about why I love essays feels on its surface very true to me, even though its particular facts do not. I was an eight-week-old fetus when my mother first read to me. And as we now know, but did not know then, a fetus at eight weeks has developed its ears but not yet the ability to hear. What this means is that anything you read to a fetus will go in one ear, but not come out.

The Next American Essay

♦

PROLOGUE

And

A papyrus fragment of a gospel written in the first century shows us Jesus on the bank of the Jordan with people around him. The fragment is torn and hard to read.

In the first line Jesus is talking but we cannot make out what he's saying: too many letters are missing from too many words to conjecture a restoration. It's as if we were too far back to hear well.

We catch some words. He is saying something about putting things in a dark and secret place. He says something about weighing things that are weightless.

The people who can hear him are puzzled and look to each other, some with apologetic smiles, for help in understanding.

Then Jesus, also smiling, steps to the very edge of the river, as if to show them something. He leans over the river, one arm reaching out. His cupped hand is full of seeds. They had not noticed a handful of seeds before.

He throws the seeds into the river.

Trees, first as sprouts, then as seedlings, then as trees fully grown, grew in the river as quickly as one heartbeat follows another. And as soon as they were there they began to move downstream with the current, and were suddenly hung with fruit, quinces, figs, apples, and pears.

That is all that's on the fragment.

We follow awhile in our imagination: the people running to keep up with the trees, as in a dream. Did the trees sink into the river? Did they flow out of sight, around a bend?

—Guy Davenport

1975

This is not a special year. We are not fighting in this year a war in Vietnam. We are not worried in this year about the price of gas. We are not celebrating in this year the American bicentennial. Instead, in this year, we are "doing the hustle." We are on the moon, again, for the eighteenth time. And we are oblivious of a teenager in his college dorm in Cambridge, who is fiddling with his computer and slowly changing the world. In this year we are reading a new novel called *Ragtime*. We love it, say the critics, because it isn't quite a novel. It is history, biography, description, fact. It is, says the *Post,* "something else." Elsewhere, in this year, with much less hoopla, a writer named John McPhee is publishing his twelfth and thirteenth books in that genre known sometimes as "something else." Years before, in high school, he began by writing poetry, then in college wrote a novel, and afterward was hired to write scripts for live TV. He finally turned to "articles" in order to pay the bills. In this year, one of the books he publishes will be called by *Time* magazine "the best book ever written about bark canoes." The other—a collection of essays—will be completely ignored. Some of us, in this year, are born.

JOHN McPHEE

The Search for Marvin Gardens

Go. I roll the dice—a six and a two. Through the air I move my token, the flatiron, to Vermont Avenue, where dog packs range.

▼▲▼

The dogs are moving (some are limping) through ruins, rubble, fire damage, open garbage. Doorways are gone. Lath is visible in the crumbling walls of the buildings. The street sparkles with shattered glass. I have never seen, anywhere, so many broken windows. A sign—"Slow, Children at Play"—has been bent backward by an automobile. At the lighthouse, the dogs turn up Pacific and disappear. George Meade, Army engineer, built the lighthouse—brick upon brick, six hundred thousand bricks, to reach up high enough to throw a beam twenty miles over the sea. Meade, seven years later, saved the Union at Gettysburg.

▼▲▼

I buy Vermont Avenue for $100. My opponent is a tall, shadowy figure, across from me, but I know him well, and I know his game like a favorite tune. If he can, he will always go for the quick kill. And when it is foolish to go for the quick kill he will be foolish. On the whole, though, he is a master assessor of percentages. It is a mistake to underestimate him. His eleven carries his top hat to St. Charles Place, which he buys for $140.

▼▲▼

The sidewalks of St. Charles Place have been cracked to shards by through-growing weeds. There are no buildings. Mansions, hotels once stood here. A few street lamps now drop cones of light on broken glass and vacant space behind a chain-link fence that some great machine has in places bent

9

to the ground. Five plane trees—in full summer leaf, flecking the light—
are all that live on St. Charles Place.

▼▲▼

Block upon block, gradually, we are cancelling each other out—in the
blues, the lavenders, the oranges, the greens. My opponent follows a plan
of his own devising. I use the Hornblower & Weeks opening and the
Zuricher defense. The first game draws tight, will soon finish. In 1971, a
group of people in Racine, Wisconsin, played for seven hundred and sixty-
eight hours. A game begun a month later in Danville, California, lasted
eight hundred and twenty hours. These are official records, and they stun
us. We have been playing for eight minutes. It amazes us that Monopoly is
thought of as a long game. It is possible to play to a complete, absolute, and
final conclusion in less than fifteen minutes, all within the rules as written.
My opponent and I have done so thousands of times. No wonder we are
sitting across from each other now in this best-of-seven series for the international singles championship of the world.

▼▲▼

On Illinois Avenue, three men lean out from second-story windows. A girl
is coming down the street. She wears dungarees and a bright-red shirt, has
ample breasts and a Hadendoan Afro, a black halo, two feet in diameter.
Ice rattles in the glasses in the hands of the men.

"Hey, sister!"

"Come on up!"

She looks up, looks from one to another to the other, looks them flat in
the eye.

"What for?" she says, and she walks on.

▼▲▼

I buy Illinois for $240. It solidifies my chances, for I already own Kentucky
and Indiana. My opponent pales. If he had landed first on Illinois, the
game would have been over then and there, for he has houses built on
Boardwalk and Park Place, we share the railroads equally, and we have can-
celled each other everywhere else. We never trade.

▼▲▼

In 1852, R. B. Osborne, an immigrant Englishman, civil engineer, surveyed the route of a railroad line that would run from Camden to Absecon Island, in New Jersey, traversing the state from the Delaware River to the barrier beaches of the sea. He then sketched in the plan of a "bathing village" that would surround the eastern terminus of the line. His pen flew glibly, framing and naming spacious avenues parallel to the shore—Mediterranean, Baltic, Oriental, Ventnor—and narrower transsecting avenues: North Carolina, Pennsylvania, Vermont, Connecticut, States, Virginia, Tennessee, New York, Kentucky, Indiana, Illinois. The place as a whole had no name, so when he had completed the plan Osborne wrote in large letters over the ocean, "Atlantic City." No one ever challenged the name, or the names of Osborne's streets. Monopoly was invented in the early nineteen-thirties by Charles B. Darrow, but Darrow was only transliterating what Osborne had created. The railroads, crucial to any player, were the making of Atlantic City. After the rails were down, houses and hotels burgeoned from Mediterranean and Baltic to New York and Kentucky. Properties—building lots—sold for as little as six dollars apiece and as much as a thousand dollars. The original investors in the railroads and the real estate called themselves the Camden & Atlantic Land Company. Reverently, I repeat their names: Dwight Bell, William Coffin, John DaCosta, Daniel Deal, William Fleming, Andrew Hay, Joseph Porter, Jonathan Pitney, Samuel Richards—founders, fathers, forerunners, archetypical masters of the quick kill.

▼▲▼

My opponent and I are now in a deep situation of classical Monopoly. The torsion is almost perfect—Boardwalk and Park Place versus the brilliant reds. His cash position is weak, though, and if I escape him now he may fade. I land on Luxury Tax, contiguous to but in sanctuary from his power. I have four houses on Indiana. He lands there. He concedes.

▼▲▼

Indiana Avenue was the address of the Brighton Hotel, gone now. The Brighton was exclusive—a word that no longer has retail value in the city. If you arrived by automobile and tried to register at the Brighton, you were sent away. Brighton-class people came in private railroad cars. Brighton-class people had other private railroad cars for their horses—dawn rides on the firm sand at water's edge, skirts flying. Colonel Anthony J. Drexel

Biddle—the sort of name that would constrict throats in Philadelphia—
lived, much of the year, in the Brighton.

▼▲▼

Colonel Sanders' fried chicken is on Kentucky Avenue. So is Clifton's Club
Harlem, with the Sepia Revue and the Sepia Follies, featuring the Honey
Bees, the Fashions, and the Lords.

▼▲▼

My opponent and I, many years ago, played 2,428 games of Monopoly in a
single season. He was then a recent graduate of the Harvard Law School,
and he was working for a downtown firm, looking up law. Two people we
knew—one from Chase Manhattan, the other from Morgan, Stanley—
tried to get into the game, but after a few rounds we found that they were
not in the conversation and we sent them home. Monopoly should always
be *mano a mano* anyway. My opponent won 1,199 games, and so did I.
Thirty were ties. He was called into the Army, and we stopped just there.
Now, in Game 2 of the series, I go immediately to jail, and again to jail
while my opponent seines property. He is dumbfoundingly lucky. He wins
in twelve minutes.

▼▲▼

Visiting hours are daily, eleven to two; Sunday, eleven to one; evenings, six
to nine. "NO MINORS, NO FOOD, Immediate Family Only Allowed in Jail."
All this above a blue steel door in a blue cement wall in the windowless interior of the basement of the city hall. The desk sergeant sits opposite the
door to the jail. In a cigar box in front of him are pills in every color, a banquet of fruit salad an inch and a half deep—leapers, co-pilots, footballs,
truck drivers, peanuts, blue angels, yellow jackets, redbirds, rainbows. Near
the desk are two soldiers, waiting to go through the blue door. They are
about eighteen years old. One of them is trying hard to light a cigarette.
His wrists are in steel cuffs. A military policeman waits, too. He is a year or
so older than the soldiers, taller, studious in appearance, gentle, fat. On a
bench against a wall sits a good-looking girl in slacks. The blue door rattles,
swings heavily open. A turnkey stands in the doorway. "Don't you guys kill
yourselves back there now," says the sergeant to the soldiers.

"One kid, he overdosed himself about ten and a half hours ago," says the M.P.

The M.P., the soldiers, the turnkey, and the girl on the bench are white. The sergeant is black. "If you take off the handcuffs, take off the belts," says the sergeant to the M.P. "I don't want them hanging themselves back there." The door shuts and its tumblers move. When it opens again, five minutes later, a young white man in sandals and dungarees and a blue polo shirt emerges. His hair is in a ponytail. He has no beard. He grins at the good-looking girl. She rises, joins him. The sergeant hands him a manila envelope. From it he removes his belt and a small notebook. He borrows a pencil, makes an entry in the notebook. He is out of jail, free. What did he do? He offended Atlantic City in some way. He spent a night in the jail. In the nineteen-thirties, men visiting Atlantic City went to jail, directly to jail, did not pass Go, for appearing in topless bathing suits on the beach. A city statute requiring all men to wear full-length bathing suits was not seriously challenged until 1937, and the first year in which a man could legally go bare-chested on the beach was 1940.

▾▲▾

Game 3. After seventeen minutes, I am ready to begin construction on overpriced and sluggish Pacific, North Carolina, and Pennsylvania. Nothing else being open, opponent concedes.

▾▲▾

The physical profile of streets perpendicular to the shore is something like a playground slide. It begins in the high skyline of Boardwalk hotels, plummets into warrens of "side-avenue" motels, crosses Pacific, slopes through church missions, convalescent homes, burlesque houses, rooming houses, and liquor stores, crosses Atlantic, and runs level through the bombed-out ghetto as far—Baltic, Mediterranean—as the eye can see. North Carolina Avenue, for example, is flanked at its beach end by the Chalfonte and the Haddon Hall (908 rooms, air-conditioned), where, according to one biographer, John Philip Sousa (1854–1932) first played when he was twenty-two, insisting, even then, that everyone call him by his entire name. Behind these big hotels, motels—Barbizon, Catalina—crouch. Between Pacific and Atlantic is an occasional house from 1910—wooden porch, wooden mullions, old yellow paint—and two churches, a package store, a strip show, a dealer in fruits and vegetables. Then, beyond Atlantic Avenue, North Carolina moves on into the vast ghetto, the bulk of the city, and it looks like Metz in 1919, Cologne in 1944. Nothing has actually exploded. It is not bomb damage. It is deep and complex decay. Roofs are off. Bricks are scattered in the street. People sit on porches, six deep, at nine on a Monday morning. When they go off to wait in unemployment lines, they wait sometimes two hours. Between Mediterranean and Baltic runs a chain-link fence, enclosing rubble. A patrol car sits idling by the curb. In the back seat is a German shepherd. A sign on the fence says, "Beware of Bad Dogs."

Mediterranean and Baltic are the principal avenues of the ghetto. Dogs are everywhere. A pack of seven passes me. Block after block, there are three-story brick row houses. Whole segments of them are abandoned, a thousand broken windows. Some parts are intact, occupied. A mattress lies in the street, soaking in a pool of water. Wet stuffing is coming out of the mattress. A postman is having a rye and a beer in the Plantation Bar at nine-fifteen in the morning. I ask him idly if he knows where Marvin Gardens is. He does not. "HOOKED AND NEED HELP? CONTACT N.A.R.C.O." "REVIVAL NOW GOING ON, CONDUCTED BY REVEREND H. HENDERSON OF TEXAS." These are signboards on Mediterranean and Baltic. The second one is upside down and leans against a boarded-up window of the Faith Temple Church of God in Christ. There is an old peeling poster on a warehouse wall showing a figure in an electric chair. "The Black Panther Manifesto" is the title of the poster, and its message is, or was, that "the fascists have already decided in advance to murder Chairman Bobby Seale in the electric chair." I pass an old woman who carries a bucket. She wears blue sneakers, worn through. Her feet spill out. She wears red socks, rolled at the knees. A white handkerchief, spread over her head, is knotted at the corners. Does she know where Marvin Gardens is? "I sure don't know," she says, setting down the bucket. "I sure don't know. I've heard of it somewhere, but I just can't say where." I walk on, through a block of shattered glass. The glass crunches underfoot like coarse sand. I remember when I first came here—a long train ride from Trenton, long ago, games of poker in the train—to play basketball against Atlantic City. We were half black, they were all black. We scored forty points, they scored eighty, or something like it. What I remember most is that they had glass backboards—

glittering, pendent, expensive glass backboards, a rarity then in high schools, even in colleges, the only ones we played on all year.

I turn on Pennsylvania, and start back toward the sea. The windows of the Hotel Astoria, on Pennsylvania near Baltic, are boarded up. A sheet of unpainted plywood is the door, and in it is a triangular peephole that now frames an eye. The plywood door opens. A man answers my question. Rooms there are six, seven, and ten dollars a week. I thank him for the information and move on, emerging from the ghetto at the Catholic Daughters of America Women's Guest House, between Atlantic and Pacific. Between Pacific and the Boardwalk are the blinking vacancy signs of the Aristocrat and Colton Manor motels. Pennsylvania terminates at the Sheraton-Seaside—thirty-two dollars a day, ocean corner. I take a walk on the Boardwalk and into the Holiday Inn (twenty-three stories). A guest is registering. "You reserved for Wednesday, and this is Monday," the clerk tells him. "But that's all right. We have *plenty* of rooms." The clerk is very young, female, and has soft brown hair that hangs below her waist. Her superior kicks her.

He is a middle-aged man with red spiderwebs in his face. He is jacketed and tied. He takes her aside. "Don't say 'plenty,'" he says. "Say 'You are fortunate, sir. We have rooms available.'"

The face of the young woman turns sour. "We have all the rooms you need," she says to the customer, and, to her superior, "How's that?"

▾▲▾

Game 4. My opponent's luck has become abrasive. He has Boardwalk and Park Place, and has sealed the board.

▾▲▾

Darrow was a plumber. He was, specifically, a radiator repairman who lived in Germantown, Pennsylvania. His first Monopoly board was a sheet of linoleum. On it he placed houses and hotels that he had carved from blocks of wood. The game he thus invented was brilliantly conceived, for it was an uncannily exact reflection of the business milieu at large. In its depth, range, and subtlety, in its luck-skill ratio, in its sense of infrastructure and socio-economic parameters, in its philosophical characteristics, it reached to the profundity of the financial community. It was as scientific as the stock market. It suggested the manner and means through which an underdeveloped world had been developed. It was chess at Wall Street level. "Advance token to the nearest Railroad and pay owner twice the rental to which he is otherwise entitled. If Railroad is unowned, you may buy it from the Bank. Get out of Jail, free. Advance token to nearest utility. If unowned, you may buy it from Bank. If owned, throw dice and pay owner a total ten times the amount thrown. You are assessed for street repairs: $40 per house, $115 per hotel. Pay poor tax of $15. Go to Jail. Go directly to Jail. Do not pass Go. Do not collect $200."

▼▲▼

The turnkey opens the blue door. The turnkey is known to the inmates as Sidney K. Above his desk are ten closed-circuit-TV screens—assorted viewpoints of the jail. There are three cellblocks—men, women, juvenile boys. Six days is the average stay. Showers twice a week. The steel doors and the equipment that operates them were made in San Antonio. The prisoners sleep on bunks of butcher block. There are no mattresses. There are three prisoners to a cell. In winter, it is cold in here. Prisoners burn newspapers to keep warm. Cell corners are black with smudge. The jail is three years old. The men's block echoes with chatter. The man in the cell nearest Sidney K. is pacing. His shirt is covered with broad stains of blood. The block for juvenile boys is, by contrast, utterly silent—empty corridor, empty cells. There is only one prisoner. He is small and black and appears to be thirteen. He says he is sixteen and that he has been alone in here for three days.

"Why are you here? What did you do?"

"I hit a jitney driver."

▼▲▼

The series stands at three all. We have split the fifth and sixth games. We are scrambling for property. Around the board we fairly fly. We move so fast because we do our own banking and search our own deeds. My opponent grows tense.

▼▲▼

Ventnor Avenue, a street of delicatessens and doctors' offices, is leafy with plane trees and hydrangeas, the city flower. Water Works is on the mainland. The water comes over in submarine pipes. Electric Company gets power from across the state, on the Delaware River, in Deepwater. States Avenue, now a wasteland like St. Charles, once had gardens running down the middle of the street, a horse-drawn trolley, private homes. States Avenue was as exclusive as the Brighton. Only an apartment house, a small motel, and the All Wars Memorial Building—monadnocks spaced widely apart—stand along States Avenue now. Pawnshops, convalescent homes, and the Paradise Soul Saving Station are on Virginia Avenue. The soul-saving station is pink, orange, and yellow. In the windows flanking the door of the Virginia Money Loan Office are Nikons, Polaroids, Yashicas, Sony TVs, Underwood typewriters, Singer sewing machines, and pictures of Christ. On the far side of town, beside a single track and locked up most of the time, is the new railroad station, a small hut made of glazed fire-brick, all that is left of the lines that built the city. An authentic phrenologist works on New York Avenue close to Frank's Extra Dry Bar and a church where the sermon today is "Death in the Pot." The church is of pink brick, has blue and amber windows and two red doors. St. James Place, narrow and twisting, is lined with boarding houses that have wooden porches on each of three stories, suggesting a New Orleans made of salt-bleached pine. In a vacant lot on Tennessee is a white Ford station wagon stripped to the chassis. The windows are smashed. A plastic Clorox bottle sits on the driver's seat. The wind has pressed newspaper against the chain-link fence around the lot. Atlantic Avenue, the city's principal thoroughfare, could be seventeen American Main Streets placed end to end—discount vitamins and Vienna Corset shops, movie theatres, shoe stores, and funeral homes. The Boardwalk is made of yellow pine and Douglas fir, soaked in pentachlorophenol. Downbeach, it reaches far beyond the city. Signs everywhere—on windows, lampposts, trash baskets—proclaim "Bienvenue Canadiens!" The salt air is full of Canadian French. In the Claridge Hotel, on Park Place, I ask a clerk if she knows where Marvin Gardens is. She says, "Is it a floral shop?" I ask a cabdriver, parked outside. He says, "Never heard of it." Park Place is one block long, Pacific to Boardwalk. On the roof of the Claridge is the Solarium, the highest point in town—panoramic view of the ocean, the bay, the saltwater ghetto. I look down at the rooftops of the side-avenue motels and into swimming pools. There are hundreds of people around the rooftop pools, sunbathing, reading—many more people than are on the beach. Walls, windows, and a block of sky are all that is visible from these pools—no sand, no sea.

The pools are craters, and with the people around them they are counter-sunk into the motels.

▼▲▼

The seventh, and final, game is ten minutes old and I have hotels on Oriental, Vermont, and Connecticut. I have Tennessee and St. James. I have North Carolina and Pacific. I have Boardwalk, Atlantic, Ventnor, Illinois, Indiana. My fingers are forming a "V." I have mortgaged most of these properties in order to pay for others, and I have mortgaged the others to pay for the hotels. I have seven dollars. I will pay off the mortgages and build my reserves with income from the three hotels. My cash position may be low, but I feel like a rocket in an underground silo. Meanwhile, if I could just go to jail for a time I could pause there, wait there, until my opponent, in his inescapable rounds, pays the rates of my hotels. Jail, at times, is the strategic place to be. I roll boxcars from the Reading and move the flatiron to Community Chest. "Go to Jail. Go directly to Jail."

▼▲▼

The prisoners, of course, have no pens and no pencils. They take paper napkins, roll them tight as crayons, char the ends with matches, and write on the walls. The things they write are not entirely idiomatic; for example, "In God We Trust." All is in carbon. Time is required in the writing. "Only humanity could know of such pain." "God So Loved the World." "There is no greater pain than life itself." In the women's block now, there are six blacks, giggling, and a white asleep in red shoes. She is drunk. The others are pushers, prostitutes, an auto thief, a burglar caught with pistol in purse. A sixteen-year-old accused of murder was in here last week. These words are written on the wall of a now empty cell: "Laying here I see two bunks about six inches thick, not counting the one I'm laying on, which is hard as brick. No cushion for my back. No pillow for my head. Just a couple scratchy blankets which is best to use it's said. I wake up in the morning so shivery and cold, waiting and waiting till I am told the food is coming. It's on its way. It's not worth waiting for, but I eat it anyway. I know one thing when they set me free I'm gonna be good if it kills me."

▼▲▼

How many years must a game be played to produce an Anthony J. Drexel Biddle and chestnut geldings on the beach? About half a century was the original answer, from the first railroad to Biddle at his peak. Biddle, at his peak, hit an Atlantic City streetcar conductor with his fist, laid him out with one punch. This increased Biddle's legend. He did not go to jail. While John Philip Sousa led his band along the boardwalk playing "The Stars and Stripes Forever" and Jack Dempsey ran up and down in training for his fight with Gene Tunney, the city crossed the high curve of its parabola. Al Capone held conventions here—upstairs with his sleeves rolled, apportioning among his lieutenant governors the states of the Eastern seaboard. The natural history of an American resort proceeds from Indians to French Canadians via Biddles and Capones. French Canadians, whatever they may be at home, are Visigoths here. Bienvenue Visigoths!

▼▲▼

My opponent plods along incredibly well. He has got his fourth railroad, and patiently, unbelievably, he has picked up my potential winners until he has blocked me everywhere but Marvin Gardens. He has avoided, in the fifty-dollar zoning, my increasingly petty hotels. His cash flow swells. His railroads are costing me two hundred dollars a minute. He is building hotels on States, Virginia, and St. Charles. He has temporarily reversed the current. With the yellow monopolies and my blue monopolies, I could probably defeat his lavenders and his railroads. I have Atlantic and Ventnor. I need Marvin Gardens. My only hope is Marvin Gardens.

▼▲▼

There is a plaque at Boardwalk and Park Place, and on it in relief is the leonine profile of a man who looks like an officer in a metropolitan bank—"Charles B. Darrow, 1889–1967, inventor of the game of Monopoly." "Darrow," I address him, aloud. "Where is Marvin Gardens?" There is, of course, no answer. Bronze, impassive, Darrow looks south down the Boardwalk. "Mr. Darrow, please, where is Marvin Gardens?" Nothing. Not a sign. He just looks south down the Boardwalk.

▼▲▼

My opponent accepts the trophy with his natural ease, and I make, from notes, remarks that are even less graceful than his.

▼▲▼

Marvin Gardens is the one color-block Monopoly property that is not in Atlantic City. It is a suburb within a suburb, secluded. It is a planned compound of seventy-two handsome houses set on curvilinear private streets under yews and cedars, poplars and willows. The compound was built around 1920, in Margate, New Jersey, and consists of solid buildings of stucco, brick, and wood, with slate roofs, tile roofs, multi-mullioned porches, Giraldic towers, and Spanish grilles. Marvin Gardens, the ultimate outwash of Monopoly, is a citadel and sanctuary of the middle class. "We're heavily patrolled by police here. We don't take no chances. Me? I'm living here nine years. I paid seventeen thousand dollars and I've been offered thirty. Number one, I don't want to move. Number two, I don't need the money. I have four bedrooms, two and a half baths, front den, back den. No basement. The Atlantic is down there. Six feet down and you float. A lot of people have a hard time finding this place. People that lived in Atlantic City all their life don't know how to find it. They don't know where the hell they're going. They just know it's south, down the Boardwalk."

1976

Cicero was an essayist because he wrote with much at stake. Two-thousand twenty years before the Fall of this one, when 820 million yards of denim jeans are sold and CNN is launched and the Supreme Court decides to constitutionalize a state's rights to put its prisoners to death, Rome is in a flutter because Caesar has been murdered, the Republic's 3 most powerful men control 1/4 of the known world, and a 62-year-old man is giving speeches in the Forum, warning his fellow citizens against the evils of Empire. Rome is not yet an Empire. Rome is in a transition between "Republic" and "Empire." It is the kind of historic moment during which one is aware of its historic importance fully. There is, in other words, much at stake. The speeches that Cicero is giving now are the essays we love or hate him for. They are heavy purple dramas encrusted with golden ornaments. Each crashes toward its climax by way of a periodic sentence, a rhetorical device employed in speeches in order to keep an audience captive, hanging on every word, anticipating the main verb, held always till the end, like the punch line to a joke that's taking too long. No one in the ancient world did this better than Cicero. He didn't exactly invent the essay; he perfected it instead. An anonymous biographer describes for us in a second-century fragment the afternoon in 44 B.C. during which Cicero spoke to an audience of "over ten thousand men" for "three and a half hours" as they stood in wool tunics in the August Italian sun. There are some who even believe that the long contentious transition between the Republic and Empire wouldn't even have occurred if Cicero hadn't been around to stall the city's history. He was that good. He had much at stake. Cicero was literally trying to save the very world as he knew it. Even he, however, could not stall forever; every periodic must come to an end. And so, with assassinations in the Senate, the Roman army advancing, and the great orator's own health wavering with pneumonia, Cicero's political influence foundered. On a fall evening in 43 B.C. Marc Antony, having lost his patience, sent a gang of five men to Cicero's small Palatine home. They chased him out of the city, then killed him in the street. The next morning in the Forum Cicero's severed head could be found nailed to the public Rostrum, the famous lectern outisde the Senate where he delivered all his essays. It was a warning to Roman citizens that there indeed was much at stake. It is hard today to imagine writing any kind of essay without at least first acknowledging the seriousness of its roots. Therefore, in this year: Saul Bellow's *To Jerusalem and Back,* Ron Kovic's *Born on the Fourth of July,* and Maxine Hong Kingston's *The Woman Warrior.* Also, in this year, there is a first book by Barry Lopez, a young essayist who is trying to remedy the seriousness of the world around him by instilling it with fable, drama, wonder. He writes: "I know I can derive something useful from this world if I can get a reader to say, 'I am an adult, I have a family, I pay bills, I live in a world of chicanery and subterfuge and atomic weaponry and inhumanity and round-heeled politicians and garrulous, insipid television personalities, but still I have wonder.'"

BARRY LOPEZ

The Raven

I am going to have to start at the other end by telling you this: there are no crows in the desert. What appear to be crows are ravens. You must examine the crow, however, before you can understand the raven. To forget the crow completely, as some have tried to do, would be like trying to understand the one who stayed without talking to the one who left. It is important to make note of who has left the desert.

To begin with, the crow does nothing alone. He cannot abide silence and he is prone to stealing things, twigs and bits of straw, from the nests of his neighbors. It is a game with him. He enjoys tricks. If he cannot make up his mind the crow will take two or three wives, but this is not a game. The crow is very accommodating and he admires compulsiveness.

Crows will live in street trees in the residential areas of great cities. They will walk at night on the roofs of parked cars and peck at the grit; they will scrape the pinpoints of their talons across the steel and, with their necks outthrust, watch for frightened children listening in their beds.

Put all this to the raven: he will open his mouth as if to say something. Then he will look the other way and say nothing. Later, when you have forgotten, he will tell you he admires the crow.

The raven is larger than the crow and has a beard of black feathers at his throat. He is careful to kill only what he needs. Crows, on the other hand, will search out the great horned owl, kick and punch him awake, and then, for roosting too close to their nests, they will kill him. They will come out of the sky on a fat, hot afternoon and slam into the head of a dozing rabbit and go away laughing. They will tear out a whole row of planted corn and eat only a few kernels. They will defecate on scarecrows and go home and sleep with 200,000 of their friends in an atmosphere of congratulation. Again, it is only a game; this should not be taken to mean that they are evil.

There is however this: when too many crows come together on a roost there is a lot of shoving and noise and a white film begins to descend over the crows' eyes and they go blind. They fall from their perches and lie on the ground and starve to death. When confronted with this information, crows will look past you and warn you vacantly that it is easy to be misled.

The crow flies like a pigeon. The raven flies like a hawk. He is seen only at a great distance and then not very clearly. This is true of the crow too, but if you are very clever you can trap the crow. The only way to be sure what you have seen is a raven is to follow him until he dies of old age, and then examine the body.

Once there were many crows in the desert. I am told it was like this: you could sit back in the rocks and watch a pack of crows working over the carcass of a coyote. Some would eat, the others would try to squeeze out the vultures. The raven would never be seen. He would be at a distance, alone, perhaps eating a scorpion.

There was, at this time, a small alkaline water hole at the desert's edge. Its waters were bitter. No one but crows would drink there, although they drank sparingly, just one or two sips at a time. One day a raven warned someone about the dangers of drinking the bitter water and was overheard by a crow. When word of this passed among the crows they felt insulted. They jeered and raised insulting gestures to the ravens. They bullied each other into drinking the alkaline water until they had drunk the hole dry and gone blind.

The crows flew into canyon walls and dove straight into the ground at forty miles an hour and broke their necks. The worst of it was their cartwheeling across the desert floor, stiff wings outstretched, beaks agape, white eyes ballooning, surprising rattlesnakes hidden under sage bushes out of the noonday sun. The snakes awoke, struck and held. The wheeling birds strew them across the desert like sprung traps.

When all the crows were finally dead, the desert bacteria and fungi bored into them, burrowed through bone and muscle, through aqueous humor and feathers until they had reduced the stiff limbs of soft black to blue dust.

After that, there were no more crows in the desert. The few who watched from a distance took it as a sign and moved away.

Finally there is this: one morning four ravens sat at the edge of the desert waiting for the sun to rise. They had been there all night and the dew was like beads of quicksilver on their wings. Their eyes were closed and they were as still as the cracks in the desert floor.

The wind came off the snow-capped peaks to the north and ruffled their breath feathers. Their talons arched in the white earth and they smoothed their wings with sleek, dark bills. At first light their bodies swelled and their eyes flashed purple. When the dew dried on their wings they lifted off from the desert floor and flew away in four directions. Crows would never have had the patience for this.

If you want to know more about the raven: bury yourself in the desert so that you have a commanding view of the high basalt cliffs where he lives. Let only your eyes protrude. Do not blink—the movement will alert the raven to your continued presence. Wait until a generation of ravens has passed away. Of the new generation there will be at least one bird who will find you. He will see your eyes staring up out of the desert floor. The raven is cautious, but he is thorough. He will sense your peaceful intentions. Let him have the first word. Be careful: he will tell you he knows nothing.

If you do not have the time for this, scour the weathered desert shacks for some sign of the raven's body. Look under old mattresses and beneath loose floorboards. Look behind the walls. Sooner or later you will find a severed foot. It will be his and it will be well preserved.

Take it out in the sunlight and examine it closely. Notice that there are three fingers that face forward, and a fourth, the longest and like a thumb, that faces to the rear. The instrument will be black but no longer shiny, the back of it sheathed in armor plate and the underside padded like a wolf's foot.

At the end of each digit you will find a black, curved talon. You will see that the talons are not as sharp as you might have suspected. They are made to grasp and hold fast, not to puncture. They are more like the jaws of a trap than a fistful of ice picks. The subtle difference serves the raven well in the desert. He can weather a storm on a barren juniper limb; he can pick up and examine the crow's eye without breaking it.

1977

But we don't read Cicero anymore, do we? We read Seneca, instead. He's more personable, we say; less critical, we think. We do not read Confucius for this same reason, but Sei Shōnagon in his place. Not Bacon, but Montaigne. Not Emerson; Thoreau. "It is somewhat of a burden to be thought of as an essayist," Susan Sontag remarked in a *New York Times* interview, 1976. But we are no longer living in 1976. This is 1977, and Bing Crosby is dead, and Charlie Chaplin is dead, and Elvis Presley is dead. The last known case of smallpox is eradicated, *Star Wars* is in theaters, and one more year has been added to history, one more leap made from the past. "The distinctions between art and science are false and irrelevant," Sontag told us, in 1966, a decade ahead of herself.

SUSAN SONTAG

Unguided Tour

I took a trip to see the beautiful things. Change of scenery. Change of heart. And do you know?

What?

They're still there.

Ah, but they won't be there for long.

I know. That's why I went. To say good-bye. Whenever I travel, it's always to say good-bye.

Tile roofs, timbered balconies, fish in the bay, the copper clock, shawls drying on the rocks, the delicate odor of olives, sunsets behind the bridge, ochre stone. "Gardens, parks, forests, woods, canals, private lakes, with huts, villas, gates, garden seats, gazebos, alcoves, grottoes, hermitages, triumphal arches, chapels, temples, mosques, banqueting houses, rotundas, observatories, aviaries, greenhouses, icehouses, fountains, bridges, boats, cascades, baths." The Roman amphitheater, the Etruscan sarcophagus. The monument to the 1914–18 war dead in every village square. You don't see the military base. It's out of town, and not on the main road.

Omens. The cloister wall has sprung a long diagonal crack. The water level is rising. The marble saint's nose is no longer aquiline.

This spot. Some piety always brings me back to this spot. I think of all the people who were here. Their names scratched into the bottom of the fresco.

Vandals!

Yes. Their way of being here.

The proudest of human-made things dragged down to the condition of natural things. Last Judgment.

You can't lock up all the things in museums.

Aren't there any beautiful things in your own country?

No. Yes. Fewer.

Did you have guidebooks, maps, timetables, stout shoes?

I read the guidebooks when I got home. I wanted to stay with my—

Immediate impressions?

You could call them that.

But you did see the famous places. You didn't perversely neglect them.

I did see them. As conscientiously as I could while protecting my ignorance. I don't want to know more than I know, don't want to get more attached to them than I already am.

How did you know where to go?

By playing my memory like a roulette wheel.

Do you remember what you saw?

Not much.

It's too sad. I can't love the past that's trapped within my memory like a souvenir.

Object lessons. Grecian urns. A pepper-mill Eiffel Tower. Bismarck beer mug. Bay-of-Naples-with-Vesuvius scarf. David-by-Michelangelo cork tray.

No souvenirs, thanks. Let's stay with the real thing.

The past. Well, there's always something ineffable about the past, don't you think?

In all its original glory. The indispensable heritage of a woman of culture.

I agree. Like you, I don't consider devotion to the past a form of snobbery. Just one of the more disastrous forms of unrequited love.

I was being wry. I'm a fickle lover. It's not love that the past needs in order to survive, it's an absence of choices.

And armies of the well-off, immobilized by vanity, greed, fear of scandal, and the inefficiency and discomfort of travel. Women carrying parasols and pearl handbags, with mincing steps, long skirts, shy eyes. Mustached men in top hats, lustrous hair parted on the left side, garters holding up their silk socks. Seconded by footmen, cobblers, ragpickers, blacksmiths, buskers, printer's devils, chimney sweeps, lacemakers, midwives, carters, milkmaids, stonemasons, coachmen, turnkeys, and sacristans. As recently as that. All gone. The people. And their pomp and circumstance.

Is that what you think I went to see?

Not the people. But their places, their beautiful things. You said they were still there. The hut, the hermitage, the grotto, the park, the castle. An aviary in the Chinese style. His Lordship's estate. A delightful seclusion in the midst of his impenetrable woods.

I wasn't happy there.

What did you feel?

Regret that the trees were being cut down.

So you have a hazy vision of natural things. From too much indulgence in the nervous, metallic pleasures of cities.

Unequal to my passions, I fled the lakes, I fled the woods, I fled the fields pulsing with glowworms, I fled the aromatic mountains.

Provincial blahs. Something less solitary is what you need.

I used to say: Landscapes interest me only in relation to human beings. Ah, loving someone would give life to all this . . . But the emotions that human beings inspire in us also sadly resemble each other. The more that places, customs, the circumstances of adventures are changed, the more we see that we amidst them are unchanging. I know all the reactions I shall have. Know all the words that I am going to utter again.

You should have taken me along instead.

You mean him. Yes, of course I wasn't alone. But we quarreled most of the time. He plodding, I odious.

They say. They say a trip is a good time for repairing a damaged love.

Or else it's the worst. Feelings like shrapnel half worked out of the wound. Opinions. And competition of opinions. Desperate amatory exercises back at the hotel on golden summer afternoons. Room service.

How did you let it get that dreary? You were so hopeful.

Rubbish! Prisons and hospitals are swollen with hope. But not charter flights and luxury hotels.

But you were moved. Sometimes.

Maybe it was exhaustion. Sure I was. I am. The inside of my feelings is damp with tears.

And the outside?

Very dry. Well—as dry as is necessary. You can't imagine how tiring it is. That double-membraned organ of nostalgia, pumping the tears in. Pumping them out.

Qualities of depth and stamina.

And discrimination. When one can summon them.

▼▲▼

I'm bushed. They aren't all beautiful, the beautiful things. I've never seen so many squabby Cupids and clumsy Graces.

Here's a café. *In the café.* The village priest playing the pinball machine. Nineteen-year-old sailors with red pompons watching. Old gent with amber worry beads. Proprietor's granddaughter doing her homework at a deal table. Two hunters buying picture postcards of stags. He says: You can drink the acidic local wine, become a little less odious, unwind.

Monsieur René says it closes at five.

Each picture. "Each picture had beneath it a motto of some good intention. Seeing that I was looking carefully at these noble images, he said: 'Here everything is natural.' The figures were clothed like living men and women, though they were far more beautiful. Much light, much darkness, men and women who are and yet are not."

Worth a detour? Worth a trip! It's a remarkable collection. Still possessed its aura. The things positively importuned.

The baron's zeal in explaining. His courteous manner. He stayed all through the bombardment.

A necessary homogeneity. Or else some stark, specific event.

I want to go back to that antique store.

"The ogival arch of the doorway is Gothic, but the central nave and the flanking wings—"

You're hard to please.

Can't you imagine traveling not to accumulate pleasures but to make them rarer?

Satiety is not my problem. Nor is piety.

There's nothing left but to wait for our meals, like animals.

Are you catching a cold? Drink this.

I'm perfectly all right. I beg you, don't buy the catalogue. Or the postcard-size reproductions. Or the sailor sweater.

Don't be angry, but—did you tip Monsieur René?

Say to yourself fifty times a day: I am not a connoisseur, I am not a romantic wanderer, I am not a pilgrim.

You say it.

"A permanent part of mankind's spiritual goods."

Translate that for me. I forgot my phrase book.

▾▴▾

Still, you saw what you came to see.

The old victory of arrangement over accumulation.

But sometimes you were happy. Not just in spite of things.

Barefoot on the mosaic floor of the baptistery. Clambering above the flying buttresses. Irradiated by a Baroque monstrance shimmering indistinctly in the growing dusk of the cathedral. Effulgence of things. Voluminous. Resplendent. Unutterable bliss.

You send postcards on which you write "Bliss." Remember? You sent one to me.

I remember. Don't stop me. I'm flying. I'm prowling. Epiphany. Hot tears. Delirium. Don't stop me. I stroke my delirium like the balls of the comely waiter.

You want to make me jealous.

Don't stop me. His dainty skin, his saucy laughter, his way of whistling, the succulent dampness of his shirt. We went into a shed behind the restaurant. And I said: Enter, sir, this body. This body is your castle, your cabin, your hunting lodge, your villa, your carriage, your luxury liner, your drawing room, your kitchen, your speedboat, your tool shed . . .

Do you often do that sort of thing when he's around?

Him? He was napping at the hotel. A mild attack of heliophobia.

In the hotel. Back at the hotel, I woke him up. He had an erection. I seated myself on his loins. The nub, the hub, the fulcrum. Gravitational lines of force. In a world of perfect daylight. Indeed, a high-noon world, in which objects cast no shadows.

Only the half wise will despise these sensations.

I'm turning. I'm a huge steering wheel, unguided by any human hand. I'm turning . . .

And the other pleasures? The ones you came for.

"In the entire visible world there is hardly a more powerful mood-impression than that experienced within one of the Gothic cathedrals just as the sun is setting."

Pleasures of the eye. It had to be emphasized.

"The eye can see nothing beyond those glimmering figures that hover overhead to the west in stern, solemn rows as the burning evening sun falls across them."

Messengers of temporal and spiritual infinity.

"The sensation of fire permeates all, and the colors sing out, rejoicing and sobbing."

There, in truth, is a different world.

▼▲▼

I found a wonderful old Baedeker, with lots of things that aren't in the Michelin. *Let's*. Let's visit the caves. Unless they're closed.

Let's visit the World War I cemetery.

Let's watch the regatta.

This spot. He committed suicide right here, by the lake. With his fiancée. In 1811.

I seduced a waiter in the restaurant by the port two days ago. *He said.* He said his name was Arrigo.

I love you. And my heart is pounding.

So is mine.

What's important is that we're strolling in this arcade together.

That we're strolling. That we're looking. That it's beautiful.

Object lessons. Give me that suitcase, it's heavy.

One must be careful not to wonder if these pleasures are superior to last year's pleasures. They never are.

That must be the seduction of the past again. But just wait until now becomes then. You'll see how happy we were.

I'm not expecting to be happy. *Complaints.* I've already seen it. I'm sure it'll be full. It's too far. You're driving too fast, I can't see anything. Only two showings of the movie, at seven and at nine. There's a strike, I can't telephone. This damned siesta, nothing's open between one and four. If everything came out of this suitcase, I don't understand why I can't cram it all back in.

You'll soon stop fretting over these mingy impediments. You'll realize you're carefree, without obligations. And then the unease will start.

Like those upper-middle-class Protestant folk who experience revelations, become hysterical, suffer breakdowns under the disorienting impact of Mediterranean light and Mediterranean manners. You're still thinking about the waiter.

I said I love you, I trust you, I didn't mind.

You shouldn't. I don't want that kind of revelation. I don't want to satisfy my desire, I want to exasperate it. I want to resist the temptation of melancholy, my dear. If you only knew how much.

Then you must stop this flirtation with the past invented by poets and curators. We can forget about their old things. We can buy their postcards, eat their food, admire their sexual nonchalance. We can march in their workers' festivals and sing the "Internationale," for even we know the words.

I'm feeling perfectly all right.

I think it's safe to. Pick up hitchhikers, drink unbottled water, try to score some hash in the piazza, eat the mussels, leave the camera in the car, hang out in waterfront bars, trust the hotel concierge to make the reservation, don't you?

Something. Don't you want to do something?

Does every country have a tragic history except ours?

This spot. See? There's a commemorative plaque. Between the windows.

Ruined. Ruined by too many decades of intrepid appreciation. Nature, the whore, cooperates. The crags of the Dolomites made too pink by the sun, the water of the lagoon made too silver by the moon, the blue skies of Greece (or Sicily) made too deep a blue by the arch in a white wall.

Ruins. These are ruins left from the last war.

Antiquarian effrontery: our pretty dwelling.

It was a convent, built according to a plan drawn up by Michelangelo. Turned into a hotel in 1927. Don't expect the natives to take care of the beautiful things.

I don't.

They say. They say they're going to fill in the canal and make it a highway, sell the duchess's rococo chapel to a sheik in Kuwait, build a condominium on that bluff with a stand of pine, open a boutique in the fishing village, put a sound-and-light show in the ghetto. It's going fast. International Committee. Attempting to preserve. Under the patronage of His Excellency and the Honorable. Going fast. You'll have to run.

Will I have to run?

Then let them go. Life is not a race.

Or else it is.

Any more. Isn't it a pity they don't write out the menus in purple ink any more. That you can't put your shoes outside the hotel room at night.

Remember. Those outsize bills, the kind they had until the devaluation.

Last time. There weren't as many cars last time, were there?

▼▲▼

How could you stand it?

It was easier than it sounds. With an imagination like a pillar of fire. And a heart like a pillar of salt.

And you want to break the tie.

Right.

Lot's wife!

But his lover.

I told you. I told you, you should have taken me along instead.

▼▲▼

Lingering. In the basilica. In the garden behind the inn. In the spice market. In bed, in the middle of the golden afternoon.

Because. It's because of the fumes from the petrochemical factories nearby. It's because they don't have enough guards for the museums.

"Two groups of statuary, one depicting virtuous toil, the other unbridled licentiousness."

Do you realize how much prices have gone up? Appalling inflation. I can't conceive how people here manage. With rents almost as high as back home and salaries half.

"On the left of the main road, the Tomb of the Reliefs (the so-called Tomba Bella) is entered. On the walls round the niches and on the pillars, the favorite objects of the dead and domestic articles are reproduced in painted stucco relief: dogs, helmets, swords, leggings, shields, knapsacks and haversacks, bowls, a jug, a couch, pincers, a saw, knives, kitchen vessels and utensils, coils of rope, etc."

I'm sure. I'm sure she was a prostitute. Did you look at her shoes? I'm sure they're giving a concert in the cathedral tonight. *Plus they said.* Three stars, I'm sure they said it had three stars.

This spot. This is where they shot the scene in that movie.

Quite unspoiled. I'm amazed. I was expecting the worst.

They rent mules.

Of course. Every wage earner in the country gets five weeks' paid vacation.

The women age so quickly.

Nice. It's the second summer for the Ministry of Tourism's "Be Nice" campaign. This country where ruined marvels litter the ground.

It says. It says it's closed for restoration. It says you can't swim there any more.

Pollution.

They said.

I don't care. Come on in. The water's almost as warm as the Caribbean.

I want you, I feel you. Lick my neck. Slip off your trunks. Let me . . .

Let's. Let's go back to the hotel.

"The treatment of space in Mannerist architecture and painting shows this change from the 'closed' Renaissance world order to the 'open,' 'loose,' and deviating motions in the Mannerist universe."

What are you trying to tell me?

"The harmony, intelligibility, and coherence of the Renaissance world-view were inherent in the symmetrical courtyards of Italian palaces."

I don't want to flatter my intelligence with evidence.

If you don't want to look at the painting, look at me.

See the sign? You can't take the boat that way. We're getting near the nuclear-submarine base.

Reports. Five cases of cholera have been reported.

This piazza has been called a stage for heroes.

It gets much cooler at night. You have to wear a sweater.

Thanks to the music festival every summer. You should see this place in the winter. It's dead.

The trial is next week, so now they're having demonstrations. Can't you see the banner? And listen to that song.

Let's not. I'm sure it's a clip joint.

They said. Sharks, I think they said.

Not the hydrofoil. I know it's faster, but they make me sick.

▼▲▼

"The sun having mounted and the heat elsewhere too extreme for us, we have retired to the tree-shaded courtyard." It's not that I loved him. But in a certain hour of physical fatigue . . .

At the mercy of your moods.

Contented sometimes. Even blissful.

Doesn't sound like it. Sounds like struggling to savor.

Maybe. Loss of judgment in the necropolis.

Reports. There's a civil war raging in the north. The Liberation Front's leader is still in exile. Rumors that the dictator has had a stroke. But everything seems so—

Calm?

I guess . . . calm.

▾▲▾

This spot. On this spot they massacred three hundred students.

I'd better go with you. You'll have to bargain.

I'm starting to like the food. You get used to it after a while. Don't you?

In the oldest paintings there is a complete absence of chiaroscuro.

I feel well here. There's not so much to see.

"Below the molding, small leafy trees, from which hang wreaths, ribbons, and various objects, alternate with figures of men dancing. One man is lying on the ground, playing the double flute."

Cameras. The women don't like to be photographed.

We may need a guide.

It's a book on the treasures they unearthed. Pictures, bronzes, and lamps.

That's the prison where they torture political suspects. Terror incognita.

Covered with flies. That poor child. Did you see?

Omens. The power failure yesterday. New graffiti on the monument this morning. Tanks grinding along the boulevard at noon. *They say.* They say the radar at the airport has been out for the last seventy-two hours.

They say the dictator has recovered from his heart attack.

No, bottled water. Hardier folk. Quite different vegetation.

And the way they treat women here! Beasts of burden. Hauling those sacks up azure hills on which—

They're building a ski station.

They're phasing out the leprosarium.

Look at his face. He's trying to talk to you.

Of course we could live here, privileged as we are. It isn't our country. I don't even mind being robbed.

"The sun having mounted and the heat elsewhere too extreme for us, we have retired to the shade of an oasis."

▾▲▾

Sometimes I did love him. Still, in a certain hour of mental fatigue . . .

At the mercy of your moods.

My undaunted caresses. My churlish silences.

You were trying to mend an error.

I was trying to change my plight.

I told you, you should have taken me along instead.

It wouldn't have been different. I went on from there alone. I would have left you, too.

Mornings of departure. With everything prepared. Sun rising over the most majestic of bays (Naples, Rio, or Hong Kong).

But you could decide to stay. Make new arrangements. Would that make you feel free? Or would you feel you'd spurned something irreplaceable?

The whole world.

That's because it's later rather than earlier. "In the beginning, all the world was America."

How far from the beginning are we? When did we first start to feel the wound?

This staunchless wound, the great longing for another place. To make this place another.

In a mosque at Damietta stands a column that, if you lick it until your tongue bleeds, will cure you of restlessness. It must bleed.

A curious word, wanderlust. I'm ready to go.

I've already gone. Regretfully, exultantly. A prouder lyricism. It's not Paradise that's lost.

Advice. Move along, let's get cracking, don't hold me down, he travels fastest who travels alone. Let's get the show on the road. Get up, slugabed. I'm clearing out of here. Get your ass in gear. Sleep faster, we need the pillow.

She's racing, he's stalling.

If I go this fast, I won't see anything. If I slow down—

Everything.—then I won't have seen everything before it disappears.

Everywhere. I've been everywhere. I haven't been everywhere, but it's on my list.

Land's end. But there's water, O my heart. And salt on my tongue.

The end of the world. This is not the end of the world.

1978

Or: Maybe the essay is just a conditional form of literature—less a genre in its own right than an attitude that's assumed in the midst of another genre.

JAMAICA KINCAID

Girl

Wash the white clothes on Monday and put them on the stone heap; wash the color clothes on Tuesday and put them on the clothesline to dry; don't walk barehead in the hot sun; cook pumpkin fritters in very hot sweet oil; soak your little cloths right after you take them off; when buying cotton to make yourself a nice blouse, be sure that it doesn't have gum on it, because that way it won't hold up well after a wash; soak salt fish overnight before you cook it; is it true that you sing benna in Sunday school?; always eat your food in such a way that it won't turn someone else's stomach; on Sundays try to walk like a lady and not like the slut you are so bent on becoming; don't sing benna in Sunday school; you mustn't speak to wharf-rat boys, not even to give directions; don't eat fruits on the street—flies will follow you; *but I don't sing benna on Sundays at all and never in Sunday school*; this is how to sew on a button; this is how to make a buttonhole for the button you have just sewed on; this is how to hem a dress when you see the hem coming down and so to prevent yourself from looking like the slut I know you are so bent on becoming; this is how you iron your father's khaki shirt so that it doesn't have a crease; this is how you iron your father's khaki pants so that they don't have a crease; this is how you grow okra—far from the house, because okra tree harbors red ants; when you are growing dasheen, make sure it gets plenty of water or else it makes your throat itch when you are eating it; this is how you sweep a corner; this is how you sweep a whole house; this is how you sweep a yard; this is how you smile to someone you don't like too much; this is how you smile to someone you don't like at all; this is how you smile to someone you like completely; this is how you set a table for tea; this is how you set a table for dinner; this is how you set a table for dinner with an important guest; this is how you set a table for lunch; this is how you set a table for breakfast; this is how to behave in the presence of men who don't know you very well, and this way they won't recognize immediately the slut I have warned you against becoming; be sure to wash every day, even if it is with your own spit; don't squat down to play marbles—you are not a boy, you know; don't pick people's flowers—you might catch something; don't throw stones at blackbirds, because it might not be a blackbird at all; this is how to make a bread pudding; this is how to make doukona; this is how to make pepper pot; this is how to make a good medicine for a cold; this is how to make a good medicine to throw away a child before it even becomes a child; this is how to catch a fish; this is how to throw back a fish you don't like, and that way something bad won't fall on you; this is how to bully a man; this is how a man bullies you; this is how to love a man, and if this doesn't work there are other ways, and if they don't work don't feel too bad about giving up; this is how to spit up in the air if you feel like it, and this is how to move quick so that it doesn't fall on you; this is how to make ends meet; always squeeze bread to make sure it's fresh; *but what if the baker won't let me feel the bread?*; you mean to say that after all you are really going to be the kind of woman who the baker won't let near the bread?

1979

Now we are worried about gas. Now Three Mile Island. Now Afghanistan, now Iran, now Northern Ireland. Now my parents are divorced. In this year they are reading *The Executioner's Song* by Norman Mailer, a book Joan Didion calls in review "absolutely astonishing." But no one in this year will call Joan Didion's new book astonishing. Perhaps because it is a collection of essays that fail to function as essays should. "We tell ourselves stories in order to live" is the promising, famous first line in the collection's opening essay; "but writing has not helped me to see what it means" is the last. Between these two conflicting expressions is the arc along which we as readers hope, and finally droop. Allowing us to watch as she struggles to make sense of her subject—gathering interviews, compiling lists, stringing together data in sections numbered like an arrow aimed for bull's-eye—Didion involves us in her pursuit. When she fails, as she claims, to package the Sixties in an easily portable container for us, we fail, too. Or at least we feel more tangibly what was at stake in this pursuit. In the end those numbered sections stand stiffly like a skeleton guarding the essay's entrails. Its finely ordered structured, its neatly bulleted form, its taut and commanding syntax is not, in the end, mimetic of the essay's chaotic, amorphous, and phantasmagoric subject, but elegiac of it instead.

JOAN DIDION

The White Album

1

We tell ourselves stories in order to live. The princess is caged in the consulate. The man with the candy will lead the children into the sea. The naked woman on the ledge outside the window on the sixteenth floor is a victim of accidie, or the naked woman is an exhibitionist, and it would be "interesting" to know which. We tell ourselves that it makes some difference whether the naked woman is about commit a mortal sin or is about to register a political protest or is about to be, the Aristophanic view, snatched back to the human condition by the fireman in priest's clothing just visible in the window behind her, the one smiling at the telephoto lens. We look for the sermon in the suicide, for the social or moral lesson in the murder of five. We interpret what we see, select the most workable of the multiple choices. We live entirely, especially if we are writers, by the imposition of a narrative line upon disparate images, by the "ideas" with which we have learned to freeze the shifting phantasmagoria which is our actual experience.

Or at least we do for a while. I am talking here about a time when I began to doubt the premises of all the stories I had ever told myself, a common condition but one I found troubling. I suppose this period began around 1966 and continued until 1971. During those five years I appeared, on the face of it, a competent enough member of some community or another, a signer of contracts and Air Travel cards, a citizen: I wrote a couple of times a month for one magazine or another, published two books, worked on several motion pictures; participated in the paranoia of the time, in the raising of a small child, and in the entertainment of large numbers of people passing through my house; made gingham curtains for spare bedrooms, remembered to ask agents if any reduction of points would be *pari passu* with the financing studio, put lentils to soak on Saturday night for lentil soup on Sunday, made quarterly F. I.C.A. payments and renewed my driver's license on time, missing on the written examination only the question about the financial responsibility of California drivers. It was a time of my life when I was frequently "named." I was named godmother to children. I was named lecturer and panelist, colloquist and conferee. I was even named, in 1968, a *Los Angeles Times* "Woman of the Year," along with Mrs. Ronald Reagan, the Olympic swimmer Debbie Meyer, and ten other California women who seemed to keep in touch and do good works. I did no good works but I tried to keep in touch. I was responsible. I recognized my name when I saw it. Once in a while I even answered letters addressed to me, not exactly upon receipt but eventually, particularly if the letters had come from strangers. "During my absence from the country these past eighteen months," such replies would begin.

This was an adequate enough performance, as improvisations go. The only problem was that my entire education, everything I had ever been told or had told myself, insisted that the production was never meant to be improvised: I was supposed to have a script, and had mislaid it. I was supposed to hear cues, and no longer did. I was meant to know the plot, but all I knew was what I saw: flash pictures in variable sequence, images with no "meaning" beyond their temporary arrangement, not a movie but a cutting-room experience. In what would probably be the middle of my life I wanted still to believe in the narrative and in the narrative's intelligibility, but to know that one could change the sense with every cut was to begin to perceive the experience as rather more electrical than ethical.

During this period I spent what were for me the usual proportions of time in Los Angeles and New York and Sacramento. I spent what seemed to many people I knew an eccentric amount of time in Honolulu, the particular aspect of which lent me the illusion that I could at any minute order from room service a revisionist theory of my own history, garnished with a vanda orchid. I watched Robert Kennedy's funeral on a verandah at the Royal Hawaiian Hotel in Honolulu, and also the first reports from My Lai. I reread all of George Orwell on the Royal Hawaiian Beach, and I also read, in the papers that came one day late from the mainland, the story of Betty Lansdown Fouquet, a 26-year-old woman with faded blond hair who put her five-year-old daughter out to die on the center divider of Interstate 5 some miles south of the last Bakersfield exit. The child, whose fingers had to be pried loose from the Cyclone fence when she was rescued twelve hours later by the California Highway Patrol, reported that she had run after the car carrying her mother and stepfather and brother for "a long time." Certain of these images did not fit into any narrative I knew.

Another flash cut:

> *"In June of this year patient experienced an attack of vertigo, nausea, and a feeling that she was going to pass out. A thorough medical evaluation elicited no positive findings and she was placed on Elavil, Mg 20, tid. . . . The Rorschach record is interpreted as describing a personality in process of deterioration with abundant signs of failing defenses and increasing inability of the ego to mediate the world of reality and to cope with normal stress. . . . Emotionally, patient has alienated herself almost entirely from the world of other human beings. Her fantasy life appears to have been virtually completely preempted by primitive, regressive libidinal preoccupations many of which are distorted and bizarre. . . . In a technical sense basic affective controls appear to be intact but it is equally clear that they are insecurely and tenuously maintained for the present by a variety of defense mechanisms including intellectualization, obsessive-compulsive devices, projection, reaction-formation, and somatization, all of which now seem inadequate to their task of controlling or containing an underlying psychotic process and are therefore in process of failure. The content of patient's responses is highly unconventional and frequently bizarre, filled with sexual and anatomical preoccupations, and basic reality contact is obviously and seriously impaired at times. In quality and level of sophistication patient's responses are characteristic of those of individuals of high average or superior intelligence but she is now functioning intellectually in impaired fashion at barely average level. Patient's thematic productions on the Thematic Apperception Test emphasize her fundamentally pessimistic, fatalistic, and depressive view of the world around her. It is as though she feels deeply that all human effort is foredoomed to failure, a conviction which seems to push her further into a dependant, passive withdrawal. In her view she lives in a world of people moved by strange, conflicted,*

*poorly comprehended, and, above all, devious motivations which
commit them inevitably to conflict and failure . . ."*

The patient to whom this psychiatric report refers is me. The tests mentioned—the Rorschach, the Thematic Apperception Test, the Sentence
Completion Test and the Minnesota Multiphasic Personality Index—were
administered privately, in the outpatient psychiatric clinic at St. John's
Hospital in Santa Monica, in the summer of 1968, shortly after I suffered
the "attack of vertigo and nausea" mentioned in the first sentence and
shortly before I was named a *Los Angeles Times* "Woman of the Year." By
way of comment I offer only that an attack of vertigo and nausea does not
now seem to me an inappropriate response to the summer of 1968.

                                      2

In the years I am talking about I was living in a large house in a part of
Hollywood that had once been expensive and was now described by one of
my acquaintances as a "senseless-killing neighborhood." This house on
Franklin Avenue was rented, and paint peeled inside and out, and pipes
broke and window sashes crumbled and the tennis court had not been
rolled since 1933, but the rooms were many and high-ceilinged and, during
the five years that I lived there, even the rather sinistral inertia of the neighborhood tended to suggest that I should live in the house indefinitely.
    In fact I could not, because the owners were waiting only for a zoning
change to tear the house down and build a high-rise apartment building,
and for that matter it was precisely this anticipation of imminent but not
exactly immediate destruction that lent the neighborhood its particular
character. The house across the street had been built for one of the Tal-
madge sisters, had been the Japanese consulate in 1941, and was now, although boarded up, occupied by a number of unrelated adults who seemed
to constitute some kind of therapy group. The house next door was owned
by Synanon. I recall looking at a house around the corner with a rental sign
on it: this house had once been the Canadian consulate, had 28 large rooms
and two refrigerated fur closets, and could be rented, in the spirit of the
neighborhood, only on a month-to-month basis, unfurnished. Since the in-
clination to rent an unfurnished 28-room house for a month or two is a distinctly special one, the neighborhood was peopled mainly by rock-and-roll

bands, therapy groups, very old women wheeled down the street by practical nurses in soiled uniforms, and by my husband, my daughter and me.

> Q. *And what else happened, if anything. . . .*
> A. *He said that he thought that I could be a star, like, you know, a young Burt Lancaster, you know, that kind of stuff.*
> Q. *Did he mention any particular name?*
> A. *Yes, sir.*
> Q. *What name did he mention?*
> A. *He mentioned a lot of names. He said Burt Lancaster. He said Clint Eastwood. He said Fess Parker. He mentioned a lot of names. . . .*
> Q. *Did you talk after you ate?*
> A. *While we were eating, after we ate. Mr Novarro told our fortunes with some cards and he read our palms.*
> Q. *Did he tell you you were going to have a lot of good luck or bad luck or what happened?*
> A. *He wasn't a good palm reader.*

These are excerpts from the testimony of Paul Robert Ferguson and Thomas Scott Ferguson, brothers, ages 22 and 17 respectively, during their trial for the murder of Ramon Novarro, age 69, at his house in Laurel Canyon, not too far from my house in Hollywood, on the night of October 30, 1968. I followed this trial quite closely, clipping reports from the newspapers and later borrowing a transcript from one of the defense attorneys. The younger of the brothers, "Tommy Scott" Ferguson, whose girlfriend testified that she had stopped being in love with him "about two weeks after Grand Jury," said that he had been unaware of Mr. Novarro's career as a silent film actor until he was shown, at some point during the night of the murder, a photograph of his host as Ben-Hur. The older brother, Paul Ferguson, who began working carnivals when he was 12 and described himself at 22 as having had "a fast life and a good one," gave the jury, upon request, his definition of a hustler: "A hustler is someone who can talk—not just to men, to women, too. Who can cook. Can keep company. Wash a car. Lots of things make up a hustler. There are a lot of lonely people in this town, man." During the course of the trial each of the brothers accused the other of the murder. Both were convicted. I read the transcript several times, trying to bring the picture into some focus which did not suggest that I lived, as my psychiatric report had put it, "in a world of people moved by strange, conflicted, poorly comprehended and, above all, devious motivations"; I never met the Ferguson brothers.

I did meet one of the principals in another Los Angeles County murder trial during those years: Linda Kasabian, star witness for the prosecution in what was commonly known as the Manson Trial. I once asked Linda what she thought about the apparently chance sequence of events which had brought her first to the Spahn Movie Ranch and then to the Sybil Brand Institute for Women on charges, later dropped, of murdering Sharon Tate Polanski, Abigail Folger, Jay Sebring, Voytek Frykowski, Steven Parent, and Rosemary and Leno LaBianca. "Everything was to teach me something," Linda said. Linda did not believe that chance was without pattern. Linda operated on what I later recognized as dice theory, and so, during the years I am talking about, did I.

It will perhaps suggest the mood of those years if I tell you that during them I could not visit my mother-in-law without averting my eyes from a framed verse, a "house blessing," which hung in a hallway of her house in West Hartford, Connecticut.

> *God bless the corners of this house,*
> *And be the lintel blest—*
> *And bless the hearth and bless the board*
> *And bless each place of rest—*
> *And bless the crystal windowpane that lets the starlight in*
> *And bless each door that opens wide, to stranger as to kin.*

This verse had on me the effect of a physical chill, so insistently did it seem the kind of "ironic" detail the reporters would seize upon, the morning the bodies were found. In my neighborhood in California we did not bless the door that opened wide to stranger as to kin. Paul and Tommy Scott Ferguson were the strangers at Ramon Novarro's door, up on Laurel Canyon. Charles Manson was the stranger at Rosemary and Leno La-Bianca's door, over in Los Feliz. Some strangers at the door knocked, and invented a reason to come inside: a call, say, to the Triple A, about a car not in evidence. Others just opened the door and walked in, and I would come across them in the entrance hall. I recall asking one such stranger what he wanted. We looked at each other for what seemed a long time, and then he saw my husband on the stair landing. "Chicken Delight," he said finally, but we had ordered no Chicken Delight, nor was he carrying any. I took the license number of his panel truck. It seems to me now that during those years I was always writing down the license numbers of panel trucks, panel trucks circling the block, panel trucks parked across the street, panel trucks idling at the intersection. I put these license numbers in a dressing-table drawer where they could be found by the police when the time came.

That the time would come I never doubted, at least not in the inaccessible places of the mind where I seemed more and more to be living. So many encounters in those years were devoid of any logic save that of the dreamwork. In the big house on Franklin Avenue many people seemed to come and go without relation to what I did. I knew where the sheets and towels were kept but I did not always know who was sleeping in every bed. I had the keys but not the key. I remember taking a 25-mg. Compazine one Easter Sunday and making a large and elaborate lunch for a number of people, many of whom were still around on Monday. I remember walking barefoot all day on the worn hardwood floors of that house and I remember "Do You Wanna Dance" on the record player, "Do You Wanna Dance" and "Visions of Johanna" and a song called "Midnight Confessions." I remember a baby-sitter telling me that she saw death in my aura. I remember chatting with her about reasons why this might be so, paying her, opening all the French windows and going to sleep in the living room.

It was hard to surprise me in those years. It was hard to even get my attention. I was absorbed in my intellectualization, my obsessive-compulsive devices, my projection, my reaction-formation, my somatization, and in the transcript of the Ferguson trial. A musician I had met a few years before called from a Ramada Inn in Tuscaloosa to tell me how to save myself through Scientology. I had met him once in my life, had talked to him for maybe half an hour about brown rice and the charts, and now he was telling me from Alabama about E-meters, and how I might become a Clear. I received a telephone call from a stranger in Montreal who seemed to want to enlist me in a narcotics operation. "Is it cool to talk on this telephone?" he asked several times. "Big Brother isn't listening?"

I said that I doubted it, although increasingly I did not.

"Because what we're talking about, basically, is applying the Zen philosophy to money and business, dig? And if I say we are going to finance the underground, and if I mention major money, you know what I'm talking about because you know what's going down, right?"

Maybe he was not talking about narcotics. Maybe he was talking about turning a profit on M-1 rifles: I had stopped looking for the logic in such calls. Someone with whom I had gone to school in Sacramento and had last seen in 1952 turned up at my house in Hollywood in 1968 in the guise of a private detective from West Covina, one of very few licensed women private detectives in the State of California. "They call us Dickless Tracys," she said, idly but definitely fanning out the day's mail on the hall table. "I have a lot of very close friends in law enforcement," she said then. "You might want to meet them." We exchanged promises to keep in touch but never met again: a not atypical encounter of the period. The Sixties were over before it occurred to me that this visit might have been less than entirely social.

3

It was six, seven o'clock of an early spring evening in 1968 and I was sitting on the cold vinyl floor of a sound studio on Sunset Boulevard, watching a band called The Doors record a rhythm track. On the whole my attention was only minimally engaged by the preoccupations of rock-and-roll bands (I had already heard about acid as a transitional stage and also about the Maharishi and even about Universal Love, and after a while it all sounded like marmalade skies to me), but The Doors were different, The Doors interested me. The Doors seemed unconvinced that love was brotherhood and the Kama Sutra. The Doors' music insisted that love was sex and sex was death and therein lay salvation. The Doors were the Norman Mailers of the Top Forty, missionaries of apocalyptic sex. *Break on through,* their lyrics urged, and *Light my fire,* and:

> *Come on baby, gonna take a little ride*
> *Goin' down by the ocean side*
> *Gonna get real close*
> *Get real tight*

Baby gonna drown tonight—
Goin' down, down, down.

On this evening in 1968 they were gathered together in uneasy symbio-
sis to make their third album, and the studio was too cold and the lights
were too bright and there were masses of wires and banks of the ominous
blinking electronic circuitry with which musicians live so easily. There
were three of the four Doors. There was a bass player borrowed from a
band called Clear Light. There were the producer and the engineer and the
road manager and a couple of girls and a Siberian husky named Nikki with
one gray eye and one gold. There were paper bags half filled with hard-
boiled eggs and chicken livers and cheeseburgers and empty bottles of
apple juice and California rosé. There was everything and everybody The
Doors needed to cut the rest of this third album except one thing, the
fourth Door, the lead singer, Jim Morrison, a 24-year-old graduate of
U.C.L.A. who wore black vinyl pants and no underwear and tended to suggest some range of the possible just beyond a suicide pact. It was Morrison
who had described The Doors as "erotic politicians." It was Morrison who
had defined the group's interests as "anything about revolt, disorder, chaos,
about activity that appears to have no meaning." It was Morrison who got
arrested in Miami in December of 1967 for giving an "indecent" performance. It was Morrison who wrote most of The Doors' lyrics, the peculiar
character of which was to reflect either an ambiguous paranoia or a quite
unambiguous insistence upon the love-death as the ultimate high. And it
was Morrison who was missing. It was Ray Manzarek and Robby Krieger
and John Densmore who made The Doors sound the way they sounded,
and maybe it was Manzarek and Krieger and Densmore who made seventeen out of twenty interviewees on *American Bandstand* prefer The Doors
over all other bands, but it was Morrison who got up there in his black
vinyl pants with no underwear and projected the idea, and it was Morrison
they were waiting for now.

"Hey listen," the engineer said. " I was listening to an FM station on the
way over here, they played three Doors songs, first they played 'Back Door
Man' and then 'Love Me Two Times' and 'Light My Fire.'"

"I heard it," Densmore muttered. "I heard it."

"So what's wrong with somebody playing three of your songs?"

"This cat dedicates it to his family."

"Yeah? To his family?"

"To his family. Really crass."

Ray Manzarek was hunched over a Gibson keyboard. "You think *Morrison's* going to come back?" he asked to no one in particular.

No one answered.

"So we can do some *vocals?*" Manzarek said.

The producer was working with the tape of the rhythm track they had just recorded. "I hope so," he said without looking up.

"Yeah," Manzarek said. "So do I."

My leg had gone to sleep, but I did not stand up; unspecific tensions seemed to be rendering everyone in the room catatonic. The producer played back the rhythm track. The engineer said that he wanted to do his deep-breathing exercises. Manzarek ate a hard-boiled egg. "Tennyson made a mantra out of his own name," he said to the engineer. "I don't know if he said 'Tennyson Tennyson Tennyson' or 'Alfred Alfred Alfred' or 'Alfred Lord Tennyson,' but anyway, he did it. Maybe he just said 'Lord Lord Lord.'"

"Groovy," the Clear Light bass player said. He was an amiable enthusiast, not at all a Door in spirit.

"I wonder what Blake said," Manzarek mused. "Too bad *Morrison's* not here. *Morrison* would know."

It was a long while later. Morrison arrived. He had on his black vinyl pants and he sat down on a leather couch in front of the four big blank speakers and he closed his eyes. The curious aspect of Morrison's arrival was this: no one acknowledged it. Robby Krieger continued working out a guitar passage. John Densmore tuned his drums. Manzarek sat at the control console and twirled a corkscrew and let a girl rub his shoulders. The girl did not look at Morrison, although he was in her direct line of sight. An hour or so passed, and still no one had spoken to Morrison. Then Morrison spoke to Manzarek. He spoke almost in a whisper, as if he were wresting the words from behind some disabling aphasia.

"It's an hour to West Covina," he said. "I was thinking maybe we should spend the night out there after we play."

Manzarek put down the corkscrew. "Why?" he said.

"Instead of coming back."

Manzarek shrugged. "We were planning to come back."

"Well, I was thinking, we could rehearse out there."

Manzarek said nothing.

"We could get in a rehearsal, there's a Holiday Inn next door."

"We could do that," Manzarek said. "Or we could rehearse Sunday, in town."

"I guess so." Morrison paused. "Will the place be ready to rehearse Sunday?"

Manzarek looked at him for a while. "No," he said then.

I counted the control knobs on the electronic console. There were seventy-six. I was unsure in whose favor the dialogue had been resolved, or if it had been resolved at all. Robby Krieger picked at his guitar, and said that he needed a fuzz box. The producer suggested that he borrow one from the Buffalo Springfield, who were recording in the next studio. Krieger shrugged. Morrison sat down again on the leather couch and leaned back. He lit a match. He studied the flame awhile and then very slowly, very deliberately, lowered it to the fly of his black vinyl pants. Manzarek watched him. The girl who was rubbing Manzarek's shoulders did not look at anyone. There was a sense that no one was going to leave the room, ever. It would be some weeks before The Doors finished recording this album. I did not see it through.

4

Someone once brought Janis Joplin to a party at the house on Franklin Avenue: she had just done a concert and she wanted brandy-and-Benedictine in a water tumbler. Music people never wanted ordinary drinks. They wanted sake, or champagne cocktails, or tequila neat. Spending time with music people was confusing, and required a more fluid and ultimately a more passive approach than I ever acquired. In the first place time was never of the essence: we would have dinner at nine unless we had it at eleven-thirty, or we could order in later. We would go down to U.S.C. to see the Living Theater if the limo came at the very moment when no one had just made a drink or a cigarette or an arrangement to meet Ultra Violet at the Montecito. In any case David Hockney was coming by. In any case Ultra Violet was not at the Montecito. In any case we would go down to U.S.C. and see the Living Theater tonight or we would see the Living Theater another night, in New York, or Prague. First we wanted sushi for twenty, steamed clams, vegetable vindaloo and many rum drinks with gardenias for our hair. First we wanted a table for twelve, fourteen at the most, although there might be six more, or eight more, or eleven more: there would never be one or two more, because music people did not travel in groups of "one" or "two." John and Michelle Phillips, on their way to the hospital for the birth of their daughter Chynna, had the limo detour into Hollywood in order to pick up a friend, Anne Marshall. This incident, which I often embroider in my mind to include an imaginary second detour, to the Luau for gardenias, exactly describes the music business to me.

5

Around five o'clock on the morning of October 28, 1967, in the desolate district between San Francisco Bay and the Oakland estuary that the Oakland police call Beat 101A, a 25-year-old black militant named Huey P. Newton was stopped and questioned by a white police officer named John Frey, Jr. An hour later Huey Newton was under arrest at Kaiser Hospital in Oakland, where he had gone for emergency treatment of a gunshot wound in his stomach, and a few weeks later he was indicted by the Alameda County Grand Jury on charges of murdering John Frey, wounding another officer, and kidnapping a bystander.

In the spring of 1968, when Huey Newton was awaiting trial, I went to see him in the Alameda County Jail. I suppose I went because I was interested in the alchemy of issues, for an issue is what Huey Newton had by then become. To understand how that had happened you must first consider Huey Newton, who he was. He came from an Oakland family, and for a while he went to Merritt College. In October of 1966 he and a friend named Bobby Seale organized what they called the Black Panther Party. They borrowed the name from the emblem used by the Freedom Party in Lowndes County, Alabama, and, from the beginning, they defined themselves as a revolutionary political group. The Oakland police knew the Panthers, and had a list of the twenty or so Panther cars. I am telling you neither that Huey Newton killed John Frey nor that Huey Newton did not kill John Frey, for in the context of revolutionary politics Huey Newton's guilt or innocence was irrelevant. I am telling you only how Huey Newton happened to be in the Alameda County Jail, and why rallies were held in his name, demonstrations organized whenever he appeared in court. LET'S

SPRING HUEY, the buttons read (fifty cents each), and here and there on the courthouse steps, among the Panthers with their berets and sunglasses, the chants would go up:

> *Get your M-*
> *31.*
> *'Cause baby we gonna*
> *Have some fun.*
> *BOOM BOOM. BOOM BOOM.*

"Fight on, brother," a woman would add in the spirit of a good-natured amen. "Bang-bang."

> *Bullshit bullshit*
> *Can't stand the game*
> *White man's playing.*
> *One way out, one way out.*
> *BOOM BOOM. BOOM BOOM.*

In the corridor downstairs in the Alameda County Courthouse there was a crush of lawyers and CBC correspondents and cameramen and people who wanted to "visit Huey."

"Eldridge doesn't mind if I go up," one of the latter said to one of the lawyers.

"If Eldridge doesn't mind, it's all right with me," the lawyer said. "If you've got press credentials."

"I've got kind of dubious credentials."

"I can't take you up then. *Eldridge* has got dubious credentials. One's bad enough. I've got a good working relationship up there, I don't want to blow it." The lawyer turned to a cameraman. "You guys rolling yet?"

On that particular day I was allowed to go up, and a *Los Angeles Times* man, and a radio newscaster. We all signed the police register and sat around a scarred pine table and waited for Huey Newton. "The only thing that's going to free Huey Newton," Rap Brown had said recently at a Panther rally in Oakland Auditorium, "is gunpowder." "Huey Newton laid down his life for us," Stokely Carmichael had said the same night. But of course Huey Newton had not yet laid down his life at all, was just here in the Alameda County Jail waiting to be tried, and I wondered if the direction these rallies were taking ever made him uneasy, ever made him suspect that in many ways he was more useful to the revolution behind bars than on the street. He seemed, when he finally came in, an extremely likable young man, engaging, direct, and I did not get the sense that he had intended to become a political martyr. He smiled at us all and waited for his lawyer, Charles Garry, to set up a tape recorder, and he chatted softly with Eldridge Cleaver, who was then the Black Panthers' Minister of Information. (Huey Newton was still the Minister of Defense.) Eldridge Cleaver wore a black sweater and one gold earring and spoke in an almost inaudible drawl and was allowed to see Huey Newton because he had those "dubious credentials," a press card from *Ramparts*. Actually his interest was in getting "statements" from Huey Newton, "messages" to take outside; in receiving a kind of prophecy to be interpreted as needed.

"We need a statement, Huey, about the ten-point program," Eldridge Cleaver said, "so I'll ask you a question, see, and you answer it . . ."

"How's Bobby?" Huey Newton asked.

"He's got a hearing on his misdemeanors, see . . ."

"I thought he had a felony."

"Well, that's another thing, the felony, he's also got a couple of misdemeanors . . ."

Once Charles Garry had set up the tape recorder Huey Newton stopped chatting and started lecturing, almost without pause. He talked, running the words together because he had said them so many times before, about "the American capitalistic-materialistic system" and "so-called free enterprise" and "the fight for the liberation of black people throughout the world." Every now and then Eldridge Cleaver would signal Huey Newton and say something like, "There are a lot of people interested in the Executive Mandate Number Three you've issued to the Black Panther Party, Huey. Care to comment?"

And Huey Newton would comment. "Yes. Mandate Number Three is this demand from the Black Panther Party speaking for the black community. Within the Mandate we admonish the racist police force . . ." I kept wishing that he would talk about himself, hoping to break through the wall of rhetoric, but he seemed to be one of those autodidacts for whom all things specific and personal present themselves as minefields to be avoided even at the cost of coherence, for whom safety lies in generalization. The newspaperman, the radio man, they tried:

> Q. *Tell us something about yourself, Huey, I mean your life be-*
> *fore the Panthers.*
> A. *Before the Black Panther Party my life was very similar to*
> *that of most black people in this country.*
> Q. *Well, your family, some incidents you remember, the influ-*
> *ences that shaped you—*
> A. *Living in America shaped me.*
> Q. *Well, yes, but more specifically—*
> A. *It reminds me of a quote from James Baldwin: "To be black*
> *and conscious in America is to be in a constant state of rage."*

"To be black and conscious in America is to be in a constant state of rage," Eldridge Cleaver wrote in large letters on a pad of paper, and then he added: *"Huey P. Newton quoting James Baldwin."* I could see it emblazoned above the speakers' platform at a rally, imprinted on the letterhead of an ad hoc committee still unborn. As a matter of fact almost everything Huey Newton said had the ring of being a "quotation," a "pronouncement" to be employed when the need arose. I had heard Huey P. Newton On Racism ("The Black Panther Party is against racism"), Huey P. Newton On Cultural Nationalism ("The Black Panther Party believes that the only culture worth holding on to is revolutionary culture"), Huey P. Newton On White Radicalism, On Police Occupation of the Ghetto, On the European Versus the African. "The European started to be sick when he denied his sexual nature," Huey Newton said, and Charles Garry interrupted then, bringing it back to first principles. "Isn't it true, though, Huey," he said, "that racism got its start for *economic* reasons?"

This weird interlocution seemed to take on a life of its own. The small room was hot and the fluorescent light hurt my eyes and I still did not know to what extent Huey Newton understood the nature of the role in which he was cast. As it happened I had always appreciated the logic of the Panther position, based as it was on the proposition that political power began at the end of the barrel of a gun (exactly what gun had even been specified, in an early memorandum from Huey P. Newton: *"Army .45;*

carbine; 12-gauge Magnum shotgun with 18" barrel, preferably the brand of High Standard; M-16; .357 Magnum pistols; P-38"), and I could appreciate as well the particular beauty in Huey Newton as "issue." In the politics of revolution everyone was expendable, but I doubted that Huey Newton's political sophistication extended to seeing himself that way: the value of a Scottsboro case is easier to see if you are not yourself the Scottsboro boy. "Is there anything else you want to ask Huey?" Charles Garry asked. There did not seem to be. The lawyer adjusted his tape recorder. "I've had a request, Huey," he said, "from a high-school student, a reporter on his school paper, and he wanted a statement from you, and he's going to call me tonight. Care to give me a message for him?"

Huey Newton regarded the microphone. There was a moment in which he seemed not to remember the name of the play, and then he brightened. "I would like to point out," he said, his voice gaining volume as the memory disks clicked, *high school, student, youth, message to youth,* "that America is becoming a very young nation . . ."

> *I heard a moaning and a groaning, and I went over and it was—this Negro fellow was there. He had been shot in the stomach and at the time he didn't appear in any acute distress and so I said I'd see, and I asked him if he was a Kaiser, if he belonged to Kaiser, and he said, "Yes, yes. Get a doctor. Can't you see I'm bleeding? I've been shot. Now get someone out here." And I asked him if he had his Kaiser card and he got upset at this and he said, "Come on, get a doctor out here, I've been shot." I said, "I see this, but you're not in any acute distress."* . . . *So I told him we'd have to check to make sure he was a member.* . . . *And this kind of upset him more and he called me a few nasty names and said, "Now get a doctor out here right now, I've been shot and I'm bleeding." And he took his coat off and his shirt and he threw it on the desk there and he said, "Can't you see all this blood?" And I said, "I see it." And it wasn't that much, and so I said, "Well, you'll have to sign our admission sheet before you can be seen by a doctor." And he said, "I'm not signing anything." And I said, "You cannot be seen by a doctor unless you sign the admission sheet," and he said, "I don't have to sign anything" and a few more choice words . . .*

This is an excerpt from the testimony before the Alameda County Grand Jury of Corrine Leonard, the nurse in charge of the Kaiser Foundation Hospital emergency room in Oakland at 5:30 A.M. on October 28, 1967. The "Negro fellow" was of course Huey Newton, wounded that morning during the gunfire which killed John Frey. For a long time I kept a copy of this testimony pinned to my office wall, on the theory that it illustrated a collision of cultures, a classic instance of an historical outsider confronting the established order at its most petty and impenetrable level. This theory was shattered when I learned that Huey Newton was in fact an enrolled member of the Kaiser Foundation Health Plan, i.e., in Nurse Leonard's words, "a Kaiser."

6

One morning in 1968 I went to see Eldridge Cleaver in the San Francisco apartment he then shared with his wife, Kathleen. To be admitted to this apartment it was necessary to ring first and then stand in the middle of Oak Street, at a place which could be observed clearly from the Cleavers' apartment. After this scrutiny the visitor was, or was not, buzzed in. I was, and I climbed the stairs to find Kathleen Cleaver in the kitchen frying sausage and Eldridge Cleaver in the living room listening to a John Coltrane record and a number of other people all over the apartment, people everywhere, people standing in doorways and people moving around in one another's peripheral vision and people making and taking telephone calls. "When can you move on that?" I would hear in the background, and "You can't bribe me with a dinner, man, those *Guardian* dinners are all Old Left, like a wake." Most of these other people were members of the Black Panther Party, but one of them, in the living room, was Eldridge Cleaver's parole officer. It seems to me that I stayed about an hour. It seems to me that the three of us—Eldridge Cleaver, his parole officer and I—mainly discussed the commercial prospects of *Soul on Ice,* which, it happened, was being published that day. We discussed the advance ($5,000). We discussed the size of the first printing (10,000 copies). We discussed the advertising budget and we discussed the bookstores in which copies were or were not available. It was a not unusual discussion between writers, with the difference that one of the writers had his parole officer there and the other had stood out on Oak Street and been visually frisked before coming inside.

7

TO PACK AND WEAR:

> *2 shirts*
> *2 jerseys or leotards*
> *1 pullover sweater*
> *2 pair shoes*
> *stockings*
> *bra*
> *nightgown, robe, slippers*
> *cigarettes*
> *bourbon*
> *bag with:*
>> *shampoo*
>> *toothbrush and paste*
>> *Basis soap*
>> *razor, deodorant*
>> *aspirin, prescriptions, Tampax*
>> *face cream, powder, baby oil*

TO CARRY:

> *mohair throw*
> *typewriter*
> *2 legal pads and pens*
> *files*
> *house key*

This is a list which was taped inside my closet door in Hollywood during those years when I was reporting more or less steadily. The list enabled me to pack, without thinking, for any piece I was likely to do. Notice the deliberate anonymity of costume: in a skirt, a leotard, *and stockings,* I could pass on either side of the culture. Notice the mohair throw for trunk-line flights (i.e., no blankets) and for the motel room in which the air conditioning could not be turned off. Notice the bourbon for the same motel room. Notice the typewriter for the airport, coming home: the idea was to turn in the Hertz car, check in, find an empty bench, and start typing the day's notes.

It should be clear that this was a list made by someone who prized control, yearned after momentum, someone determined to play her role as if she had the script, heard her cues, knew the narrative. There is on this list one significant omission, one article I needed and never had: a watch. I needed a watch not during the day, when I could turn on the car radio or ask someone, but at night, in the motel. Quite often I would ask the desk for the time every half hour or so, until finally, embarrassed to ask again, I would call Los Angeles and ask my husband. In other words I had skirts, jerseys, leotards, pullover sweater, shoes, stockings, bra, nightgown, robe, slippers, cigarettes, bourbon, shampoo, toothbrush and paste, Basis soap, razor, deodorant, aspirin, prescriptions, Tampax, face cream, powder, baby oil, mohair throw, typewriter, legal pads, pens, files and a house key, but I didn't know what time it was. This may be a parable, either of my life as a reporter during this period or of the period itself.

8

Driving a Budget Rent-A-Car between Sacramento and San Francisco one rainy morning in November of 1968 I kept the radio on very loud. On this occasion I kept the radio on very loud not to find out what time it was but in an effort to erase six words from my mind, six words which had no significance for me but which seemed that year to signal the onset of anxiety or fright. The words, a line from Ezra Pound's "In a Station of the Metro," were these: *Petals on a wet black bough.* The radio played "Wichita Lineman" and "I Heard it on the Grapevine." *Petals on a wet black bough.* Somewhere between the Yolo Causeway and Vallejo it occurred to me that during the course of any given week I met too many people who spoke favorably about bombing power stations. Somewhere between the Yolo Causeway and Vallejo it also occurred to me that the fright on this particular morning was going to present itself as an inability to drive this Budget Rent-A-Car across the Carquinas Bridge. *The Wichita Lineman was still on the job.* I closed my eyes and drove across the Carquinas Bridge, because I had appointments, because I was working, because I had promised to watch the revolution being made at San Francisco State College and because there was no place in Vallejo to turn in a Budget Rent-A-Car and because nothing on my mind was in the script as I remembered it.

9

At San Francisco State College on that particular morning the wind was blowing the cold rain in squalls across the muddied lawns and against the lighted windows of empty classrooms. In the days before there had been fires set and classes invaded and finally a confrontation with the San Francisco Police Tactical Unit, and in the weeks to come the campus would become what many people on it were pleased to call "a battlefield." The police and the Mace and the noon arrests would become the routine of life on the campus, and every night the combatants would review their day on television: the waves of students advancing, the commotion at the edge of the frame, the riot sticks flashing, the instant of jerky camera that served to suggest at what risk the film was obtained; then a cut to the weather map. In the beginning there had been the necessary "issue," the suspension of a 22-year-old instructor who happened as well to be Minister of Education for the Black Panther Party, but that issue, like most, had soon ceased to be the point in the minds of even the most dense participants. Disorder was its own point.

I had never before been on a campus in disorder, had missed even Berkeley and Columbia, and I suppose I went to San Francisco State expecting something other than what I found there. In some not at all trivial sense, the set was wrong. The very architecture of California state colleges tends to deny radical notions, to reflect instead a modest and hopeful vision of progressive welfare bureaucracy, and as I walked across the campus that day and on later days the entire San Francisco State dilemma—the gradual politicization, the "issues" here and there, the obligatory "Fifteen Demands," the continual arousal of the police and the outraged citizenry— seemed increasingly off-key, an instance of the *enfants terribles* and the Board of Trustees unconsciously collaborating on a wishful fantasy (Revolution on Campus) and playing it out in time for the six o'clock news. "Adjet-prop committee meeting in the Redwood Room," read a scrawled note on the cafeteria door one morning; only someone who needed very badly to be alarmed could respond with force to a guerrilla band that not only announced its meetings on the enemy's bulletin board but seemed innocent of the spelling, and so the meaning, of the words it used. "Hitler Hayakawa," some of the faculty had begun calling S. I. Hayakawa, the semanticist who had become the college's third president in a year and had incurred considerable displeasure by trying to keep the campus open.

"Eichmann," Kay Boyle had screamed at him at a rally. In just such broad strokes was the picture being painted in the fall of 1968 on the pastel campus at San Francisco State.

The place simply never seemed serious. The headlines were dark that first day, the college had been closed "indefinitely," both Ronald Reagan and Jesse Unruh were threatening reprisals; still, the climate inside the Administration Building was that of a musical comedy about college life. "No *chance* we'll be open tomorrow," secretaries informed callers. "Go skiing, have a good time." Striking black militants dropped in to chat with the deans; striking white radicals exchanged gossip in the corridors. "No interviews, no press," announced a student strike leader who happened into a dean's office where I was sitting; in the next moment he was piqued because no one had told him that a Huntley-Brinkley camera crew was on campus. "We can still plug into that," the dean said soothingly. Everyone seemed joined in a rather festive camaraderie, a shared jargon, a shared sense of moment: the future was no longer arduous and indefinite but immediate and programmatic, aglow with the prospect of problems to be "addressed," plans to be "implemented." It was agreed all around that the confrontations could be "a very healthy development," that maybe it took a shutdown "to get something done." The mood, like the architecture, was 1948 functional, a model of pragmatic optimism.

Perhaps Evelyn Waugh could have gotten it down exactly right: Waugh was good at scenes of industrious self-delusion, scenes of people absorbed in odd games. Here at San Francisco State only the black militants could be construed as serious: they were at any rate picking the games, dictating the rules, and taking what they could from what seemed for everyone else just an amiable evasion of routine, of institutional anxiety, of the tedium of the academic calendar. Meanwhile the administrators could talk about programs. Meanwhile the white radicals could see themselves, on an investment of virtually nothing, as urban guerrillas. It was working out well for everyone, this game at San Francisco State, and its peculiar virtues had never been so clear to me as they became one afternoon when I sat in on a meeting of fifty or sixty SDS members. They had called a press conference for later that day, and now they were discussing "just what the format of the press conference should be."

"This has to be on our terms," someone warned. "Because they'll ask very leading questions, they'll ask *questions*."

"Make them submit any questions in writing," someone else suggested. "The Black Student Union does that very successfully, then they just don't answer anything they don't want to answer."

"That's it , don't fall into their trap."

"Something we should stress at this press conference is *who owns the media.*"

"You don't think it's common knowledge that the papers represent corporate interests?" a realist among them interjected doubtfully.

"I don't think it's *understood.*"

Two hours and several dozen hand votes later, the group had selected four members to tell the press who owned the media, had decided to appear *en masse* at an opposition press conference, and had debated various slogans for the next day's demonstration. "Let's see, first we have 'Hearst Tells It Like It Ain't', then 'Stop Press Distortion'—that's the one there was some political controversy about. . . ."

And, before they broke up, they had listened to a student who had driven up for the day from the College of San Mateo, a junior college down the peninsula from San Francisco. "I came up here today with some Third World students to tell you that we're with you, and we hope you'll be with *us* when we try to pull off a strike next week, because we're really into it, we carry our motorcycle helmets all the time, can't think, can't go to class."

He had paused. He was a nice-looking boy, and fired with his task. I considered the tender melancholy of life in San Mateo, which is one of the richest counties per capita in the United States of America, and I considered whether or not the Wichita Lineman and the petals on the wet black bough represented the aimlessness of the bourgeoisie, and I considered the illusion of aim to be gained by holding a press conference, the only problem with press conferences being that the press asked questions. "I'm here to tell you that at College of San Mateo we're living like *revolutionaries,*" the boy said then.

10

We put "Lay Lady Lay" on the record player, and "Suzanne." We went down to Melrose Avenue to see the Flying Burritos. There was a jasmine vine grown over the verandah of the big house on Franklin Avenue, and in the evenings the smell of jasmine came in through all the open doors and windows. I made bouillabaisse for people who did not eat meat. I imagined that my own life was simple and sweet, and sometimes it was, but there were odd things going around town. There were rumors. There were stories. Everything was unmentionable but nothing was unimaginable. This mystical flirtation with the idea of "sin"—this sense that it was possible to go "too far," and that many people were doing it—was very much with us in Los Angeles in 1968 and 1969. A demented and seductive vortical tension was building in the community. The jitters were setting in. I recall a time when the dogs barked every night and the moon was always full. On August 9, 1969, I was sitting in the shallow end of my sister-in-law's swimming pool in Beverly Hills when she received a telephone call from a friend who had just heard about the murders at Sharon Tate Polanski's house on Cielo Drive. The phone rang many times during the next hour. These early reports were garbled and contradictory. One caller would say hoods, the next would say chains. There were twenty dead, no, twelve, ten, eighteen. Black masses were imagined, and bad trips blamed. I remember all of the day's misinformation very clearly, and I also remember this, and wish I did not: *I remember that no one was surprised.*

11

When I first met Linda Kasabian in the summer of 1970 she was wearing her hair parted neatly in the middle, no makeup, Elizabeth Arden "Blue Grass" perfume, and the unpressed blue uniform issued to inmates at the Sybil Brand Institute for Women in Los Angeles. She was at Sybil Brand in protective custody, waiting out the time until she could testify about the murders of Sharon Tate Polanski, Abigail Folger, Jay Sebring, Voytek Frykowski, Steven Parent, and Rosemary and Leno LaBianca, and, with her lawyer, Gary Fleischman, I spent a number of evenings talking to her there. Of these evenings I remember mainly my dread at entering the prison, at leaving for even an hour the infinite possibilities I suddenly perceived in the summer twilight. I remember driving downtown on the Hollywood Freeway in Gary Fleischman's Cadillac convertible with the top down. I remember watching a rabbit graze on the grass by the gate as Gary Fleischman signed the prison register. Each of the half-dozen doors that locked behind us as we entered Sybil Brand was a little death, and I would emerge after the interview like Persephone from the underworld, euphoric, elated.

Once home I would have two drinks and make myself a hamburger and eat it ravenously.

"Dig it," Gary Fleischman was always saying. One night when we were driving back to Hollywood from Sybil Brand in the Cadillac convertible with the top down he demanded that I tell him the population of India. "Take a guess," he prompted. I made a guess, absurdly low, and he was disgusted. He had asked the same question of his niece ("a college girl"), of Linda, and now of me, and none of us had known. It seemed to confirm some idea he had of women, their essential ineducability, their similarity under the skin. Gary Fleischman was someone of a type I met only rarely, a comic realist in a porkpie hat, a business traveler on the far frontiers of the period, a man who knew his way around the courthouse and Sybil Brand and remained cheerful, even jaunty, in the face of the awesome and impenetrable mystery at the center of what he called "the case." In fact we never talked about "the case," and referred to its central events only as "Cielo Drive" and "LaBianca." We talked instead about Linda's childhood pastimes and disappointments, her high-school romances and her concern for her children. This particular juxtaposition of the spoken and the unspeakable was eerie and unsettling, and made my notebook a litany of little ironies so obvious as to be of interest only to dedicated absurdists. An example: Linda dreamed of opening a combination restaurant-boutique and pet shop.

12

Certain organic disorders of the central nervous system are characterized by periodic remissions, the apparent complete recovery of the afflicted nerves. What happens appears to be this: as the lining of a nerve becomes inflamed and hardens into scar tissue, thereby blocking the passage of neural impulses, the nervous system gradually changes its circuitry, finds other, unaffected nerves to carry the same messages. During the years when I found it necessary to revise the circuitry of my mind I discovered that I was no longer interested in whether the woman on the ledge outside the window on the sixteenth floor jumped or did not jump, or in why. I was interested only in the picture of her in my mind: her hair incandescent in the floodlights, her bare toes curled inward on the stone ledge.

In this light all narrative was sentimental. In this light all connections were equally meaningful, and equally senseless. Try these: on the morning of John Kennedy's death in 1963 I was buying, at Ransohoff's in San Francisco, a short silk dress in which to be married. A few years later this dress of mine was ruined when, at a dinner party in Bel-Air, Roman Polanski accidently spilled a glass of red wine on it. Sharon Tate was also a guest at this party, although she and Roman Polanski were not yet married. On July 27, 1970, I went to the Magnin-Hi Shop on the third floor of I. Magnin in Beverly Hills and picked out, at Linda Kasabian's request, the dress in which she began her testimony about the murders at Sharon Tate Polanski's house on Cielo Drive. "Size 9 Petite," her instructions read. "Mini but not extremely mini. In velvet if possible. Emerald green or gold. Or: A Mexican peasant-style dress, smocked or embroidered." She needed a dress that morning because the district attorney, Vincent Bugliosi, had expressed doubts about the dress she had planned to wear, a long white homespun shift. "Long is for evening," he had advised Linda. Long was for evening and white was for brides. At her own wedding in 1965 Linda Kasabian had worn a white brocade suit. Time passed, times changed. Everything was to teach us something. At 11:20 on that July morning in 1970 I delivered the dress in which she would testify to Gary Fleischman, who was waiting in front of his office on Rodeo Drive in Beverly Hills. He was wearing his porkpie hat and he was standing with Linda's second husband, Bob Kasabian, and their friend Charlie Melton, both of whom were wearing long white robes. Long was for Bob and Charlie, the dress in the I. Magnin box was for Linda. The three of them took the I. Magnin box and got into Gary Fleischman's Cadillac convertible with the top down and drove off in the sunlight toward the freeway downtown, waving back at me. I believe this to be an authentically senseless chain of correspondences, but in the jingle-jangle morning of that summer it made as much sense as anything else did.

13

I recall a conversation I had in 1970 with the manager of a motel in which I was staying near Pendleton, Oregon. I had been doing a piece for *Life* about the storage of VX and GB nerve gas at an Army arsenal in Umatilla County, and now I was done, and trying to check out of the motel. During the course of checking out I was asked this question by the manager, who was a Mormon: *If you can't believe you're going to heaven in your own body and on a first-name basis with all the members of your family, then what's the point of dying?* At that time I believed that my basic affective controls were no longer intact, but now I present this to you as a more cogent question than it might at first appear, a kind of koan of the period.

14

Once I had a rib broken, and during the few months that it was painful to turn in bed or raise my arms in a swimming pool I had, for the first time, a sharp apprehension of what it would be like to be old. Later I forgot. At some point during the years I am talking about here, after a series of periodic visual disturbances, three electroencephalograms, two complete sets of skull and neck X rays, one five-hour glucose tolerance test, two electromyelograms, a battery of chemical tests and consultations with two ophthalmologists, one internist and three neurologists, I was told that the disorder was not really in my eyes, but in my central nervous system. I might or might not experience symptoms of neural damage all my life. These symptoms, which might or might not appear, might or might not involve my eyes. They might or might not involve my arms or legs, they might or might not be disabling. Their effects might be lessened by cortisone injections, or they might not. It could not be predicted. The condition had a name, the kind of name usually associated with telethons, but the name meant nothing and the neurologist did not like to use it. The name was multiple sclerosis, but the name had no meaning. This was, the neurologist said, an exclusionary diagnosis, and meant nothing.

I had, at this time, a sharp apprehension not of what it was like to be old but of what it was like to open the door to the stranger and find that the stranger did indeed have the knife. In a few lines of dialogue in a neurologist's office in Beverly Hills, the improbable had become the probable, the norm: things which happened only to other people could in fact happen to me. I could be struck by lightning, could dare to eat a peach and be poisoned by the cyanide in the stone. The startling fact was this: my body was offering a precise physiological equivalent to what had been going on in my mind. "Lead a simple life," the neurologist advised. "Not that it makes any difference we know about." In other words it was another story without a narrative.

15

Many people I know in Los Angeles believe that the Sixties ended abruptly on August 9, 1969, ended at the exact moment when word of the murders on Cielo Drive traveled like brushfire through the community, and in a sense this is true. The tension broke that day. The paranoia was fulfilled. In another sense the Sixties did not truly end for me until January of 1971, when I left the house on Franklin Avenue and moved to a house on the sea. This particular house on the sea had itself been very much a part of the Sixties, and for some months after we took possession I would come across souvenirs of that period in its history—a piece of Scientology literature beneath a drawer lining, a copy of *Stranger in a Strange Land* stuck deep on a closet shelf—but after a while we did some construction, and between the power saws and the sea wind the place got exorcised.

I have known, since then, very little about the movements of the people who seemed to me emblematic of those years. I know of course that Eldridge Cleaver went to Algeria and came home an entrepreneur. I know that Jim Morrison died in Paris. I know that Linda Kasabian fled in search of the pastoral to New Hampshire, where I once visited her; she also visited me in New York, and we took our children on the Staten Island Ferry to see the Statue of Liberty. I also know that in 1975 Paul Ferguson, while serving a life sentence for the murder of Ramon Novarro, won first prize in a PEN fiction contest and announced plans to "continue my writing." Writing had helped him, he said, to "reflect on experience and see what it means." Quite often I reflect on the big house in Hollywood, on "Midnight Confessions" and on Ramon Novarro and on the fact that Roman Polanski and I are godparents to the same child, but writing has not yet helped me to see what it means.

1980

In this year, James Wright dies. Among the few new poems he leaves behind is a technically perfect sonnet. It scans perfectly, turns perfectly, makes its case perfectly in the Italian Petrarchan tradition: the first quatrain states a thesis or supposition; the second elaborates upon that theme; the succeeding tercet offers a piece of evidence as example; and the final three lines provide a spin on the exposition. It is, in other words, a poetic argument presented with the same kind of formal perfection that is admired in the essay's traditional "five-paragraph" form. But it is also, for some reason, a sonnet in prose. A decade from this year, as I begin to enter high school and am trained for a lifetime of five-paragraph essays, an accidental encounter with James Wright's sonnet leaves me with the suspicion that there are essays somewhere to love.

JAMES WRIGHT

May Morning

Deep into spring, winter is hanging on. Bitter and skillful in his hopelessness, he stays alive in every shady place, starving along the Mediterranean: angry to see the glittering sea-pale boulder alive with lizards green as Judas leaves. Winter is hanging on. He still believes. He tries to catch a lizard by the shoulder. One olive tree below Grottaglie welcomes the winter into noontime shade, and talks as softly as Pythagoras. Be still, be patient, I can hear him say, cradling in his arms the wounded head, letting the sunlight touch the savage face.

1981

"The ore being ground, they divide it in several heaps and then begin to essay," wrote one anonymous scientist, 1368, in a treatise he contributed to a book of natural philosophy. The use of the word here is as a verb meaning "to weigh metals"— not the most common current meaning of the word *essay*, but certainly the oldest. In the ancient, Byzantine, and medieval worlds, people could be found in the streets of Europe essaying plums, gold, bricks, slaves, the advice of local priests. To *essay* has meant "to weigh" longer than it has meant "an experiment." Even as Cicero essayed the perils of the looming Roman Empire, he was doing so etymologically in the spirit of a sack of plums. It took the Renaissance to elevate the word, at last, to metaphor. It took someone so steeped in ancient literature that he spoke nothing but Latin until he was six, yet who grew up in a world already aware of the existence of the Americas. It took someone who knew by heart, according to his biographer, "all of Christopher Marlowe," yet who died before Shakespeare first published a play. It took someone who lived on a farm, alone, oblivious to the violent religious wars around him. Around the same time that Montaigne publishes his first collection of essays, Copernicus is publishing his sun-centered theories, Mercator displays the world's first projection map, the microscope is invented accidentally in Denmark, and the first African slaves are delivered to North America. In his retirement, Montaigne can be seen on the streets of Bordeaux wearing an inscribed pewter medallion: "Que sais-je?" "If I had even the slightest grasp upon my own faculties, I would not make essays," he writes, in 1569, "I would make decisions." It took someone at leisure in the world around him—someone, in other words, with much less urgently at stake than Cicero—to let the essay, at last, become a noun.

HARRY MATHEWS

Country Cooking from Central France: Roast Boned Rolled Stuffed Shoulder of Lamb *(Farce Double)*

for Maxine Groffsky

Here is an old French regional dish for you to try. Attempts by presumptuous chefs to refine it have failed to subdue its basically hearty nature. It demands some patience, but you will be abundantly rewarded for your pains.

Farce double—literally, double stuffing—is the speciality of La Tour Lambert, a mountain village in Auvergne, that rugged heart of the Massif Central. I have often visited La Tour Lambert: the first time was in late May, when *farce double* is traditionally served. I have observed the dish being made and discussed it with local cooks.

The latter were skeptical about reproducing *farce double* elsewhere— not out of pride, but because they were afraid the dish would make no sense to a foreigner. (It is your duty to prove them wrong—and nothing would make them happier if you did.) Furthermore, they said, certain ingredients would be hard to find. Judicious substitution is our answer to that. Without it, after all, we would have to forgo most foreign cooking not out of a can.

The shoulder of lamb itself requires attention. You must buy it from a butcher who can dress it properly. Tell him to include the middle neck, the shoulder chops in the brisket, and part of the foreshank. The stuffing will otherwise fall out of the roast.

In Auvergne, preparing the cut is no problem, since whole lambs are roasted: the dish is considered appropriate for exceptional, often communal feasts, of a kind that has become a rarity with us.

All bones must be removed. If you leave this to the butcher, have him save them for the deglazing sauce. The fell or filament must be kept intact, or the flesh may crumble.

Set the boned forequarter on the kitchen table. Do not slice off the purple inspection stamps but scour them with a brush dipped in a weak solution of lye. The meat will need all the protection it can get. Rinse and dry.

Marinate the lamb in a mixture of 2 qts of white wine, 2 qts of olive oil, the juice of 16 lemons, salt, pepper, 16 crushed garlic cloves, 10 coarsely chopped yellow onions, basil, rosemary, melilot, ginger, allspice, and a handful of juniper berries. The juniper adds a pungent, authentic note. In Auvergne, shepherds pick the berries in late summer when they drive their flocks from the mountain pastures. They deposit the berries in La Tour Lambert, where they are pickled through the winter in cider brandy. The preparation is worth making, but demands foresight.

If no bowl is capacious enough for the lamb and its marinade, use a wash-tub. Without a tub, you must improvise. Friends of mine in Paris resort to their bidet; Americans may have to fall back on the kitchen sink, which is what I did the first time I made *farce double*. In La Tour Lambert, most houses have stone marinating troughs. Less favored citizens use the municipal troughs in the entrance of a cave in the hillside, just off the main square.

The lamb will have marinated satisfactorily in 5 or 6 days.

Allow yourself 3 hours for the stuffings. The fish balls or quenelles that are their main ingredient can be prepared a day in advance and refrigerated until an hour before use.

The quenelles of La Tour Lambert have traditionally been made from *chaste,* a fish peculiar to the mountain lakes of Auvergne. The name, a dialect word meaning "fresh blood," may have been suggested by the color of its spreading gills, through which it ingests its food. (It is a mouthless fish.) It is lured to the surface with a skein of tiny beads that resemble the larvae on which it preys, then bludgeoned with an underwater boomerang. *Chaste* has coarse, yellow-white flesh, with a mild but inescapable taste. It has been vaguely and mistakenly identified as a perch; our American perch, however, can replace it, provided it has been caught no more than 36 hours before cooking. Other substitutes are saltwater fish such as silver hake or green cod. If you use a dry-fleshed fish, remember to order beef-kidney fat at the butcher's to add to the fish paste. (Be sure to grind it separately.)

To a saucepan filled with 2½ cups of cold water, add salt, pepper, 2 pinches of grated nutmeg, and 6 tbsp of butter. Boil. Off heat, begin stirring in 2½ cups of flour and continue as you again bring the water to a boil. Take off heat. Beat in 5 eggs, one at a time, then 5 egg whites. Let the liquid cool.

Earlier, you will have ground 3¾ lbs of fish with a mortar and pestle—heads, tails, bones, and all—and forced them through a coarse sieve. Do *not* use a grinder, blender, or Cuisinart. The sieve of La Tour Lambert is an elegant sock of meshed copper wire, with a fitted ashwood plunger. It is kept immaculately bright. Its apertures are shrewdly gauged to mince the bones without pulverizing the fish. Into the strained fish, mix small amounts of salt, white pepper, nutmeg, and chopped truffles—fresh ones, if possible. (See TRUFFLE.)

Stir fish and liquid into an even paste.

Two hours before, you will have refrigerated 1 cup of the heaviest cream available. Here, of course, access to a cow is a blessing.

The breathtaking viscid cream of La Tour Lambert is kept in specially excavated cellars. Those without one use the town chiller, in the middle depths—cool but not cold—of the cave mentioned earlier. Often I have watched the attendant women entering and emerging from that room, dusky figures in cowls, shawls, and long grey gowns, bearing earthenware jugs like offerings to a saint.

Beat the cool cream into the paste. Do it slowly: think of those erect, deliberate Auvergnat women as they stand in the faint gloom of the cave, beating with gestures of timeless calm. It should take at least 15 minutes to complete the task.

At some previous moment, you will have made the stuffing for the quenelles. (This is what makes the stuffing "double.") It consists of the milt of the fish and the sweetbreads of the lamb, both the neck and stomach varieties. (Don't forget to mention *them* to your butcher.) The milt is rapidly blanched. The sweetbreads are diced, salted, spiced with freshly ground hot pepper, and tossed for 6 minutes in clarified butter. Both are then chopped very fine (blender permitted) and kneaded into an unctuous mass with the help of 1 cup of lamb marrow and 3 tbsp of aged Madeira.

I said at the outset that I am in favor of appropriate substitutions in preparing *farce double:* but even though one eminent authority has suggested it, stuffing the quenelles with banana peanut butter is not appropriate.

The quenelles must now be shaped. Some writers who have discoursed at length on the traditional Auvergnat shape urge its adoption at all costs. I disagree. For the inhabitants of La Tour Lambert, who attach great significance to *farce double,* it may be right to feel strongly on this point. The same cannot be said for families in Maplewood or Orange County. You have enough to worry about as it is. If you are, however, an incurable stickler, you should know that in Auvergne molds are used. They are called *beurdes* (they are, coincidentally, shaped like birds), and they are available here. You can find them in any of the better head shops.

But forget about bird molds. Slap your fish paste on to a board and roll it flat. Spread on stuffing in parallel ½-inch bands 2 inches apart. Cut paste midway between bands, roll these strips into cylinders, and slice the cylinders into sections no larger than a small headache. Dip each piece in truffle crumbs. (See TRUFFLE.)

I refuse to become involved in the pros and cons of pre-steaming the quenelles. The only steam in La Tour Lambert is a rare fragrant wisp from the dampened fire of a roasting pit.

We now approach a crux in the preparation of *farce double:* enveloping the quenelles and binding them into the lamb. I must make a stern observation here; and you must listen to it. You must take it absolutely to heart.

If the traditional ways of enveloping the quenelles are arduous, they are in no way gratuitous. On them depends an essential component of *farce double,* namely the subtle interaction of lamb and fish. While the quenelles (and the poaching liquid that bathes them) must be largely insulated from the encompassing meat, they should not be wholly so. The quenelles must not be drenched in roasting juice or the lamb in fishy broth, but an exchange should occur, definite no matter how mild. Do not *under any circumstances* use a Baggie or Saran Wrap to enfold the quenelles. Of course it's easier. So are TV dinners. For once, demand the utmost of yourself: the satisfaction will astound you, and *there is no other way.*

I mentioned this misuse of plastic to a native of La Tour Lambert. My interlocutor, as if appealing for divine aid, leaned back, lifted up his eyes, and stretched forth his arms. He was standing at the edge of a marinating trough; its edges were slick with marinade. One foot shot forward, he teetered for one moment on the brink, and then down he went. Dripping oil, encrusted with fragrant herbs, he emerged briskly and burst into tears.

There are two methods. I shall describe the first one briefly: it is the one used by official cooks for public banquets. Cawl (tripe skin) is scraped free of fat and rubbed with pumice-stone to a thinness approaching non-existence. This gossamer is sewn into an open pouch, which is filled with the quenelles and broth before being sewn shut. The sealing of the pouch is preposterously difficult. I have tried it six times; each time, ineluctable burstage has ensued. Even the nimble-fingered, thimble-thumbed seam-stresses of La Tour Lambert find it hard. In their floodlit corner of the fes-tal cave, they are surrounded by a sizeable choir of wailing boys whose task is to aggravate their intention to a pitch of absolute sustained concentra-tion. If the miracle always occurs, it is never less than miraculous.

The second method is to seal the quenelles inside a clay shell. This de-mands no supernatural skills, merely attention.

Purveyors of reliable cooking clay now exist in all major cities. The best are Italian. In New York, the most dependable are to be found in east Queens. (For addresses, see APPENDIX.)

Stretch and tack down two 18-inch cheesecloth squares. Sprinkle until soaking (mop up puddles, however). Distribute clay in pats and roll flat until entire surface is evenly covered. The layer of clay should be no more than 1/16-inch thick. Scissor edges clean.

Drape each square on an overturned 2-qt bowl. Fold back flaps. Mold into hemispheres. Check fit, then dent edge of each hemisphere with fore-finger so that when dents are facing each other, they form a 3/4-inch hole.

Be sure to prepare the shell at least 48 hours in advance so that it hard-ens properly. (If you are a potter, you can bake it in the oven; if not, you risk cracking.) As the drying clay flattens against the cheesecloth, tiny holes will appear. Do *not* plug them. Little will pass through them: just enough to allow the necessary exchange of savors.

Make the poaching liquid—3 qts of it—like ordinary fish stock (q.v.). The wine used for this in Auvergne is of a local sparkling variety not on the market; but any good champagne is an acceptable substitute.

By "acceptable substitute," I mean one acceptable to me. Purists have cited the fish stock as a reason for not making *farce double* at all. In La Tour Lambert, they rightly assert, the way the stock is kept allows it to evolve without spoiling: in the amphora-like jars that are stored in the coldest depths of the great cave, a faint, perpetual fermentation gives the perennial brew an exquisite, violet-flavored sourness. This, they say, is inimitable. *I* say that 30 drops of decoction of elecampane blossoms will reproduce it so perfectly as to convince the most vigilant tongue.

Fifteen minutes before roasting time, put the quenelles in one of the clay hemispheres. Set the other against it, dent to dent. Seal the seam with clay, except for the hole, and thumb down well. Hold the sphere in one hand with the hole on top. With a funnel, pour in *hot* poaching liquid until it overflows, then empty 1 cup of liquid. This is to keep the shell from bursting from within when the broth reaches a boil.

Be sure to keep the shell in your hand: set in a bowl, one bash against its side will postpone your dinner for several days at least. In La Tour Lambert, where even more fragile gut is used, the risks are lessened by placing the diaphanous bags in woollen reticules. It is still incredible that no damage is ever done to them on the way to the stuffing tables. To avoid their cooling, they are carried at a run by teenage boys, for whom this is a signal honor: every Sunday throughout the following year, they will be allowed to wear their unmistakable lily-white smocks.

Earlier in the day, you will have anointed the lamb, inside and out: inside, with fresh basil, coriander leaves, garlic, and ginger thickly crushed into walnut oil (this is a *must*); outside, with mustard powder mixed with—ideally—wild-boar fat. I know that wild boars do not roam our woods (sometimes, on my walks through Central Park, I feel I may soon meet one): bacon fat will do—about a pint of it.

You will have left the lamb lying outside down. Now nestle the clay shell inside the boneless cavity. Work it patiently into the fleshy nooks, then urge the meat in little bulges around it, pressing the lamb next to the shell, not against it, with the gentlest possible nudges. When the shell is deeply ensconced, fold the outlying flaps over it, and shape the whole into a regular square cushion roast. Sew the edges of the meat together, making the seams hermetically tight.

If the original roasting conditions will surely exceed your grasp, a description of them may clarify your goals.

In Auvergne, the body of the lamb is lowered on wetted ropes into a roasting pit. It comes to rest on transverse bars set close to the floor of the pit. Hours before, ash boughs that have dried through three winters are heaped in the pit and set ablaze: by now they are embers. These are raked against the four sides and piled behind wrought-iron grids into glowing walls. The cast-iron floor stays hot from the fire. When the lamb is in place, a heated iron lid is set over the pit. The lid does more than refract the heat from below. Pierced with a multitude of small holes, it allows for aspersions of water on coals that need damping and the sprinkling of oil on the lamb, which is thus basted throughout its roasting in a continuous fine spray. Previously, I might add, the lamb has been rapidly seared over an open fire. Four senior cooks manage this by standing on high step-ladders and manipulating the poles and extensible thongs used to shift the animal, which they precisely revolve over the flames so that it receives an even grilling.

Thus the onslaught of heat to which the lamb is subjected is, while too restrained to burn it, intense enough to raise the innermost broth to the simmering point.

Carefully lower the lamb into a 25-inch casserole. (If you have no such casserole, buy one. If it will not fit in your oven, consider this merely one more symptom of the shoddiness of our age, which the popularity of dishes like *farce double* may someday remedy.) Cover. You will have turned on the oven at maximum heat for 45 minutes at least. Close the oven door and lower the thermostat to 445°. For the next 5 hours, there is nothing to do except check the oven thermometer occasionally and baste the roast with juices from the casserole every 10 minutes. If you feel like catnapping, have no compunctions about it. Do *not* have anything to drink—considering what lies in store for you, it is a foolish risk. The genial cooks of La Tour Lambert may fall to drinking, dancing, and singing at this point, but remember that they have years of experience behind them; and you, unlike them, must act alone.

One song always sung during the roasting break provides valuable insight into the character of the Auvergnat community. It tells the story of a blacksmith's son who sets out to find his long-lost mother. She is dead, but he cannot remember her death, nor can he accept it. His widowed father has taken as second wife a pretty woman younger than himself. She is hardly motherly towards her stepson: one day, after he has grown to early manhood, she seduces him—in the words of the song, "she does for him what mother never did for her son." This line recurs throughout as a refrain.

It is after the shock of this event that the son leaves in quest of his mother. His father repeatedly tries to dissuade him, insisting that she is dead, or that, if she is alive, it is only in a place "as near as the valley beyond the hill and far away as the stars." In the end, however, he gives his son a sword and a purse full of money and lets him go. The stepmother, also hoping to keep the son from leaving, makes another but this time futile attempt to "do for him what mother never did for her son."

At the end of three days, the son comes to a city. At evening he meets a beautiful woman with long red hair. She offers him hospitality, which he accepts, and she attends lovingly to his every want. Pleasure and hope fill his breast. He begins wondering. He asks himself if this woman might not be his lost mother. But when night falls, the red-haired woman takes him into her bed and "does for him what mother never did for her son." The son knows she cannot be the one he seeks. Pretending to sleep, he waits for an opportunity to leave her; but, at midnight, he sees her draw a length of strong, sharp cord from beneath her pillow and stretch it towards him. The son leaps up, seizes his sword, and confronts the woman. Under its threat, she confesses that she was planning to murder him for the sake of his purse, as she has done with countless travelers: their corpses lie rotting in her cellar. The son slays the woman with his sword, wakes up a nearby priest to assure a Christian burial for her and her victims, and goes his way.

Three days later, he arrives at another city. As day wanes, a strange woman again offers him hospitality, and again he accepts. She is even more beautiful than the first; and her hair is also long, but golden. She lavishes her attentions on the young man, and in such profusion that hope once again spurs him to wonder whether she might not be his lost mother. But with the coming of darkness, the woman with the golden hair takes him into her bed and "does for him what mother never did for her son." His hopes have again been disappointed. Full of unease, he feigns sleep. Halfway through the night he hears footsteps mounting the stairs. He scarcely has time to leap out of bed and grasp his sword before two burly villains come rushing into the room. They attack him, and he cuts them down. Then, turning on the woman, he forces her at swordpoint to confess that she had hoped to make him her prisoner and sell him into slavery. Saracen pirates would have paid a high price for one of such strength and beauty. The son slays her, wakes up a priest to see that she and her henchmen receive Christian burial, and goes his way.

Another three days' journey brings him to a third city. There, at end of day, the son meets still another fair woman, the most beautiful of all, with flowing, raven-black hair. Alone of the three, she seems to recognize him; and when she takes him under her roof and bestows on him more comfort and affection than he had ever dreamed possible, he knows that this time his hope cannot be mistaken. But when night comes, she takes him into her bed, and she, like the others, "does for him what mother never did for her son." She has drugged his food. He cannot help falling asleep; only, at midnight, the touch of cold iron against his throat rouses him from his stupor. Taking up his sword, he points it in fury at the breast of the woman who has so beguiled him. She begs him to leave her in peace, but she finally acknowledges that she meant to cut his throat and suck his blood. She is an old, old witch who has lost all her powers but one, that of preserving her youth. This she does by drinking the blood of young men. The son runs her through with his sword. With a weak cry, she falls to the floor a wrinkled crone. The son knows that a witch cannot be buried in consecrated ground, and he goes his way.

But the young man travels no further. He is bitterly convinced of the folly of his quest; he has lost all hope of ever finding his mother; wearily he turns homeward.

On his way he passes through the cities where he had first faced danger. He is greeted as a hero. Thanks to the two priests, all know that it was he who destroyed the evil incarnate in their midst. But he takes no pride in having killed two women who "did for him what mother never did for her son."

On the ninth day of his return, he sees, from the mountain pass he has reached, the hill beyond which his native village lies. In the valley between, a shepherdess is watching her flock. At his approach she greets him tenderly, for she knows the blacksmith's son and has loved him for many years. He stops with her to rest. She has become, he notices, a beautiful young woman—not as beautiful, perhaps, as the evil three: but her eyes are wide and deep, and her long hair is brown.

The afternoon goes by. Still the son does not leave. At evening, he partakes of the shepherdess's frugal supper. At night-time, when she lies down, he lies down beside her, and she, her heart brimming with gladness, "does for him what mother never did for her son." The shepherdess falls asleep. The son cannot sleep; and he is appalled, in the middle of the night, to see the shepherdess suddenly rise up beside him. But she only touches his shoulder as if to waken him and points to the starry sky. She tells him to look up. There, she says, beyond the darkness, the souls of the dead have gathered into one blazing light. With a cry of pain, the son asks, "Then is my mother there?" The shepherdess answers that she is. His mother lives beyond the stars, and the stars themselves are chinks in the night through which the fateful light of the dead and the unborn is revealed to the world. "Oh, Mother, Mother," the young man weeps. The shepherdess then says to him, "Who is now mother to your sleep and waking? Who else can be the mother of your joy and pain? I shall henceforth be the mother of every memory; and from this night on, I alone am your mother—even if now, and tomorrow, and all the days of my life, I do for you what mother never did for her son." In his sudden ecstasy, the blacksmith's son understands. He has discovered his desire.

And so, next morning, he brings the shepherdess home. His father, when he sees them, weeps tears of relief and joy; and his stepmother, sick with remorse, welcomes them as saviors. Henceforth they all live in mutual contentment; and when, every evening, the approach of darkness kindles new yearning in the young man's heart and he turns to embrace his wife, she devotedly responds and never once fails, through the long passing years, to "do for him what mother never did for her son."

The connection of this song with *farce double* lies, I was told, in an analogy between the stars and the holes in the lid of the roasting pit.

When your timer sounds for the final round, you must be in fighting trim: not aggressive, but supremely alert. You now have to work at high speed and with utmost delicacy. The meat will have swelled in cooking: it is pressing against the clay shell harder than ever, and one jolt can spell disaster. Do not coddle yourself by thinking that this pressure is buttressing the shell. In La Tour Lambert, the handling of the cooked lamb is entrusted to squads of highly trained young men: they are solemn as pallbearers and dextrous as shortstops, and their virtuosity is eloquent proof that this is no time for optimism.

Slide the casserole slowly out of the oven and gently set it down on a table covered with a thrice-folded blanket. You will now need help. Summon anyone—a friend, a neighbor, a husband, a lover, a sibling, even a guest—so that the two of you can slip four broad wooden spatulas under the roast, one on each side, and ease it on to a platter. The platter should be resting on a soft surface such as a cushion or a mattress (a small hammock would be perfect). Wait for the meat to cool before moving it on to anything harder. Your assistant may withdraw.

Meanwhile attend to the gravy. No later than the previous evening, you will have made 1½ qts of stock with the bones from the lamb shoulder, together with the customary onions, carrots, celery, herb bouquet, cloves, scallions, parsnips, and garlic (see STOCK), to which you must not hesitate to add any old fowl, capon, partridge, or squab carcasses that are gathering rime in your deep freeze, or a young rabbit or two. Pour out the fat in the casserole and set it on the stove over high heat. Splash in enough of the same good champagne to scrape the casserole clean, and boil. When the wine has largely evaporated, take off heat, and add 2 cups of rendered pork fat. Set the casserole over very low heat and make a quick *roux* or brown sauce with 3 cups of flour. Then slowly pour in 2 cups of the blood of the lamb, stirring it in a spoonful at a time. Finally, add the stock. Raise the heat to medium high and let the liquid simmer down to the equivalent of 13 cupfuls.

While the gravy reduces, carefully set the platter with the roast on a table, resting one side on an object the size of this cookbook, so that it sits at a tilt. Place a broad shallow bowl against the lower side. If the clay shell now breaks, the poaching broth will flow rapidly into the bowl. Prop the lamb with a wooden spoon or two to keep it from sliding off the platter.

Slit the seams in the meat, spread its folds, and expose the clay shell. Put on kitchen gloves—the clay will be scalding—and coax the shell from its depths. Set it in a saucepan, give it a smart crack with a mallet, and remove the grosser shards. Ladle out the quenelles and keep them warm in the oven in a covered, buttered dish with a few spoonfuls of broth. Strain the rest of the liquid, reduce it quickly to a quarter of its volume, and then use what is left of the champagne to make a white sauce as explained on p. 888. Nap the quenelles with sauce and serve.

If you have worked fast and well, by the time your guests finish the quenelles, the lamb will have set long enough for its juices to have withdrawn into the tissues without its getting cold. Pour the gravy into individual heated bowls. Place a bowl in front of each guest, and set the platter with the lamb, which you will have turned outside up, at the center of the table. The meat is eaten without knives and forks. Break off a morsel with the fingers of the right hand, dip it in gravy, and pop it into your mouth. In Auvergne, this is managed with nary a dribble; but lobster bibs are a comfort.

(Do not be upset if you yourself have lost all desire to eat. This is a normal, salutary condition. Your satisfaction will have been in the doing, not in the thing done. But observe the reaction of your guests, have a glass of wine [see below], and you may feel the urge to try one bite, and perhaps a second . . .)

It is a solemn moment when, at the great communal spring banquet, the mayor of La Tour Lambert goes from table to table and with shining fingers gravely breaks the skin of each lamb. After this ceremony, however, the prevailing gaiety reasserts itself After all, the feast of *farce double* is not only a time-hallowed occasion but a very pleasant one. It is a moment for friendships to be renewed, for enemies to forgive one another, for lovers to embrace. At its origin, curiously enough, the feast was associated with second marriages (some writers think this gave the dish its name). Such marriages have never been historically explained; possibly they never took place. What is certain is that the feast has always coincided with the arrival, from the lowlands, of shepherds driving their flocks to the high pastures where they will summer. Their coming heralds true spring and its first warmth; and it restores warmth, too, between the settled mountain craftsmen of La Tour Lambert and the semi-nomadic shepherds from the south. The two communities are separate only in their ways of life. They have long been allied by esteem, common interest, and, most important, by blood. Marriages between them have been recorded since the founding of the village in the year one thousand; and if many a shepherd's daughter has settled in La Tour Lambert as the wife of a wheelwright or turner, many an Auvergnat son, come autumn, has left his father's mill or forge to follow the migrant flocks towards Les Saintes-Maries-de-la-Mer. Perhaps the legend of second marriages reflects a practice whereby a widow or a widower took a spouse among the folk of which he was not a member. The eating of *farce double* would then be exquisitely appropriate; for there is no doubt at all that the composition of the dish—lamb from the plains by the sea, fish from lakes among the grazing lands—deliberately embodies the merging of these distinct peoples in one community. I should add that at the time the feast originated, still another group participated harmoniously in its celebration: pilgrims from Burgundy on their way to Santiago de Compostela. Just as the people of La Tour Lambert provided fish for the great banquet and the shepherds contributed their lambs, the pilgrims supplied kegs of new white wine that they brought with them from Chassagne, the Burgundian village now called Chassagne-Montrachet. Their wine became the invariable accompaniment for both parts of *farce double;* and you could hardly do better than to adopt the custom. Here, at least, tradition can be observed with perfect fidelity.

It is saddening to report that, like the rest of the world, La Tour Lambert has undergone considerable change. Shepherds no longer walk their flocks from the south but ship them by truck. The lakes have been fished out, and a substitute for *chaste* is imported frozen from Yugoslavia. The grandson of the last wheelwright works in the tourist bureau, greeting latter-day pilgrims who bring no wine. He is one of the very few of his generation to have remained in the village. (The cement quarry, which was opened with great fanfare ten years ago as a way of providing jobs, employs mainly foreign labor. Its most visible effect has been to shroud the landscape in white dust.) I have heard, however, that the blacksmith still earns a good living making wrought-iron lamps. Fortunately, the future of *farce double* is assured, at least for the time being. The festal cave has been put on a commercial footing, and it now produces the dish for restaurants in the area all year round (in the off season, on weekends only). It is open to the public. I recommend a visit if you pass nearby.

Eat the quenelles ungarnished. Mashed sorrel goes nicely with the lamb. Serves thirteen.

1982

Or: Maybe every essay automatically is in some way experimental—less an outline traveling toward a foregone conclusion than an unmapped quest that has sprung from the word *question.*

ANNIE DILLARD

Total Eclipse

I

It had been like dying, that sliding down the mountain pass. It had been like the death of someone, irrational, that sliding down the mountain pass and into the region of dread. It was like slipping into fever, or falling down that hole in sleep from which you wake yourself whimpering. We had crossed the mountains that day, and now we were in a strange place—a hotel in central Washington, in a town near Yakima. The eclipse we had traveled here to see would occur early the next morning.

I lay in bed. My husband, Gary, was reading beside me. I lay in bed and looked at the painting on the hotel room wall. It was a print of a detailed and lifelike painting of a smiling clown's head, made out of vegetables. It was a painting of the sort which you do not intend to look at, and which, alas, you never forget. Some tasteless fate presses it upon you; it becomes part of the complex interior junk you carry with you wherever you go. Two years have passed since the total eclipse of which I write. During those years I have forgotten, I assume, a great many things I wanted to remember—but I have not forgotten that clown painting or its lunatic setting in the old hotel.

The clown was bald. Actually, he wore a clown's tight rubber wig, painted white; this stretched over the top of his skull, which was a cabbage. His hair was bunches of baby carrots. Inset in his white clown makeup, and in his cabbage skull, were his small and laughing human eyes. The clown's glance was like the glance of Rembrandt in some of the self-portraits: lively, knowing, deep, and loving. The crinkled shadows around his eyes were string beans. His eyebrows were parsley. Each of his ears was a broad bean. His thin, joyful lips were red chili peppers; between his lips were wet rows of human teeth and a suggestion of a real tongue. The clown print was framed in gilt and glassed.

To put ourselves in the path of the total eclipse, that day we had driven five hours inland from the Washington coast, where we lived. When we tried to cross the Cascades range, an avalanche had blocked the pass.

A slope's worth of snow blocked the road; traffic backed up. Had the avalanche buried any cars that morning? We could not learn. This highway was the only winter road over the mountains. We waited as highway crews bulldozed a passage through the avalanche. With two-by-fours and walls of plyboard, they erected a one-way, roofed tunnel through the avalanche. We drove through the avalanche tunnel, crossed the pass, and descended several thousand feet into central Washington and the broad Yakima valley, about which we knew only that it was orchard country. As we lost altitude, the snows disappeared; our ears popped; the trees changed, and in the trees were strange birds. I watched the landscape innocently, like a fool, like a diver in the rapture of the deep who plays on the bottom while his air runs out.

The hotel lobby was a dark, derelict room, narrow as a corridor, and seemingly without air. We waited on a couch while the manager vanished upstairs to do something unknown to our room. Beside us on an overstuffed chair, absolutely motionless, was a platinum-blond woman in her forties wearing a black silk dress and a strand of pearls. Her long legs were crossed; she supported her head on her fist. At the dim far end of the room, their backs toward us, sat six bald old men in their shirtsleeves, around a loud television. Two of them seemed asleep. They were drunks. "Number six!" cried the man on television, "Number six!"

On the broad lobby desk, lighted and bubbling, was a ten-gallon aquarium containing one large fish; the fish tilted up and down in its water. Against the long opposite wall sang a live canary in its cage. Beneath the cage, among spilled millet seeds on the carpet, were a decorated child's sand bucket and matching sand shovel.

Now the alarm was set for six. I lay awake remembering an article I had read downstairs in the lobby, in an engineering magazine. The article was about gold mining.

In South Africa, in India, and in South Dakota, the gold mines extend so deeply into the earth's crust that they are hot. The rock walls burn the miners' hands. The companies have to air-condition the mines; if the air conditioners break, the miners die. The elevators in the mine shafts run very slowly, down, and up, so the miners' ears will not pop in their skulls. When the miners return to the surface, their faces are deathly pale.

Early the next morning we checked out. It was February 26, 1979, a Monday morning. We would drive out of town, find a hilltop, watch the eclipse, and then drive back over the mountains and home to the coast. How familiar things are here; how adept we are; how smoothly and professionally we check out! I had forgotten the clown's smiling head and the hotel lobby as if they had never existed. Gary put the car in gear and off we went, as off we have gone to a hundred other adventures.

It was before dawn when we found a highway out of town and drove into the unfamiliar countryside. By the growing light we could see a band of cirrostratus clouds in the sky. Later the rising sun would clear these clouds before the eclipse began. We drove at random until we came to a range of unfenced hills. We pulled off the highway, bundled up, and climbed one of these hills.

II

The hill was five hundred feet high. Long winter-killed grass covered it, as high as our knees. We climbed and rested, sweating in the cold; we passed clumps of bundled people on the hillside who were setting up telescopes and fiddling with cameras. The top of the hill stuck up in the middle of the sky. We tightened our scarves and looked around.

East of us rose another hill like ours. Between the hills, far below, was the highway which threaded south into the valley. This was the Yakima valley; I had never seen it before. It is justly famous for its beauty, like every planted valley. It extended south into the horizon, a distant dream of a valley, a Shangri-la. All its hundreds of low, golden slopes bore orchards. Among the orchards were towns, and roads, and plowed and fallow fields. Through the valley wandered a thin, shining river; from the river extended fine, frozen irrigation ditches. Distance blurred and blued the sight, so that the whole valley looked like a thickness or sediment at the bottom of the sky.

Directly behind us was more sky, and empty lowlands blued by distance, and Mount Adams. Mount Adams was an enormous, snow-covered volcanic cone rising flat, like so much scenery.

Now the sun was up. We could not see it; but the sky behind the band of clouds was yellow, and, far down the valley, some hillside orchards had lighted up. More people were parking near the highway and climbing the hills. It was the West. All of us rugged individualists were wearing knit caps and blue nylon parkas. People were climbing the nearby hills and setting up shop in clumps among the dead grasses. It looked as though we had all gathered on hilltops to pray for the world on its last day. It looked as though we had all crawled out of spaceships and were preparing to assault the valley below. It looked as though we were scattered on hilltops at dawn to sacrifice virgins, make rain, set stone stelae in a ring. There was no place out of the wind. The straw grasses banged our legs.

Up in the sky where we stood the air was lusterless yellow. To the west the sky was blue. Now the sun cleared the clouds. We cast rough shadows on the blowing grass; freezing, we waved our arms. Near the sun, the sky was bright and colorless. There was nothing to see.

It began with no ado. It was odd that such a well-advertised public event should have no starting gun, no overture, no introductory speaker. I should have known right then that I was out of my depth. Without pause or preamble, silent as orbits, a piece of the sun went away. We looked at it through welders' goggles. A piece of the sun was missing; in its place we saw empty sky.

I had seen a partial eclipse in 1970. A partial eclipse is very interesting. It bears almost no relation to a total eclipse. Seeing a partial eclipse bears the same relation to seeing a total eclipse as kissing a man does to marrying him, or as flying in an airplane does to falling out of an airplane. Although the one experience precedes the other, it in no way prepares you for it. During a partial eclipse the sky does not darken—not even when 94 percent of the sun is hidden. Nor does the sun, seen colorless through protective devices, seem terribly strange. We have all seen a sliver of light in the sky; we have all seen the crescent moon by day. However, during a partial eclipse the air does indeed get cold, precisely as if someone were standing between you and the fire. And blackbirds do fly back to their roosts. I had seen a partial eclipse before, and here was another.

What you see in an eclipse is entirely different from what you know. It is especially different for those of us whose grasp of astronomy is so frail that, given a flashlight, a grapefruit, two oranges, and fifteen years, we still could not figure out which way to set the clocks for Daylight Saving Time. Usually it is a bit of a trick to keep your knowledge from blinding you. But during an eclipse it is easy. What you see is much more convincing than any wild-eyed theory you may know.

You may read that the moon has something to do with eclipses. I have never seen the moon yet. You do not see the moon. So near the sun, it is as completely invisible as the stars are by day. What you see before your eyes is the sun going through phases. It gets narrower and narrower, as the waning moon does, and, like the ordinary moon, it travels alone in the simple sky. The sky is of course background. It does not appear to eat the sun; it is far behind the sun. The sun simply shaves away; gradually, you see less sun and more sky.

The sky's blue was deepening, but there was no darkness. The sun was a wide crescent, like a segment of tangerine. The wind freshened and blew steadily over the hill. The eastern hill across the highway grew dusky and sharp. The towns and orchards in the valley to the south were dissolving into the blue light. Only the thin river held a trickle of sun.

Now the sky to the west deepened to indigo, a color never seen. A dark sky usually loses color. This was a saturated, deep indigo, up in the air. Stuck up into that unworldly sky was the cone of Mount Adams, and the alpenglow was upon it. The alpenglow is that red light of sunset which holds out on snowy mountaintops long after the valleys and tablelands are dimmed. "Look at Mount Adams," I said, and that was the last sane moment I remember.

I turned back to the sun. It was going. The sun was going, and the world was wrong. The grasses were wrong; they were platinum. Their every detail of stem, head, and blade shone lightless and artificially distinct as an art photographer's platinum print. This color has never been seen on earth. The hues were metallic; their finish was matte. The hillside was a nineteenth-century tinted photograph from which the tints had faded. All the people you see in the photograph, distinct and detailed as their faces look, are now dead. The sky was navy blue. My hands were silver. All the distant hills' grasses were finespun metal which the wind laid down. I was watching a faded color print of a movie filmed in the Middle Ages; I was standing in it, by some mistake. I was standing in a movie of hillside grasses filmed in the Middle Ages. I missed my own century, the people I knew, and the real light of day.

I looked at Gary. He was in the film. Everything was lost. He was a platinum print, a dead artist's version of life. I saw on his skull the darkness of night mixed with the colors of day. My mind was going out; my eyes were receding the way galaxies recede to the rim of space. Gary was light-years away, gesturing inside a circle of darkness, down the wrong end of a telescope. He smiled as if he saw me; the stringy crinkles around his eyes moved. The sight of him, familiar and wrong, was something I was remembering from centuries hence, from the other side of death: yes, *that* is the way he used to look, when we were living. When it was our generation's turn to be alive. I could not hear him; the wind was too loud. Behind him the sun was going. We had all started down a chute of time. At first it was pleasant; now there was no stopping it. Gary was chuting away across space, moving and talking and catching my eye, chuting down the long corridor of separation. The skin on his face moved like thin bronze plating that would peel.

The grass at our feet was wild barley. It was the wild einkorn wheat which grew on the hilly flanks of the Zagros Mountains, above the Euphrates valley, above the valley of the river we called *River*. We harvested the grass with stone sickles, I remember. We found the grasses on the hillsides; we built our shelter beside them and cut them down. That is how he used to look then, that one, moving and living and catching my eye, with the sky so dark behind him, and the wind blowing. God save our life.

From all the hills came screams. A piece of sky beside the crescent sun was detaching. It was a loosened circle of evening sky, suddenly lighted from the back. It was an abrupt black body out of nowhere; it was a flat disk; it was almost over the sun. That is when there were screams. At once this disk of sky slid over the sun like a lid. The sky snapped over the sun like a lens cover. The hatch in the brain slammed. Abruptly it was dark night, on the land and in the sky. In the night sky was a tiny ring of light. The hole where the sun belongs is very small. A thin ring of light marked its place.

There was no sound. The eyes dried, the arteries drained, the lungs hushed. There was no world. We were the world's dead people rotating and orbiting around and around, embedded in the planet's crust, while the earth rolled down. Our minds were light-years distant, forgetful of almost everything. Only an extraordinary act of will could recall to us our former, living selves and our contexts in matter and time. We had, it seems, loved the planet and loved our lives, but could no longer remember the way of them. We got the light wrong. In the sky was something that should not be there. In the black sky was a ring of light. It was a thin ring, an old, thin silver wedding band, an old, worn ring. It was an old wedding band in the sky, or a morsel of bone. There were stars. It was all over.

III

It is now that the temptation is strongest to leave these regions. We have seen enough; let's go. Why burn our hands any more than we have to? But two years have passed; the price of gold has risen. I return to the same buried alluvial beds and pick through the strata again.

I saw, early in the morning, the sun diminish against a backdrop of sky. I saw a circular piece of that sky appear, suddenly detached, blackened, and backlighted; from nowhere it came and overlapped the sun. It did not look like the moon. It was enormous and black. If I had not read that it was the moon, I could have seen the sight a hundred times and never thought of the moon once. (If, however, I had not read that it was the moon—if, like most of the world's people throughout time, I had simply glanced up and seen this thing—then I doubtless would not have speculated much, but would have, like Emperor Louis of Bavaria in 840, simply died of fright on the spot.) It did not look like a dragon, although it looked more like a dragon than the moon. It looked like a lens cover, or the lid of a pot. It materialized out of thin air—black, and flat, and sliding, outlined in flame.

Seeing this black body was like seeing a mushroom cloud. The heart screeched. The meaning of the sight overwhelmed its fascination. It obliterated meaning itself. If you were to glance out one day and see a row of mushroom clouds rising on the horizon, you would know at once that what you were seeing, remarkable as it was, was intrinsically not worth remarking. No use running to tell anyone. Significant as it was, it did not matter a whit. For what is significance? It is significance for people. No people, no significance. This is all I have to tell you.

In the deeps are the violence and terror of which psychology has warned us. But if you ride these monsters deeper down, if you drop with them farther over the world's rim, you find what our sciences cannot locate or name, the substrate, the ocean or matrix or ether which buoys the rest, which gives goodness its power for good, and evil its power for evil, the unified field: our complex and inexplicable caring for each other, and for our life together here. This is given. It is not learned.

The world which lay under darkness and stillness following the closing of the lid was not the world we know. The event was over. Its devastation lay round about us. The clamoring mind and heart stilled, almost indifferent, certainly disembodied, frail, and exhausted. The hills were hushed, obliterated. Up in the sky, like a crater from some distant cataclysm, was a hollow ring.

You have seen photographs of the sun taken during a total eclipse. The corona fills the print. All of those photographs were taken through telescopes. The lenses of telescopes and cameras can no more cover the breadth and scale of the visual array than language can cover the breadth and simultaneity of internal experience. Lenses enlarge the sight, omit its context, and make of it a pretty and sensible picture, like something on a Christmas card. I assure you, if you send any shepherds a Christmas card on which is printed a three-by-three photograph of the angel of the Lord, the glory of the Lord, and a multitude of the heavenly host, they will not be sore afraid. More fearsome things can come in envelopes. More moving photographs than those of the sun's corona can appear in magazines. But I pray you will never see anything more awful in the sky.

You see the wide world swaddled in darkness; you see a vast breadth of hilly land, and an enormous, distant, blackened valley; you see towns' lights, a river's path, and blurred portions of your hat and scarf; you see your husband's face looking like an early black-and-white film; and you see a sprawl of black sky and blue sky together, with unfamiliar stars in it, some barely visible bands of cloud, and over there, a small white ring. The ring is as small as one goose in a flock of migrating geese—if you happen to notice a flock of migrating geese. It is one 360th part of the visible sky.

The sun we see is less than half the diameter of a dime held at arm's length.

The Crab Nebula, in the constellation Taurus, looks, through binoculars, like a smoke ring. It is a star in the process of exploding. Light from its explosion first reached the earth in 1054; it was a supernova then, and so bright it shone in the daytime. Now it is not so bright, but it is still exploding. It expands at the rate of seventy million miles a day. It is interesting to look through binoculars at something expanding seventy million miles a day. It does not budge. Its apparent size does not increase. Photographs of the Crab Nebula taken fifteen years ago seem identical to photographs of it taken yesterday. Some lichens are similar. Botanists have measured some ordinary lichens twice, at fifty-year intervals, without detecting any growth at all. And yet their cells divide; they live.

The small ring of light was like these things—like a ridiculous lichen up in the sky, like a perfectly still explosion 4,200 light-years away: it was interesting, and lovely, and in witless motion, and it had nothing to do with anything.

It had nothing to do with anything. The sun was too small, and too cold, and too far away, to keep the world alive. The white ring was not enough. It was feeble and worthless. It was as useless as a memory; it was as off kilter and hollow and wretched as a memory.

When you try your hardest to recall someone's face, or the look of a place, you see in your mind's eye some vague and terrible sight such as this. It is dark; it is insubstantial; it is all wrong.

The white ring and the saturated darkness made the earth and sky look as they must look in the memories of the careless dead. What I saw, what I seemed to be standing in, was all the wrecked light that the memories of the dead could shed upon the living world. We had all died in our boots on the hilltops of the Yakima, and were alone in eternity. Empty space stoppered our eyes and mouths; we cared for nothing. We remembered our living days wrong. With great effort we had remembered some sort of circular light in the sky—but only the outline. Oh, and then the orchard trees withered, the ground froze, the glaciers slid down the valleys and overlapped the towns. If there had ever been people on earth, nobody knew it. The dead had forgotten those they had loved. The dead were parted one from the other and could no longer remember the faces and lands they had loved in the light. They seemed to stand on darkened hilltops, looking down.

IV

We teach our children one thing only, as we were taught: to wake up. We teach our children to look alive there, to join by words and activities the life of human culture on the planet's crust. As adults we are almost all adept at waking up. We have so mastered the transition we have forgotten we ever learned it. Yet it is a transition we make a hundred times a day, as, like so many will-less dolphins, we plunge and surface, lapse and emerge. We live half our waking lives and all of our sleeping lives in some private, useless, and insensible waters we never mention or recall. Useless, I say. Valueless, I might add—until someone hauls their wealth up to the surface and into the wide-awake city, in a form that people can use.

I do not know how we got to the restaurant. Like Roethke, "I take my waking slow." Gradually I seemed more or less alive, and already forgetful. It was now almost nine in the morning. It was the day of a solar eclipse in central Washington, and a fine adventure for everyone. The sky was clear; there was a fresh breeze out of the north.

The restaurant was a roadside place with tables and booths. The other eclipse-watchers were there. From our booth we could see their cars' California license plates, their University of Washington parking stickers. Inside the restaurant we were all eating eggs or waffles; people were fairly shouting and exchanging enthusiasms, like fans after a World Series game. Did you see . . . ? Did you see . . . ? Then somebody said something which knocked me for a loop.

A college student, a boy in a blue parka who carried a Hasselblad, said to us, "Did you see that little white ring? It looked like a Life Saver. It looked like a Life Saver up in the sky."

And so it did. The boy spoke well. He was a walking alarm clock. I myself had at that time no access to such a word. He could write a sentence, and I could not. I grabbed that Life Saver and rode it to the surface. And I had to laugh. I had been dumbstruck on the Euphrates River, I had been dead and gone and grieving, all over the sight of something which, if you could claw your way up to that level, you would grant looked very much like a Life Saver. It was good to be back among people so clever; it was good to have all the world's words at the mind's disposal, so the mind could begin its task. All those things for which we have no words are lost. The mind—the culture—has two little tools, grammar and lexicon: a decorated sand bucket and a matching shovel. With these we bluster about the continents and do all the world's work. With these we try to save our very lives.

There are a few more things to tell from this level, the level of the restaurant. One is the old joke about breakfast. "It can never be satisfied, the mind, never." Wallace Stevens wrote that, and in the long run he was right. The mind wants to live forever, or to learn a very good reason why not. The mind wants the world to return its love, or its awareness; the mind wants to know all the world, and all eternity, and God. The mind's sidekick, however, will settle for two eggs over easy.

The dear, stupid body is as easily satisfied as a spaniel. And, incredibly, the simple spaniel can lure the brawling mind to its dish. It is everlastingly funny that the proud, metaphysically ambitious, clamoring mind will hush if you give it an egg.

Further: while the mind reels in deep space, while the mind grieves or fears or exults, the workaday senses, in ignorance or idiocy, like so many computer terminals printing out market prices while the world blows up, still transcribe their little data and transmit them to the warehouse in the skull. Later, under the tranquilizing influence of fried eggs, the mind can sort through this data. The restaurant was a halfway house, a decompression chamber. There I remembered a few things more.

The deepest, and most terrifying, was this: I have said that I heard screams. (I have since read that screaming, with hysteria, is a common reaction even to expected total eclipses.) People on all the hillsides, including, I think, myself, screamed when the black body of the moon detached from the sky and rolled over the sun. But something else was happening at that same instant, and it was this, I believe, which made us scream.

The second before the sun went out we saw a wall of dark shadow come speeding at us. We no sooner saw it than it was upon us, like thunder. It roared up the valley. It slammed our hill and knocked us out. It was the monstrous swift shadow cone of the moon. I have since read that this wave of shadow moves 1,800 miles an hour. Language can give no sense of this sort of speed—1,800 miles an hour. It was 195 miles wide. No end was in sight —you saw only the edge. It rolled at you across the land at 1,800 miles an hour, hauling darkness like plague behind it. Seeing it, and knowing it was coming straight for you, was like feeling a slug of anesthetic shoot up your arm. If you think very fast, you may have time to think, "Soon it will hit my brain." You can feel the deadness race up your arm; you can feel the appalling, inhuman speed of your own blood. We saw the wall of shadow coming, and screamed before it hit.

This was the universe about which we have read so much and never before felt: the universe as a clockwork of loose spheres flung at stupefying, unauthorized speeds. How could anything moving so fast not crash, not veer from its orbit amok like a car out of control on a turn?

Less than two minutes later, when the sun emerged, the trailing edge of the shadow cone sped away. It coursed down our hill and raced eastward over the plain, faster than the eye could believe; it swept over the plain and dropped over the planet's rim in a twinkling. It had clobbered us, and now it roared away. We blinked in the light. It was as though an enormous, loping god in the sky had reached down and slapped the earth's face.

Something else, something more ordinary, came back to me along about the third cup of coffee. During the moments of totality, it was so dark that drivers on the highway below turned on their cars' headlights. We could see the highway's route as a strand of lights. It was bumper-to-bumper down there. It was eight-fifteen in the morning, Monday morning, and people were driving into Yakima to work. That it was as dark as night, and eerie as hell, an hour after dawn, apparently meant that in order to *see* to drive to work, people had to use their headlights. Four or five cars pulled off the road. The rest, in a line at least five miles long, drove to town. The highway ran between hills; the people could not have seen any of the eclipsed sun at all. Yakima will have another total eclipse in 2086. Perhaps, in 2086, businesses will give their employees an hour off.

From the restaurant we drove back to the coast. The highway crossing the Cascades range was open. We drove over the mountain like old pros. We joined our places on the planet's thin crust; it held. For the time being, we were home free.

Early that morning at six, when we had checked out, the six bald men were sitting on folding chairs in the dim hotel lobby. The television was on. Most of them were awake. You might drown in your own spittle, God knows, at any time; you might wake up dead in a small hotel, a cabbage head watching TV while snows pile up in the passes, watching TV while the chili peppers smile and the moon passes over the sun and nothing changes and nothing is learned because you have lost your bucket and shovel and no longer care. What if you regain the surface and open your sack and find, instead of treasure, a breast which jumps at you? Or you may not come back at all. The winches may jam, the scaffolding buckle, the air conditioning collapse. You may glance up one day and see by your head-lamp the canary keeled over in its cage. You may reach into a cranny for pearls and touch a moray eel. You yank on your rope; it is too late.

Apparently people share a sense of these hazards, for when the total eclipse ended, an odd thing happened.

When the sun appeared as a blinding bead on the ring's side, the eclipse was over. The black lens cover appeared again, backlighted, and slid away. At once the yellow light made the sky blue again; the black lid dissolved and vanished. The real world began there. I remember now: we all hurried away. We were born and bored at a stroke. We rushed down the hill. We found our car; we saw the other people streaming down the hillsides; we joined the highway traffic and drove away.

We never looked back. It was a general vamoose, and an odd one, for when we left the hill, the sun was still partially eclipsed—a sight rare enough, and one which, in itself, we would probably have driven five hours to see. But enough is enough. One turns at last even from glory itself with a sigh of relief. From the depths of mystery, and even from the heights of splendor, we bounce back and hurry for the latitudes of home.

1983

Who is America's great modern essayist? How about postmodern? Some say the essay is the only American genre to never have made a transition into the twentieth century. Would this be the case if those American writers who ostensibly work in essayistic forms called the work that they produced essays? David Antin improvises his poems during performances he gives in front of live audiences. He composes in the tradition of "man on his feet, talking," he says, a tradition based on the earliest Greek ideas of poetry—*dianoia,* traveling bards—an associative, meditative, process-oriented way of making art, reminiscent of the conversations conducted during walks in Arcadia by the earliest men who talked on their feet: "if robert lowell is a poet i don't want to be a poet / if robert frost is a poet i don't want to be a poet / if socrates was a poet i'll consider it."*

---

* Socrates was an essayist.

DAVID ANTIN

The Theory and Practice of Postmodernism: A Manifesto

about two years ago ellie and I decided we needed a new
mattress   or maybe ellie decided it   because i didnt pay much
attention to the problem
                            we had an old mattress we'd had it for
years and the salesman we bought it from had assured us it would
last us a lifetime   and it was getting older and lumpy or lumpy
in some places and hollowed out in others and   i just assumed
    it was part of a normal process of aging   it was getting
older we were getting older and we'd get used to it

but eleanor has a bad back and she was getting desperate
to get rid of   this mattress   that had lived with us for such
a long time   and so loyally   that i thought i knew all of its
    high points and low points   its eminences and pitfalls   and
i was sure that at night my body worked its way carefully around
the lumps   dodging the precipices   and moving to solider
    ground whenever it could
                            but maybe eleanor sleeps more heavily
than i do   i have a feeling that i spent much of my life at night
    avoiding the pitfalls of this mattress that i was used to   and it
    was a skill i'd acquired over the ten or fifteen years of this
mattress's life   so i felt there was no reason to get rid of this
    mattress that had been promised to us by a salesman who said
it would last the rest of our lives   i figured we were going to live
    long lives i didnt think we were anywhere close to dying   so

neither was the mattress   but eleanor kept waking up with
   backaches

            still i figured it was a good mattress and that ellie just
didnt have enough skill at avoiding the lumps   it never
   occurred to me that the mattress was at fault   so i didnt do
anything   and ellie didnt do anything because she's not into
   consumer products and she hates to go shopping   but by the end
of a year ellie convinced me   because she has a sensitive back
and i dont   that she had a more accurate understanding of this
   business than i did   so i said sure eleanor   let's get a new
mattress   we're rebuilding the house   as long as we're going
to have a new house   we may as well have a new mattress   but
   eleanor said how will i know its a good one   i don't want to get
another mattress that gets hollowed out and lumpy and gives me
backaches when i wake up   how will i know how to get a good
   one?

            i said we'll open the yellow pages and we'll look up
   mattresses and therell be several places that sell them   and
i'll close my eyes and point a finger at one of these places   and
   it will be a place that has lots of mattresses where we can make
   a choice as to what constitutes a good one by lying on them

            now ellie really knew that you cant just walk into a
   place and buy a mattress   she knows this about american
consumer goods   and she knows that these places would be
equipped with rich delusional capabilities whatever they might be
      we would go to a great warehouse with subdued lighting where
      they played somniferous music   that encouraged you into
   restful comfort while people would be heard talking in hushed
voices walking about examining the mattresses or testing them by
gently reclining on them   "oh are you buying that one   my
   aunt sylvie had one just like it and practically lived on it"
      "that's a wonderful mattress   my uncle everett suffered for
years from lumbago that never let him sleep   he bought that
mattress and slept like a baby ever since"   "my aunt agnes had

asthma and she used to wake up every hour gasping for breath
       since she's been sleeping on this mattress she sleeps like a
log   she rises fresh every morning and plays three sets of tennis
every afternoon   and she's seventy-three"

              so eleanor said i cant deal with that and i said okay el
    what are you going to do?   she said i'll call carol
                                             carol is
    our expert   carol has been an expert in anything domestic that
we've ever done all our lives because we're definitely not   carol
has been our great expert on everything   gardeners carpenters
    schools   eleanor calls carol   and its hard sometimes   carol
may have a new husband   and then she's living somewhere else
    and youve got to find her   she's an expert on everything but
    men or she is an expert on men   but   she changes them
    fairly often   she's been married five times and each time it seems
fine   but then it turns out after a while its not fine   or not
fine any more   so she has to change men   and probably
changes mattresses with them   so she should be an expert on
    mattresses

              but for some reason carol is unavailable   she's on a
jury or she's managing somebody's election campaign or consulting
    on somebody's math program   she's inaccessible and cant
return ellie's phone calls   i said well   youre going to have to
    call somebody   how about a chiropractor   why dont you
call a chiropractor   youve got two chiropractors   they ought
    to know whats good for your back
                                        she said which one should i call?
       i said call them both   she said which one should i call first?
       i dont know i said   why dont you call akasha?   akasha
is a sikh   not from india but from los angeles   he's a wonderful
chiropractor but he's a los angeles kid who grew up to be a
    vegetarian and a los angeles dodger fan and a sikh   he has a
pale white bread looking face under his white turban but he knows
    all about diet and he can stick you all over with little pins and he
has wonderful hands   and when he presses your back your pains

magically go away sooner or later   and we dont go to him for the
    diet or the exercises he can teach or for classes in shamanism
        or even for the little pins   but for his wonderful hands
          he has more excellences than we can rightly enjoy   but we
go to him for his wonderful hands and we have conversations about
the dodgers and the padres while he makes our back pains go away
          and eleanor calls him but it turns out that mattresses are
not part of his expertise   he tells eleanor he knows nothing
    about what could separate a poor mattress from a good mattress
and he suggests we call nikolai   he should know more about it
        he lives in del mar

                i find this frankly puzzling   nikolai is our sloe eyed
weight lifter chiropractor who used to be part of the sixties
    alternative scene in la jolla that ran the *unicorn*   a theater that
showed only classics   and ran *mithras*   a bookstore that
    specialized in spiritual healing   but now that the sixties and
seventies were over he's become a chiropractor to upscale del mar
    and has to control a taste for rich food in pricey italian restaurants
        akasha figured he would know about mattresses   i wasnt
sure of the logic but nikolai had played the weight lifter in eleanor's
    last movie and i figured he'd be willing to share whatever
knowledge he had
                            but he was attending a conference on chiropractic
somewhere near aspen and ellie couldnt reach him

            ellie i said if you want a mattress today and you wont
come back into the house without a new mattress   we're going
    here   and i point to an ad in the yellow pages that says THE
MATTRESS WAREHOUSE
                            but they have two locations   one is in
encinitas eight miles to the north of us and the other is on miramar
about five miles to the south   so ellie worries   should we go
    to the encinitas one or the miramar?   i'd made the mistake
    of not looking before i showed it to her
                                        i said we could call them
and find out which one has a bigger stock   i dial the number a

woman answers and i say i have a serious question   do you have
a bigger selection of mattresses in miramar or encinitas   she
says "what?"   i explain   if i was looking for a mattress and
wanted to make the most responsible connoisseur choice of the
    mattress of mattresses to which of your two stores should i go
        she said i don't think theres any difference   i said you mean
you dont have a bigger inventory in one place than the other   she
    said i dont know   i really dont think so   so i said eleanor
lets go to miramar   its a little closer   she said but what if
    the encinitas store is better?   i said lets go to miramar and if
you dont like what you see there we can go right to encinitas
        we'll go to both of them and then you make your decision

        we drive out to the one on miramar   and its in one of
    those little malls with a vietnamese restaurant, a shoe store and
an aerobic studio for women   and there's a big empty looking
    storefront that says THE MATTRESS WAREHOUSE   its encouraging
i say   theres a big truck outside filled with mattresses   she
    says yes   but the place looks as blank as a tire store   its
unimpressive looking   i said well   the mattresses are all
    lying down on the floor and youre looking in the window

        so i get her into the store and we start looking around
    trying to figure out where to start   and there is a helpful
little man   an elderly irishman with freckles and gray hair and
    very laid back and he wants to know if he can help us
        can you tell me where the better mattresses are asks
eleanor
        it all depends on what you want
        i want something eleanor says thats firm but comfortable
        no i said   eleanor you want it to be more than firm
    every time you talk to me about a mattress you want it to be
    hard because youre afraid youll sink into it
        the little man smiles   if you really want it to be hard
    you want one of these he says pointing to a pastel blue
mattress right next to us   but if you want it to be luxuriant and
    hard at the same time you want one of these   and he leads us

a little further into the showroom   the mattress he's showing
us is a salmon colored one with some odd looking padding on the top
   that makes it softer   my wife he says loves this one   she
wakes up fresh every morning and makes me breakfast all because
of this mattress   he runs his hand lovingly over its padded surface
      go on try it he says try them all

            now this mattress is only some incredible price like $890
or $750 i dont really remember   but it was some outandish price
   to somebody like me who figures you pay around a hundred dollars
   for an okay mattress   but this is a special top of the line
mattress   i can see that   for somebody with a sensitive back
      so i say nothing and he tells elly   go on try it   try them
all   you can only tell what you like by trying them   so elly
starts trying mattresses

            she's lying down on one mattress and then she's popping
up and lying down on another and then she's beckoning me to lie
   down there with her to make sure that she really likes it   and
she's somewhat liking all of them   because theyre all new and
   better than our old mattress to start off with   but mostly she's
not sure and we're lying on them and reclining on them in different
   positions and i'm beginning to get a little embarrassed by all this
because other people are starting to come in   and theyre looking
   at mattresses too and looking at us to see how we're lying on our
mattress   and there are certain things you do on mattresses that
   youre not going to try out in public either   so i'm not really
   sure either

            meanwhile workmen are bringing in more mattresses
and people are walking around looking and feeling mattresses and
   looking at us because we're a little less uptight about lying
around in public   and i'm beginning to feel a bit like a specimen
   in a laboratory or zoo but elly isnt disturbed about it at all and
   keeps running around looking for new mattresses with different
   kinds of support systems that our nice little irishman kindly
shows us

but the proof is in the pudding he says   in the end its
your bed and youve got to lie in it

so elly keeps on testing and ive
bailed out because i'm not really into this   ive been doing it
sort of   but i keep thinking that what you do with a
mattress is you learn to live with it   you know?   somehow
you learn to live with a mattress   you buy one that seems
roughly humanly adequate   and then you learn to live with
its defects   everything made in america is built with defects
right?   i figure that defects are the name of the american
consumption game

but eleanor believes in perfection   and marcia thats
my sister-in-law has already told eleanor that if you want a great
mattress   a really great mattress   you have to get it custom
made   i said eleanor forget it   i wouldnt know what to tell
them to custom make would you   what do you mean custom
made   i would have to know what constitutes its greatness
do you know what constitutes mattress greatness?   do you
know what constitutes its greatness

she said no   so i said forget
custom made   custom made is for people who are geniuses
they know all there is to know about what mattresses should
do   i dont have any idea what a mattress should do   except
that theyre there to be slept on   and not get up and bite me
i want a mattress that leaves me alone and i'll leave it alone
but we're going through this whole mattress trial routine
and finally eleanor has narrowed it down to two mattresses
meanwhile our friendly irishman has told us his life story
he is it turns out the nephew of a famous cinematographer
who made a lot of famous bad movies with great cinematography
and its through the inheritance from this dignitary that our
friend lives in a comfortable house in encinitas where he spends a
lot of time when he's not selling mattresses puttering around his
garden   or watching public television   he's found out that we
work in an art department and has some questions he wants to
ask us about a program he saw last tuesday about an artist named

botticelli what did i think of him   he's pretty good i said
        yeah there was this one painting   it was beautiful   you
mean the springtime lady i said   thats right she was coming
   out of the water and she had long hair   and she was stepping
out of a seashell i said   very beautiful he said   yeah i said
very beautiful   not anybody could draw like that he said   so
exact   you could tell every line he put down was just where he
wanted it to go   thats right i said just where he wanted it to
go   then   this other artist who painted a ceiling for the pope
        that must have been very hard to do lying on his back all the
time

                 very hard indeed i said   it took him years to paint it
he must have had a very good mattress to lie on his back that long
   and get it right
                           thats the kind of mattress you want he said
        yeah eleanor wants a mattress that would last long enough for
her to paint the sistine ceiling   fifteen years or more   or
   whatever would be necessary while the pope kept bugging her
           i believe this might be the right mattress for you he said to
eleanor who'd just returned from an exploration of the furthest
corner of the showroom   and he pointed to a mattress with a
   particularly elaborate cushioning on top   eleanor pops into it
lies flat for a moment then pops up again   i dont think so she
says   it was not rigorous enough   it was hard enough
   underneath but it was too soft on top   and you could sink
four inches in before you hit rock bottom   four inches and my
   back goes out she said   at least i think so

                 at this point i am getting slightly desperate i want to
get out of there   eleanor i say if you dont like this one why
dont you take the one next to it   it has no padding and its
soid rock all the way down   this is no solution but she finally
makes a choice   and the mattress of her choice is as hard as a
   rock   i figure i can sleep on this fucking rock and our little
irishman is writing us up while the other salesmen are telling us

what a great choice we made   we're out the door and into the
car and eleanor says   i think i made a mistake   so we go back
   into the showroom and eleanor says   i'm really sorry to trouble
you   but our friend is not troubled   my dear its no trouble
     its your choice and we want you to be happy with it

          so eleanor goes back and starts in all over again but she
decides fairly quickly this time that it was the other one of the two
   finalists   the pastel blue one with a little padding over the rock
shelf   am i right she asks   youre right i say   and he writes
   it up   but this one is going to be delivered to us in a week and
we could have had the other one the next day   so we'll still
have to sleep on our old one that i'm used to   which is fine with
me because i'm used to it   its my old friend   i know its hills
   and valleys   and i'm happy driving home

          we're halfway down miramar when eleanor says to me
david   do you think we made a mistake?   i said no   i didnt
make any mistake   no mistake i said
                                        but what if its the wrong
one she said   we'll get used to it i said   but seriously she said
     what if its the wrong one?   i said what would be the right
one?   eleanor forget it   it doesnt matter   you know what
   luther said when he was confronted by the student who wanted to
   know what to do if he wasnt sure whether or not he was in a state
of grace   he said "sin bravely!"   i said dammit we dont know
   if we got the right mattress   we dont know if we got the right
mix master   we dont know if we got the right anything
     theres no way to know   let us live cheerfully in our
   ignorance   and we went home

          two weeks later the mattress arrived   for fifteen
   minutes ellie wasn't sure theyd sent us the right mattress because
we couldnt remember the name of the mattress she'd chosen
        but i said i'm sure they gave us the right mattress   why
would they send us another one?   but before we got into that we

found the bill   and the numbers and name on the bill appeared
   to correspond fairly reasonably with the label on the mattress
      we think

            so now we're sleeping on the great mattress that eleanor
selected so carefully for us   and she still has back troubles
      but theyre not as bad as the ones she used to have   so either
   this is the best possible mattress for her and for us   or not and
      this is the situation that i think best describes our postmodern
condition   with respect to which i believe in taking descartes
advice   if youre lost in a forest and you have no idea which way
   to go   go for it straight ahead   because its not likely to be
any worse than anything else

1984

Born in Greece a century after Cicero died, Plutarch sometimes bulleted his essays with as many as a hundred numbered sections. Sometimes Plutarch eschewed traditional narratives altogether, and simply listed. His essay "Sayings by Spartan Women" itemizes quotations from unknown Spartan mothers, wives, daughters, and widows on a variety of topics without any transitional narratives between them, without exposition, interpretation, or any suggestion whatsoever as to how we might read the texts, or even, for that matter, why. If Cicero, as they say, is all smooth conclusion and marble floor, then Plutarch is the muddy boot print trampling across the form. His descendants are those essayists who rely more heavily on documentation than they do on interpretation. Georges Perec in France, Eduardo Galeano in Ecuador, Eliot Weinberger in America. These are writers who incorporate perhaps the "truest" nonfiction materials—names, rules, maps, dates, lists, symbols, etc.—cobbling together these elements into literary texts, creating a form that clings to facts, that cleaves the world, and that celebrates through the presumed certainties of data the confidence that once characterized the essay in Plutarch's day, back when a fact could supposedly speak for itself. In this year, documentary photographer Ansel Adams dies. There is famine in Ethiopia. A song called "Like a Virgin" is on the radio in America.

ELIOT WEINBERGER

The Dream of India

(c. 1492)

For India was named by Noah, and its king is called the King of Knowledge.

For Paradise is in India, and in Paradise is the living fountain from which the four great rivers flow.

In India a year has two summers and two winters.

In India the land is always green.

Shadows there fall south in summer and north in winter.

In India there are twelve thousand seven hundred islands, some made entirely of gold, and some of silver. There is an island where pearls are so plentiful the people wear no clothes, but cover themselves in pearls.

In India wine is made from the milk of palmtrees. There is a tree whose fruit is a kind of bread.

In India there is a worm which cannot live without fire.

Snakes crawl about in the streets there.

In India they sleep on mattresses of silk on beds of gold. They eat at tables with silver vessels, and everyone, no matter of what rank, wears pearls and rings with precious stones.

There is a race of people there with eight toes on each foot and eight fingers on each hand. Their hair is white until they are thirty, and then it begins to turn black.

They have no poor people there, and all strangers are welcome.

In India crabs turn to stone the minute they are exposed to air.

There is a race of people there who live on the smell of an apple. And when they travel they must take an apple with them, for without the smell of it they will die.

It was so hot the people never left their houses.

Horses there are few and wretched, for they are fed with boiled meat and boiled rice.

In India they have a class of philosophers devoted to astronomy and the prediction of future events. And I saw one among them who was three hundred years old, a longevity so miraculous that wherever he went he was followed by children.

There are no liars there.

In India it is the custom for foreign traders to stay at inns. There the food is cooked for the guest by the landlady, who also makes the bed and sleeps with the stranger.

There is a race of people whose ears hang down to their knees.

In India there is a fountain guarded by deadly snakes. It is the only water in that place, and if anyone wishes to drink, he must take off all his clothes, for the snakes fear nudity more than fire.

There is a race of people there whose upper lip is so large they cover their faces with it when they sleep in the sun.

And I saw a king walking with two men before him sounding trumpets; two men behind him holding colored parasols over his head to shade him from the sun; and on each side of him a panegyrist, each rivaling the other in his invention of praises to the king.

In India there is a fruit, round as a calabash, which has three fruits inside, each with a different taste.

In India they worship the sun in a large temple outside of town. Every morning at sunrise the inhabitants rush out to this place and burn incense to a huge idol which, in a manner I cannot explain, turns around and makes a great noise.

In India they tell the future from the flight of birds.

In India if a man wants to burn himself alive, it is cause for great rejoicing. His family prepares a feast, then leads him on horse or on foot to the edge of a ditch. There he throws himself into the flames to the sound of music and celebration. Three days later he comes back to make his last will known; then he is gone forever.

In India it is very crowded because they have no pestilence. The number of people there exceeds belief. I saw armies of a million men or more.

It was so hot men's balls hung down to their knees, and the men had to tie them up and apply special ointments.

In India there is a bird called a *gookook* that flies in the night crying "gookook." Fire flashes from its beak. And if it lands on a roof, someone in that house will die that night.

In India they are much addicted to wantonness, but the unnatural crimes are unknown among them.

In India the dead are mourned for by women, who stand around the body, naked to the waist, and beat their breasts, crying "Alas! Alas!"

There is a race of barking people with the heads of dogs.

In India the ships are sewn like dresses, without a nail or a piece of iron in them, for there the rocks at sea draw iron to them, and any ship made with nails will crash against the rocks.

There is a race of horned people who grunt like pigs.

In India there are wells with hot water at night and cold during the day.

They clean their teeth with toothpicks.

In India the people are black. The blacker they are, the more beautiful they are thought to be. So every week they take their babies and rub them with oil till they become as black as devils. (Except that, in India, their gods are black and their devils white.)

In India each woman has many husbands, each with a specific duty. The wife lives in one house and her husbands in another. And they divide up the day so that each husband lives in his wife's house at certain hours, during which time no other husband may enter.

On one day of the year they light innumerable lamps of oil.

In India there are trees with leaves so big five or six men can stand in the shade of them.

They wash their feet first and then their faces. They wash before sleeping with their wives.

In India they worship the cow, and if one kills the cow he is immediately put to death. Some, particularly on holidays, even take the dung of the cow and rub it on their foreheads instead of perfume.

There are no adulterers there.

And I saw a temple high on a hill, and in it there was a single amethyst the size of a large pine cone, the color of fire, flashing from a distance as the sunbeams played about it.

In India there is a mountain called Albenigaras which is full of diamonds, but it swarms with venomous animals and serpents; no man can approach it. Next to it, however, is a higher mountain, and at certain times of the year the people climb it with oxen which they then cut to pieces. By means of machines they have invented, they throw the warm and bleeding hunks of meat below, onto the slopes of Albenigaras. Diamonds stick to the meat. Then vultures come and snatch the meat for food, flying off to places where they will be safe from the serpents. There the men go, and collect the diamonds that have fallen from the flesh.

In India the wise men can produce and quell great winds. For this reason they eat in secret.

In India the women wear wigs of black, the color they favor most. Some cover their heads with painted leaves, but none of them paint their faces.

There is a race of feathered people there who can leap into trees.

In India the men have no beards, but their hair is long and they tie it with a cord of silk and let it flow over their backs. In this way they go to war.

In India there is a fish whose skin is so hard that men make their houses out of it.

There is not a single tailor in India, for everyone goes naked.

In India it is very crowded, for the people are of a sort who are loathe to leave their own country.

In India they worship an idol, half man, half ox. And the idol speaks through its mouth and demands the blood of forty virgins. In one city I saw them carry their idol on a great chariot, and such was the fervor of the people that many cast themselves under the wheels of the chariot, that they may be crushed to death, as their god requires.

In India there is an animal called a *rhinoceros* because he has a horn over his nostril. And when he walks his horn jogs about, but when he becomes enraged by what he is looking at, his horn erects, and it becomes so rigid he can uproot a tree with it. His skin when it is dried is four fingers thick, and some people use it instead of iron for their plows, and they plow the earth with it.

There is a race of people there who are only one foot tall, and must always be on guard lest the storks carry them away. They are adult at age four and old men at eight.

In India there are roses everywhere—growing everywhere, for sale in the market, in wreaths around the necks of men and braided in the hair of the women. It seems they could hardly live without roses.

In India women sleep with their husbands in the day, but at night they go to foreign men and sleep with them and even pay them for it, for they like white people. And when a woman conceives a child by a stranger the husband pays him. If the child is born white the stranger receives eighteen tenkas extra; if it is black he gets nothing.

There is a race of people with backward feet.

In India there are long serpents called *cockodrilles* which live on land by day and in the water at night. In the winter they do not eat, but lie there dreaming. They kill men and devour them weeping.

In India there is a river known as the Arotani, where the fish are so abundant they can be caught by hand. But if anyone holds those fish in his hand for a short time he is immediately attacked by fever. As soon as he puts the fish down his health returns to him.

They use turbans for trousers.

They beat cymbals with a stick.

They kill their parents when they are old and use the flesh for food.

In India there is a tree, some three cubits high, which bears no fruit, and which is called, in their language, the tree of modesty. For if a man approaches it, it contracts and draws up all its branches, expanding again when he departs.

In India the girls have such firm flesh that you cannot squeeze it or pinch it anywhere. For a small coin they'll let a man pinch them as much as he likes. On account of this firmness, their breasts do not hang down at all, but stand straight out in front.

Peacocks run in the forest there.

And I saw a temple cast of solid bronze with an idol of solid gold the size of a man. Its eyes were made of two rubies, so skillfully done they seemed to be watching me.

They sit cross-legged on the ground.

In India the women go naked, and when a woman marries she is set on a horse, and her husband gets on the crupper and holds a knife pointed at her throat, and they both have nothing on except a tall cap on their heads like a miter, wrought with white flowers. And all the maidens of the place go singing in a row in front of them till they reach the house, and there the bride and groom are left alone, and when they get up in the morning they go as naked as before.

In India there are some who cut off their own heads, that they may go to Heaven. They use a strange sort of scissors.

In India if a man walks out of his house and hears someone sneeze he immediately goes back inside and does not leave—for they think it is a bad omen.

There are people with ears like winnowing fans, and at night they lie on one and cover themselves with the other.

In India the men wear female dress; they use cosmetics, wear earrings, arm-rings, golden seal-rings on the ring finger as well as on the toes of the feet.

They eat alone, one by one, on a tablecloth of dung. After eating they throw the plates away.

They cohabit like a snake entwined by a vine, or rather, while their wives move back and forth as if they were plowing, the husbands remain motionless.

In India there is a bird called a *semenda* whose beak has several distinct pipes with many openings. When death approaches, this bird collects a quantity of dry wood in its nest, and sitting upon it, sings so sweetly with all its pipes that it attracts and soothes all listeners to a marvelous degree. Then, igniting the wood by flapping its wings, it allows itself to be burnt to death.

I asked them about their religion and they replied, "We believe in Adam."

In India the wife throws herself on her husband's funeral pyre, and if she will not do so, the people throw her there.

It was so hot swords melted in their scabbards, and the gems in their handles turned to coal.

There are headless men with eyes in their stomachs.

There are people who walk about on all fours.

In India there is a dragon called a *basilisk,* whose breath can pulverize a rock. Its tail can kill any animal except the elephant. It is said that when a man and a basilisk meet, if the creature sees the man first, the man dies; but if the man sees the basilisk first, then the creature will die.

In India when they dive for pearls they take their wise men with them, for the fish where the pearls are found are treacherous to man, but the wise men chant in such a way so as to stupefy the fish.

It is so cold that water turns to crystal, and on those crystals real diamonds grow. And the diamonds and the crystals mate and multiply and are nourished by the dew of heaven.

One morning a man of great stature and with a snowy white beard, naked from the waist up with only a mantle thrown about him and a knotted cord, appeared at my lodgings. He prostrated himself full length upon the sand, beating his head three times against the ground. Then he raised himself, and seeing my bare feet, wanted to kiss them, but I refused. And he told me that he came from an island across the sea, that he had been traveling for two years, and that he had come in search of me. For his attachment to his idols was so pure and devout that God had spoken to him, showed him my face, and told him to find me that he may be instructed in the true path.

There are warrior women with silver weapons, for they have no iron.

There are women with beards growing from their breasts.

And I saw, deep in the interior, Venetian ducats in circulation, and gold coins twice the size of our florins.

In India, they do not cut any hair of the body, not even the hair of the genitals, for they believe that cutting that hair increases carnal desire and incites to lust.

In India when they travel they like to have someone riding behind them.

In all emergencies they take the advice of women.

In India on one day of the year they set up poles like the masts of ships and hang from them pieces of beautiful cloth, interwoven with gold. On the top of each pole sits a man of pious aspect who prays for all. These men are assailed by the people, who pelt them with spoiled oranges, lemons, and other rank fruit, and the holy men must bear it all with equanimity.

In India when a child is born people show particular attention to the man, not to the woman. Of two children they give preference to the younger, for they maintain that the elder owes his birth to predominant lust, while the younger owes his origin to mature reflection and a calm proceeding.

There is a race of people there who have only one enormous foot, and when they want to rest in the noonday sun, they lie on their backs and raise their foot like a parasol. They are great runners.

In India they let their nails grow long, and glory in idleness.

There are little people who have no mouth, but only a small hole in their face, and they must suck their food through a straw.

In India they write the title of a book at the end.

And I saw one of their holy men, standing nude, facing the sun, cloaked with a panther skin, and I continued on my way. Sixteen years later I happened to return to the same place—and there he was, unmoved.

It was so hot fish at the bottom of the river burned like silk touched by a flame.

And I saw far off the coast of that land a thing in the sky, huge as a cloud, but black and moving faster than the clouds. I asked what that thing could be, and they said it is the great bird Rokh. But the wind was blowing off the coast, and the Rokh went with it, and I never got a closer look.

In India the birds and animals are completely different from ours, except for one: the quail.

All of the imagery and some of the language are derived from works written in the five hundred years prior to 1492. India, of course, is where Columbus thought he was going.

1985

Days after *Dictee,* her first book, is published, Theresa Hak Kyung Cha is murdered. The book is about her struggles with dislocation. It's about Korea and Persephone and America and Joan of Arc, about reading French and Demeter and Jesus Christ and Cha. It is a book that is made up of fragments, mostly. There is white space, therefore. Ghosts coming and going, adding and subtracting, rearranging the air.

THERESA HAK KYUNG CHA

ERATO   LOVE POETRY

She is entering now. Between the two white columns. White and stone. Abrasive to the touch. Abrasive. Worn. With the right hand she pulls the two doors, brass bars that open towards her.

The doors close behind her. She purchases the ticket, a blue one. She stands on line, and waits.

The time is 6:35 p.m. She turns her head exactly to the left. The long hand is on 6 and the short hand on 7. She hands her ticket to the usher and climbs three steps, into the room. The whiteness of the screen takes her back wards almost half a step. Then she proceeds again to the front. Near front. Close to the screen. She takes the fourth seat from the left. The utmost center of the room. She sees on her left the other woman, the same woman in her place as the day before.

She enters the screen from the left, before the titles fading in and fading out. The white subtitles on the black background continue across the bottom of the screen. The titles and names in black appear from the upper right hand corner, each letter moving downwards on to the whiteness of the screen. She is drawn to the white, then the black. In the whiteness the shadows move across, dark shapes and dark light.

Columns. White. Stone. Abrasive and worn.

Whiteness of the screen. Takes her backwards.

Drawn to the white, then the black. The shadows moving across the whiteness, dark shapes and dark light.

Extreme Close Up shot of her face. Medium Long shot of two out of the five white columns from the street. She enters from the left side, and camera begins to pan on movement as she enters between the two columns, the camera stop at the door and she enters. Medium Close Up shot of her left side as she purchases the ticket her full figure from head to foot. Camera holds for a tenth of a second. The camera is now behind her, she is at the end of the queue. Long shot. Cut to Medium Close Up shot of her from the back. She turns her head sharply to her left. cut. The clock in Extreme Close Up. Same shot of her head turning back. She leaves the camera, other faces enter, of the others in line, and camera is stationary for a brief tenth of a second. Close Up shot of her feet from the back on the three steps leading into the theatre, camera following her from the back. She stops. Her left foot lifts back half a step then resumes. Camera is stationary, tilts upward and remains stationary. Pans to the right, while zooming out, the entire theatre in view. The theatre is empty, she is turning right into the aisle and moving forward. She selects a row near the front, fourth seat from the left and sits. Medium Close Up, directly from behind her head. She turns her head to the left, on her profile. Camera pans left, and remains still at the profile of another woman seated. Camera pans back to the right, she turns her head to the front. The screen fades to white.

Mouth moving. Incessant. Precise. Forms the words heard. Moves from the mouth to the ear. With the hand placed across on the other's lips moving, form-

One expects her to be beautiful. The title which
carries her name is not one that would make her
anonymous or plain. "The portrait of . . ." One seems
to be able to see her. One imagines her, already. Already before the title. She is not seen right away. Her
image, yet anonymous suspends in one's mind. With
the music on the sound track you are prepared for her
entrance. More and more. You are shown the house
in which she lives, from the outside.

Then you, as a viewer and guest, enter the house. It is
you who are entering to see her. Her portrait is seen
through her things, that are hers. The arrangement of
her house is spare, delicate, subtly accentuating,

ing the words. She forms the words with her mouth as the other utter across from her. She shapes her lips accordingly, gently she blows whos and whys and whats. On verra. O-n. Ver-rah. Verre. Ah. On verra-h. Si. S-i. She hears, we will see. If we will have to see if. If. We would wait. Wait to see, We would have to wait to see, Wait and see. If. For a second time. For another time. For the other overlapping time. Too fast. Slow your pace. Please. Slower, much slower. For me to follow. Doucement. Lentement. Softly and slowly. For a second time. For another time. Two times. Together. Twofold. Again. And again. Separately, together. Different place. Same times. Same day. Same Year. Delays, by hours. By night and day. At the same time. to the time. twice. At the same hour. Same time. All the same time. At the time. On time. Always. The time.

rather, the space, not the objects that fill the space. Her movements are already punctuated by the movement of the camera, her pace, her time, her rhythm. You move from the same distance as the visitor, with the same awe, same reticence, the same anticipation. Stationary on the light never still on her bath water, then slowly moving from room to room, through the same lean and open spaces. Her dress hangs on a door, the cloth is of a light background, revealing the surface with a landscape stained with the slightest of hue. Her portrait is not represented in a still photograph, nor in a painting. All along, you see her without actually seeing, actually having seen her. You do not see her yet. For the moment, you see only her traces.

"Letter of Invitation to the Wedding of Sister Thérèse of the Child Jesus and the Holy Face.

God Almighty, Creator of Heaven and Earth, Sovereign Ruler of the Universe, the Most Glorious Virgin Mary, Queen of the Heavenly Court, announce to you the Spiritual Espousal of Their August Son, Jesus, King of kings, and Lord of lords, with little Therese Martin, now Princess and Lady of His Kingdoms of the Holy Childhood and the Passion, assigned to her in dowry by her Divine Spouse, from which kindoms she holds her titles of nobility-of the Child Jesus and the Holy Face.

Monsieur Louis Martin, Proprietor and Master of the Domains of Suffering and Humiliation and Mme Martin, Princess and Lady of Honor of the Heavenly Court, wish to have you take part in the Marriage of

Until then. The others relay her story. She is married
to her husband who is unfaithful to her. No reason is
given. No reason is necessary except that he is a man.
It is a given.

He is the husband, and she is the wife. He is the man.
She is the wife. It is a given. He does as he is the man.
She does as she is the woman, and the wife. Stands
the distance between the husband and wife the distance of heaven and hell. The husband is seen. Entering the house shouting her name, calling her name.
You find her for the first time as he enters the room
calling her. You only hear him taunting and humiliating her. She kneels beside him, putting on his
clothes for him. She takes her place. It is given. It is
the night of her father's wake, she is in mourning.

their Daughter, Thérèse, with Jesus, the Word of God, the Second Person of the Adorable Trinity, who through the operation of the Holy Spirit was made Man and Son of Mary, Queen of Heaven.

Being unable to invite you to the Nuptial Blessing which was given on Mount Carmel, September 8, 1890, (the heavenly court alone was admitted), you are nevertheless asked to be present at the Return from the Wedding which will take place Tomorrow, the Day of Eternity, on which day Jesus, Son of God, will come on the Clouds of Heaven in the splendor of His Majesty, to judge the Living and the Dead.

The hour being as yet uncertain, you are invited to hold yourself in readiness and watch."

Her marriage to him, her husband. Her love for him, her husband, her duty to him, her husband.

Still the apprenticeship of the wife to her husband.
He leaves the room. She falls to the floor, your eyes
move to the garden where water is dripping into the
stone well from the bark of a tree. And you need not
see her cry.

She moves slowly. Her movements are made gradual, dull, made to extend from inside her, the
woman, her, the wife, her walk weighted full to the
ground. Stillness that follows when she closes the
door. She cannot disturb the atmosphere. The space
where she might sit. When she might. She moves in
its pauses. She yields space and in her speech, the
same. Hardly speaks. Hardly at all. The slowness of
her speech when she does. Her tears her speech.

   She climbs the steps slowly. While she climbs, the
lake changes from the lake at dawn the lake at day
the lake at dusk the lake at moonlight. The time passing over the lake. The time it takes her to climb the
steps.

"I still cannot understand why women are so easily excommunicated in Italy, for every minute someone was saying: "Don't enter here! Don't enter there, you will be excommunicated!" Ah poor women, how they are misunderstood! And yet they love God in much larger numbers than men do and during the Passion of Our Lord, women had more courage than the apostles since they braved the insults of the soldiers and dared to dry the adorable Face of Jesus." He allows misunderstanding to be their lot on earth since, He chose it for Himself. In heaven, He will show that His thoughts are not men's thoughts, for then the last will be first."

Upon seeing her you know how it was for her. You know how it might have been. You recline, you lapse, you fall, you see before you what you have seen before. Repeated, without your even knowing it. It is you standing there. It is you waiting outside in the summer day. It is you waiting and knowing to wait. How to. Wait. It is you walking a few steps before the man who walks behind you. It is you in the silence through the pines, the hills, who walks exactly three steps behind her. It is you in the silence. His silence all around the unspoken the unheard, the apprenticeship to silence. Observed for so long and not ending. Not immediately. Not soon. Continuing. Contained. Muteness. Speech less ness.

It is you who know to hear it in the music so late in the night. Then it becomes you, the man, her companion, the live-in student accompanying her to school how many times as a young girl. It is you who hears his music for her while she sleeps. It is you sitting behind him looking at the moon the clouds the lake shimmering. You are she, she speaks you, you speak her, she cannot speak. She goes to the piano while he plays. You know that he cannot speak either. The muteness. The void muteness. Void after uttering. Of. Each phrase. Of each word. All but. Punctuation, pauses. Void after uttering of each phrase. Of each word. All but. Punctuations. Pauses.

They do not touch. It is not like that. The touching made so easy the space filled full with touch. The entire screen. To make the sequences move. In close up. To fabricate the response. So soon. Too

immediate. To make fully evident the object. The touch. Making void the reticence of space the inner residence of space. Not this one. It's not like that.

He plays the piano, his own composition as he would on the ancient string instrument. Abstract, but familiar to you. Ancient and familiar. You think you have seen this before. Somewhere else. In *Gertrude*. It is her, with her elbows on the piano. It is you seeing her suspended, in a white mist, in white layers of memory. In layers of forgetting, increasing the density of mist, the opaque light fading it to absence, the object of memory. You look through the window and the music fills and breaks the entire screen from somewhere. Else. From else where.

You know how it was. Same. For her. She would do the same. She would sit at the piano as her sadness grew in her breath without any destination. She would set before each note until the music would induce her and she would acquiesce.

From the other room you knew as she would begin playing. You walk inside the room, you sit behind her you knew the music, which ones.

Mother you who take the child from your back to your breast you who unbare your breast to the child her hunger is your own the child takes away your pain with her nourishment

Mother you you who take the husband from your back to your breast you who unbare your breast to the husband his hunger your own the husband takes away your pain with his nourishment

She asks if you want to sing a song and you move next to her on the bench and you sing for her as she plays for you.

Perhaps she loved him. Her husband. Perhaps after all she did. Perhaps in the beginning it was not this way. In the beginning it was different. Perhaps she loved him inspite of. Inspite of the arrangement that she was to be come his wife. A stranger. Stranger to her. The one that she should espouse. Decided for her. Now she would be long to him. Perhaps she learned to love him. Perhaps it was never a question. It was given. She took whatever he would give her because he gave her so little. She takes she took them without previous knowledge of how it was supposed to be how it is supposed to be. She deserved so little. Being wife. How it was. How it had been. Being

"I am only a child, powerless and weak, and yet it is my weakness that gives me the boldness of offering myself as *VICTIM of your love, O Jesus!* In times past, victims, pure and spotless, were the only ones accepted by the Strong and Powerful God. To satisfy Divine *Justice*, perfect victims were necessary, but the *Law of Love* has succeeded to the law of fear, and *Love* has chosen me as a holocaust, me, a weak and imperfect creature. Is not this choice worthy of *Love?* Yes, in order that I ove be fully satisfied, it is necessary that It lower itself, and that It lower Itself to nothingness and transform this nothingness into *fire.*

O Jesus, I know it, love is repaid by love alone, and so I searched and I found the way to solace my heart by giving you Love for Love."

woman. Never to question. Never to expect but the given. Only the given. She was his wife his possession she belonged to him her husband the man who claimed her and she could not refuse. Perhaps that was how it was. That was how it was then. Perhaps now.

It is the husband who touches. Not as husband. He touches her as he touches all the others. But he touches her with his rank. By his knowledge of his own rank. By the claim of his rank. Gratuity is her body her spirit. Her non-body her non-entity. His privilege possession his claim. Infallible is his ownership. Imbues with mockery at her refusal of him, but her very being that dares to name herself as if she possesses a will. Her own.

One morning. The next morning. It does not matter. So many mornings have passed this way. But this one. Especially. The white mist rising everywhere, constant gathering and dispersing. This is how it fills the screen.

Already there are folds remnant from the previous foldings now leaving a permanent mark. This cloth

She forgets. She tries to forget. For the moment. For the duration of these moments.

She opens the cloth again. White. Whitest of beige. In the whiteness, subtle hues outlining phoenix from below phoenix from above facing each other in the weave barely appearing. Disappearing into the whiteness.

once in certain mind to prepare a quilt now left unattended to some future time. Its purpose having
been expended she opens it, spreads it again as if following a habitual gesture. She looks at it once more
with a vague uneasiness as though she was missing a
part to this very gesture that she could not remember.

It stings her inside. All sudden. Summons. Move. To
simply move. Her body. Renounce no more the will
inhabiting her. Complete. She changes her dress,
shed to the ground, left as it fell.

She moves now. Quickly. You trace her steps just
after, as soon as, she leaves the frame. She leaves
them empty. You are following her. Inside the mist.
Close. She is buried there. You lose her. It occurs to
you, her name. Suddenly. Snow. The mist envelops
her she appears from it. Far. On top of the hill. You
have seen her there many times. The lake she has
visited often. The lake behind her on her steps. The
waiter comes out to greet her he says how early she is
this morning she says she came to see the lake he says
he will bring her tea. Everything is seen from above.
Very far above. The two figures inside the mist mass
shifting in constant motion. You are made to follow
the waiter inside while he prepares tea made to wait
with him and when you return with him you find her
gone. The white table the two white chairs the waiter
in his white jacket the mist thick and rising. Very far.
Above. Again from above the waiter inside the large
white corners running back and forth calling her
name. Hardly visible. The corners.

"The smallest act of PURE LOVE is of more value to her than all other works together."

"Martyrdom was the dream of my youth and this dream has grown with me within Carmel's cloisters. But here again, I feel that my dream is a folly, for I cannot confine myself to desiring one kind of martyrdom. To satisfy me I need all. Like You, my Adorable Spouse, I would be scourged and crucified. I would die flayed like St. Bartholomew. I would be plunged into boiling oil like St. John; I would undergo all the tortures inflicted upon the martyrs. With St. Agnes and St. Cecilia, I would present my neck to the sword, and like Joan of Arc, my dear sister, I would whisper at the stake Your Name, O JESUS."

It had been snowing. During the while.
Interval. Recess. Pause.
It snowed. The name. The term. The noun.
It had snowed. The verb. The predicate. The act of.
Fell.
Luminescent substance more so in black night.
Inwardly luscent. More. So much so that its entry
closes the eyes
Interim. Briefly.
In the enclosed darkness memory is fugitive.
Of white. Mist offers to snow self
In the weightless slow all the time it takes long
ages precedes time pronounces it alone on its own
while. In the whiteness
no distinction her body invariable no dissonance
synonymous her body all the time de composes
eclipses to be come yours.

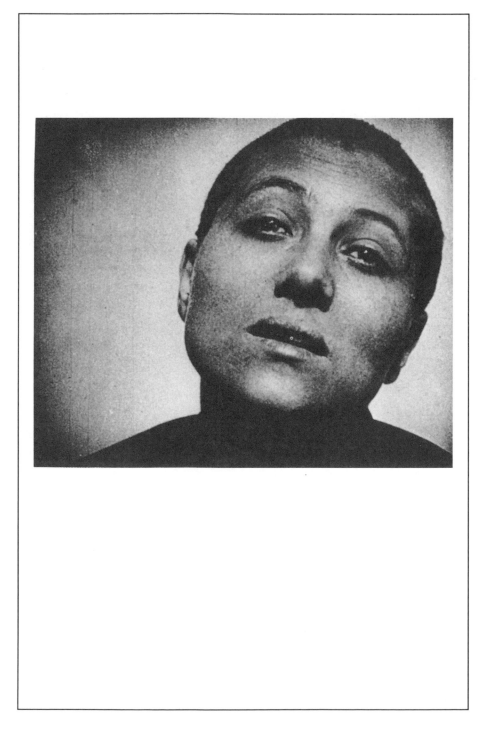

1986

In this year I am fired from my position as News editor of my fifth-grade class's in-house newspaper, and reassigned as the editor of a new section, "Features." Mrs. Tuttle, who fires me, says I don't know the difference between nonfiction and art. Mom says to take this as a compliment. To this day, however, I still don't know what to do with things like Dennis Silk's "The Marionette Theatre"—an essay that appears in his highly acclaimed collection of criticism on theatre, but which nonetheless is not the kind of essay I would turn to if I desperately needed to learn something about puppets. Why, then, do I turn to it?

DENNIS SILK

The Marionette Theatre

PART ONE

Shutters shut and open. So do queens.

GERTRUDE STEIN

I

A Japanese traveler, Saikaku, has a tricky story about umbrellas. Twenty of them hung outside the temple at Kwannon. People borrowed them in bad weather. In spring 1649, an unlucky umbrella-borrower had it blown out of his hand by a divine wind. Traveling further maybe than Saikaku, the umbrella landed at the village of Amazato. No one there had seen an umbrella. But from its ribs, numbering forty, and the unusual luminosity of its oil-paper, they knew the sun-god had landed at Amazato. They built a shrine to the umbrella.

Saikaku does not describe the landing of the umbrella. But it must descend slowly on Amazato from *up there,* slowly and in considered spirals as a god should. After the vigorous theophany of its descent, it lies stranded in the market-square. Yet everyone understands the umbrella is latent. A farmer closes his fingers around its handle as around a staff-hook. They travel gingerly up the limb of this god, they feel a metal obstruction then a yielding. The umbrella shuts. *Deus absconditus.* But what shuts opens, like fingers. Open shut. This farmer becomes the attendant of the opening and shutting god.

169

II

The umbrella teases. It opens. Then folds back on itself. Really, it's two umbrellas. Yet it's one. A villager would have to have two minds to grasp this. Moreover, its mode of arrival draws attention to itself. So they build a shrine to it. Best to abandon it to mystery. Amazato bundles away the umbrella in a shrine.

And it's a jealous god. There is no god but the umbrella. That's because Amazato doesn't pay attention. In the street outside, the small red spinning top has been hoarding its conversation a long time. Gathering itself together for a definitive statement. Speech after a long silence. And its cousin, the yo-yo, opens and shuts shop. Here is the eight-year-old shopkeeper. His balloon declared itself at half-past nine this morning. Then went back into tininess. The god sulks.

The umbrella should make a place for them in the shrine. It should hold a nest of gods. Umbrella, yo-yo, spinning top, balloon. A cotton-reel. And an eight-year-old boy to play a concertina for the gods. Wheezy Anna sucking its breath in and out. Now we're leaving Amazato. We're high as an umbrella. This flag over the shrine waits. Waits for a lucky wind to give it life. Unfolds and flaps in the wind.

III

The queer pendulum life ferries us there, and back. *There* is the seed-life. (Or of dead grain.) *Here* is here. The two-fold tribe are performers, they perform their two lives. They're like an actor waiting to go on, so half-way perhaps between two lives he could scarcely tell you who he is. The life of the flag above the shrine is also two-fold. First, stiff, folded back on itself, then declaring itself for movement. But the flag is performed rather than a performer. And a bale of cloth is performed in the street. This street-salesman unfolds an arm's-length of it, then teasingly folds it back on itself. Again a mystery. But the cloth itself scarcely performs.

The same for this regiment of tin soldiers preparing for war. They're the played rather than the players. And of this marble wanting to be flicked. What's this needle doing? There and back. There and back. The seamstress hides her thinking under her eyelids. Pins and needles—seamstresses' cathedrals.

Needles are used rather than performed. Or unused. Till someone makes much of them. They too are in the folded and unfolding life. Like this savage tribe of the kitchen. It screams in the drawer, or on the shelf, it demands conscription. Here are the drones, or proles, of this tribe: cheese-grater, potato-peeler, corkscrew, pestle, rolling-pin, cake-pattern, coffee-mill. Here's the managerial class: knife, fork, spoon, plate, cup, glass. They all belong to the *rending* tribe, the tribe of tooth. They're at continual war with the seamstress in her *remembering* room: the life in things is put together there, patched up, reconstituted. It's in alliance with certain lives in the children's playroom next door: scattered pieces of jig-saw remembering the original puzzle, building bricks planning a town, alphabet blocks working out language. What are we to say about the seamstress? She remembers, retrieves. Yet her molars aren't there for nothing.

IV

We say *animism.* Then we put it back on the shelf with the other relegated religions. Maybe our flight from animism is our flight from madness. We're afraid of the life we're meagre enough to term inanimate. Meagre because we can't cope with those witnesses. Rainer Maria Rilke hesitates whether to abandon a bar of soap in a hotel-room. During Gilles de Raïs' confession, the Bishop of Nantes covers the Cross. (The world of wood, incarnate in the Cross, rejects Gilles.) If a cross is a witness, why not a loaf of bread, or a shoe-tree, or a sugar-tongs, or a piece of string? We should have an All Souls' Night for dead objects, and confer on them some hours of the life we deny them.

V

His heavy, dangling life marks out what's possible. Whatever came out of lumpishness to dance to us. It's the marionette from Lyon, the transformation dancer. Incorporating coffins, and chairs, and tables. A coat-hanger. A hat rack. Needle and thread. Dancing for them to us. It's All Souls' Night. Dancing in a muck-sweat. Two-fold life's thick in this man. He marks out his tiny patch. Fights for three feet of life. He dances for the sake of a pair of shoe-laces, for a bereaved hat. Privileged ghostly spectators cram the stage. Caskets and cupboards. A commode on its last legs. They're like a group of one-legged men watching a good dancer. They have their best chance in him.

The unexpected charge of all these souls fuses the lights. Lights Lights we shout. The man from Lyon stands there striking matches. Lighting up possibility. Terror! A struck match.

VI

The marionette salaams to us, shuts his eyes. A mahogany wardrobe observes his trance-strong face. He's propped up in a corner. He's in *samadhi.* Traveling for everyone.

The marionette, in *samadhi,* controls the audience by the strength of his will. It's like a commode with locked drawers that fascinate us.

He hasn't fluffed his exit or muffed his lines. (Unlike the spinning top.) He's more tricks up his sleeve than an umbrella. Now he's in the folded life. But he could lash out and scare everyone.

PART TWO

*King Charles walked and talked
an hour after his head was cut off.*

I

The marionette is a poet from Peru who got education. He comes from a long way off to talk to us. He talks of bread and trousers and the crease in a shirt. Because he is safe among things, because he is himself a thing, "a thing thing," he allows himself our town-talk. He kneels to talk to dismembered man.

He doesn't have the impediments of an actor. An actor's body is so untalented. It doesn't have doors, it doesn't take in pain, it can't play us the world-tooth rending and shredding. It merely walks and talks around that tooth. The marionette—because it is a thing and yet a man—because it is this poet from Peru—plays us this mastication of things, and of ourselves. The marionette is shredded over the suburbs. He plays us the world-breakfast. His well-jointed body speaks for us. He uses the nearest grammar to hand. "I simply couldn't contain myself," he says. And comes apart at the joints.

"Pull yourself together," he's admonished. His scattered parts do their best to come together. "I couldn't keep my eyes off her," he confesses. She removes his eyes with distaste from her private parts.

He's an accurate grammarian. He's devoured and disgorged. He contracts and expands. He does acts of nut-cracker cruelty, expiates them with his own head, plucks out his eye for a woman, performs Caesareans, swells to the balloon he flies off in, opens like a Queen-for-One-Night-Only, shuts like Venus-Fly-Trap. His head observes its trunk making off down a side-street. He's a man about town, a man about town on his last legs. His head sings the complete man: buttocks and toes and fingers and eyes, that reconstituted man he thought about in Peru. "I'll be very changed," he says, "before I'm changed."

II

Mother fork, grandmother fork, ex-father fork, the child says, laying the cutlery out on the playroom floor. (Tooth and memory, two machines working against each other.) The head of the stacking toy lies on the playroom floor. All you can see is the back of this head. He seems to be inquiring deeply of a tile. His dismantled parts call out Help from the battlefield. Heroes have come apart at the joints. They ask to get kitted out again. This deficiency can tell against them in the long run.

The head starts traveling across the floor. Probably he's looking for a way back. Probably the other parts of this dismembered man are craning their necks to find the legal instrument. (After all, a head does have jurisdiction over his parts.) His yellow throat must be craning its neck, his red trunk—in the corner over there—must be craning its neck, all the *disjecta membra* of this man's body must be remembering him. Blocks of wood thinking about the original tree.

In the meantime, the head's traveling. It confronts the camp of the enemy. Fatigues and drill. Everything you think of when you say Khaki. But the head soldiers on. He travels this playroom floor the entire day looking for the parts of a man. Saluting meccano. Attending parades for a foundered horse. He could spend a day and playroom night inspecting this floor. And nothing accomplished.

The head is a foot-soldier sent out to foreign parts. Made use of by Empire. He knows he is a head but no longer knows what a head is. Everything's so topsy-turvy on a battle-field. (His trunk just tried to get a message through to him but was outflanked by the cavalry.) And say he found his trunk, here, on this battle-field blurred in jig-saw, what would happen? He could think his trunk his head, or his head his trunk. Now he remembers what a hand is but no longer remembers its name. It's lucky he remembers fingers are gloved in shoes. He could think his great left toe his big right thumb if he hadn't remembered his right ankle is his left wrist. Now that boy-soldier from Hong-Kong has banged his drum into his head. Is it? Say his head is his head, his trunk his trunk. What's next? Say he slips his trunk on right, he'll screw the head on back to front. Such junketings!

III

Index finger says Yes. But it's Thumbs down, anyway. Small finger says Maybe. Big brother middle finger says Calm down, everyone. Number four says All right.

Right hand sugar. Left hand salt.

Molars grind. Heart says sorry.

He put his best foot forward. His worst foot went to sleep.

▼▲▼

He redeems his promissory notes to the world-bank with toes and fingers, buttocks and eyes. His bereaved trousers limp off to the bank to redeem the last note.

▼▲▼

A Caesarean performed on a hearty-eater marionette. Out comes a baby marionette clutching a butcher's bill:

> 1 lb. lambchops
> 3 lb. salt beef
> Whose intestines?

A waiter interviews this new arrival: Is that an Indian scripture you have there, sir? *(Indicating butcher's bill.)* A saving gospel from up there? *(Indicating sky.)*

The new-born puppet begins greedily to steal from the hearty eater's plate. *(Who withdrawing his plate appeals to the waiter.)* Let me keep my meat in your safe. *(He opens the waiter, hides the meat in his insides.)*

▼▲▼

Opening the door in his head he takes out his still-born child.
Closing the door in his chest he hides his still-born child.
To-day, he says, I feel the whole world is a door.

▼▲▼

Fingers skillfully, restlessly, empty pockets. Their master directs them from bed. (This pickpocket never travels to work with his body because he's afraid of being identified.)

▼▲▼

The day before her wedding she visits the dressmaker. Forget about that wedding-dress, she says. I'm betrothed to a headless groom. Have you the sewing machine that will put him together again?

▼▲▼

At the doll-hospital: two old ladies insert the stuffing in dolls, their hair, their eyes.

IV
Cut-Out

a

Your head won't need its hat any more. It lies here oddly intact without its trunk. Was it some Judith who cut it off? Your arms like dolphins fly about their business. Your feet stand in their pumps at the Coroner's. Someone has made a cut-out of all your parts.

b

Won't you join the dance? I won't, you say, no I can't. I don't have a breath long enough. I've the left lung of a suicide, it refuses to breathe in. What's that musician trying to do? My left leg keeps Greenwich Time, my right's gone to sleep in New York. Is that a wedding-march he's trying to strike up? But my ring-finger's divorced its hand. My hat's an affront to this street. Merely tooth marries air. Greedyguts, saying All right. (But it is not right not to publish these banns.)

C

A whistle blows. Someone is directing the traffic. For the wedding, in the next street, of dismembered man. Careful, you say, gingerly. I can scarcely pull myself together, scarcely stand up. With a somewhat sheepish smile you ransack your memory. Send your leg down looking for your ankle. A scouting party to look for your wrist. Eight then ten fingers. Ditto toes. Two or so eyes. (They are not glass.) You're kitted out. Tear-ducts and memory. You put your best foot forward. You're a man of parts.

PART THREE

We're in the sleeping life. A hundred strings play the dream.

A. TRYPHON

I

It's the Fantoccini man, the master of the marionettes. Sitting down, in the nineteenth century, to his fowl and wine. He wears a frock-coat buttoned at the waist, a high black stock, turkey-grease runs down the entire length of the shirt front. He's dining out on the takings. Bones on his plate remind him of his come-apart marionettes. He worked them, tonight, in "the very first of drawing rooms." A menu of marionettes for the London aristocrats. But he's stolen the royalty from his marionettes. These favorites of heaven came unstuck in London. They're the dream of a mechanic. He reviews his dream. *Item:* A Scaramouch with no head and afterwards all head. His neck shot up to a great man's ceiling. Ceiling not sky. The connection is with pockets. *Item:* Judy Callaghan with six figures jumping out of *her* pocket. *Item:* A Nondescript juggling with his head. First of all Somebody, afterwards Nobody. *Item:* The Parson in his Pulpit. (But an atheist among marionettes.) *Item:* The Polander balancing a chair and two poles. You'll gape spreadeagled, Polander. *Item:* A Policeman splitting down the middle. And he doesn't blow his whistle for the real theft. This Fantoccini man has stripped his puppet-shreds of all their valuables. Gutted their memory. No more sending memory down side-streets for news of themselves. They lie here like freethinkers. They're retrieved by the perfectly organized secular strings in the hard hands of this Fantoccini man. Now it's time for knife and fork. After a hard evening of snapping orders at Judy Callaghan. Fifty strings I worked for that Judy. Hot and hidden managing that bitch.

II

The dream-shreds lie scattered on the carpet. Secular children for a Victorian mansion. The Polander's fallen between two fools. The first fool is the hard fool, the Fantoccini man, with clicking heels, martial handshake, waxed look in Victorian sleep. The second fool's the soft fool, the contemporary fool. He's a teddy-bear courting a totem. Cuddling his dream now. Performing his parlor tricks, this puppeteer disowns his own marionettes. Paderewski at the piano. Christopher Robin saying his prayers. Charming assumptions have put the puppeteer to sleep. The marionette's doing his best to stay awake through all this. He begins to realize his position isn't easy. Such a soft master to make such a hard thing. And master doesn't know he has a dangerous object on his hands. He's like a sapper defusing the mines he plants. He likes the blue eyes of his marionette too much to see what they focus on. He can't follow the straight road of the marionette he's made . . . Actually, he doesn't want to. He likes children, he likes pillows.

III

The abused marionette appeals to us. Use me, please use me. Don't kill me in a dream. Send me out. This hand of mine could win the Punic Wars. This head of mine is the entire family of Zen Patriarchs.

The puppeteer doesn't listen. His own family's gone to sleep, his whole body's a big puppeteering yawn. He indomitably yawns.

We're sleepy, too. Sleep runs down our face, we try to wipe it out of our eyes in the morning, our foot's gone to sleep over some trying task. Lazybones.

Sleepy love-affairs. Bowing and scraping before the absent heart. That heart went out the window in sleep last night. It's playing leap-frog in the courtyard. Some other woman smiles at you.

Snoozing over tea-break and heart-break. Snoozing kid.

▼▲▼

A puppeteer, waking, would study the difference between sleepers and men. Study lovers like spinning-tops, or ninepins in a bowling-alley. Nothing royal. Study their wooden luck. For the lovers are all in the lock-up, the toy-theatre.

IV

The hero of Hoffmann's "The Sandman" falls in love with Olympia, who the same time every night plays the harp at her window. Later he dances with her at a ball, she never speaks to him but she's a marvellous dancer. Of course she's an automaton, a perfect doll.

Fascination of automatons, of the perfect response lost in clockwork. Had Hoffmann written for the puppet-theatre, a young automaton would discover, with what horror, the clockwork in Olympia.

V

A Houdini bill from 1914:

DARING DIVE!

—

This Wednesday, July 15— 12:30 P.M. sharp —Battery, Near The Aquarium

HARRY HOUDINI

Now Appearing At Hammerstein's Victoria Theatre and Roof Garden

Securely handcuffed and leg-ironed will be placed in a heavy packing case, which will be nailed and roped, then encircled by steel bands, firmly nailed. Two hundred pounds of iron weights will then be lashed to this box containing HOUDINI. The box will then be THROWN INTO THE RIVER. Houdini will undertake to release himself whilst submerged under water.

There's a puppet-vocabulary in Houdini: the handcuffed soul, the straight-jacketed soul, the soul locked in a filing-cabinet at the river-bottom. The sleepwalker down there sends up bubbles to comfort the family.

PART FOUR

This is the place, gentlemen.

Abraca dabraca banana. This puppeteer, plausible mountebank, does his spiel for the populace. He plays them his entire stock: marionettes grated round town like cheese, or peeling themselves like that Norwegian going into an onion. (Cold now, in late October, without a coat.) He knows the language of coats and toes. Of four-fingered men. Of marionettes confiscating each other's parts. "I confiscate your right eye, Edward Grey. You've been such a naughty boy." Marionette-orphans of broken-down kitchens. Tripes billow from their mouths like balloons in a comic-strip. Tripes and smiles. Cries of No more No more. A hearty-eater marionette throws his own head to the populace. Hardy little boys throw it back laughing. (They don't know it's serious to have a head thrown at you in October.)

Marionettes open like umbrellas in late October. These rain-clouds are waiting to say something. The mountebank looks up carefully at the sky. Mounts his bench and chatters. Assistants carry out a coffin from his booth. (Should I tell this town my secrets? he asks himself. Shouldn't I have locked the door of that booth?) He stands there in apparent surprise. What do you have here for us? he asks these mourners. It seems they don't know. With an effort he forces the coffin-lid. To go by his look, it can't really be empty down there. He addresses the populace. "Ladies and gentlemen, you don't know what it is to serve the dead. I do. I got this grammar-book *(holding it up)* from their own mouths. That one there *(indicating a rival puppeteer),* that one there just leafs through the dictionary. Ladies and gentlemen, I give you Cesare the somnambulist." And raises Cesare by a primitive rod to the head. Waxen Cesare opens his eyes very slowly. From a coffin to a crowd. Looks wildly at outside. Clearly he's thinking about this and that. Now he's decided on something. Opening the door of his chest he shows, painted inside, the body of his soul. A childlook to that painting. Raising his right arm, he copies the gesture of the interior arm. "Here is the place," he says, "here."

1987

In 1895, when Oscar Wilde was on trial, the distinctions between nonfiction and poetry were brought to issue when he
decided to call a love letter to his protege, Lord Alfred Douglas,
a poem. "A man who was not an artist could not have written
that letter," Wilde testified. What was the big deal? If Wilde
had called what he wrote to Douglas a letter, then he could
have been convicted of "lewd and immoral" behavior. But if
Wilde called what he wrote a poem, then he could try to
argue his way out of a conviction on the grounds of artistic li-
cence. In other words: poetry could be art; nonfiction could
not—

COURT: Where was Lord Alfred Douglas staying when you
        wrote that letter to him?
WILDE: At the Savoy; and I was at the Babbacombe.
COURT: It was a letter in answer to something he had sent you?
WILDE: Yes, a poem.
COURT: Mr. Wilde, why should a man your age address a
        boy nearly twenty years younger as "My Own Boy"?
WILDE: I was fond of him; I have always been fond of him.
COURT: Do you adore him?
WILDE: No, but I have always liked him. I think it is a beau-
        tiful letter. It is a poem. I was not writing an ordi-
        nary letter. You might as well cross-examine me as
        to whether a sonnet of Shakespeare were proper.
COURT: Apart from art, Mr. Wilde?
WILDE: I cannot answer apart from art.

ANNE CARSON

Kinds of Water

St. Jean Pied de Port ▶ 20th of June

The good thing is we know the glasses are for drinking.

MACHADO

At the foot of the port of Roncesvalles, a small town bathes itself. Thunderstorms come down from the mountains at evening. Balls of fire roll through the town. Air cracks apart like a green fruit. Underneath my hotel window is a river (La Nive) with a sizable waterfall. There is a dark shape at the edge of the falls, as I look down, knocking this way and that in the force of the current. It would seem to be a drowned dog. It *is* a drowned dog. And I stand, mind burning, looking down. No one is noticing the dog. Should I mention it? I do not know the word for "drowned." Am I on the verge of an ancient gaffe? Waiters come and go on the terrace of the hotel bar, bending deeply from the waist to serve *potage*. A fathom below them the dark body slaps. At the foot of the falls, where water is rushing away, a fisherman casts his line over it. What sense could there be in things? I have come through countries, centuries of difficult sleep and hard riding and still I do not know the sense of things when I see it, when I stand with the pieces in my hands. Could there be a sculpture of a drowned dog on the ledge of an ancient waterfall? I watch and pass, hours pass. My mind a laughingstock. Evening falls, the shape is still there. Fisherman gone, waiters whisking tablecloths on the terrace. What is it others know?

Pilgrims were people who loved a good riddle.

▼▲▼

from St. Jean Pied de Port ▶ 21st of June

*Presently, to a distant tinkling of bells, they turned and
started off. The retreating figures made Kaname think of a
line from the pilgrim's canticle they had practiced so earn-
estly with the innkeeper the evening before:*
    Hopefully we take the path from afar
    to the temple where blooms
    the flower of the good law.

TANIZAKI

It rained during the night. We sit on the hotel terrace drinking coffee.
Morning sparkles on us. I watch the dog. One soaked paw has moved over
the ledge and is waving back and forth as water streams around it. The man
I am traveling with peers vaguely towards it. "Ah!" and returns to eating
bread. His concern is with the more historical aspects of pilgrimage.
Pilgrims, for example, were traditionally gracious people and wore wide-
brimmed hats in order that they might doff them to other pilgrims. The
man that I am traveling with demonstrates how this should be done. I
think I will call him "My Cid." It speeds up the storytelling. Besides, he is
one "who in a happy hour was born," as the famous poem says. You will see
this as the journey proceeds, see him sailing through danger and smiling at
wounds. Perhaps I—no, he is waiting for me. I doff my hat in the general
direction of the waterfall, and we set off. Behold now this good fortune.

By afternoon it is darker, thunder comes down the hills. Presently we
are in Spain. In the bar where we stop, a press of people, a small cup of coffee. I wipe the table with my hat: paws still dripping.

When is a pilgrim like a sieve? When he riddles.

▼▲▼

Buergete ▶ 22nd of June

unmoved the melons
don't seem to recall
a drop
of last night's downpour

SODO

The small hotel of Buergete is made of water. Outside, rain streams all night. Roofs pour, the gutters float with frogs and snails. You would not see me—I lie in the dark listening, swirling. Walls of the hotel are filled with water. Plumbing booms and sluices. A water clock, embedded in the heart of the building, measures out our hours in huge drops. Wheels and gears turn in the walls, the roaring of lovers washes over the ceiling, the staircase is an aqueduct of cries. From below I can hear a man dreaming. A deep ravine goes down to the sea, he calls out, rushes over the edge. The mechanisms that keep us from drowning are so fragile: and why us?

In the morning the hotel is dark, no sign of life, no smell of coffee. Old clock ticking in the deserted hall. Dining room empty, shutters drawn, napkins in glasses. Morning drifts on. I peer into the kitchen: still as a church. Everyone has been washed away in the night. We pile money on the table in the hall, leave without breakfast, without ado! as they say in my country. Outside is silent, street dissolving, far hills running down in streaks. We filter westward.

Pilgrims were people who figured things out as they walked. On the road you can think forward, you can think back, you can make a list to remember to tell those at home.

▼▲▼

to Pamplona ▶ 23rd of June

*When he thought of the fragile O-hisa made over to look
like the winsome pilgrim of the Kabuki and of the old man
at her side ringing a pilgrim's bell and intoning a canticle
from one holy place to the next, Kaname could not help
feeling a little envious. The old man chose his pleasures well.
Kaname had heard that it was not uncommon for men of
taste in Osaka to dress a favorite geisha as a pilgrim and do
the Awaji circuit with her every year. The old man, much
taken with the idea, announced that he would make this
the first of an annual series. Always afraid of sunburn,
O-hisa was less enthusiastic. "How does it go? We sleep at
Hachikenya, is it? Where do you suppose Hachikenya is?"*

                                                    TANIZAKI

Kinds of water drown us. Kinds of water do not. My water jar splashes
companionably on my back as I walk. A pool of thoughts tilts this way and
that in me. Socrates, after bathing, came back to his cell unhurriedly and
drank the hemlock. The others wept. Swans swam in around him. And he
began to talk about the coming journey, to an unknown place far from
their tears, which he did not understand. People really understand very
little of one another. Sometimes when I speak to him, My Cid looks very
hard and straight into my face as if in search of something (a city on a
map?) like someone who has tumbled off a star. But he is not the one who
feels alien—ever, I think. He lives in a small country of hope, which is his
heart. Like Socrates he fails to understand why travel should be such a chal-
lenge to the muscles of the heart, for other people. Around every bend of
the road is a city of gold, isn't it?

   I am the kind of person who thinks no, probably not. And we walk,
side by side, in different countries.

   Pilgrims were people in scientific exile.

                                   ▼▲▼

Puente la Reina ▶ 24th of June

the world so unsure, unknowable
the world so unsure, unknowable
who knows—our griefs may hold
our greatest hopes

ZEAMI

A bridge is a meeting point, where those who started out how many, now how many nights ago? come together. Hearts uneasy in their depths. It was in the medieval city of Puente la Reina that all the pilgrims heading for Compostela, from France and Spain and Italy and other points of origin, met at the crossing of the River Arga. Except, in those days, there was no crossing. Boatmen plied the river—many of them not honest men at all but sordid assassins who took advantage of the pilgrims! Kinds of water drown us. Evil boatmen threw many a pilgrim to his watery death. Then an act of grace supervened. The queen of Spain was moved to pity for the pilgrims' difficult situation. She gave it some thought. How could she defend them? Why not a bridge! A beautiful, antic, keyholed construction, washed by gold shadows on the underside (photograph). She smiled, when she saw it, out of the side of her eyes: *curva peligrosa* says the sign on the bridge to this day. *Deadly slant.* There were stars in the plane trees and stars in her eyes. There were pilgrims singing on the bridge. There were boatmen who turned to worse crime. Such is the balance of human efforts.

Pilgrims were people wondering, wondering. Whom shall I meet now?

▾▲▾

Estella ▸ 25th of June

like lame-wheeled carrriages
we creep forth reluctantly
on the journey from the capital

ZEAMI

On dark mornings in Navarre the fall-off hills rise in masses, flat on top. White clouds bite down on them like teeth. In my country too it is morning now, they are making coffee, they are getting out the black bread. No one eats black bread here. Spanish bread is the same color as the stones that lie along the roadside—gold. True, I often mistake stones for bread. Pilgrim's hunger is a curious thing.

The road itself was built by the pilgrims of ancient times as they walked. Each carried a stone and set it in place. As is clear from the photographs, these were in general stones of quite good size. While the pilgrims trudged, they would pretend the stones were loaves of bread and, to keep spirits high, they sang songs about bread, or about the rock that was following them. *¡No me mates con tomate, mátame con bacalao!* You can hear this one still, in bars, some nights. *Don't kill me with tomato, kill me with cod!* What is it that keeps us from drowning in moments that rise and cover the heart?

Pilgrims were people whose recipes were simple.

▼▲▼

to Nájera ▸ 27th of June

we pick spring greens
in the little field of Ikuta
a sight so charming
the traveler stops to watch
foolishness! all these questions

KAN-AMI

Rain during the night. No guests in the hotel except My Cid and me. Yet, just before dawn, someone made his way down the stairs and past our rooms to the bath. Much noise of taps and other facilities. A rough cough. I fell asleep, when I woke he was gone. In the plaza we find bars and shops already open, how surprising. We purchase blood oranges and eat them very fast. It is already late when you wake up inside a question. Rose petals are being swept from the church steps as we pass, and faces in the doorway are lit with vague regret. Someone has roused the town, not me. Someone has been gained and lost, someone of value. Are there two ways of knowing the world? a submissive and a devouring way. They end up roughly the same place.

Pilgrims were people who tried not to annoy the regular inhabitants.

▼▲▼

Nájera ▶ 28th of June

moon drifts in cloud
I have a mind
to borrow
a small ripe melon

SHIKI

We are moving on the edge of the Meseta. Hills are harsher, terraced, red soil shows through the green like sunburn. Small trees line up in spikes on the horizon. No more deep woods shaded for battle. No more long winds rolling down from Roland's eyes.

You see that uncertainty along the horizon (photograph)? Not rain. It is heat haze on the plain of León.

Water is less, and less.

In Nájera are buried the kings of Navarre. They lie on their tombs long-limbed and cool as water plants. The stone faces are full of faith but rather private, with a characteristic set to the lips: one straight incision across like the first cut made by a man peeling his orange with a knife. My Cid, as you know, prefers the speckled kind called blood oranges, which are quick to eat but slow to peel. Cleaning his knives reminds him of a story. There was once a pilgrim who carried a turnip all the way from France. A turnip of quite good size. He had in mind to feast his fellow pilgrims on the last hill outside Compostela and be king of their hearts for a while.

Thieves broke his head open, just as he came to the top of the hill. The good man's name has not come down to us, but the hill is still there and is called Monte del Gozo. From where you are perhaps you can see it. Mountain of Joy. My Cid tells these old stories wonderfully well. He has two knives, for different sizes of oranges.

Pilgrims were people who carried knives but rarely found joy.

▼▲▼

Santo Domingo de la Calzada ▶ 29th of June

waited for you along the road, I did—
silent, silent, walking alone
but today again the darkness falls

GENSEI

As we move into Castile we are accompanied on either side of the road by aqueducts and other more modern systems of irrigation, for the water grows less. Like pastries of red lava the rocks rise in visible layers. Fields are no longer dark and edged close with woods but stretch out and roll away beneath the eye, sectioned in areas of ocher and amber and red. *Nine months of winter, three months of hell* is the proverbial description of climate on the Meseta. No dark green wheat riding in waves under the wind here, as there was all through Navarre. No wind at all. That smell is light, ready to fall on us. One day closer to the plain of León.

We live by waters breaking out of the heart.

My Cid loves heat and is very elated. He rarely gets thirsty. "I was born in the desert." Twice a day, at meals, he drinks a lot of wine, staring at the glass in genial amazement as it empties itself again and again. He grows heavier and heavier like a piece of bread soaking, or a fish that floats dreamily out of my fingers down deeper and deeper in the tank, turning round now and then to make dim motions at me with its fins, as if in recognition, but in fact it does not recognize me—gold shadows flash over it, out of reach, gone. Who is this man? I have no idea. The more I watch him, the less I know. What are we doing here, and why are our hearts invisible? Once last winter when we were mapping out the pilgrimage on his kitchen table, he said to me, "Well, what are you afraid of, then?" I said nothing. "Nothing." Not an answer. What would your answer be?

We think we live by keeping water caught in the trap of the heart. *Coger en un trampa* is a Spanish idiom meaning "to catch in a trap." *Coger por el buen camino* is another, constructed with the same verb, that means "to get the right road." And yet to ensnare is not necessarily to take the right road.

Afraid I don't love you enough to do this.

Pilgrims were people who got the right verb.

▼▲▼

Villamayor del Río ▶ 30th of June

As I look back over the many years of my frivolous life, I re-member at one time I coveted an official post with a tenure of land and at another time I was anxious to confine myself within the walls of a monastery. Yet I kept aimlessly wan-dering on like a cloud in the wind.. . . It is because I believe there is no place in this world that is not an unreal dwelling. At this point I abandoned the line of thinking and went to sleep.

BASHO

The town of Villamayor del Río, My Cid observes, is three ways a lie. "It is not a town, it is not big and there is no river." The observations are correct. Notwithstanding, we lunch, and over lunch a conversation—about action, in which he does not believe. I would relate the conversation and outline the theory of his belief but theories elude me unless I write them down at the time. Instead, I was watching his dreamy half smile. It floats up through his face from the inside, like water filling an aquarium, when he talks about God. For his conversations about action (we have had more than one) are all descriptions of God, deep nervous lover's descriptions.

I should have taken photographs. A theory of action is hard to catch, and I know only glimpses of his life—for instance, at home he makes his own bread (on Saturday morning, very good bread). He thought about being a priest (at one time). He could have made a career on the concert stage, and instead built a harpsichord (red) in the dining room. The harpsichord goes unmentioned in Villamayor del Río. I am telling you this because a conversation is a journey, and what gives it value is fear. You come to understand travel because you have had conversations, not vice versa. What is the fear inside language? No accident of the body can make it stop burning.

▼▲▼

to Burgos ▶ 2nd of July

what does he do—
the man next door
in the abode in late autumn?

BASHO

"The land is lean indeed!" He quotes from the poem as we begin our long, cold climb up the windswept plateau of Burgos. Cold is the mountain road that goes curving up. Cold are the woods where winds come roaring out at us as of we were enemies—or birds, for here are tiny birds walking about on the road, who have strolled out of their homes in the treetops now level with the road as we ascend—and there is no one else. The wind is too loud to talk. He walks ahead, eyes front.

In the city of Burgos lies El Cid himself—beside Ximena he rests in an eternal conversation. Beneath the transept of Burgos cathedral they have lain since 1921, and before that, in a burial place in the city from the year 1835, and previously, seven hundred years in the monastery of San Pedro outside the city walls. By now she must know every word he is going to say. Yet she kisses his mouth and the eyes of his face, she kisses his hands, his truth, his marrow. What is the conversation of lovers? Compared with ordinary talk, it is as bread to stone. My heart gets dizzy. It is the most difficult photograph I have tried to take so far: up the scaffolding, hand over hand and out onto the pinnacles they blow, her hair like a red sail as they veer around storks' nests in the wind and clutch wide at the railings, leaning out over the tiny city, its clockwork shadows so crazily far below. One shriek goes flaring and flattening away down the valley. Gone. She kisses him on the shoulder in the Moorish custom. They look at one another. They look into the light. They jump.

There is no question I covet that conversation. There is no question I am someone starving. There is no question I am making this journey to find out what the appetite is. And I see him free of it, as if he had simply crossed to the other side of a bridge, I see desire set free in him like some ray of mysterious light. Now tell me the truth, would you cross that bridge if you came to it? And where, if you made the grave choice to give up bread, would it take you? You see what I fear. One night I dreamed of such a world. I rowed upon the surface of the moon and there was no wind, there were no moments, for the moon is as empty as the inside of an eye and not even the sound of a shadow falling falls there. I know you want me to tell you that hunger and silence can lead you to God, so I will say it, but I awoke. As the nail is parted from the flesh, I awoke and I was alone.

Ahead of me walks a man who knows the things I want to know about bread, about God, about lovers' conversations, yet mile after tapping mile goes by while I watch his heels rise and fall in front of me and plant my feet in rhythm to his pilgrim's staff as it strikes the road, white dust puffing up to cover each step, left, right, left.

When is a pilgrim like a letter of the alphabet? When he cries out.

▼▲▼

from Burgos ▶ 3rd of July

now I return to the burning house
but where is the place I used to live?

KAN-AMI

Cold Burgos is beautiful to leave along the avenue of dark plane trees that line the river. Whiteness floats on the water. At the bend of the river a water bird stands on one long, chill leg. He turns an eye. *Adiós.* Gladly and bravely we go—how surprising. Burgos was to have been for us a major interval, some four days of luxury and recuperation, according to our original itinerary. Instead, we stay just long enough to mend our trousers and tie new straps on our hats. The cloud-moving wind calls through our sleep: we rise too early, look at one another, set off again. It is an open secret among pilgrims and other theoreticians of this traveling life that you become addicted to the horizon. There is a momentum of walking, hunger, roads, empty bowl of thoughts that is more luxurious—more *civil*, than any city.

Even the earliest *Pilgrim's Guide,* published in A.D. 1130, contains remarks touching the dilemma of the pilgrim who reaches his destination and cannot bear to stop. But that is not my question, presently.

My questions, as you know, concern pilgrims' traditions. Animals ride on top of one another. Animals ensnare themselves in plants and tendrils. These are two motifs that may be seen repeatedly in reliefs and other works of art along the pilgrim's route. Signs are given to us like a voice within flesh, that is my question. Signs point our virtue. I want to ask how is it this man and I are riding on top of one another, and how ensnared, for it is not in the customary ways. We take separate rooms in hotels. Carnal interest is absent. Yet tendrils are not. A pilgrim is a person who is up to something. What is it? A pilgrim is a person who works out an attitude to tendrils and other things that trammel the feet, what should that be? Chop them as fast as they grow with my sharp pilgrim's knife? Or cherish them, hoarding drops of water of every kind to aid their struggle? Love is the mystery inside this walking. It runs ahead of us on the road like a dog, out of the photograph.

▼▲▼

to Castrogeriz ▶ 4th of July

twisting up hemp
I spin a thread that has no use
the tears that fall
are not beads for stringing

TSURAYUKI

We walk for hours through a single wheat field stretching as far as the eye can see in every direction to the sky. Hills come lower. Horizon flattens. Color begins to bleach out of the landscape as we move onto the Meseta. No more red clay. Where soil shows through the vegetation now it is white, or the porous grey of pumice, and powders off in the wind. Trees are short and clenched like fists in a Goya painting. No rivers at all today until just outside the town of Castrogeriz we cross the Río Odra, a dry gully.

My Cid has taken to wearing a goatskin bag *(odra)* for carrying water. He is rarely thirsty but likes the effect of it slung across his body like a gangster's gun, and he is perfecting the knack of shooting water from the goatskin into his mouth with one hand while reading a map in the other as he walks. Half smile. Very ordinary behavior can be striking when it plays in the shapes of things like a sage, or a child biting into a pear. In the photograph the two of us are bending over the map, looking for Castrogeriz which has been obscured by water drops. Here is an enlargement. You can see, within each drop, a horizon stretching, hard, in full wind. Enlarged further, faint dark shapes become visible, gathering on the edge of the plain of León. *¡Corazón arriba!*

▼▲▼

Castrogeriz ▶ 4th of July

*I will gaze at the moon
and cleanse my heart*

ZEAMI

Castrogeriz is a pile of history. It is layered upward from the dry ravine of the Odra to the ancient remains of a Roman camp high on top of the rock. This smashed Roman grin commands the rock and the town and the whole valley below. It stands behind every sound, like something dripping.

Why then, I wonder, in the town of Castrogeriz, do they turn the water off at night? Not only in each house, but in the fountain of the central square and also in all the fountains of the lesser plazas. A surprise, and a long dry night for me. I walk back to the hotel, hands hanging down. Surprises make a child of us: here is another. A moon rising, edge so sharp you can feel it in your back teeth. By the time she is full, there will be two grave children walking the plain of León. Unexpectedness moves us along. And the moon—so perfectly charted, never fails to surprise us, I wonder why. The moon makes a traveler hunger for something bitter in the world, what is it? I will vanish, others will come here, what is that? An old question.

Well, a pilgrim is like a Nō play. Each one has the same structure, a question mark.

▼▲▼

to Frómista ▶ 5th of July

daybreak comes on distinctly
with sounds of a punted boat
does not the dissolving moon
stay yet in the sky?

SHOHAKU

Every morning as I walk behind him, I gather a handful of flowers which My Cid pins to his hat. Flowers are banal between lovers but this is not that. Mine are much less an offering to My Cid than an entangling of him in an offering to the saint, which is in turn an entangling of the saint in an offering to God, as the pin snares the flower stalks and the hat gives occasion to the whole. As you know from the photographs, Saint James in his day was insouciance itself—with his great hat tilted low over one eye and his blue cloak unfurling around him like the first notes of paradise. Morning is clear. The hearths smoke. Distances go silent.

Pilgrims were debonair people.

▼▲▼

Frómista ▶ 7th of July

as one turns about the moon
understands one's very heart

SOZEI

Hills continue to pale and scarify. They look shaved, like old heads of women in an asylum. What is the breaking point of the average pilgrim? I feel so lonely, like childhood again. What kind of ensnaring can touch the loneliness of animals? Nothing can touch it. No, maybe that is not altogether correct. This evening My Cid gave me a back rub and spoke to me, more kindly than he has before, about his mother, who suffers from a wasting disease. Once, when he first learned of her illness, his heart broke. Then he set about taking care of her, with back rubs and other attentions. A voice coming from behind your back can be different. Animals who ride on top of one another do not have to see each other's face. Sometimes that is better.

▼▲▼

Carrión de los Condes ▸ 7th of July

as usual with men who are blind
my ears are sharp, you know
you just called me "a man without feelings"
don't go on saying things like that!

ZEAMI

The morning is clear. The morning is immensely clear. Lower the lance and lean forward in the saddle. It is time to question him about the loneliness. His answer both surprises me and does not.

He has not been lonely since he was thirty, when he took the decision to channel his sadness into forms "more metaphysical." He began to think about penance. Like a blind poet of ancient times, he built his hut on a meeting slope, chose a small number of objects and waited for friends. Fish dart out of gold regions. His loves are deep, sudden services. And his delight is of a very particular kind. "You have a passion for people who are pelted, Dan," says Sir Hugo to Daniel Deronda in a novel I read once. My Cid lives this novel; his friends are ones in affliction. *She is someone who has known hardship,* he often begins. Has a bad back, father abandoned her, gives all her money away to the poor, history of lunacy, lost the whole family, royalty—fallen, nowhere to go. He loves these stories—they make people seem real. Nonetheless there are difficulties. People mistake his intentions, especially women, and some do drown.

For women may regard a story as the beginning of something, like a love affair. Serious mistake. For him it is already the end: *se abandona.* Persons studying the photographs from different angles may see different tendrils, but for him these entanglements are not a problem. It is you who are lonely.

And in the end, his tendency to rescue maidens is not something I can explain to you, nor dramatize—I am a pilgrim (not a novelist) and the only story I have to tell is the road itself. Besides, no one can write a novel about a road, any more than you can write a novel about God, simply because you cannot get round the back of it. A round character is one you can see round. He changes according to the company he keeps. He moves but your movements are always larger, and circumnavigate his. Inside the minds of other characters you see him flicker past, suddenly funny—or evil. Now I think it is true to say of the road, and also of God, that it does not move. At the same time, it is everywhere. It has a language, but not one I know. It has a story, but I am in it. So are you. And to realize this is a moment of some sadness. When we are denied a story, a light goes off—Daniel Deronda vanishes; do we vanish too? I am asking you to study the dark.

▾▲▾

Sahagún ▸ 8th of July

no wind, yet the windbells
keep on ringing

Shiren

The light is astounding, a hammer. Horizon no closer, ever. Hills again change color: gold and dark gold and darker gold. Whole fields are nothing but slabs of this gold soil, smashed up in chunks for cultivation, as if the massive altar at Castrogeriz had toppled straight across León. The pieces of bread that line the pilgrims' road have the color and shape of the round loaves of León, many show bites taken out. They were famished people who built this road.

My Cid and I have our first open anger today. It cut like glass. Animals entangle themselves in one another, and grow enraged. (What is rage?)

When I spoke to him about the loneliness I didn't mean out in the wheat fields. There is a loneliness that opens up between two people sitting in a bar, not in love with one another, not even certain they like the way they are entangled with one another, one taps a glass with a spoon, stops. There is a silence that pounds down on two people. More astounding than the light that hammers the plain of León, at least for those animals who choose to fear it. (Is it a choice?)

▾▲▾

El Burgo Ranero ▸ 9th of July

your autumn leaves—
it is because they fall we love them
so why not launch our Takase river boat?

SHIKIBU

It would be an almost perfect love affair, wouldn't it? that between the pilgrim and the road. No mistake, it is a beautiful thing, the *camino*. It stretches away from you. It leads to real gold: look at the way it shines. And it asks only one thing. Which happens to be the one thing you long to give. You step forward. You shiver in the light. Nothing is left in you but desire for that perfect economy of action, using up the whole heart, no residue, no mistake: *camino*. It would be as simple as water, wouldn't it? If there were any such thing as simple action for animals like us.

Pilgrims were people glad to take off their clothing, which was on fire.

▼▲▼

Mansilla de las Mulas ▸ 10th of July

bones on the moor
wind blows on them through my heart

BASHO

Meseta colder than expected. Distances crushing. Horizon beats on the eyes.

Everything is gold. I cannot describe the gold. I have shown you the photographs (or have I?) but they don't come near it. You get almost no warning. Something is coming along the edge of the wheat, drumming the plain like a horseman, you stop, listen, begin to turn—don't!

It is life taken over, *esa es la verdad.*

▼▲▼

to León ▶ 11th of July

the rumor is already
in circulation
yet when I began to love
there was not a soul who knew

TADAMINE

Water abandons itself. Gold does not. Gold takes life over. There are drownings on the Meseta. I will show you the photographs if you like but, really, in this case they are not helpful. Because the light is not something you *see,* exactly. You don't look at it, or breathe, you feel a pressure but you don't look. It is like being in the same room as a man you love. Other people are in the room. He may be smoking a cigarette. And you know you are not strong enough to look at him (yet) although the fact that he is there, silent and absent beside a thin wisp of cigarette smoke, hammers you. You rest your chin on your hand, like a saint on a pillar. Moments elongate and drop. A radiance is hitting your skin from somewhere, every nerve begins to burn outward through the surface, your lungs float in a substance like rage, sweet as rage, no!—don't look. Something falling from your mouth like bits of rust.

Well, the photograph—after all it may give some idea of the thing. From outside it all, looking down: two tiny figures moving on the Meseta. Two animals enraged with one another. How can you tell? Pay particular attention to the nerves. Every one is visible. See, as they burn, you can look right down the heart's core. See it crumble like old dry bread.

▼▲▼

to León ► 11th of July

In the Nō play Obasute, *at the line "I feel ashamed to see the moon," there exists a moment when the acting can be so effective that (as they say) "gold is picked up in the middle of the road."*

ZEAMI

A baking hot morning. I can feel you watching. I shrug and go on.

In allegorical renderings of the pilgrimage to Compostela, days spent crossing the plain of León stand for the dark night of the soul—how can it help being that way? Although we taste everything and take on every animal, although your true love exists (and maybe it does), we continue to behave more or less like the people we are, even on a pilgrimage. No soul ever goes dark enough for you. Look again at the photograph. Two figures moving on the Meseta, running slowly on a table of gold. Running with arms out, mouths open. Two small ensnared animals howling toward Finisterre.

You can lead a pilgrim to water.

▼▲▼

León ► 12th of July

when in the clear water
at Ausaka border
it sees its reflection
the tribute horse from Mochizuki
will surely shy away

ZEAMI

Various dangers come at you from water. We cross the top of the world and descend into the city of León in conditions much different than expected. Lashing rain and slate-grey winds, horizontal and cold as winter. Something is being prepared on the plain of León. The city itself is a bright animal, bustling, turning, restless to lie down. We find lodgings and fall asleep. Storms pass over the city. My Cid dreams of leviathans coming up out of the water to kill him. He impales one of them on his pilgrim's staff and hurls it back. Losing his staff (I point out). But the creature will (he feels sure) be purified on its journey downstream to the ends of the earth. A clean gold animal clambering ashore at the end of the world, isn't that so? I am the kind of person who says let's wait and see.

▾▴▾

Arzoá ▸ 12th of July

she at once capped his verses

SHIKIBU

My Cid and I are very polite with one another. At the same time, somewhat dialectical—that is, I contradict everything he says. I have been trying to curb this habit by picking up pieces of bread from along the roadside to gnaw as I walk. It must have been, in origin, for this purpose that pilgrims began to put the bread there.

An origin is not an action, although it occurs (perhaps loudly) at the very start and may open an action (as in breaking a gun). How long ago it seems we started out. In the photographs from this leg of the journey you will notice a certain absence of scale clues, so that a bullet-pocked rock seems to hold the heavens.

Pilgrims were people who took a surprisingly long time to cross the head of a pin.

▾▴▾

Órbigo ▸ 13th of July

since my house burned down
I now own
a better view
of the rising moon

MASAHIDE

Color begins to return to the fields as we move towards the edge of the Meseta. There are green potato fields cut by canals. Avenues of poplar trees turn their bright soles to the wind. Horizon closing in. Behind the light, towards the west, (darkish) shadows are gathering. That would be animals on the rim of the plain. That would be the wolf.

The pieces of bread along the roadside are blacker now and more wildly bitten. At the same time, in some places you see whole loaves thrown down untouched. Curious. Insouciance may escalate to proportions of madness at this stage in the pilgrimage. Breaking points appear.

▼▲▼

Astorga ▸ 14th of July

the dried sardine is broiled at noon
but in this back country
the use of coins is not yet heard of
what a bother to travelers

BASHO

Those things that cut across the time are what you remember, voices cutting across sleep.

"*¡Agua! ¡Agua!*" ripping through my siesta like a color.

Red. The color red speeds through the land as we move into the mountains again. Sections of brick-red soil mark out the green plantings of the hills as they rise. Poppies flash along the roadside, amid dark chunks of rusted bread. At noon, the cicadas let their red throats crack open. Red, My Cid informs me, is the only color wolves see: this is taken as clear testimony, in ancient Celtiberian belief, that they are genuinely royal animals.

It is over lunch that we talk of wolves, and My Cid has ordered trout. The scales and eyes are gold as it sizzles on the plate. He cuts in. The flesh is a deep rose color. After lunch we proceed to the museum to see a twelfth-century statue called *The Virgin of the Trout,* with wooden cheeks of the same rose color. Her smile an underwater bell. Ancient pilgrims traveled from far and wide, on delicately tinted feet, to visit her. And there is still more red, as we move from the museum to the cathedral, for the cathedral at Astorga wears a deep blush. Its porch of rose limestone is inscribed with scenes of shame: Christ expelling moneylenders from the temple, and others. Now we are close to the heart of the color. Shame. Look at the photograph. Yes, it is a picture of a hole in a wall.

The hole dates from medieval times. It is located in the west wall of the cathedral at a height of about two meters above the head of My Cid. Behind it is a pit opening into the wall and, in front, iron bars. Women once placed themselves inside the pit and lived there, taking as sustenance only what was offered by those passing by. Many a pilgrim on his way to Compostela shared his meager rations with the women, handing in water or pieces of bread or whatever he had. Others passed with their eyes on the road. Some tossed stones through the bars. It is a strange economy that shame set up, isn't it? almost as strange as that of honor. Pilgrims blush in broad daylight. Women blush in a hole. They trade morsels of gold through a grillwork and so all live to overcome another day. What is a blush?

Dum pudeo pereo (as I blush, I die) says an old love song. Blood rushes to the face, at the same time the heart seems to wither in on itself and snap, like the eye socket of a trout when it hits the hot oil. Shame is the presence of someone right up against me. Hot because her eyes are closer to me than my own honor. She is a woman in a pit in a wall with a stone hot as the midday sun in her hands: listen, footsteps go fading down the street. She is My Cid cut open by a word from me, him weeping within me. Kinds of water drown us.

The women in the wall were called *las emparedadas* (the walled-in ones). What is a pilgrim's life after he quits the *camino?* There is an ancient tradition: the afterlife of a pilgrim is three ways shame. Never hungry again. He will eat and eat and taste nothing. Never free again, according to the terms of the freedom he finds while bound to the road. Never angry again, with that kind of rage that scorches two animals ensnared on the Meseta. It is an anger hard to come back from as death, or so it seems to me now as I recollect the day near Sahagun when My Cid and I cut ourselves open on a moment of anger, and blasphemed your name. Let's take out the photographs again, *momentito*. There is something here that deserves to be studied, there is a sense of the excitement and danger of the night. And yet it was broad day: look.

▾▲▾

from today the dew
will erase the inscription on my hat
"I am one of two traveling together"

Basho

I have never felt life to be as slow and desperate as that day on the Meseta with the sky empty above us, hour after hour unmoving before us and a little wind whistling along the bone of my ear. Walking across the top of the world. Hours give no shade. Wind gives no shade.

Sky does not move. Sky crushes all that moves.

We had been out since sunrise, we were growing black. Then we saw water.

A plane tree in the middle of the desert with a spring beside it. We ran to it and drank, drank more, grew arrogant. Here I am swaggering like a *torero* around the little oasis, or so it looks (photograph), water all over my face. Now I ask My Cid a question—and what follows—well, it may seem to be nothing at all. But in fact it was sackcloth of hair and the moon became blood. He begins to answer the question (I don't remember what it was). And he has a certain way of answering a question (as we all do). And I know what he is going to say (as soon as he begins). And all at once I am enraged. My sharp pilgrim's knife flashes once. *"I know!"* right across his open face.

I know. I know what you say. I know who you are. I know all that you mean. Why does it enrage an animal to be given what it already knows? Speaking as someone who is as much in love with knowledge as My Cid is in love with the light on the plain of León, I would say that knowing is a road. The metaphor is unoriginal but now you may set it beside the photographs of the pit in the wall and see what it signifies to me.

You reach out your hand for bread and grasp a stone. You touch stone, you feel sweat running down your body. Sweat running, day going black, it is a moment that does not move. How I did waste and exhaust my heart. Something darker appears to be running down the body of the saint in the photograph, but it is just an effect of the light filter we were using on the Meseta. There is nothing darker (than the second death).

Now that I study them, however, I have to confess the photographs of the *emparedadas* are something of an embarrassment. I tried to angle my lens so as to shoot through the bars but the grillwork was too high. None of them printed properly. Look at this one, for instance—it could be a picture of a woman with something in her hands. It could be a drowned dog floating in bits of stone. Can you make it out? The picture has been taken looking directly into the light, a fundamental error. As I was considering these matters, he had gone his way, footsteps fading down the street like the last drops of water running out of a basin. I hurry after him. Kinds of water drown us. Kinds of water blister the negatives irremediably (prints look burned). Perhaps I will have time to put these through again later.

▼▲▼

Molinaseca ▸ 16th of July

voice of wind in pines
makes the solitude familiar
who will do such waking for each dawn?

SOGI

Mountains. We have come over the mountains of León. It takes a whole day from light to light. The road goes winding, winding, winding up. The road goes plunging down. You understand these were *words* before: up, down. It is nearly my limit, nearly stupor, whereas he grows lighter and lighter as he walks. What is penance?

Up.

On top of the mountains of León is an iron cross. Here we stop. A wind whistles up one side of the mountains from early times, mornings, much too far away and still those mornings, down on the plain of León. "Somewhere down there we were hot," he says. Somewhere down there we were drowning. I fall over on a flat rock and fall asleep, while he watches. Wolves come and go, browsing at my back. At sunset we get up and start down the other side of the mountains.

Down.

Gorge after gorge, turning, turning. Caverns of sunset, falling, falling away—just a single vast gold air breathed out by beings—they must have been marvelous beings, those gold-breathers. Down. Purple and green islands. Cleft and groined and gigantically pocked like something left behind after all the oceans vanished one huge night: the mountains. Their hills fold and fold again, fold away, down. Folded into the dens and rocks of the hills are ghost towns. Broken streets end in them, like a sound, nowhere. Shadow is inside. We walk (oh quietly) even so—breaking lines of force, someone's. Houses stand in their stones. Each house an empty socket. Some streaked with red inside. Words once went on in there—no. I don't believe that. Words never went on there.

Down.

We circle, circle, circle again. Around each bend of the road, another, bending back. It is sunset. Look down: at the foot of the mountain something comes into view. Clustered on the water like wings, something, shining. Something, marveling, at the float of its wings around it on the water—how they change and turn gold! That is what an evening was in the beginning, you once told me. *Y la paloma volvió a él a la hora de la tarde.* The photograph has been taken with the light behind it so that the two figures stand out clear against the mountains, which crush them from behind. They appear to be running—not because of the wolves who, as you see, are merely watching from this peak or that in mild curiosity. An effect of immediacy has been achieved by showing the figures close up and cut off at the knees. *And the dove came into him in the evening.*

Pilgrims were people to whom things happened that happen only once.

▼▲▼

Trabadelo ▸ 17th of July

great moor
answering heart
oh do not forget
the bounds of life keep shifting

SOCHO

All day we steer along the edge of the mountains, looking up: the massif of
Galicia. Tomorrow, climb again. "We will strike them in the name of God
and of Saint James!" He is blithe. I am not. With folded paws they watch
us, wait.

▾▲▾

Cebreiro ▸ 18th of July

in the town of Kowata
there were horses to hire
but I loved you so much
I walked barefoot all the way

KAN-AMI

So we climb to the top of the world once more. Straight up a rocky goat
track, teetering, panting, pouring with sweat, plastered in dust to the pass
of Cebreiro. At the top the wind is suddenly wide open and cold as a river.
Look back—now it all pulls away at our feet, a thousand miles straight
down straight back to the morning we began, it was a good bright morning
in the eleventh century and we must have been very young to judge from
the photograph. So white was I when I went to harvest.

   "I do not wish to sound Socratic, " between angry bites of tortilla, "but
what is your definition of penance?" He is annoyed with me today. He does
not find my definition adequate. Pilgrims who go on foot but sleep in hotels (like us) are, in his view, more authentic than pilgrims who drive cars
but sleep on the ground. Well, Galicia is a surprising place, is my view. And
authenticity is surprisingly well defended here. For example, in this hotel,
one huge white wolf guards us through the night. He has a huge, slow gaze

and lies in the lettuces, still as a sculpture except for his huge, black eyes which rove tirelessly back and forth over the moon-washed grounds. Who would have thought we would reach the zone of greatest danger to find that the wolves are the hospitalers here? Penance can be a surprising study and pilgrims, even very authentic ones, raven in ways they do not expect. I have seen men die of the waters because they had learned to crave only wormwood. What sense could there be in that? What sense is there in pain at all—however we contrive it for ourselves as we cast about for ways to bind up the wound between us and God? The penitent in the act of binding up pain with pain is a photograph I have tried (unsuccessfully) a number of times to capture.

On the edge of the world is a black row of trees, shaking. Moon like a piece of skin above.

When is a pilgrim like a photograph? When the blend of acids and sentiment is just right.

▼▲▼

to Samos

ah, for her too, it is the midnight
pilgimage
how many of them there are! is this
the work of hell?

CHIKAMATSU

What is the relation of rage to penance? Of entanglement?

It is a room of women. The night is black. In the photograph you can see an eyelid outlined in light from the street, here. The wall streaked with darker moisture, there. We listen to each other breathe. A cicada has got in here tonight and with his tiny rasp is nicking our nerve ends open. Even among the living, sometimes it seems a night will never end. A woman begins now to shriek, softly. I am not one to interfere, but sadness is sadness. Maybe a little song—my mother used to sing to me, sometimes at night, old ballads from the civil war:

as each hour passes Miguel my love
you grow more dear:
is that the reason Miguel my love
you are not here?

Ah. The shrieking has stopped. The others are breathing. The room grows quiet. Sometimes it is enough just to recognize a *camino.* Your bitter heart heals my heart, oh stay with me.

▼▲▼

Samos ▶ 19th of July

"Yes," he says, "for your sake."
What is he saying?

ZEAMI

Penance is something broken off and thrown back, like a sweetness that pierces your thoughts when all at once you remember someone you dreamed of last night. It was someone unknown. Just at dawn he was there, gleaming, shuffling. It makes the night transparent to think of. It makes the night incomparable. You dreamed of black arms shaking on the edge of the world. Reaching back for that, you drop through a freedom so clear it is simply pain. *Corazón nuevo* means "new heart." It is a place you reach for through your skin, which goes silver, through shame burned black on you, through a thirst that we cannot describe, to where he is cooling his wings in the stars like a pond, looking down at them trailing around him on the dark water—look, there he is, vaguely marveling—oh beloved, who could catch your eye?

▼▲▼

Palas del Rey ▶ 21st of July

two petals fall
and the shape of the peony
is wholly changed

Shikibu

Climbing and tracking through the bottomlands of Galicia in deep fog.
Shapes of life loom and vanish at us, grow grotesque. Fog invents the imagination. We do not like to be surrounded by meaningless grotesquerie, we
are animals who take it upon us to find form in the misshapen. There
(photographs) is Velázquez on a cabbage stalk, and the pine trees here a
row of teeth? a fortress? dice? and this fence post has the outline of the
Dead Sea, I believe.

Shapes of life change as we look at them, change us for looking. Take
wolves. You may think you know what a wolf looks like: Queen Lupa
thought so. For the countryside around Palas del Rey was once thick with
wolves and Lupa was their queen, commanding them from a rough fort
called the Castro Lupario. Strange her yellow eyes should fasten one day on
Saint James himself.

He had come through Galicia in the first century A.D. on his way to
Finisterre, bent on Chrisianizing the uttermost edge of the known world,
and returned some years later to Palestine to be martyred. Whereupon his
disciples took the body and embarked on a boat. They reached Galicia,
within sight of the Castro Lupario: see Lupa's eyes narrow. She goes to
meet them and offers them land to bury the saint. Her speech is fluent, her
face empty as a pocket and her plan is to kill them with death. That very
night she sends the holy men out with the body on a cart. What are those
animals yoked to the cart? Oxen, says Lupa. They look somehow darker,
but at night who can say? Of course they are Lupa's own wolves—is this
just a name? As they walk through the dark the wolves become oxen and
pull the cart to a good high hill. There the apostles build their tomb and
offer thanks. Lupa's eyes widen. She studies the photographs under various
magnifying lenses and, in the end, converts to the new religion.

Animals who ride on top of one another become entangled in ways
they do not expect. From behind its back you may see a wolf as a queen, or

a hill as a holy body, or action as a fact. But facts form themselves this way and that, when we look for them in photographs or historical accounts.

Penance is one form we find, one form we insist on.

▼▲▼

to Compostela ▶ 23rd of July

it's not easy to tell which end
is which of a resting snail

KYORAI

Your voice I know. It had me terrified. When I hear it in dreams, from time to time all my life, it sounds like a taunt—but dreams distort sound, for they send it over many waters. During these hard days I, a pilgrim, am giving my consideration to this. I trudge along the bottom of the river and the questioning goes on in me. What are we made of but hunger and rage? His heels rise and fall in front of me. How surprised I am to be entangled in the knowledge of some other animal. I know the animal. Does that mean I hand myself over? What is knowing? That is the question no one was asking, although I went from place to place and watched and listened to all that they said. I began to suspect some code was in operation. It had me terrified. Why? It plunged me in a pit, why? Because it is your question.

Your question I leave to you. There is in it a life of love I can scarcely look at, except in dreams. Or from time to time in photographs. Here is an old picture of My Cid with his mother. He is reaching up to put his hat on her head. Even before her illness she disliked being exposed to the afternoon sun. Yet she never brought a hat, and I believe they walked most afternoons. "Must get a hat," she would say every time, bending her head. Half smile.

How is a pilgrim like a blacksmith? He bends iron. Love bends him.

▼▲▼

to Compostela ▸ 24th of July

why, my dear pilgrim hat
you must accompany me
to view the plum trees!

BASHO

It takes a long time to arrive from not very far away. Just before the end we climb the small hill called Monte del Gozo. On achieving this height, from which the long-desired city can suddenly be seen half a league distant, ancient pilgrims would fall to their knees, shed tears of joy and begin to sing the Te Deum. "They felt like seafarers on reaching a haven after a tempest at sea," says one old account, which My Cid is reading aloud as he walks ahead of me. His voice is joy, his steps are joy, moved along like a water wheel in water. While for my part I feel I have broken in half. Every pilgrim hits the mark in his own way.

Stars are spitting out of the cathedral as we enter Compostela: the cathedral! No, it is not a mirage, this stupendous humming hulk of gold that stands as if run aground upon the plaza at the center of the city of Santiago. Built in the early years of the twelfth century, it was embellished towards the end of that century by one Master Mateo, who added the Portal of Glory to replace the original entrance. That was an act of grace. An entrance is important to a pilgrim: there can be only one.

An entrance should be a door built as a kiss, so Master Mateo understood it. All over his Portal are creatures in glory, harping with the harps of God. Smiles and half smiles fall from them like music. Animals and prophets, angels and the unnamed people of God raise their hands (surprised) and lean together in joy. Some show a small blush on each cheek. Through this portal, since the twelfth century, pilgrims enter. Won and not cheaply! They go straight in. They go to greet the Master of the place, entering with hand outstretched—I did it too (photograph). You approach the tree of Jesse, carved on the main column shaft by Master Mateo in 1195. You fit your hand into the five hollows visible at shoulder height among the tendrils of the tree. With your fingers in the hollows you can just lean down and kiss the head of Master Mateo, who has sculpted himself into the column base amid entangled leaves and animals. So many pilgrims' lips have brushed the hard plane of the Master's forehead that is has been worn into a convex pool, where rainwater and other moistures collect. *Se abandona*. (I like this photograph of two hurried visitors mistaking Master Mateo for a font.)

Stars, as I say, are shooting from the cathedral high into the air as we make our way across the plaza. They drop to the ground and lie in white fire. My Cid is bending down, in the photograph, to see whether he has one lodged in the sole of his sandal: in fact he does—problematic, you would think. But this is an example of the way trials turn to joy for him. Since an accident in childhood his legs have been of unequal length, but now, with a star in his shoe he is walking evenly for the first time in years. It has tripled his insouciance. He embraces a statue of Saint James. He embraces me—and I fall over (I have had several glasses today)—my good black beret rolling in the dust. "Why, I'm drunk!" "Why, I know." Half smile. With a certain flourish he replaces my beret.

▼▲▼

Compostela ▶ 25th of July

since you are blind
your sense of poetry
can't be expected to show on your face

ZEAMI

At midnight, fireworks in the plaza. No photographs—you know what fireworks are like. Tawdry, staggering, irresistible, like human love. Live stars fall on twenty thousand people massed in a darkened square. Some cry out, get burned, applaud. No star falls on me, although I try to position myself. Will you say you cannot make out my face in the dark? you heartless creature.

At the end of the fireworks we burn down the cathedral, as is traditional. So dazed with light and sulphur by now, there is no question it is the appropriate finale. Tomorrow morning, when we try to celebrate Saint James's solemn mass amid the charred ruins, we will think again. But fireworks are always now, aren't they? like human love. *¡Corazón arriba!*

When is a pilgrim like the middle of the night? When he burns.

▼▲▼

Compostela ▸ 25th of July

even I who have no lover
I love this time
of new kimonos

ONTSURA

Notwithstanding a rainy morning in Compostela, solemn mass in honor of Saint James is a debonair event. Pilgrims stand knee-deep in gold rubble, beneath swaying shreds of the high lantern, from which fire is still dropping in lit flakes. Soot and rain stream down on their shoulders unnoticed. The chancel is rumored to be a molten lake and small animals drowning in the side aisles, but we cannot see past a barrier of klieg lights and recording apparatus that has been set up in the central vault by National Spanish Television (the festival mass will be broadcast live, with excerpts for the six o'clock news). Camera crews, trying to string booms across the nave, dodge and curse as they wade on the glassy sea.

There are several fine moments, for example, just about midway through the Credo the central chandelier begins to short circuit—exploding a drizzle of stars over pilgrims in the front pews, quite spectacular. All applaud. But I see you peering hard at another photograph. Oh yes.

That solid silver asteroid is the *botafumeiro,* a vessel from which incense is dispensed at the close of the festival mass, to sanctify the crowds. It hangs straight down from the lantern of the church on a silver rope, about the size of a full-grown wolf. Beneath it, as you see, crowds of pilgrims are packed tight as fish all down the central aisle of the church, while the transepts are empty—why? It is to create a sort of runway: when the crowds are blessed, the *botafumeiro* is swung the whole width of the church—sixty-five meters from transept to transept—in great fuming swerves that carry our prayer up to God and drown the stench of new hearts as they burn below. Saint James tilts his brim: sixty-five meters across! Never was My Cid so happy.

Tomorrow, the ultimate absurdity. We will hire a car and drive to Finisterre.

▼▲▼

Compostela ▶ 26th of July

*the eye you see isn't
an eye because you see it
it's an eye because it sees you*

MACHADO

Just as no mountain ends at the top, so no pilgrim stops in Santiago. The city and the saint buried there are a point of thought, but the road goes on. It goes west: Finisterre. So, although a pilgrim arrives in Compostela thinking he wants nothing more than to stop, and although the city entangles his feet so that for a day or two days or a week he stands still, or walks from statue to statue kissing Saint James, or lies on a bed in a dream, comes a day he awakens. Morning is cutting open its blue eyes. Time is a road. Time to go: Finisterre.

It would not be amiss to mention here one or two things about this place. The farthest western point of the land mass of Europe, a point sought by the earliest Celtic inhabitants of the continent and made the object of pilgrimages centuries before Saint James was born, it is located on a spit of the Atlantic coast of Spain called *Cabo de Finisterre*. You can walk there. You can walk no farther (west).

Why did pilgrims and others searching to pinpoint the end of the world go always towards the west? For gold, says My Cid. As you travel west, days are longer: gold, more gold, and still more gold. However that may be, it is an endeavor as old as civilization to set out on a road that is supposed to take you to the very end of things, if you keep going. What do you find there? That is a good question. Who would you be if you knew the answer? There is one way to find out. So a pilgrim sets off. One thing is certain, one item is constant in the set of beliefs with which he travels. It is simply this, that when you reach the place called the end of the world, you fall off into the water. Some pilgrims drown, some do not. *Claro.*

How is a pilgrim like a Nō play? His end is not the point. And yet it is indispensable, to the honor and to the shame.

▼▲▼

to Finisterre ▸ 26th of July

if we pick them
we'll pick by guessing
while chrysanthemums
when first frost has settled
and deceives the eye

Mitsune

In all honesty I am, when the time comes, unenthusiastic about proceeding to Finisterre. I slept heavily through the night and dreamt I was a criminal on the run from the local authorities. When they corner me in a cellar I hurl at them with marrow bones, which explode in the air like live stars. Now dark and unshaven I crouch over my breakfast and jump! when My Cid comes up behind my back. Conversation is balky. He taps a glass with a spoon. I page through the guidebook and find no entry for Finisterre. Is it a place of any interest? He grasps his beard. "Perhaps not." Half smile. "There is nothing there except the end of the world." And so we go to Finisterre.

There is only one road out of Compostela and we take it. Fog closes over us as we drive west. Hours pass. Blurring. Whitening. Fog keeps folding in. Outside—there is no outside. No presence at all out there. Abruptly the road ends. We stop. Disembark. Lock the car. Start to walk. A path is visible now and again through rents in the fog. We make our way along it for some time. Suddenly the path vanishes. There is not a cry. Not a living thing. Just white. Boulders come forward. We begin to climb over them, down, slipping, clutching at roots and lichen. Until the rocks go no farther. We grope this way. That way. There is nowhere to go. Still, we are not at the end. Eyes sting with peering. Cold air from some ice age is pulsing up out of the raw lungs under the sea. Foghorns go round, go off. Distances pass each other, far out. And a cry of some animal—white. Cold. "Shall we go back?" We begin to retreat the way we came, hand over hand, up the rocks. Fog is still shifting in, white, burning. Nothing is visible. And by now we are utterly lost. Let me revise that. I am lost. Suddenly pressingly alert I look around. No one is here but me. And there is no road.

How is a pilgrim like an epigram? Ask me tomorrow.

▾▴▾

Finisterre

a dried salmon
a pilgrim's gauntness
both in the coldest season

BASHO

There is a fearful ashy light falls on the end of the world. It makes the photographs slow. But you can see the scorched place and the immense hour. Eyes search the shore. There is no wind. There is no shadow. One flat event moves out in a ripple over the whole expanse of the water towards the line of the horizon. Still as watchers they stand, they look, moving their lips. They begin to approach. Now they are browsing at my back, where I have fallen at the edge of the water, knocking back and forth slightly in the force of the waves. They are leaning over me. What is it they are saying? Perhaps—no. Words never went on in me.

But one of them is bending closer. Fear shakes me. As it sometimes will just when we are about to be handed over. Your action is simple. You take hold of my paws and cross them on my breast: as a sign that I am one who has been to the holy city and tasted its waters, its kinds.

Pilgrims were people who carried little. They carried it balanced on their heart.

▼▲▼

¡E ultreja e sus eja Deus adiuva nos!

1988

Or: Maybe we're wrong; maybe the essay really is just a philosophical investigation that, masked as it sometimes is by the infusion of other forms—by story or memoir or lyric or fable—we're just ignoring its most basic form.

FABIO MORABITO

Oil

Oil is water that has lost its get up and go, its cheeky forward drive. Having exhausted all its routes, it's discovered treading over ground it trod before. It is water that has turned its back on the world. It is *de trop*. It has forfeited its old rights of way across the floor and now has to step to one side in favor of fluids younger and grander. It is luxury water, which after so much flowing has felt the weight of experience, maybe bitter experience. It's as if it had other water at its service; hence its sumptuousness, not far from prostration, for where there is sumptuousness, there's always somebody on his knees, tied with bonds. So oil is a form of water that needs to prop itself up on another form, one hand placed over another hand—that's the fundamental nature of oil—and this disability makes it uneasy. It's water clogged with sand, a water that went astray on a hairpin bend that cut down its progress and couldn't shake off the sand, so it said good-bye to foam and withdrew into itself, taciturn, choked with grit. It is water that is weak at the knees.

Incapable of running, of instinctively shaking off hazards, of stepping warmly on every stone, of producing a crystal-clear diction, oil has turned snooty, calculating, sedentary. After it used up all its routes, it became reflexive. It ruminates and shilly-shallies like somebody who cautiously returns to his home ground and rather than walk further, occupies it, seizes possession. All possessive forces keep going over the same ground, and oil is back home again. It is water with a predatory air. While young waters disinterestedly investigate the earth, oils get on their high horse, develop ambitions. They are water on the up and up. Their sandiness lets them climb up things slowly but steadily. Without oils, in fact, our world would lack surprises, would be constantly heading downhill, tyrannized by gravity, a place of limitless flatness. In the long run a world without oil would become

221

geometric. But oil puts a stop to that possibility by being anti-doctrinaire. It proves this by cautious progress, its sounding things out. It is water with its hopes shattered. It forms around objects a zone of confusion that saves them from being brutally scrubbed by the world. It encloses them in a hypnotic state. That's how lubrication works. Any piece that is lubricated subtly washes its hands of other pieces, it achieves autonomy, and within the mechanism as a whole, it recaptures the rhythms of its own individual will, or at least the illusion of them.

Oil really does project an individual temperament; it comprehends and knows how to listen. Hence where water, distracted and gullible, charges ahead, oil turns back, full of guile, and holds itself in check and takes in its surroundings. It neither tosses things away nor draws conclusions. Instead, it discerningly imprints a face and an age on whatever it touches. Everything oily has a name. Without oil there would be no culture, no commerce, no transportation. Oil is water with a burden to carry. Thanks to oil, our world has different hues, and things swap postures and places, and open themselves up to unsuspected uses. Oil, if we may put it this way, acts like a butler; it's the bridge or the mattress which make affable contact possible between things. It legitimates relationships and bestows a lasting stamp on them. It doesn't throw its weight around; it applies pressure with finesse, gets chatty, reanimates, civilizes.

Deprived of oil, we'd be subject to water's monastic lifestyle and forever uncouth. Kinkiness and hope would be tabooed. We'd live without cunning, but also without grace. Water searches for channels and always finds them. It loves order and repetition. Oil, which travels at one or two gears lower than water, has a multitude of eyes and that induces it to spill over and not exclude. It has lots of community spirit and is inventive. Where water settles disputes and gives each his own, oil jumbles things up in a utopian fashion. Every jumble contains a trace of utopia and puts rumors and spirited efforts to the test. It is a circus strongman.

Its job involves rigmarole. The oil that covers over a certain material, that lubricates it—a pipe or whatever—is subtly duplicating it, like an echo. It extends it microscopically in order to take away its claws and to help it relax. Oiled materials collide with no more than a shrug. The curtain of oil functions like an evangelizing fire and individual points of friction lose their gleaming sharpness. A sense of overall enthusiasm prevails, for oil is like the pump that vitalizes the whole contraption, getting the parts to pass from a state of sleepiness to excitement, and then to humility, setting aside their private concerns the more they pitch in on the main job, whose whole point is mutual contact.

Oil, therefore, is the speediest of messengers, leaving nobody uninformed or confused. Its masterpiece, or rather its whole *raison d'être,* is hugging things, mixing them together, cooking them, rounding them out to perfection. Unlike water which heads toward the sea, oil takes any route it can to produce a stew, a sense of communion.

Translated by Geoff Hargreaves

1989

"The lifespan of a fact is shrinking," the famous biologist has come to say; "It's shrinking, I can feel it. And I don't think there is time to save it." I am in high school in this year, at an assembly. It is a fall afternoon, the north shore of America. The famous biologist has come from the city in order to warn us against advances in science: "Sometimes a fact should just be left alone." It used to be that a fact would last as long as its people, he says; as long as kingdoms stood, or legacies lived, or myths endured their skeptics. But now, he says, facts have begun to dwindle to the length of a generation, to the lifespans and memories of wars and plagues and depressions. Once the earth was flat, he says, but now we say it's round. Once we were the center of a vast but known universe; now we're just a speck in a vast and chaotic jumble. Once we thought we could sail west easily to the Indies. Now we think differently: that a New World is there. In this year, the Berlin Wall comes crumbling down, Paris allows a foreigner to build a glass pyramid at the Louvre, and America's longest stretch of wild protected shoreline is ruined by an oil spill of ten million gallons. This is the year I am given a book by George W. S. Trow. "And you," says the biologist, pointing out to the crowd—to our young burning faces; townsfolk crammed into the aisles; all our teachers lined up along the edges of the room; to the coughing, the sneezing, the legs crossing, uncrossing, squeaking in their chairs—"how long will facts last when *you* inherit the earth?"

George W. S. Trow

Needs

First, what I need you to do is give me permission to drive you completely insane by using the word "need" in places where another word, like "want" or "order," would be more "honest." We're going to be doing this (with your permission, of course—but we need you to give your permission) in phrases such as *I* (or *we*—the editorial "we") *need you to do this* and *we need you to do that*. Also, as part of this process, I need you to totally accept and validate the phrase *we need for you . . .* to do this or that, even if that phrase makes you want to stand up and hit me. I need for you to do it. That's it. That's all there is to it. If it were just a matter of what I *wanted*—hey, it would be different. In this case, my needs are involved, and I just can't back down. So bear with me, because I also need for you to initial where I reserve the right to use the repulsive phrase *what you need to do is*.

I want you to get to know me, OK? I (we) am (are) not comfortable thinking of myself (ourself) as a person who ruthlessly and rudely demands things of persons like yourself. When I (we) shove a rental-car agreement in front of you, I (we) want (need for) you to have the feeling that life is a matter of:

       1. Fine Options

and

       2. Splendid Choices.

At the same time, I (we) need for you to do very specific things—things so specific you would never dream them up in one million years. So why not accept a little guidance?

▼▲▼

You are now ready to check in with our Guidance Department. Ready? Now you need to read and understand why you have to sign, date, and initial the paragraph beginning "other word choices—surrendering the right to require the use of."

☐ Other Word Choices—Surrendering The Right To Require The Use Of.

We need for you to sign this paragraph. Right now. Just do it. That's the Nike ad. "Just do it." Remember the handsome young athlete running through the decayed city? Think about him, how he's running and running and not asking a single question. We need for you to think about that, how *he* isn't asking any questions—just running and running—and then we need you to sign.

X _____

Signature

Thanks! OK. We're out of novice level now, and you did great. But you didn't date it. What you need to do—oh, there he is, that runner! He's better-looking than ever! Look at those muscles! How does he get such a great body, living where he does, where the poor people live? Tempts you to ask questions, doesn't it? But *he's* not asking questions. *Doesn't have the time,* what with his TV work, etc. Guess *you* aren't going to bother with the old read-for-detail drag-o-rama, what with your high ambitions and goals—for the fulfillment of which there is barely time! And you already at a level where you breathe and hold down a job! Whew! Am I impressed! But before we can process your application we need for you to give us a thousand dollars. OK. Thank you. You're great! But, uh, this thousand dollars is in *dollars.* We need to have you transfer that to *Swiss* dollars— which they call *"francs"* in one of the quaint *patois* they use over there in Switzerland. We need for you to do that, and while you are asking your financial institution to handle the foreign-exchange problem, we need for you to write a short essay on the Swiss—their historic neutrality, their cleanliness, and so on. THAT'S THE ESSAY QUESTION. THEN THERE ARE SOME MULTIPLE CHOICE. What you need to do is take the essay question home with you, bring it in tomorrow, and do the multiple choice now.

Actually, there's only one multiple choice. By the way, are you sure you want to decline collision? Now here's your question.

The word "patois" indicates:

(a) Provincial speech—as found, for instance, in backward, rural areas
(b) Substandard housing
(c) A big patio

OK. Now you are at our highest level. What you did so far is fine, but you should know that in some states insurance coverage isn't what it should be, because lax regulators have let the whole thing go down the drain, so as a service to you we've made the optional coverage automatic. If you don't want the optional protection, we need for you to swear before a federal court judge bad, because then you've missed the point. We need for you to try harder to get the point so we can release the steaming hot dinner and the delicious frozen Margarita to your custody. We need for you to watch *48 Hours* for forty-eight hours. That usually does the trick in problem cases. The overtime is five dollars and twenty-two cents. We need for you to consider if it shouldn't have more of a multicultural aspect. Are you sure you want to decline the collision? Think it over. I'll be waiting on the big patio.

1990

There is Basho's *Narrow Road* and Michel Butor's *Mobile* and Mary Rowlandson's *Narrative of the Captivity.* There is Osip Mandelstam's *Journey to Armenia.* Thoreau's "Walking." Audubon's journals. There is the definitive travelogue, in my mind—*Conundrum,* by Jan Morris—in which the famous travel writer journeys just a few miles east from her family home in Europe to an undisclosed office somewhere else in Europe, in order to then travel from her old male body to her new female one. It is always this kind of traveling that strikes me hardest in an essay—the transformations that can happen when even movement does not. If essays are experiments then they are journeys, too. "I do not want to know where this journey ends," Basho wrote in the first journal he carried deep into the north. "Otherwise," he wrote, "why call this action 'journey'?" Basho gave away everything he owned before making his footway across long Japan. He gave away his job, he gave away his home, he gave away his clothing, said farewell to all his friends. What Basho brought with him on his month-long journey deep into the north was only enough food for one meal on one day. Why bother conducting an experiment at all if you know what results it will yield?

Notes Toward a History of Scaffolding

1

Hotel Inghilterra, Via Boca di Leone, Rome (April 24)

Once the *cameriera* has pulled open the heavy draperies and cranked out shutters so thick they would protect even an insomniac from the most insistent noise and dazzle, there it is: cobbles and clatter of light, squeak of pulleys, the dash, the rattling, shouts and anvil bangs—all the canon and commotion of Rome sung, swung, and wafted with one deft heave of the *cameriera*'s arm, along with smells of coffee and fresh baked *cornetti,* butter curlicues on ice, milk in its pitcher. *Good for the complexion,* say the *cameriera,* pointing to the skin stretched over steaming milk. She pats her face to demonstrate how I should spread this skin over my own, then leans back to mime a woman relaxing in the bath, eyes closed, dozing under that nourishing maternal gaze. With the windows open, it seems possible to touch the other side of Via Boca di Leone and reach into the *salon di belleza* that looks into my hotel room. The beauty salon takes up the second floor of an austere seventeenth-century building, and no matter when I wake, there are women sitting under dryers. A man shakes water from a comb, and I wince as if splashed. A woman with blue hair swirled into the elaborate spines and turrets of a murex turns the pages of a magazine. Another shimmers in wrappings of aluminum foil while her feet soak in a bronze basin. A *stravaganza* creams up in rusted orange, a fantastic chess piece stolen from a Gaudi cathedral. The rubber caps with hair pulled through tiny holes, the lightning rods with tin-foil stamens, the gilded tritons and lavish conches seem a language in the making, a *tessellatura* neither Italian, nor English, nor Latin—an eccentric landscape conjugating itself into spires and spigots, *coclea* and knitting needles: *turret, turris,*

233

turricula, culcullus, curls. What a pity the dyes will be washed out, the curlers removed, the aluminum wreaths discarded, the hair brushed and brushed until the women walk out onto the Via dei Condotti merely stylish and beautiful. And what a pity the scaffold will eventually come down too. For a week the scaffold has swayed dangerously in front of the beauty salon, covering the entire building like a network of vines. On it, five workers stand, chat, tell jokes, call out to women passing by, eat breakfast, eat lunch, pet a black and white dog that runs back and forth along the narrow platform. They are cleaning the stone face of the building, air blasting what seemed its natural grey to an artificial, dazzling white. Now one of them turns the dial of a radio balanced on top of a bucket, and suddenly, a woman's voice pours out—a husky rough burlap, splintery wood: Loredana Berte singing *Sola.* The worker catches me looking at him and holds out the bun he is eating, takes a bite, waves with his mouth full. Late afternoon when the workers have gone for the day, pigeons come to roost on the scaffold. Light, golden and lazy, rests on the wooden planks. When it rains, water drips from the wood, plump rain hangs its berries. The ropes glisten. The contraption sways with every breeze. Already, it seems the scaffold has always been there.

2

Scaffold: *a usually temporary or moveable platform (as a plank) supported by a wood or metal framework, jacks, poles, or brackets or suspended (as by ropes and tackle) and used by workmen (as bricklayers, painters or miners) to stand or sit on and to support tools and material when working at considerable heights above floor or ground;*

a platform on which a criminal stands for execution, especially by hanging or beheading;

any platform at a considerable height above floor level or ground (scaffolds were used by some Native Americans to dispose of the dead);

a usually temporary stand on which a public spectacle (as a dramatic performance) is staged;

a stand for spectators at a public performance;

an accumulation of adherent, partly fused material forming an obstruction above the tuyeres in a blast furnace;

to support (as an argument) by scaffolding—i.e., with explanation and comment.

3

The way a nest of twigs and candy wrappers is held together by bird spit and mud, the word *scaffold* is held together by muddles layered and pressed between its definitions. Muddles have the convoluted energy of the snarl and the tangle, wads of sniggered string and rope: they hold *scaffold* together even when its various meanings are flying off in different directions. Without its muddles, *scaffold* would probably fall apart and have to be carted off with leftover screening and malfunctioning lights. Muddles circulate enough energy to hold the scaffold erect and keep its meanings up in the air while thinking is in progress.

Muddle One. The scaffold an artist steps up on to execute a work of art can become the scaffold a criminal steps up on to be executed. Does this mean the creative process is like a guillotine?

Muddle Two. The scaffold (as platform) is set up to support the work of art while it is in progress, but the scaffold (as dross in a furnace) is what is left over after the work of art is made. The scaffold is what makes a work of art possible and also what is made possible by a work of art—art's by-product. In either case, once the work of art is finished, the scaffold is carted off to storage or chucked out as rubbish. Why?

Muddle Three. Sometimes the dead are buried in the air. In plain view. With so much exposure, they decompose. Up there for all to see, they are easier to forget. The more visible, the more accessible, the more easily they are dispensed with. What does a work of art have in common with a corpse?

Muddle Four. A scaffold that serves as a temporary stand or stage for a public performance can also serve as a stand for spectators at a public performance. Does this mean there is no difference between the spectacle and the audience? If the spectators sat on the stands designated for the performance and the actors sat on the stands roped off for the audience, would it make any difference? And is it gauche of me to applaud the audience, to prefer the intermissions to the opera?

4

Instead of writing a history of art, I am making notes toward a history of scaffolds. Instead of a history of the finished, the permanent, the enduring, I am writing a history of the transitory, a history of flittings and fleetings, spray blown from the fingers and other mutabilia.

Look at the scaffold. So airy, birds fly in and out of it. Tall grass pokes up through it. A passerby leans against it to tie his shoe lace. If the scaffold is placed in a tidal pool, the tinted cantharis will adhere to it, the red zig-zag blotches of the nerite will suck fast, kelp will linger, sea lettuce catch and fasten. In a garden, vines will ramble over it.

Wherever it is placed, the scaffold will cast shadows. The shadows come and go like birds. Wherever it is placed, the scaffold becomes a ruin, an emblem of the transitory. Like a skull. Like a skeleton. Look at the scaffold reflected in a natural mirror—a lake or a city window. Wherever it is placed, the scaffold says: All this must come down.

5

What if the scaffold did not come down? Or, what if the work of art came down and the scaffold stayed up? If a work of art had sufficient energy, could it support the scaffold, keep it propped up indefinitely?

6

Sometimes when I start to write, I set up an ironic tone. Once the writing is under way, however, the irony comes down. So what if my foothold is precarious, I'm oblivious, too deeply engrossed in what I'm thinking to notice where I am. Where I am is made of match sticks and the shadows cast by match sticks. But with a window cleaner's bravado, I'm ready to scale walls of glass, to shimmy up high-tech polish. Of course, there's always the possibility of a fall. In fact, from time to time I drop something—cement plug, wire snippet—to determine how far below ground is. I listen for the whoosh and unfasten my seat belt. I wait for the plop when cement hits the water which is always pooling up in the excavation site. Do I do this just to scare myself? Am I merely a thrill seeker?

7

There's a story I never get tired of looking at—picture by simple picture in the thirteenth-century manuscript of the *Cantigas* of Alfonso X. A mural painter sits on the top step of a pyramid-shaped ladder and paints an image of the devil on a cathedral wall. All at once the real devil appears. He's decked out in black leather wings and the pronated horns of a steer—and he's furious. Pointing to his image on the wall, he threatens the artist for painting him ugly. Undaunted, the artist balances himself on an even more precarious platform, what appears to be a pole thrown across two other poles. Crouching on this fragile monkey rail, he calmly paints a beautiful image of the Virgin on the cathedral vault. All it would take is a huff and a puff, that's how frail his support system is—handful of pick-up-sticks, lattice work pie crust. And sure enough, in the next illumination the devil pulls down the scaffold. But just in time, the Virgin painted on the vault reaches out toward the artist and with her two strong arms clutches him to her breast.

In the Middle Ages this story was enjoyed as a miracle of the Virgin, one of the most popular of her miracles, in fact. But I prefer to read it as a parable of the creative process: at a crucial moment, the artist and the work of art must be able to stand free of all support systems. The work of art has to be self-sufficient—a separate reality with everything it needs to perpetuate itself.

But while the fall may appear to be a test of the art work's self-sufficiency, it is something far more important. The fall provides a shock that is essential to creation. In Grimm's tale of the Frog Prince, it is only when the princess hurls her frog-suitor against the bedroom wall with enough force to crack him in two that he is transformed into a handsome prince. The shock facilitates his change of form. And in *Exodus* when God commands Aaron to throw his rod on the ground, instead of breaking on impact, the rod is altered—into a serpent. Baudelaire and Yeats—they both understood the crucial role that shock, jounce, and jolt play in artistic work. Baudelaire speaks of poetic composition as a duel in which the artist screams out in fright just before he is defeated, and in one poem in *Les Fleurs du Mal,* he has this to say about creative swordplay:

> *I venture out alone to drill myself*
> *in what must seem an eerie fencing-match,*
> *duelling in dark corners for a rhyme*
> *and stumbling over words like cobblestones*
> *where now and then realities collide*
> *with lines I dreamed of writing long ago.*
>
> ("THE SUN," TRANS. RICHARD HOWARD)

The stumbles and collisions seem to shake the words and rhymes out of Baudelaire, then agitate them into poems. For Yeats, too, the poet is born in defeat and fashions his mask in disappointment: it is precisely these defeats and disappointments that supply the necessary shocks. Like Baudelaire, Yeats even envisions the creative process as a duel: ". . . when I close my eyes upon the pillow I see a foil playing before me, the button to my face. We meet always in the deep of the mind, whatever our work, wherever our reverie carries us . . ." ("Anima Hominis"). For Yeats, the poet like any hero must be "doom eager."

8

Boca Raton, Florida (June 17)

I actually saw it happen. A bird falling from the roof of a building. The bird let out a little cry as it dropped—one story, two—then, just as if it had hit something solid in the air, it bounced into flight. Hardly back on the roof, it was falling again, and falling, letting out that cry. But were the falls failed attempts at flight? The bird seemed to be throwing itself off the roof—falling on purpose. Out of the plunge perfected, flight pushed up as necessity. There was thrust behind it—the fear of falling. And with each practice fall, the cry lasted longer until the cry became a run of notes, a flutter along the avifaunal scale. Out of the fall, the cry shivered up and down, the natural embodiment of thrill. Suddenly, I understood. The bird wasn't practicing flight. It knew how to fly. The bird was teaching itself to sing.

9

Of course, an artist may come to depend on falls for thrills and chills, may even come to prefer falling to creating. Such an artist is addicted to the shocks—as well as to what shocks provoke: wild sprees of shape-shifting that refuse to settle into the complacencies of the stabilized gestalt. During the early stages of the creative process, when everything is still fluid, it's not unusual for the imagination to go on a rampage, churning up images so fast the artist may not be able to record them. "My story is there in a fluid—in an evading shape," the novelist Joseph Conrad wrote a friend. "I can't get hold of it. It is all there—to bursting, yet I can't get hold of it any more than you can grasp a handful of water. . . . The worst is that while I'm thus powerless to produce, my imagination is extremely active, whole paragraphs, whole pages, whole chapters pass through my mind." Writers' notebooks, artists' sketchbooks provide at least a glimpse of the phantasmagoric shoot-the-chutes. Shelley's notebooks are showered with marginal sketches of boats and trees and human faces, the poems jotted in sideways and upside down as if the poet had been jolted along on a roller-coaster. Picasso's sketchbooks seethe with complex sequences of images that unsettle into new series: the open-mouthed head of a woman kaleidoscoping into a slack-jawed skull which in turn flickers into a landscape of arches and grottoes. In medieval illuminations the ornate borders frequently threaten to overwhelm the central image with all the possibilities the artist must have rejected in favor of a single elegant shape—angel or saint. Stored in the peripheries, in the margins of the illumination, these cast-off images still have power: they spill over into elaborate interlaces, they tangle into endless knots, as if the ropes and tackle of the scaffold were preparing a takeover, reclaiming the vigor of the art work for the platform where the artist has stopped work in order to dream.

Dreaming, for some artists, is the irresistible temptation. "What seems to me the highest and most difficult achievement of Art," Flaubert wrote his mistress, Louise Colet, "is not to make us laugh or cry, nor to arouse our lust or rage, but to do what nature does—that is, to set us dreaming." But the artist who dreams too long usurps the stands reserved for the spectator or reader. Instead of creating for an audience, that artist becomes the audience. Such artists cannot tear themselves away from the spectacles their own minds are staging. Passively, they sit in the theaters of their imaginations. They wait for the curtain to rise. For the show to begin.

10

I have long suspected that Poe's famous story, "The Pit and the Pendulum," is about such an artist, an author who prefers the thrill of shock and fall to the drudgery of writing. Where Conrad felt frustration when paragraphs and chapters refused to crystallize into the immutable patterns of a finished work, Poe's narrator revels in the phantasmagoric—and of course in the shocks and falls needed to keep reverie in motion. "The Pit and the Pendulum" is the only story I know of that advances by falling forward. When the narrator learns that the Spanish Inquisition has sentenced him to an agonizing death, he swoons—and this swoon is described as a long fall: "Down—down—still down—till a hideous dizziness oppressed me at the mere idea of the interminableness of the descent." Swoon blurs into real fall, and the narrator regains consciousness to find himself in a subterranean prison chamber which he immediately sets out to explore, only to fall again—violently on his face: "my chin rested upon the floor of the prison, but my lips, and the upper portion of my head, although seemingly at less elevation than the chin, touched nothing. . . . I put forward my arm, and shuddered to find that I had fallen at the very brink of a circular pit, whose extent, of course, I had no means of ascertaining at the moment." Not content to have missed a fatal plunge, the narrator tries to evoke the fall by simulating it for his imagination. Breaking off a piece of his prison wall, he drops the fragment down the abyss: "For many seconds I hearkened to its reverberations as it dashed against the sides of the chasm in its descent; at length, there was a sullen plunge into water, succeeded by loud echoes." Each of those reverberations provides the shock of a real fall—and not only for the wrought-up narrator.

The narrator's prison chamber also responds to shocks, and each time the narrator survives a fall, his chamber is provoked to change its form. In this respect, it resembles the imagination of the artist: even a minimal excitement is enough to set it quivering. On his first go-round, the narrator ascertains that his chamber is irregular in shape, but after he narrowly misses falling into the pit, he discovers that the chamber is roughly square and thinks his first impression was mistaken. I doubt that it was. That chamber is the embodiment of the artist's imagination at its most elastic—and heated up. When the narrator outwits the guillotine-like machine that has been trying to shred him, the chamber becomes incensed: it gleams, it glows, it steams. And not only that. With the quick reflexes of a Venus fly-trap, it closes on its victim. Powerful, sphincter-like muscles go into action as the chamber squeezes its walls together, pressuring the narrator toward the very pit he had previously escaped. Now the narrator simply has to fall.

In a way, though, the narrator has been falling ever since he started his story. The successive falls that make up his narrative seem like slow-motion takes of one long fall, a fall that has been repeatedly interrupted and de-layed, a fall that has been drawn out with masochistic pleasure. The fall is like a long scream, the scream that the story's nineteenth-century illustrator Alphonse Legros permits the victim much sooner than Poe does. In an etching that shows the narrator strapped to a wooden platform or scaffold while rats swarm over his body and a sickle-like pendulum threatens his skeletal rib cage, the victim's mouth has opened: he is screaming. As a child, unable to tear myself away from that etching, I ran a finger round and round the victim's mouth, tracing and retracing that scream, which is of course what Poe does when he draws out and delays the fall, when he doesn't allow the story to end. This is a story where the artist's scaffold is fused with the executioner's, where the only way for the narrator to finish his tale is to let himself be finished off. In such a story, closure is indistin-guishable from closing in—for the kill.

But like the artist in the medieval miracle of the Virgin, Poe's narrator manages to fall without falling. Just as he totters on the brink, he is res-cued: "An outstretched arm caught my own as I fell, fainting, into the abyss."

II

Nevertheless: there is much to be said for delay, for not getting down to work, for prolonging the dream. When I dream, I pack more and more into the art work which expands obligingly like an udder. When I dream, the art work grows bigger, and who knows, maybe this time nothing will be left out, not even the rough, natural energies of the scaffold which is after all, a tree, and as tree, sways with every breeze, smells of resins and turpentine, and shudders forth a few splintery leaves.

Up here on the scaffold, I have set down a bottle of well-aged Barbaresco, a hearty wedge of Port du Salut, a handful of figs. Why should I leave? Up here I am beginning a journal. I call it Journal of Waste and Effluvia, Journal of Excess. In the journal I will record ladders and the mineral aura that haloes the stone cutter. I will bring in the damp mustiness the ropes exuded on rainy days and bird droppings splattered on the plastic wrappings. There will be rare dialects of grit and efflorescence and dizzying heights. Nor will I leave out *for the time being, awhile, here today and gone tomorrow, short and sweet,* and *fly-by-night.*

What do I care if some entries are stacked like canvases in an artist's studio, if they lean in ill-fitting frames against a wall. And what does it matter if another entry resembles an overstuffed sofa with broken springs and lumpy wads of filler poking through worn aqua velour. That's where I do my thinking. I rub the ornate wooden arms of the sofa, I roam the golden swags and waxy pears, I polish the red stains where wine has dripped. Here's where I contemplated a journal spare as a thick rope of water running from the tap. And here's where I imagined that other journal congested as a subway car at rush hour, its last entry caught in the door like the sleeve of a woman's coat.

Into the Journal of Excess I am packing everything I was forced to leave out of Notes Toward a History of Scaffolding.

I keep the Journal of Excess because I am too frugal to let anything go to waste.

June 13

On still days my mind drifts far into my travels. It crosses the Adriatic, the Aegean, the Mediterranean. To stop this drift, I fill my canvases with massive buildings, with old palaces and charitable institutions, with clock towers, sturdy churches, stone bridges—with *campo, piazza,* and *palazzi antichi.* Looking at my work, you will think that I am in love with solidity and permanence, with space. Well, look again. I am in love with time, with the ephemeral. My paintings are filled with flags and pennants, with regalias and parades, with laundry lines strung with wash, with puppet shows that come and go. But mainly, my paintings are hung with scaffolds, my buildings encrusted and scabbed with work in progress. I am in love with everything that comes down—with plinths and stalks, with ropes and rigging, with fragile boats and sails and clouds. If you look long enough at my work, everything becomes a scaffold. Those shadows leaning up against a church, the delicate twigs of a tower and belfry—in an hour or two they will be gone. And that night scene at S. Pietro di Castello—night too is a scaffold, and when it comes down, day goes up. What I'd most love to do is fashion an architecture of impermanence. I'll make a cottage out of a flight of stairs and put in broken fencing, casks, and surplus timbers. I'll turn everything into scaffolding—and sign it *Canaletto.*

June 16

Not me. I'll bring in sky like a furnace and what's scraped from the furnace—refuse of ores, goldskin skimmed from boiling lead, the run-off still running. What happens if you scrape flame, if you cauterize fire, that's what I'd like to know.

I'll bring in funnel and funnel cloud and the gold pores of its crust. Nor will I forget the rough stuccoes of congealed metals. I'll have magnesiums soldered to the branches of trees, the drip and spackle of zincs along telephone wires, the fused mangle of explosion and disaster. And I will not leave out the wings of Icarus, their wax still melting, the failed flight commemorated, its ashes scattered with the ashes of holocaust.

My skies I'll make out of rainbow run-off of flame, out of fire pit. I will make them electroplated and with chromium plate scummed. With oyster and chitton. With shroud and loricate and grout. Out of the excesses of disaster I shall make them. And I shall sign them *Anselm Kiefer.*

June 21

Had lunch today with K. At Max a Luna: black bean soup laced with garlic, peasanty chunks of whole wheat bread, cappucino; but passed on the wine since I planned to write later. As always with K., the conversation focused on men. No matter how diverse, K.'s men have one thing in common: they are always involved with another woman. As her relationships deepen, the other woman is talked about more and more. Whenever K. is with her man, the other woman goes up like a scaffold. Lately, no one even bothers to take her down. Too much trouble. Sitting on the scaffold, K. and her man talk, whisper sweet nothings (sometimes into the other woman's ear), go to the movies, read the *Times Book Review,* make love. They wouldn't dream of a Sunday in the country without packing the scaffold. Theirs is a relationship that can't stand on its own four feet. Without the other woman as scaffold, it would fall apart.

Lately, I find myself more interested in the scaffold than in K. I want to talk to the other woman about her job problems, her relationships with men. Of course, it's possible all I'll hear about will be K.

Boca Raton, Florida (May 4)

Went to my favorite boutique today. Sometimes I think I go there just for the poster in the dressing room: a life-size photo of a man and woman standing knee deep in the ocean. She's wearing a white bikini. His chest is bare. Their well tanned bodies gleam with salty marine saliva, and in this moment of black and white soft focus, she is starting to unzip his jeans, he is reaching for her breasts. The dressing room is so small, I have to lean against his shoulder when I unzip my own jeans. At any moment, I expect him to help me undress. Or she might take the time to unbutton my blouse. With so little space, I'll have to step into their ocean and get my feet wet. Maybe I won't bother to go out later. I could tell my date I have to find a new studio, a studio that's more like a theater.

12

Cadenza with mineral waters

Sometimes I thirst for a long pause. I go to a small café and choose a table under an awning where shade and light ripple together. From there I can look up at a building overrun with scaffolding—huge spiraling wasp nests, crisp wooden honeycombs, buckets straddling, pulleys, hoists, ropes.

I order a bottle of San Pellegrino, and as the waiter fills my glass, I watch the bubbles rise. The water tingles my lips. I am sipping minerals— magnesium, potassium, phosphorus, salts. I am drinking deep from marble springs, from iron wells. I am drinking the quarry where waters have been rising and falling for centuries. As I drink, I recall that the German word for *creator—Schopfer—*also means *scoop, ladle, dipper.*

Today I want to dip deep. I want to scoop and ladle until I reach that place where Midas rinses his face and everything reflected around him— leaves, apples, birds—turns to gold. No, deeper—I want to reach the place where Medusa bathes her hair and water is shocked to stone, where the earth rumbles and lava is stilled to pumice.

When I look at myself in the dark marble eddies of the table top, my eyes have darkened—as if they were bruised, as if I had two shiners.

13

Certain images invariably get left out of the finished work. Oddly, they are the very images that came first, that obsessed and haunted me as I sat dreaming on the scaffold, that I couldn't let go of as long as. . . . Now I wonder if it would be possible to photograph them. Some of these images have to do with light, light that becomes chilled and jagged where it touches broken cement. Light workers left covered with tarpaulin when they finished for the day. Light workers sharpened their tools on and wiped their mouths with. A ladder leans against this light. And when a boy dips his fingers into it, I have to cover his hands with gloves. This is the light I hear flapping during the night because someone forgot to tie it down, so that I have to get up and search for it while a high wind whistles overhead.

Sometimes my naïveté amazes me. Do I really believe it's possible to take these pictures? To photograph the temperature and the textures of that light and the way it never stops filtering into the basement studio where I took ballet lessons as a child, the way it keeps slipping between the curved iron bars that protected windows streaked with dirt? That light we arabesqued in to the cracked, out of tune nocturnes of Chopin? Light that felt cold at first, then gradually warmed. Light that smelled of lambswool and the sweat of dancers who had been there before me. And going home, that gritty light that overhangs West Side buildings where icicles bunch black udders, that milky light scumming a child's lips.

Or light that powders, that crumbles, peeling like old posters from walls. Filthy light in the gas station bathroom, light disinfected and bare as cement, merging with natural light falling from above, mixing with the stutter of fluorescent—light I wash my face in after writing all night.

14

Herculaneum (May 4)

—terra-cotta cooking pots as they were left on a charcoal stove nineteen hundred years ago in the kitchen (culina) of the Casa dei Cervi

—coils of rope, slightly scorched, used to draw water from a well

—marble sculpture of Sleeping Eros, the boy lying on his side, his curly hair painted red: found on the terrace of the Casa dei Cervi

—rubble, partly fused, with lizards scurrying across, with ants in every which direction

▼▲▼

the red hot fluids are called *lava*
when broken up by vapors, they form larger fragments called *bomba*
the smaller pieces are known as *lapilli* or *scoriae*
minuter portions are called volcanic ashes

it was streams of mud that proved destructive to Herculaneum, mud mingled with pumice stones and ashes from Vesuvius

in 1719 Prince Elbeuf, an Austrian, had a shaft sunk at Herculaneum and discovered the theater. The Italian word for *shaft, pozzo,* is the same word for *well.* 100 steps down it feels like a well, the theater damp and chilly and flickering in the candle light

15

Pompeii (May 7)

In the museum, the casts and models of doors, windows, shop shutters

In glass cases, several casts of human corpses. The soft parts of course decayed with time. In 1863 Giuseppe Fiorelli made an ingenious discovery: the bones of a body imbedded in lava could be removed, the cavity filled with plaster—the figures and attitudes of the bodies preserve their death struggle

—a man lying on his face
—another man lying on his side with remarkably well-preserved features
—a young girl with a ring on her finger
—and of course the dog, legs thrust out in its death agony

Corpses? Or art? Or are they too still for art? Or too lively? Too fully in view to be totally dead? Too disinterested in the spectator to be art?

16

Among the postcards my grandmother brought back from Naples, there was the cement dog and the cement man lying on his face. I played with them on the floor, along with the cameo brooch, the cameo earrings. Grandmother stroked my hair. Men had followed her through the streets of Naples, pressed close to her body in the crush of crowds. *Venere d'Oro,* they had whispered.

17

Many of the houses at Pompeii and Herculaneum are decorated with scenes from the theater. The dining room of one house is hung with theatrical masks, in other houses the walls are covered with scenes from comedies, with dressing rooms where actors take off their masks. The figures in the murals are life-size and the illusion of space so powerful that it seems possible to sit down with actors, exchange gossip, drink a toast. To enter these houses is to enter a theater, to mingle with friends as in a spectacle.

Where does illusion end and reality begin?

18

When Vesuvius erupted on August 24, 79 A.D., the Elder Pliny stayed on in Misenum, unable to tear himself away from the spectacle: broad sheets of flame falling down the mountain, the empty houses of the town on fire, ashes piling up like snowdrifts in the gardens. Pliny hurried to the place where everyone else was leaving, departing in boats. People held pillows over their heads. Bits of pumice and blackened stones were falling, along with scorched lapilli. The pumice, which was light and porous, floated in the bay. Two days later when daylight returned, Pliny's body was found intact where he had collapsed between the slaves supporting him: fully clothed, the body was uninjured, and he looked, his nephew said, as if he were sleeping.

19

After the eruption was over, restorers and other artisans were in great demand. Everyone wanted it all to look as old and as new as it had looked before.

20

Rome, Via Margutta (April 17)

From Via dei Fiori turn right into Via del Babuino, then cross over to Via Margutta, its houses gaily decorated with balconies and gardens, the doors of its first-floor ateliers nearly always open. I can't get enough of these workshops, their aroma of varnish and glue, mixed with old wood and something even older—a musty dampness that seeps out of Roman buildings, that takes me by surprise when I round the corner of a street or pause in a stairwell. Entering one of the gallery-workshops, I squeeze past a massive table. In the Middle Ages, God the Father like any good artisan was ready to roll up his sleeves, one bare foot stepping out of the blue frame of a thirteenth-century French Bible as he steadies himself: the world he is making has quartz-rough seas and a still molten core of gold waiting to be beaten and hammered. "How old is that mirror?" I ask of an ornate oval leaning up against what looks like a Renaissance chair, the mirror's frame hung with overripe fruit, gilt flowers, a tangle of woody stems chipped and peeling. "How old would you like it to be?" comes the quick reply, the artisan on his knees, doing something deft with a Q-tip dipped in mahogany stain.

I would like my scaffold to be very old, old as Homer, old as the mast Odysseus had himself strapped to so he could listen to the sirens sing.

21

Positano, Hotel Sirenusa (May 10)

I am learning to be passive, to receive each day without reaching for it. And the days wash over me like an ocean. I bathe in blue refractions, in phosphorescent pearl. At night I fall asleep listening to the Mediterranean lapping the beach far below. In the morning, I wake to sunlight breaking against stone, to wind eddying and splashing against the rocks. The tile walls and floor of the hotel room are blue and always cool. When I walk across the room, I wade through shallows, I walk under water where the sunken palaces are. I am immersed in breakfast, lunch, and dinner. I climb up and down dailiness as if it were the ladder of a boat. I am immersed in people I shall never see again, in gossip I shall forget tomorrow. Each evening I go dancing, and the delicate network of straps that crisscross the back of my dress are torn. The next day I take the dress to be mended. In the evening it tears again. That way nothing changes. The ships on the horizon don't move: they are always about to tumble, to fall off the earth. When I open the *persiani,* the thick-lidded blinds covering the windows, I think: I want to do this every morning for eternity, I want to live forever.

From my balcony, I can see I Galli, the rocky isles where Odysseus is supposed to have heard the sirens sing. Lashed to the mast of the ship, he begged the crew to set him free, so ravishing was the music of those creatures part woman, part bird, part fish.

What did Odysseus hear? If he had been a composer or a poet, he might have been able to write it down. Sometimes I think the sirens sang the dailiness of a seaside town, the repetitions of everyday pleasures, the tides rising and falling; and Odysseus, man of action that he was, immediately wanted to hurl himself into that singing—as if art were something that could be lived.

22

Do I live in order to write? Or do I write in order to live my life as I do?

23

From the Journal of Excess (May 17)

Still, it must be thrilling: high up in the cathedral vaults where it's always dusk, where bats hang like broken umbrellas and the scaffold trembles and sways. It's as if someone pulled open old theater curtains, velvet with scallops of braid, and the scaffold creaks up in a fit of dust. Is that when the wings open?—yes, like a skydiver's pack, parachute billowing upward. And it's possible to waft all night, grazing, licking the syrupy, the blackstrap, the sooted faces of gargoyle and griffin, the monster wings of basilisk and upupa and cornix and accipiter. Up here there is always a conversation going on, very low, barely audible, with sometimes a word jumping out as if a tile had suddenly broken loose from a mosaic. Or is that the wind? It's possible to keep drawing this moment out, any moment, hammering it thinner and thinner like beaten gold, like iced chablis, whipping it, whipping it to cheap perfume, each word blown to aneurysm. What if the wings feel like a tightfitting harness, what if they cramp and constrict. No one ever said the moment had to be beautiful, gritty will do . . . or painful. Up here is sweetness so cloying it has gone past midnight, past sour, creams curdled as the paste teachers said never to eat, awakening the desire to devour the salve spreading on the back of a cardboard lamb, daring the child's teeth to sink into paper wool and take the animal snout into the mouth, its picture into the mouth. Like that: the saffrons and dyes sucked and lapped . . . smell of clouds . . . something wrung out.

1991

Among those responsible for inspiring Emerson's essays was a con-artist from Germany named Johann Maelzel. In America, Maelzel is best known for creating something called The Chess Player, an automaton that could be wound up and challenged to a game. For years it toured America astonishing crowds, beating its opponents time and again. It wasn't until Edgar Allan Poe watched the automaton closely over a series of weeks that the phenomenon was exposed as just a puppet being manipulated by a man in a box. But earlier than this, in 1830, Maelzel was in America with a more legitimate wonder. No one knows exactly when Emerson first met Maelzel, but it is clear in Emerson's journals that the man's influence was profound. Emerson at this time is frustrated with writing sermons, with their "cold mechanical preparations for a delivery most decorous—fine things, pretty things, wise things—but no arrows, no axes, no nectar, no growling." He wants to find what he calls "a new literature." This is before *Self-Reliance*. This is Emerson's transition between eloquence and ecstacy. Imagine him fed up one afternoon with the approaching week's sermon, spontaneously riding into Boston from his Concord home, meeting friends for dinner, then skipping dessert to catch the last show of a contraption that's all the rage—a music box from Germany that can play whole symphonies on its own. Into the South Church Emerson and his friends walk quietly and sit. There in front of them is what looks like an organ without keys. "A panharmonicon," is what its inventor, Johann Maelzel, stands up and calls it. He cranks three times its heavy silver lever, takes three steps off to the side, and then: flutes, drums, trumpets, cymbals, trombones, a triangle, clarinets, violins. The machine spins out a whole orchestra's worth of sound. *So many sounds,* imagine Emerson thinking; *Just one voice!* The machine is playing—according to the program—an original composition written especially for it. It's a march that will soon become known as Beethoven's famous "Wellington Victory." If there is a single moment that might mark Emerson's discovery of the essay, this is it. The next day into his journal Emerson pours out the following: "Here everything is admissible—philosophy, ethics, divinity, criticism, poetry, humor, fun, mimicry, anecdotes, jokes, ventriloquism—all the breadth and versatility of the most liberal conversation, highest and lowest personal topics: all are permitted, and all may be combined into one speech." It is the new literature Emerson has been seeking all along. A literature he calls for the time being "a panharmonicon."

ALBERT GOLDBARTH

Delft

*No great and enduring volume can
ever be written on the flea, though
many there be who have tried it.*

HERMAN MELVILLE

He cometh unto his kingdom now.

Yea, he cometh unto the greased posed-open body of his belovéd, Cornelia *nee* Swalmius, where she beckons from the alcove-bed, beneath the Turkish rug flung coverlet-like for extra warmth, she of the variegated fleshy plains and amphitheatrical vastness, toe-nook, ear-maze, sweet crease under the arm, where tassel-bodied bacterial Creation loop-de-loops and only he of all gigantic unknowing humankind has witnessed its aswimming, dividing wonders. Call him Leeuwenhoek.

For the spit or the snot below his exemplary lenses is a living turkish rug, is a paisley of armies and harem houris, brigands, flagellating pilgrims, hosts and hordes, upon their skimpily cellular business. Say it LAY-wen-hook: with his pseudopods and gastropods and all the other podners in the enterprise of being alive at any glimmering instance on this planet, on up to pea pods Mendel will duly contemplate later, and the *pas de deux* of the ovaries as they practice with each other for that moment they're asked to glide out star-showered onto the ballroom floor. An-TONY-van-LAY-wen-hook. "Here . . ."

For he, himself, is overmuch drunkenly groggy with having supped on her pungent dermal delights, although he knows her busy microcitizenry is going about its daily rounds clearheadedly, in alpine height, in swampy venetian recesses. O, the krill of her! The rotifers! The roe! "Yes, that's it . . . there."

For he has seen the population of the cheesiness between her fine

253

Dutch teeth—and in the pleasures of her lips, and in the wonders of the throwing animalcules therein, he revels with equally unblinking gusto, and of the pleasure he brings her in turn, he knows: that there are levels, and under them levels, and so on, crowded.

Yea, I lift my pen as baton to all of the congregate proboscises of the globe, that join in this one blatted honorific bombastic cockadoodle, for he is Leeuwenhoek, he has studied the spires and bristles, the mitred tips and galley-oared bellies, that pass beneath our notice.

Finished, lounging in the late Delft light in afterplay, ". . . another . . . another . . ." casually tweezing the seventeenth century's fleas from the folds of her body, cracking those tiny rhinocerlings' sleek cases with his fingers.

▼▲▼

It's altered everything thereafter. As did the atomic bomb, movable type, an accurate mirror: think of a life in which you'd never clearly seen your own face.

Leeuwenhoek made the world larger by making it smaller. He wasn't the first. We have no lens for looking back in time, but Zacharias Jansen, "an obscure spectacle-maker of Middleburg," is right now choice contender for its inventor. John Faber, naturalist and physician, named it "after the model of telescope, a microscope"—reminding us we zoomed the moon's craters before our own cankered insides. And Robert Hooke, in *Micrographia,* published 57 illustrations enabled by his new optical aid—describing the honeycomb structure of cork, he uses "cell" for the first time in its modern biological sense.

But Leeuwenhoek is the reverse-Galileo from whom it's most tempting to date the birth of a wholly new understanding. Before him, sight stopped at the dot of a flea. It wasn't of course that sight could *not* go further so much as that "further" didn't exist. Our vision through knowable space was infinite.

After Leeuwenhoek, vision was finite, simply because known space came into being at which the eyes' gaze failed.

The cosmos, which had been hierarchical, now was incremental. The difference this makes. The resonances.

The flea, which had been the final blank wall of the world became the door to a new world. There, the flea was a looming leviathan. We might call those units *fleas,* by which the space between two worlds is measured—and by which we leap across.

Then Columbus extended the European planet-map by (so-many) fleas.

Alicemay Axleburr—waking in her bed in the emergency ward of a Dayton, Ohio, hospital after having been officially dead, now having light, albeit the bloodless wired-in ceiling light of her room, dance manic to hosannas in her eyes again—went out of her body by (so-many) fleas, with a round-trip ticket of ectoplasm, and made the (so-many) fleas return journey.

Yea, for he peereth long and long at this Animal Crumb and seeth both the End and the Beginning—and the compact Transport therefrom and thereto.

> *6 July:* Worm formed out of egg.
> *17 July:* Worm white all over and did spin around itself a covering web.
> *21 July:* Changed into a chrysalis of transparent white.
> *25 July:* Assumed somewhat a red colour, this growing evermore deeper.
> *30 July:* Entirely red, and in the evening the Flea it contained was hopping about in the glass.

▾▲▾

They've only pestered me once in my life, and that was at Cynthia's, courtesy of a pug-snouted marmalade tabby so evolved toward feline unapproachability, sharing its fleas with us seemed its singlemost warmhearted gesture.

In those days, though, when love was new, and I was so new that my heart squeaked like a boot fresh from the box, and sex was new and each lick of a stamp or casual glance at the butcher's display-case of glistening organ-meats was fraught with recent memory of (and promise of yet more) wondrously offered-up sexual chowchow and marzipan . . . in those days, anything bringing me back to Cynthia's especially flawless surface with its neatly trimmed (and indeed, near topiary-like) central gardenspot, was welcome. So I picked fleas off her, chasing them with a fox hunt ardor, suffering my own pink frieze of bites around the ankles as a necessary dues, and thanking that otherwise damnable cat for its smuggling-in of what seemed to be, in my godawful moon-eyed and drooly infatuee's vision, a bevy of cupid's helpers, each with its requisite arrow.

If this prose seems overlush—well, that's the boy I'm describing, now twenty years back. We'd roll, as full of the stuffings of lust as two *cannolis,* over the unkempt bed beneath the cheap print of Vermeer (his *View of Delft*) and some enraged forbidding portrait by Diane Arbus (I forget which), there might be incense that was all-too-sweetly thickening the air like jasmine jello, and the gauzy background music of rock violins . . .

The history of this specific lovers' googoo long preceded us. Tiny ceramic or lacquered containers, often described by unwitting or fastidious antique purveyors as snuff (or pomade or potpourri) holders, are boxes in which the worshipful swain would save, as tokens, corpses of the fleas he'd remove from his mistress's clefts and swells. This intimate grooming, for most of humankind at most points on the timeline, has been traditional, a natural result of, on the one hand, need for vehicles by which corporeal exploration could take place unashamedly—and, on the other hand, the age-old unstoppable day-and-night assault of sheer pestiferousness.

You put both hands together, and you have some satin-draped Renaissance dandy fondling away at a bosom made almost buttocky by its tight underlacing, tittering from both he and she, and pseudoscientific observations on the chessleap prowess of fleas beginning, by pucker and flush, to metamorphose into whatever version is current of "Oh, my little éclair cream . . . !" So, here: Cynthia and myself.

At moments like that (and remember: we were twenty, and lucky, and dumb) it seemed the hugest emotions we owned, the most gargantuan thoughts our brains could fashion (that is, what we felt toward each other, that limited range of ourselves we understood in those hazed-over days to be our whole existence) rose from deep inside us somewhere, bumping against the skin from underneath like whales about to breach. "Exhilarating" doesn't come close. "Here: you missed one." Then I'd be at The Source, transported, gobbling her up like crazy.

There is some evidence (and much popular belief) that fleas prefer a female's chemistry (*pulex,* "flea," may take its name from the Latin *puella,* "girl"). Be that as it may, the flea-trap has its own trivial place in the history of ladies' fashion. A German print shows one kind, worn as a pendant between the breasts. This trap is perforated throughout its columnar length with holes just right for a flea-sized shady siesta: inside, the flea encounters a gummy tube. Hung on a velvet ribbon, the trap is as pleasing a decoration as any. Strips of fur were also used. Lore even has it that lapdogs were selectively bred toward a similar purpose. Women carried long ivory sticks—again: this was an acceptable public statement—for scratching the scalp from amidst the intricate palps and infoldings of their Marie Antoinette coiffures.

The link between fleas and female hormonal rounds is most amazingly seen in the life of that very excellent specialist, the European rabbit-flea. It clusters on the female rabbit, and only there—it would soon die in, say, the fur of a cat or the shag along a farm rat's groin—and, in the spring, up to seventy form a community on a single rabbit's ears, the place from which attempts to dislodge them are least efficacious. There they slurp and snooze and do whatever broad-jump acrobatics the space of a rabbit's ear allows.

Every stage in the rabbit-flea's cycle—ovulating, the ripening of eggs—is triggered by hormone cues in the host-doe's blood as *she* becomes pregnant, and then by the blood of her newborn litter, to which the fleas migrate for one frenzied spate of flea sex and subsequent laying of eggs. The larvae from these will find the warren floor a rich profusion of food in the form of droppings; and then, of course, the young rabbits are there to eventually host the new flea generation. The timing of this, and its exquisitely fine-tuned dependence, is something to quicken your breath, like watching a vee of Canada geese turn *snap* on an airy dime as if it outlined a single sinuous manta ray . . . Except it's fleas we've got here, filth-colored repugnantly-ugly butt-blood suckers: fleas.

Was that interesting? While it was happening, we finished, in that moment twenty years ago: Cynthia, me. Then we lay wet and thoughtless, I was yakking probably out of nervousness, we both had residual energy and emotional hodgepodge itching under our skins, we were raw to the world's least touch, and each other's touch, *imagined* touches could rummage our psyches and pull strings taut there. What I said that did it, I don't remember; or what she said back. It might have been about that cat, a mean neurotic boneless beast at best—but that's a guess, and then I was an arrogant sonofabitch, and she was blind to her own intense Queen Termite spasms of laziness: all of the standard invective, razor-edged with intimate knowledge. We didn't fight fair; we were truthful.

And I wouldn't apologize: no.

In minutes, I was out walking the evening sidewalks of Ithaca, New York, the bile already starting to pit my tongue. It was dead-middle summer. Heat charmed out of the asphalt did snake-hulas in the air. The sky

grew eggplant black, then flat black. When the moon showed, she was pit-
ted too.

It had happened this quick: like a match to the gas. Like some one small
word to our Big Talk. Whoosh.

On Monday, the 12th of October 1654, at 10:30 A.M., in the Dutch city
of Delft, where both Vermeer and Leeuwenhoek were not only born in the
same year (1632) but entered on the same page of the church baptismal
records . . . a powder magazine exploded—*90,000 pounds of powder*—
killing untold hundreds and making wreck of the streets in a flash, so
much so that, in the words of Elizabeth Stuart, Queen of Bohemia, who
visited, "not one stone upon another" remained.

▼▲▼

We might see the past as glorious in scale, either personally (before the
Company failed, I was V.P. in charge of production . . .) or historically (the
grandeur that was Rome, ah! . . .). And the same is true of the future: any
nascent aspiration is projectable as grandiose.

But for the most part, when we extend ourselves through time it makes
us smaller. Though it's *me,* it's not the me-who's-here-imagining-this-in-
the-Present-Tense: I'm watching another "me," me-prime, recede through
temporal distance as I'd watch a figure dwindle through distance in spatial
terms. The blood-stuffed, psyche-whomping, undeniable Present Moment
is the certainty, the survival-worthy; past and future slope from it on either
side, forming a sort of equilateral triangle of perception, and the diminish-
ing "me's" who fill it to fore and aft decrease appropriately to fit their re-
spective far-offness.

Being a child again is smaller. Being very much older is smaller. If we
retrojected ourselves to seventeenth-century Delft, retaining the integrity
of a physical body, but having that body time-shrink by—let's see . . . 350
years . . .we'd be about the size of a flea.

Say this one, at the base of the wall, near the little wood-case foot-
warmer, in this room of the building that faces, on one side, the Vol-
dersgracht and its whitewash-bricked Old Woman's and Old Man's
Almshouse, which he'll also do, but now he's having Catherina unfasten
the ties of her bonnet and let the sun trowel morning onto the pleats of her
jacket he's going to get *so* right you can feel its lemon and burgundy nap in
the paint.

(And the flea—? Oh yes, we *could* be larger than that—but then we'd be correspondingly incorporeal. This is the choice that ghosts make.)

▼▲▼

If we enter Delft through his *View of Delft*—if we enter into the picture plane, as light—we face the Schiedam Gate on the Rotterdam Canal of the River Schie, from the south. The water is partly a dark, morocco brown from the last of the rain clouds, and from reflections cast by buildings on the farther bank. These buildings are themselves just coming into their own aged colors, now that the storm is passed. Beyond—and more buff, or celadon—the tower of the Nieuwe Kirk (where Vermeer was baptized) rises; and beyond that, even, we see—and where we can't, we sense—the colors of everyday human use, the salmon roof tiles and deep wine burgheress gowns and inlaid humidors of tobacco, divvying up the field of vision into its various commercial and domestic arrangements.

What we see here, then, is light in its first being shaped, from its even and definitionless travel, to being "sky"—this is "weather," the bunching mackerel-gray of the laden clouds, the emptier clouds a range of slightly soiled cotton, then the cloudless blues that shade off, near the roofline, to something almost white: a white that's been around.

And so, as we enter in, and down, we see light architectured, filling the empty lanes between buildings—so "building" bordered things, transparent structures of its own.

Now light is . . . *exemplified,* it's seven points on seven stacked apples, it's ringed in a puddle-top's ripples, it's flat, it's latticed by shadows, it's blinding.

And now it hits—no, it's so gentle I'd say it endorses—the side of a building, his building, and *some* of this light that says in representation *all* of this light, is softly entering the window that always admits light in his paintings, from the left side, onto a table like powder, crinkled over a wall-map in saurian folds, minutely flowering as many times as there are pearls in the necklace of pearls she's lifting . . . light, domesticated.

"Yes . . . so; with the strand like . . . yes . . . yes . . . Good!"

His wife is Catherina Bolnes. She is a remarkable woman, and will be for many years after her husband's death. By her decision to marry out of her religion and out of her approximate class (this Johannes Van der Meer is an innkeeper's son and the inn is a less than . . . um, *seemly* place), and by the little we know of her battles with debt in the years of her widowhood, we imagine someone of sharp-boned character, heedful of her own current. Yes, and by the nine paintings we now assume to be portraits of her, we look at a woman in whom the journey of light from the heart of the sun, through the atmosphere, onto the lace of the collar that wings her throat—is a culmination. "Like so?"

"*Fah!* You moved when you said 'Like so.'"

"But I should be like—this. You see?"

"No. Yes . . . Good! And undo the ties?" She's wearing one of those puffed white caps that look like conestoga wagon tops.

"So?"

"Yes. Good." Some paint. Long silence. "Still, now . . . still. You're beautiful, 'Thrina, it glints along your skin as if you were a guilder."

And next to *her,* Jan Vermeer loves his light. I say "his" light because this is what happens, somehow, at the sill of the world and house: the light that implicates the planet in all of its fullness, that marries the continents to the seas, becomes a personal field here, across the maps and globes of continents and seas he has in his work so often. "His" light. A solace of light.

Some paint. Long silence.

"*Ya!*"

"What! 'Thrina!"

Fussing at her waist.

"You moved. What?"

"One of the little devil-wanger imps is on me."

"Here" / sigh / "let me help with it."

at her bodice

You know what follows.

▼▲▼

O flea, thou amorist!

Thou pepper grain that spicest us to our canoodling!

▼▲▼

The poemlet often called "Fleas" (I believe it's anonymous; sometimes you find it billed as "the briefest poem in the English language"):

> *Adam*
> *Had 'em.*

places our prickler squarely at The Beginning: it was naked flesh from the word "go." (Actually, fleas date from the Cretaceous, when a two-winged ancestor scavenger-insect discovered that blood was not only a nourishing swill, but high on the findability scale; wings atrophied, legs grew resourcefully jumpworthy: this was the proto-flea.) Goldbarth has written—addressing both the antiquity and the ubiquity of this intimate relationship—an "Addendum Couplet":

> *As did*
> *Madam.*

and pretty much prides himself on it.

▾▲▾

There's a centuries-long salubrious tradition of flea as inciter to carnal cha-cha-cha. Potential lovers frisk one another in search of a barb-tipped interloper. Places best left unthought-of are flea-tickled. Raiment becomes disarrayment. The rest is so many rut and estrus dominoes tumbling, slickety-slick. The flea as excuse, as Muse of Physical Passion. Fleas and brothels are commonly linked. We still say of somebody looking to nibble a bit of the ol' hot pastrami, looking to dip in a little tuna fondue, if you get my drift, that he or she "has the itch." The flea reminds even the clergy of what stuff's stuffed out of sight down there—its enlivening jig, from Eden onward, up and down out whozee-whatsis.

This same sly service is even performed for the gods of Olympus, in Willart de Grécourt's 16-page erotic poem *L'Origine des puces*—not a great poem, no, but equally engaging an origin story as that of Cretaceous mutation. Cupid, it turns out, is vexed when an ambrosia-lubricated convocation of the deities turns sleepy under Morpheus's intervening, instead of orgiastic. He shoots an arrow, the arrow turns into a swarm of fleas, and before you know it, divine thighs and mammaries undulate winsomely from divine togas, with three days and nights of mad coupling resulting. After which, the new insects are banished to Earth, and adapt to it beautifully.

"Fleas are so much a German erotic specialty," Brendan Lehane writes, "that two learned Teutons, Herren Hugo Hayn and Alfred N. Gotendorf, applied themselves at the turn of the century to compiling a bibliography of the literature. *Floh-Litteratur,* they called it," from the sixteenth century

up. But the Germans have no monopoly here; and by the sixteenth century, something like the

> *. . . flea*
> *mankind one morning stared to see*
> *on Catherine Desroches' bared breast*
> *sucking imperturbably*

is a well-established folk *motif de prurience.* A poem ascribed to Ovid has
its narrator imagining he can—*poof*—become a flea at will, and so spelunk
flesh grottoes. Long after, a character in Marlowe's *Faust* says, "I am like to
Ovid's flea. I can creep into every corner of a wench." Lehane: "There is in
fact a whole class of erotic flea art." Night: a candle: an off-white cambric
shift uprumpled in search of some coven of spiky-snouted scoundrels, and
there you have it: the two full moons and the fertile crescent, the nasties,
the nougat, the grail.

An example of our lusty flea in the knowingmost of literary abilities
would be, of course, Donne's poem, from when he was known, still, as "a
great Visitor of Ladies, a great Frequenter of Plays, a great Writer of con-
ceited Verses." This sexy, savvy paean to the gourmandizing flea as tiny
armored-over "marriage temple" where (because "It suck'd me first, and
now sucks thee") "our two bloods mingled bee" was (a Norton anthology
says) "apparently the most popular of Donne's poems in his own century."
Donne died in 1631; Leeuwenhoek was born the year after; "The Flea" was
first published in 1633. A kind of flea Golden Age.

But if you've been waiting for gland-enflaming quotations from less-
than-literary sources, if you really want to swag the haggis, down the banana cream pie, and scramble the sugar-eggs, if you get my drift and I think
you do, *voilà,* from (purportedly) 1789 (but more likely a century later), the
caviar, the crown, the catered lazy susan's topmost radish rosette of all
flearotica (if you'll allow me the coinage), Anonymous's still-in-print
spunk-spewing classic, *The Autobiography of a Flea:*

"Born I was—but how, when, or where I cannot say. I shall not stop to
explain by what means I am possessed of human powers of thinking and
observing, but, in my lucubrations, leave you simply to perceive that I possess them and wonder accordingly. My earliest recollections lead me back . . .
I was engaged upon professional business connected with the plump white

leg of a lady, the taste of whose delicious blood I well remember, and the flavour of whose—

"But I am digressing."

The lady is Bella, domicile, provender, and means of vast travel, all three sometimes at once, to our narrator; also an endless amusement:

"They have sat her upon the edge of the table, and one by one they sucked her young parts, rolling their hot tongues round and round in the moist slit. Bella lent herself to this with joy, and opened to the utmost her plump legs to gratify them . . ."

. . . and so on, for 190 pages in my paperback edition, while our *raconteur* himself is supposedly perched at the lip-edge of waterfall torrents, lumberjack fellings, Richter-scale seismic upquakings, and mud-slide inundations of human venality.

Thou nethermost peek up the vents of taboodom!

O flea, that bearest considerable great witness!

▼▲▼

And *we*

Can witness the *flea:*

▼▲▼

The *Talmud* knew: the flea, "being one of the animals that propagate by copulation, is therefore not to be killed on the Sabbath."

But this was an isolated knowledge. Pliny the Elder had said that "leapers" were "engendered by filth, acted upon by the rays of the sun," and straight from the Romans to the moment Leeuwenhoek pincered one up from a china jar to the gaze of his *dainty Lens,* the flea was a sexless creature, springing wholly grown into life through spontaneous generation. The flea's "Originall is from dust," wrote Thomas Moufet late in the sixteenth century, "chiefly that which is moyst'ned with mans or Goats urine." That a German engraving from 1749 shows two fleas mating in accurate detail, each brushy plate of her carapace holding its own knot of light, and he, in his underposition, credibly shadowed and textured with burls and jointwork . . .

. . . this can be traced exactly to that table in Delft, the morning sun backing his finicking wire tweezers, yes and his *enduring, unprejudiced Stare.* He writes, as if both declaring and winning the war in one compact statement, "Fleas are not produced from corruption, but in the ordinary way . . ."

▾▲▾

Depending on how you mean "ordinary."

The penis of the male flea is the singlemost intricate penis known on the planet.

It consists of *two* rods, a thick and a thin, that twine about each other in his body caduceus-like. The sperm are wound like spaghetti around the thinner, longer shaft. When the two fated fleamates have found each other by whatever rarefied sense they use, crossing the Gobi and Tetons of our bodies; when he completes what Lehane endearingly dubs his "demurring zigzag" of wooing; and then when he's finally fitted beneath her, back to belly and tail to tail; THEN his rods uncoil, the thick rod snugged in a blind pouch halfway up her ample tract, the thin rod sliding in a groove along the thicker one, steadied thereby and directed, until it surpasses the thick rod, probes its way into her ultimate vaginal opening, yes and THERE it pushes its payload tangle of sperm and "somehow" releases it.

This takes maybe three hours, sometimes up to nine, and neither merrymaker halts feeding. All this while, the male is also using yet *another* organ, a kind of feather duster with which he gently strokes his own true inamorata. Really.

Returning them gingerly into the blue china jar ". . . to set the Truth before my eyes, to embrace it, in order to draw the World away from Old-Heathenish superstition, to go over to the Truth, and to cleave unto it" even, yea, for this his "very minute and despised creature." Sliding the lenses' brass slips fussily back into their oxblood leather case. Time now for an ale with Vermeer, and trading tales of an honest morning's work. Let the tavern wits turn a few easy verses.

> *A flea climbing out of my beverage*
> *Said "My wife is much taller than average.*
> *How can I keep her?*
> *I can't even leap her*
> *Without using one dick for leverage."*

▾▲▾

Okay, so Thomas Moufet was wrong about the ways fleas are engendered; so they *don't* scrabble *ex nihilo* from some log's mud-scabrous sides. But (in addition to being, as some claim, the father of *that* Miss Muffet, who comes through time to us with her fabled food and arachnophobia—plausibly so, in light of both the name and the father's interest) he was a man of learning "who," John Aubrey mentions, "hath written a Booke *De Insectis.*"

Moufet supplies us remedies for "the Torment" (including Dwarf Elder leaves, Fern root, Rue, and flowers of Pennyroyal); relates how the clever fox relieves itself of the pests (by mincing backwards into a river with a rag of moss in its teeth, until the ever-more-crowded fleas are on its snout, then just its nose, and then have no choice but to jump to what quickly becomes a moss raft floating downstream); and offers up quite a neat phrase when he wants to: of their biting, he says "they leave a red spot as a Trophie of their force."

He was one of an informal school of sixteenth-century men of letters shepherded over by Mary Herbert, Countess of Pembroke—Donne would be included here, as well as Edmund Spenser, Ben Jonson, and Thomas Nashe. She must have been an extraordinary person, "a beautiful Ladie and an excellent witt, and had the best breeding that age could afford"—it's Aubrey again. "She was a great Chymist," he tells us, with a "Laborator" to concoct in, and under her lithesome guidance "Wilton House was like a College, there were so many learned and ingeniose persons." She knew Sir Walter Raleigh. She toured with the Queen. She suggested her brother the poet Philip Sidney write his book *Arcadia,* which she revised and addended. Her own *bon mots* could be hurled in Greek, Latin, or Hebrew.

And this: "She was very salacious, and she had a Contrivance that in the Spring of the yeare, when the Stallions were to leape the Mares, they were to be brought before such a part of the house, where she had a *vidette* (a hole to peepe out at) to look on them and please herselfe with their Sport."

—Enormous wicked fun, to picture her leaning observantly into this pastime. Yes, but today I can only see Leeuwenhoek scribbling in front of me, blocking the view. I look over his shoulder: he's writing up notes on one more session spent with the flea, *endowed with as great Perfection in its kind as any large Animal.*

▼▲▼

Fact: Its leap is *80 times* its length high, *150 times* its length long. This makes the frog or the kangaroo seem anemic younger cousins.

Fact: The fleabite isn't a bite. It's a piercing and siphoning up. The responsible tool is made up of three stiletto-shaped blades—and good blades, so sharp the pierced skin doesn't relay it.

Fact: It's not this piercing that causes the itch, but enzymes in the flea's saliva, which enters the wound in a forceful injection and keeps the blood-flow from coagulating. Now the flea imbibes—for many hours, if undetected. It will suck more blood that its body can bear, and the excess spurts straight out its anus.

Fact: There are 2,000-plus flea species.

Fact: 932 hedgehog-fleas have been found on a single young hedgehog.

Fact: But monkeys *aren't* natural hosts to fleas. The picking we see is to clear their own packed, gummy body-scurf. They can, however, accidentally catch human-fleas from zoogoers.

Fact: I said the human-flea, *our* flea, *Pulex irritans:* "irritating flea." The name is lived up to.

Fact: The patient pupal flea in its case will wait alive but inactive, over a year, for a proper host to appear. It *knows*. A realtor unlocking a house abandoned for months, in which not one free flea has been leaping, can walk right through and briskly out the back door, and emerge with 150 crisscrossing snappily under his pants.

Fact: Almost everybody. Everywhere.

Fact: Every three days the priests of ancient Egypt shaved their heads (this, from Herodotus) specifically to keep their scalps flea-free. And still they scratched.

Fact: Indian noblemen had themselves hoisted dandily off the floor at night, in light cane hammocks that were dangled from the roof (according to Marco Polo) specifically to ward off the flea. And still they scratched.

Fact: A wardrobe from the court of Henry VIII was discovered, and spilling from the tucks of its clothes was a dry pour of the bodies of mummified sixteenth-century fleas. Kings scratched. Queens scratched. Viziers and flouncing extramarital favorites scratched, and scratched.

Fact: Jesus the Christ scratched fleas.

Supposition: They were, then, the first to take the "host" of Mass; the only to take it directly.

Fact: The Buddha scratched fleas.

Fact: Mohammed scratched fleas.

Fact: Cleopatra, only an hour after bathing in asses' milk and rose-petals, having had a handmaiden lotion her, then a eunuch strigil the lotion off . . . Cleopatra scratched fleas. The handmaiden scratched. The eunuch.

Fact: With his head in The World of Original Forms That Precede All Earthly Existence, Plato dug into his tummy. Thinking radium, Madame Curie rubbed an ankle abstractedly with an ankle. Then went at it good, with a pen nib. Isadora Duncan. The Czar. The Continental Congress. Scratched.

Fact: At the Barrel-and-Boar in Delft, with one proper citizen's one proper ale before him, waiting Vermeer's appearance, Leeuwenhoek (drawing a crazed but clear distinction between his cozy colony of fleas in the china jar—that is, his objects *of dear Contemplation*—and any sybaritic invader profaning the sanctum-space of his body—that is, *Vermin*) scratched a fine ten-fingered tarantella all over his butt. And fifty-six years later, his British disciple Henry Baker ("on whom seems to have fallen," says one biographical note, "the Dutch microscopist's mantle") scratched. When Baker met Daniel Defoe in 1727, Defoe was scratching. Two years later, Baker married young Sophia Defoe; the preacher, two fiddlers, and every flower-bounteous maid in the wedding party, was witnessed, off and on for that entire grand evening, scratching.

There was also the scratch of Defoe's quill pen. In 1722, in the room where his paper-tumulted desk moved into afternoon with morning light still tenaciously dabbed across it . . . Defoe is writing a fiction—though founded on fact.

Defoe is writhing *A Journal of the Plague Year*.

▼▲▼

"Then, came such a Stink upon the wind; from the bodies piled at corners in wait of the Dead Carts making their rounds; and from a City tormented by running Sores; and from the market goods and the rubbish heaps and the stores of grain and salted cuts that had, from the terrible toll of the labourers, none to attend them; and so they rotted; the Stench being such, the saying was this: the Air was of a thickness, you could climb it as if it were a ladder; each new death, being a rung.

"A girl, a Hooper's daughter, she not above Six years of age; her father and mother having exhibited the Tokens over their chests and arms, and

Expiring, both, within the same night, to the grief of an older son, who fled the City on foot, and no one has heard to this day; then the girl, when she exhibited Tokens, *viz*, the black swellings, there was none who would go near, and so she wandered the Parish for two nights sleeping in rain and all. I saw of her next on Joiner Street where it meets the earthen wall, she had swooned. And then I saw her pitiful body in Spasms, ogglddypoggldy, as if dancing or thrown about; at which her Chest bled; and at the bleeding her skin did break; and out crawls a Rat with her spleen in its jaws yet. This was the cause of her being worked from the inside like a Judy puppet. And I would fall weeping right there, save for a nasty pack of the creatures were all upon her then, with their devilish piping that squeals right through like a knife. And the morning next, she was bones."

▼▲▼

It begins: in the blood of marmots and susliks among the steppes of central and eastern Asia. And there the disease is mild (as syphilis was, in New World systems, before Columbus's men introduced it to Europe). In times of migration, however, these rodents mingle with countryside rats. Some fleas, by mistake or intent, transfer over; and with them, as in a decanter, come the bacilli.

Rats die then; some, not all. Of the surviving, some of these open-air rats will eventually come to share their fleas with the rats at the edges of cities: and here, a new player enters onstage.

For when a rat dies and its carcass cools, its population of fleas will seek a living rat; and if none is easily found, as can happen when rats by the thousands are toppling over foaming, an alternative is available. Without even trying, the horror has made its way to the top of the corporate ladder.

We first read of plague in *Samuel,* Book I, Chapter V: as punishment for stealing the Ark of the Covenant, the Philistines are smote. The populations of Gath, Ashod, and Akron: smote. First documentation, in an historical sense, is from the pandemic that decimated Justinian's Rome, beginning 542 A.D. At the height of that misery 10,000 people a day were dying, filling the air with cries and stinks we can't begin to imagine without touching madness and so we back off. This outbreak lasted sixty years, and pushed its fatal reach "to the ends of the habitable world." At its finish, the Dark Ages start.

"And a mother was dead, but the child still crawled her breast; and sucked most piteously there; to no avail, save a trickle of Rheum; and tho the child was plucked away and bathed of its Contagions, it was purple in a night; and this scene we were obliged to witness daily; until an infant was a purse of weeviled meal you heaved across your shoulder into a Pile; and called upon the Constable to shovel them into a Pit."

Lulled down to occasional, local swaths of tragedy over the centuries, plague as a pandemic reemerges with fatalities among a host of Tartars who, in 1346, besieged a colony of Italians at Caffa, a trading town in the Crimea. At no great loss for martial efficiency, Tartar war chiefs ordered their own dead catapulted over the city walls. When the siege was relieved, and the extant Italians homed again in Genoa, it was only a matter of days—a matter of fleas in half-inch switches of host and hostess—and the infamous Black Death had started gnawing away at the succulent ribmeat of Europe. Even Greenland was tortured. In three years, a quarter of Europe was dead; in less than twenty years, half.

Survivors, for as long as they remained survivors, thought it was the end of the world—and in a sense they were right. One out of every two: marked with the pustules, the cold sweats, retching, then dead. This surge lasted 300 years, its farewell performance being the Plague of 1665 Defoe writes so movingly of—100,000 Londoners were added, as a last flash, to the utter devastation. You slept beside Death, and you woke facing Death, and you caroused or fasted in excess with Death's breath on the *x* between your shoulders, pontiff or shitpicker, harlot or saint. "And now the Wagons, that they sent by once a day for the dead; they sent by twice; and this was not sufficient, the dead would tumble from their stacks and land in the Streets cracked open; and none would go near, for fear of what issued; no, not even a dog."

The Great Fire of London one year later burnt five-sixths of the city—having, perhaps as much as anything else to do with quieting the plague. Again it existed as only a fitful flicker for centuries—a rumor here, a measley 30,000 Cairoese there, a wink, a nibble. Then in January 1894 a woman in Canton fell ill. It arrived in Hong Kong and passed to Bombay—and from that city's trading vessels the third great plague pandemic spread worldwide; the most savage: *thirteen million* people dying in a calamitous heap on the steps of the twentieth century.

All this while, no one suspected the flea. (It took until 1910 for the Plague Research Commission to pinpoint the culprit.)

They burnt Jews instead. In London, in 1665, 200,000 cats and 40,000 dogs were killed, as a precaution. Some wore large dried toads as amulets. Tar was pored onto fires, to cleanse the air of its "Poisons." Coins and letters were dipped in vinegar, or handled by cups on long rods. Pepys carried a hare's foot. They burnt Arabs. They severed the heads of the poor. Jackdaws and pigeons were trapped and given over to the knife in unimaginable numbers. That the flea was never efficaciously suspect, not in 1,400 years, is testimony, of a silent but eloquent sort, to its acceptance as a fact of life. You breathed, you shat, your soul hearkened unto the Throne of the Lord, your groin was aburble with longing, the sun shone, it hailed, and you had fleas.

"And some were of an Opinion, the wind did bear it; and these would show themselves only if clothed in a cloak and gloves of cloth and a Mummer's mask; and some of the Opinion, it abided in the waters; and these drank naught, or these drank Spirits only; and some said God above; and some said Satan below; and none knew, save for this, that its Conveyance to the Humours of the body was of a common Particular, not to be avoided (withal through Chance); and in those days a man would not so much as rub his own two hands for warmth or scratch his own Fleas or with his knuckles dig the sleep out from his eyes; without prayer; or a Shudder."

▼▲▼

O flea, thou Carrier, thou millionth-gram of Oblivion.
Thou scourge, thou Humbler, thou Totterer of Goliaths.
Thou Pygmy with poison-tip dart.
Thou Death Speck, thou dillseed Accessory to the Crime.
Woe dot. Destroyer.

▼▲▼

So I apologized.

This story's this simple: the tiniest units that introduce love, conduct huge suffering. Lollapalooza hurt lives on this planet, people. No one's exempt. Why add more hurt or turn from one of the little, saving annealing-moments we're given?

Besides, I was lonely, more lonely than proud; and she was breathing out there somewhere with those freckles paprika'd over her nose, and her barrister's manner of nailing a tough question home, and that amberthatched snickerdoodle between her legs that enjoyed my own gargoyley thing. Whatever pushed me over—a crash at the corner, a classmate's leukemia, Alan's parents' divorce, or maybe I was up reading about the plague one night for a course that told me history's never finished with us, history's ever-voracious . . . I was knocking on Cynthia's door. I knew we didn't need to keep on garnishing Pain with our own small sprigs of Petulance.

No dummy, I'd brought a peace gift: this, a small ceramic lozenge case I claimed was one of those antique token-boxes in which the lovestruck swain collected his mistress's nimble leapers . . . oh, I was golden-tongued. I thought it might be an easy key back to our former intimacy, and also a way of saying (though not in words) how I accepted the place of that prissy, pissy, parasite-smuggling cat in her life and mine. No dummy, she took the case with a calculated aloofness, and required of us a gauntlet of conversational reassurances and proofs, before we were once again nuzzling each other across her sheets, her lips a remora on me, mine improvising red-hot jazz on her chickfuzz ocarina.

Now that was all so long ago, it shrinks to a postcard scene—its grandiose romance and randy rollaround are . . . "quaint," I suppose: what twenty years does. And yet the substance scribbled on that postcard's back is true, is simple but true, and I've brought you through all of this pop-historical voyeuristic pseudo-memoir Oompahpah-and-Fizz to share it:

The transmitter's size says nothing about the total jolt of the message: what *are* we if not the exquisite parquetrywork of chromosomes, retarded or voluptuous by assignment of perhaps a single gene? Oh nodes no larger than peas can double us over, and these are the casters on which well-being wheels. One scant nodded *yes* or stuttered *no* will drive an entire life from its route. We need to be attentive, to the smallest rising moon above a cuticle, to the lilliput taj mahal of blue at the center of any red flame, to the slimmest syllable love or politics utters, yes and because our forgiveness is the flimsiest mote in the galaxy's eye and our tenderness as well, we need to practice them daily, turn to someone who matters and practice them daily, as if repetition does count, for suffering's armory of small but endless plague-marks adds a grief to a grief and finally strikes with the strength of a huge blunt instrument, and even the least of our comforts and dignities needs to be archived, kept well-lubed and, when required, marshaled in attempt to be a counterbalancing force.

A stranger, some punk twenty-year-old imposter claiming my name, has sent this sentiment to me over two decades of daily fuss and kaboom, and I think I'll hearken.

He'll know Cynthia for a year more maybe, tops. She'll go to law school, then on to Japan. The squabbles won't stop with this single apologetic tryst. But for the moment, as I unwind time and see him, he's stroking her shoulders while she dozes, he's coming to see (not that the wisdom will always remain with him when it's needed, but nonetheless coming to see) we need to care about each other down to units the size of just one umber asexual freckle . . . stroking her, thinking this, idly with his other hand jiggling the little case that he brought—because he's clever, you see—at a flea market.

Cynthia's deep, damp breaths . . . the cat in its psycho slumber . . .

He looks up at, and into, her poster of the painting of Delft. One spark, no one knows whose or how, and the top of that city was blown off like a skull from a .45 at the palate. Although it's rebuilt by the time Vermeer immortalizes his view across the river, the mackerel grays that float above the water, the rich clay colors roofing the farther plane . . .

If he could ray himself to a point, he'd be of size enough to wander those backmost Delftways, past the peculiarly whitewashed jambs of that time and place, and find the Barrel-and-Boar. Vermeer has just entered. Leeuwenhoek raises his long-emptied mug in halloo.

"Hoofdman!"

▼▲▼

By the time of his death, Jan Van der Meer—Vermeer—will have fathered eleven children (eight of them still minors when he dies).

No wonder he sometimes itches sorely to vamoose, breathe-in the outside, slant a flagon with the guys. (We hope Catherina escapes sometimes as well, an empty wicker basket over her arm, and nothing but giddiness guiding her, maybe down the wharf steps, to Van Loo's, where bolts of goldshot damask are being unrolled on a large dry tarp, and sun picks over the gold like lute strings, yes . . . But today is Vermeer's.)

From what we know, it's likely he succeeded his father as the innkeeper of the Mechelen, a tipple-spot off the market square at the corner of Oudemanhuisteeg; he and Catherina would have lived in its two upper floors. So it won't do, of course. The morning's paints are drying, what he wants for some few minutes is *away.*

"*Hoofdman!*" says Leeuwenhoek on seeing him enter the tavern dimness, and raises his empty mug as if a second round might rain into it from the rafters. ("Head-man," is what it means, a big-wig in the Artist's Guild: as if a friend might yell "Yo Prez!" or "Heydeeho it's Boss Man!") Soon enough, the seventeenth-century Netherlands bullshit is batted back and forth.

"My friend"—this is three rounds later—"the shell of the beetle I have been studying under my little glass . . . it looks exactly like a *viola da gamba!*" He makes the shape in the air.

"Then it must look exactly like Gjerta there," and Vermeer nods nearimperceptibly toward the tavernmaid they like and tease, the way they like and tease each other; he makes the same shape back in the air, for Leeuwenhoek. "My dear shepherd of beetles, you've been too long with your eye at your device."

"*Faa!* You've been too long with your eye drilling over to Gjerta. You could muddy her pee, your looking is so intense. Eleven's enough!" (The seventeenth-century test for pregnancy was clarity of the urine.)

"And from your bees and beetles you've learned to sneak those little conscienceful stings of yours into a conversation. But listen, now: my *mission* is looking. Yes, and looking *impartially*"—he gestures like a balance-pans—"on the pitying face of the Virgin Herself above the font in the nave, and on the lovely plumpness peeking from Gjerta's lacings."

"*You*, look? Jan, stare out the door, at the light there. What do you see?"

"Oh, go fish with your nose in your beer."

"No, truly: What?"

"You can see it yourself. There's Houckgeest's shop. The entrance to his side lane. The front stoop. Way in back, the roofs of the street where Steen's bakery is."

"Jan . . . The light is filled with dancing motes. Look. They dazzle, then they turn the other cheek like a good dour Christian, then they flare up again. There are thousands and thousands"—he drifts his hand from front door to kitchen door—"floating in here across your chin and your dingus, man, into the shadows, all over!"

"And you could spend the afternoon counting the dancing last of them, and not see that the shaft of light you're looking straight into pours like a bath of apricot brandy, over some sumptuous Gjerta or other."

"No, listen . . ."

Etc. You get the idea. Two friends, a few hours. The nubbling of extra texture into the breath-thin lining of life.

▼▲▼

And *did* they know each other? That baptism record places them on the same page. Leeuwenhoek served well as the executor of Vermeer's (bankrupt) estate, and spent enormous energy satisfying its creditors. (This, though, might be an ordinary result of Leeuwenhoek's station in Delft burgher life at the time, as opposed to the role of longstanding family friend.) Between those parentheses Birth and Dying, the history is uncertain; experts argue differing likelihoods.

But we know Vermeer's father owned a silk-weaving business the son inherited; Leeuwenhoek was, by profession, a draper. And, writing of "Vermeer's change in style," one art historian says it "happens to coincide with Leeuwenhoek's return to Delft from Amsterdam."

Around that time, Vermeer evidently found the lenses and know-how for constructing a *camera obscura.* "The significant shift in both style and execution," says Leonard J. Slatkes, "is signaled by the *Soldier and Laughing Girl.*" The effects "preserve the optical phenomena not visible to the naked eye but clearly observable in *camera obscura* images. Vermeer's unique application of paint in small dots, or *pointilles,* also seems to be an attempt to capture the specific visual qualities of the *camera obscura* projected image. Indeed, he seems to be the only painter who attempted this."

Shimmerings over the bread of *The Milk Maid,* over the side of the boats and bridge of the *View of Delft,* like so many diatom-tiny florins and stuyvers poured out of sunlight itself . . . these dots. And Leeuwenhoek, parsing his eyesight ever more rarefied, down to what he terms the "gloubles" that add up to living.

I think it was more than one day of ale they shared. I like to see it this way:

The light from what we call the universe enters Vermeer's open window—on the level of light, it must be like a needle threaded.

The painter humanizes—*familiarizes*—this unthinkably cosmic presence. Light is given its holdable, credible bodies here: it's curlicued impasto in the picture frames, and stippled over an ermine collar, and wrinkled with geology across the faces of wall-hung maps, it's clabbered here, it's seamlessly creamy there, it's alive, we can lift it, it's something the size of a pearl on a vanity table, glowing from the grain heart of a pearl . . .

And at the far end of that room it reaches Leeuwenhoek. He's absorbed in his peering. He's funneling that light to a pinpoint, to an as-yet-never-imagined pinpoint—where it burnishes, and turns like a bright star inside of, the jet back-case of a flea.

And so they make a two-man-unit engine of increasingly finer-focused resolution and power.

We need to be attentive.

▼▲▼

/There's a submicroscopic level where color doesn't exist—the wavelengths of light are larger than any possible place to land.

/According to Frederick Turner's study, "The length of the human present moment"—the "bundles" of sensory intake by which our day is divided—is roughly three seconds. Basic units of meter, worldwide, are three seconds in reciting; conversational speech occurs in three-second bursts with milliseconds between; a listener takes in three seconds of speech at a time, to his processing centers. Below that, time in some real sense doesn't occur. Sounds separated by anything less than three-thousandths of a second are "heard" as simultaneous.

/God's seed in Mary. Christ in the wafer. Incubus. Succubus. Mercury visiting man in the guise of a peddler . . .

These are all from the realm of nonperception. Before Columbus, the map of a flat Earth drew a clear border between this realm and the known.

We might say the flea is that border, our last clear datum before we slip over into silence between black holes, electron spin, quark iffiness . . .

We might say the flea is the Edge of the World.

▼▲▼

Well, we live in *this* world. C., not two years old, went in this week to have her chest sawed open. N., just twenty-two, jumped twenty-two stories and then his father was brought to identify what they bucketed. On the other hand, my sister calls, and she and Boog and the kids are fine, and the dog is fine, and the lawn is fine; she's hanging up now and sifting with him pollen by pollen into her fine sleep . . .

If they mean anything at the last, these fleas, it's because they say us, for us, while we're busy under the eddying fires of galaxies, under mountains-diminishing Big Bang pulses of time, pretending we're pretty large stuff.

They don't say the whole poignant nuanceful range, but I hope I've implied they have (or we impart to them) the basics down pat: our grief, and our cleaving unto another. When we forget, they remind us.

—Best, perhaps, at that nowadays-nearly-defunct, but idiosyncratic, crackpot institution-of-sorts, the flea circus.

Thomas Moufet tells us of "Mark an Englishman (most skilfull in all curious work)" who created a chain of gold, with key and lock to match, for shackling a flea, which then "did draw a Coach of Gold that was every way perfect." Indeed, as a formal idea the flea circus seems to have come from sixteenth-century England.

It has its geniuses.

Flamboyant ***Signor Bertolotto*** who, in the 1830s, *"Under the Patronage of Her Royal Highness the Princess Augusta,"* included, as part of his Regent Street Flea Circus in the Cosmorama Rooms, a costumed twelve-piece flea orchestra "playing audible music"; he knew his fleas by individual name, and some of his most distinguished performers were, he let out, prolifically fed in secret by various "ladies of distinction."

Professor Leroy Heckler of Hubert's Freak Museum at Broadway and 42nd, a friend to the photographer Diane Arbus. She would finish midnight shoots of Congo the Jungle Creep, the Serpent Lady, Sealo the Seal Boy, midgets, pinheads, the chafing folds of the Fat Lady, Rudolf the Armless Man who used his toes to light his cigarette, Presto the fire Eater, Albert Alberta half-man half-woman . . . Then, with the living trash of that neighborhood starting its wee-hours rounds in the alleys outside, she'd recompose herself while Heckler fed his *artistes.* "He'd roll up his sleeves and, using tweezers, pick up the fleas out of their mother-of-pearl boxes, drop them on his forearm, and let them eat while he read the *Daily News.*"

Professor Len Tomlin struggling impresario of (in 1974, at least) "Britain's one remaining flea circus," "POSITIFLEA AN ALL LIVE SHOW"—at that time he'd brought thirty years of dedicated flea ringmastership to his craft. "Only three men in the world," he is reported as saying, "have the steadiness of eye and hand to harness fleas."

And there are the Flea Stars leaping through circus history, too: for instance, Paddy, who "was said by Mr. Heckler to have given 52,850 consecutive performances, a record scientists say is quite impossible but which Mr. Heckler liked to call 'Broadway's longest run.'" Or the star of Copenhagen's Tivoli Gardens flea circus, "caught by a dowager countess in one of the city's most exclusive districts." In keeping true to its exquisite origins, this performer (a "tightrope dancer") was attired completely in pink, its costume fashioned from the down of one of the Copenhagen zoo's pedigreed flamingos.

Locked into roles we've decreed, they act out their rough parodies of our human passions—what I called "our grief, and our cleaving unto another." Gala battles are common, with uniformed ranks of flea foot soldiers (some bayoneted or dragging cannons) and stalwart generals leading them onward to carnage—Washington, Grant, Napoleon, all swords-drawn, astride flea chargers. There are pugilists and dueling fencers. Maidens are tied by villains to flea-sized railroad tracks and wriggle there most piteously. There is wailing and gnashing of teeth.

And there are the lovers. Romeo, rapt in the garden, courting a balconied Juliet; and then, with a single bounce, he's at her side. There have been elaborate flea weddings, down to the veil and bouquet. Flea waltzers, cheek to cheek. Fleas side-by-side in their own flea Tunnel of Love car. And, when the children and ladies are ushered out of the tent, gents, how'dja like to witness the Absolutely Sensational (but Educational) Spasms of Four-poster Prowess on the Honeymoon Night . . .

▼▲▼

He covers her freckled shoulders with the sheet. Her breathing is deep and steady, it seems it must be in tune with something enormous, something as imperturbably confident as the Ithaca night sky itself. But he can't sleep one eyelash-worth of it. The dregs of sex are in him, I guess, or maybe some foreboding—who knows? I love him as I might a close friend's child. And it's so long ago . . . two decades shrinks this in size to one of those crystal globes you shake and it's snowing.

I shake it: he's holding her lightly now, the summer heat is woozying his wakefulness, he's staring through blur at the thumbtacked Vermeer, and he sees that it's snowing in Delft right now. A calm white hand is stroking the brows of its houses . . .

▼▲▼

Usually the weather is clement. Oh, it can get cold—that corpulency we at-
tribute to the figures in Dutch paintings, portly burghers and their
dumpling wives, may partly be the up-to-seven-layers of underskirting and
pants they wore. But real snow is rare. So Leeuwenhoek wants to study it,
Leeuwenhoek's out in it, flumping through great white loaves. And it's
quiet. It softens all detail. He can use a little of that.

Because eight minors is a lot of confusion for any dead man to have left
behind, and especially a poor one. And all of the documents 'Thrina needs
to sort through now, the many paper cogs of the many paper machines of
this world . . . ! So much. He wishes Jan could be here if just to complain
about it.

Even so, he's watching each individual flake in its glide—he's Leeuwenhoek. He's seeing each unduplicated face in the choir, each separate star
of descent—and then he's looking into distance, a landscape of simple
enamel-white lengths.

He thinks, "These little ones!" Some must be in his eyes now, on his
cheeks, they're damp. "These little ones, *ay-yi,* how they add up!"

1992

When Paul Metcalf was a child his family accidentally found in the ancestral home's attic the only known copy of the novel *Billy Budd*. It had been hidden there decades earlier by Metcalf's grandmother, the daughter of Herman Melville, who grew up with the embarrassment of her father's failure as a writer. *Moby-Dick* especially was considered dishonorable. Why? "The author has not given his effort here the benefit of knowing whether it is history, autobiography, gazetteer, or fantasy," wrote the *New York Globe* in 1851. There are, after all, long stretches of invention in Melville's controversial book, which are unseamlessly mixed with impeccably researched details on how to dress a whale, what cannibals believe in, and where in the world the color white is found. Unlike his grandmother, however, Paul Metcalf would not grow up with the embarrassment of his great-grandfather's unclassifiable book, but rather with the knowledge of it having once embarrassed others and the benefit of finding that amusing. He will label his first book, *Genoa,* a "novel," and then he will never bother with genre again.

PAUL METCALF

"...and nobody objected"

And there I found very many islands filled with people without number, and of them all I have taken possession for their Highnesses, by proclamation and with the royal standard displayed, and nobody objected.

CHRISTOPHER COLUMBUS, REPORTING ON HIS FIRST VOYAGE

One

Who was he? Where was he born? When was he born? Where did he come from? Where had he traveled? What had he done? Where did he study? What did he know? What was his name?

He was described as "a man from the land of Genoa, a merchant of books of print who traded in them . . ." Yet he bragged to Ferdinand and Isabella that he had gone to sea at fourteen, and that he had "been twenty-three years upon the sea without quitting it for any time long enough to be counted . . ."

Was his hair white, or was it red? Was he the son of a poor weaver who neglected his loom, ran a tavern, had to be bailed out of a Genoese jail where he had been locked up for debt?

Was Genoa a jail to Christopher, with the Mediterranean Sea at his feet, spreading outward, beckoning?

Why could his son Ferdinand, returning to Genoa years later, find no trace of the family?

Why did Christopher speak Spanish with a Portuguese accent? Why did he write in Spanish, even before he arrived in Spain? Or in Latin, with errors that a Spaniard would make?

Las Casas reported that: "In the matters of the Christian religion, no doubt he was a Catholic and of much devotion."

But was he protesting too much, laboring doubly hard to prove his Christian fervor? Was his family, in fact, Spanish Jews who had fled Spain and the Inquisition a generation or two earlier? Why did he write that "the holy spirit works in Christians, Jews, Moors . . ." and "All people receive their astronomy from the Jews"?

There were name changes: Colombo . . . Colomo . . . Colom . . . Colón . . .

It was in Portugal, before going to Spain, that he married Doña Felipa, and engendered his first son, Diego. But "wanting to go on sailing, he left his wife there."

Why does he seem so much the preincarnation of Don Quixote, who also believed in islands, who had adventure, and who set such great store by the titles and trappings of his status? (Columbus: ". . . that he should be honored and armed a Knight with golden spurs.")

He would discover islands where he would be secure against the threat that his uncertain heritage might come to light.

Or was he—for all the mysteries, the obfuscations, the clouds of black ink that, like the squid, he oozed out around the facts of his life—simply put, an outrageous, wholesale liar?

Two

It was said that Isabella "meant to finance the expedition herself by drawing on the royal treasury." Her funds, generally depleted, were perhaps enriched now by Moorish plunder, and by property and money confiscated by the Inquisition.

There was also a substantial loan (over a million *maravedis*), secured by one Luis de Santángel, keeper of accounts of the royal household, who borrowed from the *Santa Hermandad,* the Secret Police.

De Santángel imposed a fine on the citizens of the town of Palos, ordering them to build, equip, and man two caravels, at their own expense.

The fine, perhaps, was for smuggling.

Three

Who was he? Where did he come from? What went on in his head?

Was he, in truth, Don Quixote?

"He saw visions and he heard voices." And he wrote that "St. Peter, when he jumped into the sea, walked on it as long as his faith was firm."

"The [Portuguese] King, as he observed this *Christovoa Colom* to be a big talker and boastful in setting forth his accomplishments, and full of fancy imagination with his Isle Cypango than certain whereof he spoke, gave him small credit."

". . . they all considered the words of *Christovoa Colom* as vain, simply founded on imagination . . ."

The Spanish cosmographers "judged his promises and offers were impossible and vain . . . and that it was all air and there was no reason in it . . ."

". . . the said Admiral always went beyond the bounds of truth . . ."

But Isabella—with insanity touching both her mother and her daughter—was just strange enough to listen . . .

On several voyages, he deceived his crews, hoarded the charts, misled even the sovereigns as to where and how far he was sailing. He claimed to have developed a "mode of reckoning derived from astronomy which . . . resembles a prophetic vision."

When Ovando set sail, against Columbus's advice, and all but three or four of his twenty-eight ships went down in a storm, Columbus was accused of raising the tempest himself, by magic act . . .

Columbus:

"St. Augustine says that the end of this world is to come in the seventh millenary of years from its creation . . . there are only lacking 155 years to complete the 7000, in which year the world must end."

. . . condoning and justifying all brutalities against the Indians, as extreme haste must be made to convert the heathen . . .

Did he once chop the paws off a wild monkey, and throw them to a wild pig, to enjoy the battle between the two?

Four

When the flotilla set sail on the first voyage the ships were manned largely by experienced seamen, with a lesser number of jailbirds.

There were no women. Women were bad luck on the ocean.

And no priests.

On later voyages, the more extensive use of jailbirds was proposed—when it was determined that the Indians could not be made to work. Convicted criminals would be reprieved if they agreed to settle in Española. Excluded from this opportunity were those found guilty of:

> heresy
> lèse majesté
> treason
> counterfeiting of coinage
> and sodomy

Five

Columbus:

"The Paradise on Earth is a pleasant place, situated in certain regions of the Orient, at a long distance by land and by sea from our inherited world. It rises so high that it touches the lunar sphere . . ."

"I always read that the world, land and water, was spherical . . . Now I observed so much divergence, that I began to hold different views about the world and I found that it was not round . . . but pear-shaped, round except where it has a nipple, for there it is taller, as if one had a round ball and, on one side, it should be like a woman's breast, and this nipple part is the highest and closest to heaven . . ."

"There is a spring in Paradise which waters the Garden of Delights and which splays into four rivers."

"We reached the latter island near a large mountain which seemed almost to reach heaven, and in the centre of that mountain there was a peak which was much higher than all the rest of the mountain, and from which many streams flowed in different directions, especially toward the direction in which we lay. At a distance of three leagues a waterfall appeared . . . which precipitated from such a high point that it seemed to fall from heaven."

"I think the earthly paradise lies here, which no one can enter but by God's permission."

On the first voyage, early in the return, Columbus set out to discover the island of Matinino, inhabited, as the Indians told him, only by women.

"In Cariay and the neighboring country there are great enchanters of a very fearful character . . . When I arrived they sent me immediately two girls very showily dressed; the oldest could not be more than eleven years of age, and the other seven, and both exhibited so much immodesty that more could not be expected from public women . . ."

". . . the women have very pretty bodies, and they were the first to bring what they had . . ."

"On the previous day . . . he saw three mermaids, which rose well out of the sea."

In the Gulf of Paria, he observed the tiny oysters clinging to the mangrove roots, the oyster shells open, to catch from the leaves above, dewdrops that engender pearls.

Six

Pope Alexander VI:

"Alexander, bishop, servant of the servants of God, to the illustrious sovereigns, our very dear son in Christ, Ferdinand, king, and our very dear daughter in Christ, Isabella, queen, of Castile, Leon, Aragon, and Granada, health and apostolic benediction. Among other works well pleasing to the Divine Majesty and cherished of our heart, this assuredly ranks highest, that in our times especially the Catholic faith and the Christian religion be exalted and everywhere increased and spread, that the health of souls be cared for and that barbarous nations be overthrown and brought to the faith itself."

Father Ascensión:

"This will be discovering here another world, to the end that in all of it may be preached the Holy Gospel, and the conversation undertaken of many souls throughout its whole extent who live without religion or knowledge of the true God or of his most sacred law. Since all have been ransomed by the most precious blood of Our Redeemer and Lord Jesus Christ, it is a very great pity that they should be condemned for want of this light and the knowledge of the truth. May His Most Holy Majesty, for He created them and died for them, grant that to so many and various nations of lands so remote and as yet undiscovered, knowledge be given of His most holy law, that they may receive and believe it, and that by means of holy baptism their souls may be saved, and that they may enjoy it."

". . . the Spaniards can go on settling other districts and places suitable for effecting the conversion of souls, and affording them profits and advantages; for if the Spaniard does not see any advantage he will not be moved to do good, and these souls will perish without remedy if it is understood that no profit will be drawn from going there. But if they are lured by self-interest they will go on discovering new lands every day, so much, indeed, that it will be necessary to keep them in check . . ."

Columbus:

"There are many spices, and great mines of gold and other metals."

"Thus the eternal God, our Lord, gives victory to those who follow His way over apparent impossibilities."

On the Indians: "Christendom shall make good business with them."

Las Casas:

"What good tidings all over the land, and such a good show of Christian gentility and goodness."

Seven

Columbus's mission was "to reduce to the obedience of their Highnesses savage and warlike peoples who live in mountains and in the wilderness."

And yet the Sovereigns' express command, for the second voyage, was that the Indians were to be treated "well and lovingly."

He found the natives to be "well-built, with good bodies and handsome features . . . They do not bear arms, and do not know them . . ."

". . . the lands of the country cannot be more beautiful . . . nor the men more cowardly . . ."

"I did not find, as some of us had expected, any cannibals among them, but on the contrary, men of great deference and kindness."

". . . wonderfully timorous . . ."

". . . timid beyond cure . . ."

"With fifty men we could subjugate them all . . ."

"As soon as I arrived in the Indies, on the first island which I found, I took some of the natives by force . . ."

> (Las Casas: ". . . as if indeed it was necessary to instill hatred before preaching the Gospel!")

Isabella issued a slave-raiding license: "To take Indian men and women for slaves, without harming them . . . to take them as nearly as possible with their consent; and in the same manner he may take monsters and animals of any kind . . ."

Columbus sent five hundred slaves to Castile, "a cargo of human cattle." Many of them died of cold.

Las Casas:

". . . our work was to exasperate, ravage, kill, mangle and destroy . . ."

". . . each generation of men has a time appointed for its calling."

"It was a general rule among Spaniards to be cruel; not just cruel, but extraordinarily cruel so that harsh and bitter treatment would prevent Indians from daring to think of themselves as human beings or having a minute to think at all. So they would cut an Indian's hands and leave them dangling by a shred of skin and they would send them on, saying, 'Go now, spread your news to your chiefs.' They would test their swords and their manly strength on captured Indians and place bets on their slicing off of heads or the cutting of bodies in half with one blow."

In Haiti, every Indian, fourteen or older, was ordered to bring in a certain amount of gold every three months. But there were no gold fields, no mines, only dust to be gathered in the streams. Natives who failed to fill their quota had their hands cut off, or they were hunted down with dogs and killed.

Later, mines were opened: ". . . mountains are stripped from top to bottom and bottom to top a thousand times; they dig, split rocks, move stones, and carry dirt on their backs to wash it in the rivers . . ."

After six or eight months in the mines, the men were sent home where their wives had continued to work the soil alone. Husbands and wives— both—were too tired to procreate.

The naked Indians fought back, "with no other shields than their bellies."

Las Casas:
"The Spaniards found pleasure in inventing all kinds of odd cruelties, the more cruel the better, with which to spill human blood. They built a long gibbet, low enough for the toes to touch the ground and prevent strangling, and hanged thirteen of them at a time in honor of Christ Our Savior and the twelve Apostles."

> (". . . each generation has a time appointed for its calling.")

"When the Indians were thus still alive and hanging, the Spaniards tested their strength and their blades against them, ripping chests open with one blow and exposing entrails . . ."

> (". . . each generation . . .")

"Then, straw was wrapped around their torn bodies and they were burned alive . . . My eyes have seen these acts so foreign to human nature, and now I tremble as I write, not believing them myself, afraid that I was dreaming."

(One, being burned at the stake, refused baptism for fear that in heaven he would find more Christians there.)

Las Casas, on Columbus:
"His was a crafty ignorance, if indeed it was ignorance and not greed."

The Indians "fled to avoid . . . the ferocious and wild condition of the Spaniards . . ."
". . . they rushed in all directions like lunatics, women dropping and abandoning infants in the rush, running for miles without stopping, fleeing across mountains and rivers."

Masses of the natives created their own final mode of escape: ingestions of casava poison.

October 1992

In this month in which Christopher Columbus is being celebrated for the 500th time, Sherman Alexie, who has just
graduated from college, is celebrating the publication of his
very first book. He, too, in this year, has something to say
about Columbus. But it is something he will say under the
protection of the term "fiction."

Captivity

He (my captor) gave me a biscuit, which I put in my pocket, and not daring to eat it, buried it under a log, fearing he had put something in it to make me love him.

FROM THE NARRATIVE OF MRS. MARY ROWLANDSON,
WHO WAS TAKEN CAPTIVE WHEN THE WAMPANOAG
DESTROYED LANCASTER, MASSACHUSETTS, IN 1676.

1

When I tell you this story, remember it may change: the reservation recalls the white girl with no name or a name which refuses memory. October she filled the reservation school, this new white girl, daughter of a BIA official or doctor in the Indian Health Services Clinic. Captive, somehow afraid of the black hair and flat noses of the Indian children who rose, one by one, shouting their names aloud. She ran from the room, is still running, waving her arms wildly at real and imagined enemies. Was she looking toward the future? Was she afraid of loving all of us?

2

All of us heard the explosion when the two cars collided on the reservation road. Five Indians died in the first car; four Indians died in the second. The only survivor was a white woman from Springdale who couldn't remember her name.

3

I remember your name, Mary Rowlandson. I think of you now, how necessary you have become. Can you hear me, telling this story within uneasy
boundaries, changing you into a woman leaning against a wall beneath a
HANDICAPPED PARKING ONLY sign, arrow pointing down directly
at you? Nothing changes, neither of us knows exactly where to stand and
measure the beginning of our lives. Was it 1676 or 1976 or 1776 or yesterday when the Indian held you tight in his dark arms and promised you
nothing but the sound of his voice? September, Mary Rowlandson, it was
September when you visited the reservation grade school. The speech ther-
apist who tore the Indian boy from his classroom, kissed him on the lips,
gave him the words which echoed treaty: *He thrusts his fists against the posts
but still insists he sees the ghosts.* Everything changes. Both of us force the
sibilant, in the language of the enemy.

4

Language of the enemy: *heavy lightness,* house insurance, *serious vanity,*
safe-deposit box, *feather of lead,* sandwich man, *bright smoke,* second-guess,
sick health, shell game, *still-waking sleep,* forgiveness.

5

How much longer can we forgive each other? Let's say I am the fancydancer
and every step is equal to a drum beat, this sepia photograph of you and me
staring into the West of our possibilities. For now, you are wearing the cal-
ico dress that covers your ankles and wrists and I'm wearing a bone vest
wrapped around a cotton shirt, my hair unbraided and unafraid. This
must be 1876 but no, it is now, August, and this photograph will change the
story. Remember: I am not the fancydancer, am not the fancydancer, not
the fancydancer, the fancydancer, fancydancer.

6

Fancydance through the tall grass, young man, over broken glass, past
Crowshoe's Gas Station where you can buy an Indian in a Bottle. "How do

you fit that beer-belly in there?" asks a white tourist. "We do it," I tell her, "piece by piece."

7

Piece by piece, I reassemble the house where I was born, but there is a hole in the wall where there was none before. "What is this?" I ask my mother. "It's your sister," she answers. "You mean my sister made that hole?" "No," she says. "That hole in the wall is your sister." For weeks, I searched our architecture, studied the walls for imperfections. Listen: imagination is all we have as defense against capture and its inevitable changes.

8

I have changed my mind. In this story there are words fancydancing in the in-between, between then and now, between walls in the alley behind the Tribal Café where Indian boys smoke old cigarettes at halftime of the all-Indian basketball game. Mary Rowlandson, it's true, isn't it? Tobacco and sugar are the best weapons.

9

The best weapons are the stories and every time the story is told, something changes. Every time the story is retold, something changes. There are no photographs, nothing to be introduced as evidence. The 20th century overtook the reservation in 1976, but there we were, stuck in 1975. Do you remember that white boy then, who spent the summer on the reservation? I don't know how he arrived. Did his father pilot a DC-10 forced to make an emergency landing in the Trading Post parking lot? Did the BIA Forestry man find him frozen in amber? Did Irene sweep him up from the floor of a telephone booth? Lester FallsApart says he himself drank and half-swallowed the white boy out of a bottle of Annie Green Springs wine and spat him out whole into the dust. The nightwatchman at the Midnight Mine tells us he caught the white boy chewing uranium. Do you remember that white boy dove naked into Benjamin Lake? He wore the same Levi's hung low on the hips, a red bandanna wrapped around his head. He tugged at his blond hair, yes, telling us "It will grow, I promise." We beat

him often, specifically. Arnold broke the white boy's nose with a snowball
he had saved, frozen and hidden in the fridge since March. It was July 4th
when we kidnapped him and kept him captive in a chicken coop for hours.
We spat and pissed on him through the wire; Seymour shot him twice with
a pellet gun. That white boy fell backward into the nests, crushed eggs,
splintered wood, kicked chickens blindly. I was the first to stop laughing
when the white boy started digging into the dirt, shit, the past, looking for
somewhere to hide. We did not make him any promises. He was all we
had left.

10

All we had left was held captive here on the reservation, Mary Rowlandson,
and I saw you there chewing salmon strips in the corner, hiding from all the
Indians. Did you see him, Mary Rowlandson, the Indian man who has
haunted your waking for 300 years, who left you alone sipping coffee in the
reservation 7-11? I saw you there, again, as I walked home from the bar,
grinning to the stars, but all you could do was wave from the window and
mouth the eternal question: *How?*

11

How do you open a tin can without a sharp-edged dream? How do you
sleep in your post office box using junk mail for blankets? How do you see
past the iron bars someone painted on your U.S. government glasses? How
do you stop a reservation tsunami before it's too late?

12

It's too late, Mary Rowlandson, for us to sit together and dig up the past
you buried under a log, salvage whatever else you had left behind. What do
you want? I cannot say, "I love you. I miss you." June, Mary Rowlandson,
the water is gone and my cousins are eating Lysol sandwiches. They don't
need you, will never search for you in the ash after your house has burned
to the ground one more time. It's over. That's all you can depend on.

13

All we can depend on are the slow-motion replays of our lives. Frame 1: Lester reaches for the next beer. Frame 2: He pulls it to his face by memory, drinks it like a 20th-century vision. Frame 3: He tells a joke, sings another song: *Well, they sent me off to boarding school and made me learn the white man's rules.*

14

White man's rules: all of us must follow them, must remember the name of the officer who arrested us for running when the sign said DON'T WALK. It's the language of the enemy. There is no forgiveness for fancydancing on WET CEMENT. Before we move into the HUD house, we must build dreams from scratch, piece by piece, because SOME ASSEMBLY IS RE-QUIRED. Remember to insert CORRECT CHANGE ONLY when you choose the best weapons, the stories which measure all we have left. How do you know whether to use the IN or OUT door to escape? But it's too late to go now, our four-door visions have been towed from a NO PARK-ING ZONE. Leonard tells me he's waiting for the bus to the dark side of the moon, or Oz, or the interior of a drum. I load up my pockets with all my possessions and wait with him. That Greyhound leaves at 3 A.M. That's all we can depend on.

1993

Imagine, in this year, that you must contact an essayist. Imagine, for some reason, that you're desperate. What you'd like is a list of all the writers who are classified as such, a geographical breakdown of where they tend to congregate, a specific address at which to reach your favorite. Where would you turn? If you are living this year in the United States, your most logical choice would be a newly published resource entitled *The Directory of American Writers*—the most comprehensive resource of its kind, say the editors, a group of people committed to "connecting the literary community." You open up the book: *Over 7,000 listings!* the preface exclaims. Wow! you say. So you begin flipping through the book to search for some of your favorite essayists: John McPhee, let's say. But then, Oh, you tell yourself, when his name doesn't appear. Perhaps they've overlooked him. So you start flipping through the book for another essayist you love. But, Hmmm, you start thinking, when that name also doesn't appear. Well then what about _____? Or how about _____? Then surely _____ is here! You eventually realize however that no essayist who primarily is known as such can be found in this directory of the literary community because this directory of the literary community only includes listings of poets, fiction writers, and "performance poets." "To be eligible for listing in the directory you must have at least 12 publishing credits," the application for inclusion in the directory explains:

These however do not count toward points for listing: work you have edited; writing for children; publications of work in vanity presses; *any work of nonfiction, including essays, criticism, and creative nonfiction* [emphasis mine].

Therefore, were this directory to hypothetically consider writers from around the world and from all literary time, a few of those writers who would still not meet the editors' criteria for inclusion are Plato, Herodotus, Thucydides, Heraclitus, Seneca, Suetonius, St. Augustine, Yoshida Kenko, Sei Shōnagon, Christine de Pisan, Francis Bacon, Michel de Montaigne, Richard Steele, Blaise Pascal, Daniel Defoe, Charles Lamb, Samuel Johnson, Alex de Tocqueville, Meriwether Lewis, William Hazlitt, Henry David Thoreau, John Ruskin, Simone Weil, James Baldwin, H. L. Mencken, Rachel Carson, George Orwell, James Thurber, Wendell Berry, Freya Stark, Roland Barthes, Marguerite Duras, John Hersey, Primo Levi, Marguerite Yourcenar, E. B. White, Anaïs Nin, Truman Capote, Edward Abbey, Loren Eisley, Elizabeth Hardwick, Lewis Thomas, Hélène Cixous, N. Scott Momaday, Tom Wolfe, Wole Soyinka, Lawrence Weschler, Oliver Sacks, Terry Tempest Williams, Maxine Hong Kingston, Lewis Hyde, Ted Conover, Gloria Anzaldua, Richard Selzer, Umberto Eco, Susan Orlean, Bernard Cooper, Edward Hoagland, Pico Iyer, Cynthia Ozick, Joseph Epstein, David Quammen, Gretel Ehrlich . . .

SUSAN GRIFFIN

Red Shoes

The imprisonment which was at one and the same time understood as the imprisonment of the female mind has a larger boundary, and that is the shape of thought itself within Western civilization.

It is an early memory. Red shoes. Leather straps crisscrossing. The kind any child covets. That color I wanted with the hot desire of a child.

On one level, one thinks simply of the conditions of imprisonment which affected, for instance, the intellectual life of George Sand. How it was necessary for her to dress like a man in order to attend the theater with her friends. She wanted to be in the section just beneath the stage, and women were not allowed in that section. This transgression was a necessary one if she was going to, as she did, enter the realm of public discourse within her mind.

When was it I first heard the title of the film, The Red Shoes? *My older sister had seen it. Did she speak of it with my mother? I must have overheard it. I was often excluded from such conversations. I was too young. And my mother preferred my sister.*

The female world, bounded as it is, contains, as does any world, rich layers of meaning. It is not simply that a woman must stay within this world but that signification itself is kept away from it.

Whatever lies within the confines of the feminine province is defined *sui generis* as either trivial or obscene (as in housework, or lovemaking) and as such not fit for public discourse.

I was, I suppose, shopping with my grandmother in the department store with the X-ray machine that made a green picture of the bones in my feet. I have the vague feeling my grandmother finds red impractical.

In this light it is no wonder that the novel became a literary form so widely practiced by women, a genre in some of its popular manifestations, and in some phases of its development, dominated by women. The novel is allowed to describe what we think of as the private sphere of life, which is also the sphere of life given over to women. And is it any wonder that so many "classic" novels written by men have a heroine at the center of the story? *Anna Karenina. Madame Bovary.*

In my mind, as I remember my grandmother, I can feel the shape of her larger body next to mine. Her elbows are wrinkled in a way that fascinated me. The flesh on her forearms hangs in beautiful white lobes, not so different than the lobes of her breasts.

Why is it the novel can enter the private sphere in a way, for instance, that the essay cannot? One answer presents itself immediately. The novel is fiction. It is not true. It exists in an epistemological category unto itself. Yes, it is lifelike, it evokes or even, as is said metaphorically, creates realities; still the reality of fiction is not to be confused with *reality.*

I cannot remember whether or not my grandmother let me have those shoes. Despite her somberness in my presence, a mouth habitually turned down, and her air of dutiful weariness at having to raise a child at her advanced age, she has another side. I am twenty-one years old when she pulls a black silk robe out of a closet where she has kept it for years and gives it to me.

In the public imagination the feminine world has the same flavor as a fictional world. It is present but not entirely real. Men enter the home in the evening, as darkness descends. They may eat there, play with the children, make love, confess certain feelings hidden during the day to their wives, sleep, dream, but all that fades away into near obscurity with the dawn when they must emerge again into the world of work.

Perhaps she did buy me those red shoes. I can see them now in my closet which was also her second closet, the closet of the black silk robe, the place where she kept her rarer treasures, her two fur coats, worn only on the more special occasions . . . and, am I embellishing here, her sweater with the rhinestones on it, or were they pearls? Whenever I wore those red shoes, which was as often as I could, they gave me a secret sustenance, the liberatory feeling of a rebellion conspired between my grandmother and me.

Secrets within the private life are like obscurities within an obscurity. Private life is *private,* walled off, unseen, unscrutinized. To write a history of the private life is a recent departure, an ingenuous idea, and has an erotic edge, not only because of the sexuality which is part of private life, but because in doing so one penetrates a contained world. The secret alcoholism or indiscretion or sexual abuse within a family history is, being an obscurity inside an essentially obscure world, seemingly less real than the rest of private life, and has even more the flavor of fiction. At the same time the novel, being fiction, is congruous with this world. It is formed to the contours of the way we hold the private life in our minds.

When I put the red shoes on it was not only on special occasions. I wore them even on ordinary days. They followed me into a child's world, one that no adult ever saw. If I took them off to play in the sand or the mud, they witnessed me from the sidelines and kept my secrets.

In fiction the whole life of the body, of sensuality, is opened to view. The form of the novel or the short story and even more of the poem allows the reader to enter imagined experience as if within a body. Pain, pleasure, color, taste, sound, smells are evoked. The literary devices of fiction are meant to admit this material world.

I wore them walking the twelve blocks I regularly walked to school. The shoes became so much a part of me that I forgot I was wearing them. I let my mind wander. I looked into the windows of the houses along the way and imagined the lives of the inhabitants.

In depicting the sensuality of the world and our bodily experience of it, fiction is also portraying the mind itself, which always thinks in a sensual

context. Without the body, it is impossible to conceive of thought exist-
ing. Yet the central trope of our intellectual heritage is of a transcendent,
disembodied mind. As the essay moved further away from meditation and
reflection, further from what we call "confessions" and closer to science,
with its claim of objectivity, it began more and more to resemble this celes-
tially detached brain. At a fairly recent point in the history of the essay it
became a radical act to use the pronoun "I."

*Perhaps she did not buy me the red shoes. But even if that were true, the fact is
she might have.*

The idea of an entirely autonomous mind has a subtext, and that is the desire for unlimited freedom from natural limitations.

*In the lay and ken of her soul, this was a possibility. As I imagine that she gave
me the shoes, which perhaps she did, am I bringing part of her soul into being?*

And yet limitations are a necessary predisposition for any existence, including the existence of something we suppose to be abstract and cerebral, like
the essay. And when the essay is built on the purposeful "forgetting" of the
body, these limitations paradoxically grow greater. The form of the essay
circumscribes imagination. At its edges many other imagined possibilities
are hovering.

*Was this the reason for her attachment to the peach-colored bedspreads? They
covered the single beds where she and my grandfather slept. They had a luxuriant feel, suggesting an erotic dimension that otherwise was absent in her house.*

To speak of housework, or childbirth, or sexuality, or rape in the form of
the essay represents, in each instance, a crumbling of the fortifications
erected by a masculine world against the feminine world. But still, in each
instance, the sensual reality of these phenomena is stripped away so that
they may enter public discourse. And when these subjects are made into
sciences, they gain a certain legitimacy. Though it is often marginal, as in
Home Economics.

Or perhaps not entirely absent, but never more open, never so frank, as in those bedspreads. They were luminously sexual, the sort of bedcover Mae West might have had. Of course we never spoke of this quality. It could never be spoken, only suggested.

One might think that, because fiction brings one into a fully sensual world, the subject matter would be more rigidly policed. But this is not the case. The idea that fiction is untrue allows it a greater radius. I am thinking of Virginia Woolf's *Orlando*. At the time of its publication, it was her most popular novel. What she suggested about the malleability of gender was far more palatable in this form than in her essays, which treated the subject, by comparison, more conservatively.

The bedspreads were symbolic of many aspirations. She cosseted a desire to be socially elevated. In her mind we were finer than all our neighbors, though I, with the working-class language of my father, and my childish ignorance of manners, constantly endangered our superiority.

Just as the reader is protected by the supposition that fiction is not true, so too the author of fiction is shielded by this idea. Stories can be told that otherwise could not. But what is even more interesting is that, because fiction evokes particular social and natural worlds in their entirety, many possible stories exist inside the narrative world implicitly, without being explicitly described. They exist as possibilities or even likelihoods. A door to a barn is described. The narrator does not open that door. But it exists. And therefore the reader can imagine what is behind the door. The shape of circumstances in both *Jane Eyre* and *Wuthering Heights* suggest sexual abuse. One knows a racist political history has preceded *Their Eyes Were Watching God*. Neither writer nor reader needs to have delineated these events. The experience is part of the reality that is conjured.

I was fascinated by my grandparents' bedroom. The family story was that they slept in a double bed until one day my grandmother woke to find my grandfather's hands around her neck. He was having a dream. I am certain the significance of the dream was never discussed. Only thereafter they slept in single beds. I can't remember when I heard that story. Now it is as if I've always known it.

But unless one knows the history of racism or the configurations of sexual abuse, one does not see them in the narrative. They are felt perhaps, sensed, but not delineated, unnamed.

In this bedroom, they lived as if in separate worlds. I liked to watch my grandmother at her dressing table, trying on her earrings, her perfumes; I felt privileged to catch a glimpse of her fleshy body, her long pendulous breasts emerging from her corset. I preferred to look at my grandfather's desk when he was absent. What I loved best was his collection of fountain pens.

Reading a book about the documentation of torture in Brazil, I come across this distinction made by Thomas Nagel: ". . . the difference between knowledge and acknowledgment." He defines "acknowledgment" as "what happens to knowledge . . . when it becomes officially sanctioned, when it is made part of the public, cognitive scene." The essay, is a forum for the "public cognitive scene."

One evening when my grandparents went out and I was alone in the house I was pulled as if by a magnet to my grandfather's desk. I wanted to write with his fountain pen, which he never let me use in his presence. But the ink was heavy in it. Many times I had seen him shake it down to the nib, and so I did this, but not with the same experienced gesture. The ink sailed across the room in a sure trajectory toward my grandmother's satin bedspreads. Both covers were evenly spattered.

The integration of knowledge into public consciousness is more than a simple act of education. Perception itself in human consciousness is a social act. It is not only that knowledge and language are socially derived, but the moment of perception itself is prismatic. A single viewer will react differently when part of an audience. Certain responses are amplified. A small gesture made on the stage, whose meaning otherwise might be ignored or even forgotten, brings the whole theater to laughter. In the assembly of others, perception becomes a demarcated event. And, as it is said in the same book about torture in Brazil, the process of transforming knowledge into public acknowledgment is also "sacramental."

I tried to wash the spots out but only made them worse. I can feel the terror of discovery now. It is hot under my skin. I would have preferred the discovery to be private, between my grandmother and me. I was rarely physically punished. But she beat me this once, with a belt. My father and grandfather were in the next room, and I was angry at them, not because they failed to intervene but because they were witnesses at all.

Sitting in the public gardens that are close to my house, I hear a white-haired woman exclaim to her friend, "The color is so intense!" Their bent bodies are as if curled together around a rosebush. The gardens are tiered and shaped like an amphitheater and so her voice travels easily. It is an extraordinary moment. All at once I am pulled into her passion and the brightness of the roses, and I begin to think how closely twinned in human consciousness are experience and the expression of experience. Something happens, indefinable yet palpable, as all of us in the garden are pulled simultaneously toward the sound of this old woman's voice and the color of the rose.

What was it I did not want them to know? That I had committed a crime and been found out? Or that I had become abject, shamed by the pain itself of my punishment? I had been in such abject states before, when, through the neglect of my mother, I was cold, frightened, perhaps hungry. Afterward I would feel a profound embarrassment. Writing of his experience of torture, Jean Amery recalls that "one never ceases to be amazed that all those things one may . . . call his soul, or his mind, or his consciousness, or his identity are destroyed when there is that cracking and splintering in the shoulder joints." It is this that is humiliating and, as Amery writes, "The shame of destruction cannot be erased."

After a time I leave my bench and walk up the tiers of the amphitheater. I hope to catch a glimpse of these two women. In my imagination I have already given the speaker a rich mystical life. But they are gone.

Such a memory is perhaps more easily recalled when it is only an abstraction of itself. One says, "I was tortured," or "I had a difficult childhood," without entering the experience in any concrete way, and thus also without reliving the feeling of destruction. But sensuality and abstraction are mutually dependent. In the mind, the capacities are inseparable.

I had wanted to see the old woman's face. There was something in the tone of her voice which led me to believe she had crossed that barrier which we so often erect against what is seen. Did she fall into the color of the rose?

Fiction, as opposed to the essay, is often viewed as an escape from reality. The storyteller can make up a world and has no moral reason to stay loyal to this one. Shame and suffering can be left at the boundaries of this imagined world.

I imagined the color of the rose to be red. As I entered the garden I saw a rose whose deep burgundy color drew me. This red is replete with associations. Some of them wonderful. Some terrible.

But any really good story includes both pain and pleasure, sorrow and joy, in infinite complexities. And any imagined world, if it is to be believed, will soon be replete with its own requirements, consequences, and limitations, just like this world.

Falling into that color, was she not also falling into herself, as I fall into myself now, my own memories of red, and my own redness? For me this is still a color heavy with menses and childbirth, with violence and loss. But in her voice I hear something different. All that, yes, but an added dimension, a kind of lightness, an aspect of this color that comes to one perhaps only in old age.

The freedom that fiction affords is a freedom not from concrete limitations but from the limitations on the mind imposed by ideas. This is a secret liberation, the same liberation given by direct experience. For the limits of physical reality are not the same, nor as distinct in experience as the limitations described in abstraction. As John Berger writes in his long work on the peasants of Alpine France, those who live on the land "never suppose that the advance of knowledge reduces the extent of the unknown."

It is easy for me to imagine beginning to perceive another dimension of color in old age. Imagining this, I am pulled toward a future I have never until now predicted.

The extent of the unknown borders all language. One's relationship with it is erotic. One has a passion to know. But one can never entirely know what is other. Telling a story, no matter how much you know, you are very soon pulled into unexplored territory. Even the familiar is filled with unexpected blank spaces. The usual Sunday drive is all of a sudden a wild ride into terra incognita. You are glad to be going, but there is a vague feeling of discomfort. Where are you?

This is not a dimension of color acknowledged in our culture. Still, it exists within the culture. It has been painted. I am thinking of the work of Helen Frankenthaler. Color as she paints it takes a different place in the mind. Or rather one might say the mind takes place in the color. One is infused with it, the same way one is taken in by water, swallowed.

I am thinking of a Sunday drive with my grandparents. We went to the country place of friends. They had an orchard filled with peach trees. I have remembered it all of my life. The vividness of the peaches I pulled from the trees. The sharply sweet taste in my mouth, nothing like store-bought fruit.

Is this experience of color had by some in old age, and others who are artists, a return to an earlier state of mind, the beginner's mind of infancy? To a perception untutored, not yet muted by the mediating presence of language?

Now as I remember that peach, it is a taste indistinguishable from the shapes of trees, the tall grass surrounding them, the summer heat, the breeze blowing, the sight of my grandmother in a white blouse standing on the ladder. And was there a kitten, or am I confusing the memory of my great-grandmother's garden, and her kitten, with this one?

There are of course two experiences of the red color of that rose. One is acknowledged. It is the social red, the historical red, the red, as Merleau Ponty writes, "that is a punctuation in the field of red things." The other red is unacknowledged, it exists in an exiled region of consciousness. But can they be separated, these two reds? And what of the tension one feels between experience and the forms experience assumes in the imagination? One feels it while writing. The words are not quite right. They betray. Lie a little. Fail to make a perfect fit. Take off in another direction entirely on their own.

Of course I am embellishing. I doubt that my grandmother wore white. It is the color one is supposed to wear if one is a woman in a pastoral setting.

In recent critical discourse, the awareness that in the mind experience is replaced by a construction of experience has led to a despair of the possibility of describing reality. But in the sway of this despair, how do you point out a lie? How do you answer the contention that torture in Brazil never took place?

That day in the country I breathed in a certain state of mind. One that I never had before with such force. Later, when I encountered the same mood in certain paintings, certain myths, I mixed not only my memory but also my hope with these images.

I love that moment in writing when I know that language falls short. There is something more there. A larger body. Even by the failure of words I begin to detect its dimensions. As I work the prose, shift the verbs, look for new adjectives, a different rhythm, syntax, something new begins to come to the surface.

Looking back, I see a maze of associations I must have had with the color red. I know my mother also loved the color red. That she would have bought me those shoes unhesitatingly. That she wore bright red lipstick. That she used red henna on her dark brown hair. But I cannot remember if I thought of her that day I chose red shoes.

The manner of telling lies in public life is seldom direct any longer. Far more pervasive is the habit of ignoring an event of great significance. No official need argue that torture never existed. The torture is just never mentioned. No one goes to trial. No torturer is ever named. A general, vague reference is made to troubling events of the past which must be changed. The actuality of the torture begins to fade from public consciousness.

She had faded away from my life. I could not remember her at all as my mother, but only as a woman I would visit, and whom I liked. Liked her in a way un-accountable even to myself.

Among those who were tortured or those who lost a loved one to torture there are two reactions. Some wish to evade the memory at all costs. Even though the memory is always there in some form, the pain of recall is too excruciating. Others live to tell the truth, or hear it told, and never tire of the telling. Of course, this is also too simple. For most of us, who have not been tortured, but experienced lesser pains and fears, the two impulses, to remember and tell, or to deny and forget, are side by side, and mixed together.

She was not easy to remember. It was not only neglect but abuse I suffered from her, a nastiness when she drank that came from her, as if from a demon, and which she herself would forget the next day.

I underline this passage in a recent issue of the *Paris Review,* in which Nathalie Sarraute is being interviewed. ". . . it seemed impossible to me," she said, "to write in the traditional forms. They seemed to have no access to what we experienced."

It seems possible to me then that even as a child I would be drawn to the color red, and yet also welcome my grandmother's common interdiction. It is certainly not a practical color. It won't get you anywhere.

Form can be transgressed for transgression's sake, but it can also be transgressed in an attempt to lean in a certain direction. It is a tropism toward the light and heat of another knowledge. And is this knowledge a memory?

Even so I cannot forget my desire to wear red. Even if my grandmother failed to buy me those shoes, years later as an adult woman I make up another story. I investigate the possibility that she did buy them. This is not an escape from my desire. It is instead an instigator of grief. I learn more fully what it is I have lost.

What we would wish to remember and what we might wish to forget are so intricately woven. Would we perhaps like to forget the life of the body, of the inner self, the private world, the world of children and childhood, of sucking and orgasm and death? This world which is a privacy within a privacy, protected by the double walls of house and skin, the conventional forms of expression and silence.

It is not the inner place of red I am seeking but the right to wear it outwardly. To wear it brazenly. Like a sequined dress. Or a scarlet letter.

There is then a hypnotic movement of the mind. We are used to it. We move back and forth from fiction to essay. From private to public. The arc of the pendulum has put us to sleep. But when the two poles meet, and the swaying stops, someone in us awakens.

It is one thing to love the color red and quite another to wear it openly. For my mother, wearing red was an act of defiance, a flag of another kind. Despite everything, she has won some territory for me, her daughter. I am like the daughter of Madame Bovary. The daughter of the fallen woman.

Bringing the public world of the essay and the inner world of fiction together, is something sacrificed? The high ground? Perspective? Distance? Or is it instead a posture of detachment that is renounced, a position of superiority? The position of one who is not immersed, who is unaffected, untouched? (This is, of course, the ultimate "fiction.")

And she, my mother, was the daughter of a respectable woman. But that is not the whole story. My grandmother had her own rebellion. She was a club woman. In the organization that was defined as auxiliary to my grandfather's club, she was made president. The proceedings of the club were secret. It was a secret realm of power, a fictional world, closed from that other world described as real life.

But there is always the other side of the coin. Behind the "superior" stance of the essay a quality of fragility is concealed. Theory pales when faced with the complex world of experience. Almost as soon as any idea reaches the page, another argument comes to mind. And while it is true that in the realm of ideas one can diminish the reality of everything outside these ideas, this is at best a temporary diminishment and one that always rebounds upon the self. For ultimately this diminishment requires a lessening of one's own knowledge, one's perceptual experience and, even, existence.

It was to these clubs that my grandmother wore her best finery. Treasures sequestered from her closet, the closet of the fur coats and the black silk robe, which was also my closet.

On the other hand, the realm of experience longs for more than knowledge. What goes on in the private body, in the inner quarters of the mind, cannot fully be redeemed, or even understood, without public acknowledgment. I am thinking of the tears of the victim who has finally heard her assailant convicted. In this case, paradoxically, it is not an imprisonment which takes place so much as a liberation from the imprisonment of an enforced privacy.

On the nights when the family could attend dinners or occasions given by my grandmother's club we were given little party favors and corsages. These had been made by the women in their secret sessions together. They contained bits of plastic fruit, sprays of pine, sparkles, all tied together with a bit of ribbon, most often red.

Is it possible to write in a form that is both immersed and distant, farseeing and swallowed? I am thinking now that this is what women have been attempting in the last decades. Not simply to enter the world of masculine discourse but to transform it with another kind of knowledge.

My grandmother has been dead for nearly two decades, and now my mother, who is old herself, has become respectable. Yet it is an astonishing moment for me, now, to recall these two women, and myself as a child, my red shoes, my mother's rebellion, my grandmother's secret wardrobe, the inner meanings of these, and the threads of meaning that reach out like tendrils in the larger landscape of mind.

If I rise from my desk, leave my pen and paper behind, walk to the door, the play of life before me and inside is suddenly dazzling in its intensity. Is it because I am thinking about consciousness that suddenly my experience sharpens? And when I return to write will I be able to reshape the form so that more of this world falls on the page? One can spend a whole life writing, I think to myself, and still hardly begin.

.

1994

I'm in college in this year, wondering why I don't like Classics anymore. Why I'm moving from a major in Latin and Greek to a major my school is calling "Independent": an amalgam of courses in rhetoric, poetry, religion, math, sculpture, journalism, the history of science. Some essays are bastards of the mind's indecision. Some essays are poured, molten, from a pure ore of information. In this way, admittedly, essays can sometimes appear no more literary than how-to books, the TV guide, classified or personal ads. There is a body of water some essays cross, though, over which they are transported from material to incantatory prose. James Agee's *Let Us Now Praise Famous Men*—an amalgam of journalism, poetry, music, and religion, and arguably the most important book-length essay from the mid-twentieth century—sold under 500 copies when it was first released. It fell out of print for over a decade, and its first substantially positive review didn't even appear until Agee was already dead. Indeed, the essay's innate intoxication with the mathematics of language—the multiplication of data, evidence, argument—distinguishes the genre as much as it taboos it. Its occasional focus on the list as a formal device, for example, eschews the comforting narratives of fiction, the intimate lyricism of poetry, and the sensational admissions of memoir, allowing its writers to make art out of the gossip and noise and rubble and minutia that often get overlooked in literature, fashioning instead a baudy, relentless, user-unfriendly art that is not comforting, not intimate, not sensational at all, but suspicious, messy, and stubornly unresolved. A former resident of a Trappist monastery, Alexander Theroux observed a vow of silence for two full years before beginning to pour himself out into essays.

ALEXANDER THEROUX

Black

Black is the Stygian well. As a color, truculent, scary, deep and inaccessible, it appears as a kind of abstract unindividualized deficiency, a bullying blot with a dangerous genius to it. There is no ingress. It absorbs and efficiently negates all color—in spite of the fact that Claude Monet once pronounced it of all colors the most beautiful—and, with the negative aura of nothing more than itself, suggests the sinister, dissolution and the permanence of disease, destruction and death. As Jan Morris says in (and of) *Fisher's Face,* reminding me of black, "One does not like that queer withdrawal into the expressionless." It is a color rightly described in the words of Henry James as portentously "the fate that waits for one, that dark doom that rides." It shocks us in the saccade of its sudden, inky prohibition but becomes as well in the inscrutable deepness of sleep the backdrop of all our dreams, and is sometimes even a comfort. (Dickens wrote, "Darkness was cheap, and Scrooge liked it.") With its syntax of hidden and unverifiable dimension, black has no indexicality but remains for the fat prohibitive hachuring of its drawn drapes a distinct code above all colors that, like espionage, legislates no place signs or particularity. In its relentless boldness, black is both atrociously present and atrabiliously absent.

No one would deny that the color black in its solid vagabondage—forgive the paradox—barges into things, and how its bigness booms. There is nevertheless relief, arguably, in seeing the ultimate value of "reality," and it is here, perhaps, that black allows for any continuing comfort.

Is that why Henry Matisse declared, "Black is the color of light," in spite of the fact that in color theory black is the absence of light? No pure colors in fact exist. Black and white, which are banished from chroma, at least in the minds of many if not most people, in the same way 0 and 1 were once denied the status of numbers—solid Aristotle long ago defined

319

number as an accumulation or "heap"—are each other's complements just as they remain each other's opposites. Is this too paradoxical? W. H. Auden wrote,

> *Where are the brigands*
> *most commonly to be found?*
> *Where boundaries converge.*

Weirdly, black *is:* darkness truly is our destiny at both ends of life. And yet it *is not:* "And those wonderful people out there in the dark," declares creepy, decaying, old, self-deluded Norma Desmond, when there is nothing out there at all. If an object absorbs all the wavelengths. We call it black, in the same way, for example, that a leaf that absorbs red light looks green to us or a stained-glass window that absorbs blue looks orange. And yet how can we legitimately call what is so full of other colors, whether white or black, *one* color? There is beyond its almost muscular intensity an irreconcilable force to the sheen of its light and shape of its lutulence, *ut tensio sic uis:* "as the tension, so the power." Black both is and it is not: disguises appear, we use aliases, and silently stand before that unabsorbing wall. The color black is the extreme, high-gravity, bombed-out, cave-blot color of Nox, Rahu, Quashee, Hela, Erebus, Sambo, Maevis and, deader than Dead Sea fruit with black ashes inside, it is the dark side of the Manichean alternative.

More often than not, it is with black as with Gustav Mahler's *Sixth Symphony,* which in its deep complexity, in Bruno Walter's phrase, "utters a decided 'No.'"

It is a color specifically inimical to white, including its thousand shades and tints and tones, along with what is in between. (Technically speaking, *tints* are colors that also contain white; *shades,* colors that contain black; and *tones* are those colors containing gray.) We call an object black if it has absorbed all wavelengths. Ordinary sunlight (or white light) is a mixture of light at all wavelengths—or all colors. A material that we perceive to be colored, of whatever color, has absorbed certain visible wavelengths and not others. Black and white, however, as polar extremes most significantly both embody what Paul Fussell, discussing the nature of enemies, refers to as "the *versus* habit," one thing opposed to another, not, as he explains, "with some Hegelian hope of synthesis involving a dissolution of both extremes (that would suggest a 'negotiated peace,' which is anathema), but with a sense that one of the poles embodies so wicked a deficiency or flaw or perversion that its total submission is called for." In this sharp dichotomy along the lines of "us" versus "them," black *is*—legendarily, has always been—precisely that wickedness. If white is known, safe, open and visible, black, unknown, hostile, closed and opaque, is the masked and unmediated alternative. Is it not clear in the confrontation of chess?

> *The board*
> *detains them until dawn in its hard*
> *compass: the hatred of two colors*

writes Jorge Luis Borges in "Chess."

It has an unholiness all about it, does black. "Your blood is rotten! Black as your sins!" cries Bela Lugosi in the film *Murders in the Rue Morgue* (1932). Doesn't the devout Moslem pray for the Kaaba's return to whiteness, which has turned black by the sins of men? Is not black the color of chaos, witchcraft, black magic, mad alchemy and the black arts? "Some negroes who believe in the Resurrection, think that they shall rise white," writes Sir Thomas Browne in *Christian Morals* (1716). And what of the darkness of bondage? The descent into hell? Evil? The word black is, more often than not, considered somewhat of a rude and insulting adjective, especially in English, serving as a dark, maledroit, prefixal name or term like "Dutch" and "psycho" and "gypsy." What puzzle can ever be worked of the spasmodic record of all it portends? Who in the essence of its ultimate reduction does not disappear? No animal or bird can see in total darkness. What is the color of the Congo? Boom-black! Jew's pitch! Nightmare! The bituminous side of life. Coal-black trolls. Demons. Bats. Moles. Fish alone can live in the unravellable inscrutableness of darkness. Coelacanths, blind as stones! According to the song "Think Pink" in *Funny Face* (1957) what should be done with black, blue and beige, remember? Banish the black, burn the blue and bury the beige! In Sant-Saëns's *Danse Macabre,* the white skeleton may terrifyingly dance in the darkness, but it is Death playing the violin.

After the ominous scriptural caveat "Whoever touches pitch will be defiled" (Sirach 12), the color black has never stood a chance. The rule was writ. Watch, for the night is coming.

Why speak of Cimmeria and unearthly mythologies? Darkness is right above us. Space itself is perpetual night, an atmosphere as black and haunted as the Apocalypse, totipalmate, hovering, suffoblanketing our entire and endless universe in which, crouching in total enigma, we lost inchlings squat in fear with headfuls of questions. How caught we are by its vastness. Midnight, according to Henry David Thoreau, is as unexplored as the depths of central Africa. "It is darker in the woods, even in common nights, than most suppose," he wrote in his diary at Walden Pond. "I frequently had to look up at the opening between the trees above the path in order to learn my route, and where there was no cart-path, to feel with my feet the faint track which I had worn." Old-timers in New Hampshire used to say of a winter's blackness, "This is a gripper of a night." But don't we know, by what we fear, what blackness is by the state of our natural condition? Black intimidates us. As the line from the old song "Lovin' Sam (The Sheik of Alabam)," tells us, "That's what it don't do nothin' else, 'cep."

On the other hand, what with any clarity defines whiteness? No, W. B. Yeats is correct: nothing can live at the poles (". . . there's no human life at the full or the dark"). No activity can be discovered there, no incarnations. They are gloomy waste places in the extreme, noncerebral and brainless and uninhabited, recalling for me the phrase by which Laurel and Hardy were once described: "two minds without a single thought." Orthochromatics shock us, before anything else, not only in the insolence of their extremes, but in the way they are a part of the same destitution. Schiller asserted, *"Verwandt sind sich alle starke Seele"*—"All strong spirits are related."

Black suggests grief, loss, melancholy and chic. It also connotes uniformity, impersonality, discipline and, often as the symbol of imperial order, jackbooted force and Prussian dominance. It is the color of Captain Mephisto and the dark lunar half of the Zoroastrian puzzle, with the kind of legendarily subterranean and inscrutable, praealtic malignity apposite to it that conjures up the sort of words on which writers like Edgar Allan Poe and Arthur Machen and H. P. Lovecraft constantly relied, like "unutterable," "hideous," "loathsome" and "appalling." It is the color of the contrarian, the critic and the crepe-hanger. It is airless, above all, hermeneutically closed, a larcenous color which in its many morphs of mourning and concomitant glumness is wholly subject, like André Gide's brooding immoralist, to "evasive and unaccountable moods." What could be worse than to be destitute of light and at the same time incapable of reflecting it? Blackness tends to envelop and overwhelm a person by dint of the largeness of volume in which it appears or is presented to one, in the very same way that the faster you walk the more your peripheral vision narrows. The Japanese adjective *usui* means not only thin as to width but light as to color. What other color in the spectrum comes at you point-blank and so directly yet without access? It is immoderate and almost autoerotic in what subrationally but somehow inexorably it suggests of possibility in the theatrical, untiring and even violent depth of its inscrutable vastness. The darkness of black is the part of its brooding deepness inviting dreams. The soul of the color harbors in its holophrastic enigma all sorts of moods, including deliberation and delay. Didn't Rodin tell us, "Slowness is beauty"? There is gravity in the batwing-black of its weight, pull and shocking hue. It is the very medium of stark, rigorous negativity, a storm in Zanzibar, the black cataracts of Stygia, Kanchenjunga and its ferocious clouds, black maelstroms, black goat tents, catafalques, of defeaturing and helmeting shadows, rebellion and revolt, the unforgiving, spectral grimace fetched up in beetling frowns—the color of Spartacus, Robespierre, Luther, Marat, Sam Adams, Marx and Lenin and Mao, intractable Prometheus and defiant Manfred.

> *From thy own heart I then did wring*
> *The black blood in its blackest spring*

Mystery doesn't so much surround the color black as it defines it. If color symbolizes the differentiated, the manifest, the affirmation of light— and is not God, as light, ultimately the source of color?—black in turn indicates primordial darkness, the non-manifest, renunciation, dissolution, gravity. Isn't it sadly apposite to the surreptitious ways of man himself? Didn't André Malraux write perspicaciously in *The Walnut Trees of Altenburg* "Essentially a man is what he hides"? Don't we placate by our reliance on black the very color with which we most identify? A wife in Africa to be fertile often wears a black hen on her back. In Algeria, black hens are sacrificed. A black fowl in certain folklores, if buried where caught, is alleged to cure epilepsy. In medieval France, the limbs of black animals when applied warm to the limbs of the body supposedly relieved rheumatism. Chimney sweeps wear black as a totem with the same credulity that bandits in Thailand and Myanmar adorn themselves with protective tattoos. In Ireland, England—even Vermont—black wool to many people provides a cure for earache, just as in Russia it cures jaundice. Who can explain why for Rimbaud in his *Vowels* the letter A was black? Or why Beethoven thought that the key of B minor was black? No, enigma is only another word for black. We spend half our lives in curved shadows and in the sleep of dark, occlusive nights that are as "sloeblack, slow, black, crow black," as Dylan Thomas said of his own Welsh ("fishing-boat-bobbing") sea, and that are every bit as vast and profoundly mysterious.

Wet *is* black. On a gray day, in neutral light, with a faint drizzle, stones of almost any stripe quite vividly take on colors. As Adrian Stokes writes, the passing of water on stone gives a sense of organic formation and erosion, so that the stone seems "alive." Robert Frost in "The Black Cottage" notes, "A front with just a door between two windows/Fresh painted by the shower a velvet black." Cactus spines shine strangely red or gold in deserts during wet weather, just as creosote bushes become olive after rain. Most things darken when wet. And brighten when dark. And glisten when bright. Even swimmers. Harry Cohn of Columbia Pictures even said of his swimming star, Esther Williams, "Dry, she ain't much. Wet, she's a star." Darkness is also depth. The depth of black is determined by the penetration of light, which equals color when light is translated to pigment. A color with great tinting power allows in a lot of light. The stronger a tint is, the more transparent it may seem. The darker the wampum, the more valuable it was in trade. Native Americans sought *dark* clam shells from the English colonists who were compelled to use wampum in trading with them. Fr. Joseph François Lafitau, the French Jesuit, wrote in *Manners of the American Savages* in 1724 that in his time the usual strand of a wampum belt was eleven strands of 180 beads or about 1,980 beads. Three dark (or six white) beads were roughly the equivalent of an English penny. Black water in its stillness goes deeper than the ramparts of Dis. Clouds loom high above us, ominous, profoundly dark, yet shifting. There is a "black wind," the *beshabar,* a dry melancholy wind that blows northeasterly out of the Caucasus. "Even such winds as these have their own merit in proper time and place," declares Robert Louis Stevenson on the chiaroscuro wrought by wind, observing how "pleasant [it is] to see them [the clouds] brandish great masses of shadow."

Black is a maelstrom oddly inviting, winding about, ever beckoning us. It is a veiled temple, emptiness, the Balzacian abyss, "the mystery for which we are all greedy." Just as darkness is depth, corners are hidden and dark and inaccessible. Black is not only recessed but even in its most noble aspects never far from surreption and stealth. Is that not why silos are round? (Silage *spoils* in corners.) Black can be sullen as distant thunder, heavy as lead, here starkly blunt, there preternaturally atraluminous. It is also unlived-in, too authentic, embowered, conspiratorial, rarely tender-hearted, cruelly cold, uninviting, casket-heavy, thick, explosive, mum and uncatalogably dead.

I think of Peggy Lee, singing the heartbreaking "Yesterday I Heard the Rain."

> *Out of doorways*
> *black umbrellas*
> *come to pursue me*
> *Faceless people*
> *as they passed*
> *were looking through me*
> *No one knew me*

Gene Lees, who wrote it, around 1962, told me it was a song about the loss of faith.

Black is the color without light, curtain dark, the portcullis-dropping color of loss, humility, grief and shame. Although to the human eye everything visible has a color, where color exists as an optical phenomenon, with a place already constructed for it in the human imagination, what can be said of the color black? *Is* black visible? Is it even a color? Or in some kind of grim, ruinous thunderclap and with a sort of infernal and ghastly force does it somehow smother color? Wholly destitute of color, is it the result of the absence of—or the total absorption of—light? It is patently not included among Andrew Lang's color fairy books. It is, oddly, *not* the color of blindness. "I can still make out certain colors. I can still see blue and green," said Jorge Luis Borges, who added, ironically, that the one color he did not see in his blindness was black, the color of night. He said, "I, who was accustomed to seeing in total darkness, was bothered for a long time at having to sleep in this world of mist, in the greenish or bluish mist, vaguely luminous, which is the world of the blind." Achromatopsy can involve partial or complete loss of color vision, where shades of gray are seen. (Robert Boyle spoke of this phenomenon as early as 1688.) To sufferers of such color deficiency, most foods appear disgusting—things like tomatoes appear black, for example. A patient of Dr. Oliver Sacks in 1987 became a victim of such dislocating misperception: "His wife's skin seemed to him to be rat-colored," Sacks observed, "and he could not bear to make love to her. His vision at night was so acute that he could read license plates from four blocks away. He became, in his own words, 'a night person.'"

Many World War II pilots had the singular experience of actually *seeing* black, when, during "blackouts," pulling out of a dive—they could often hear but not see—blood quickly drained out of their heads and flowed into their abdomen and legs, whereupon immediately they "sticked" high to gain altitude and usually came fully alert. There are no commercial airplanes painted black. It is far too inkily deathful and crepuscular a hue. Most modern aircraft, in fact, have bright white fuselage tops largely to reflect sunlight and reduce cabin temperatures. Flight data recorders, introduced in 1965 and dubbed "black boxes" by the media, in spite of the fact that they are invariably orange, traditionally share that nickname with any electronic "box of tricks," as I learned when, teaching at MIT, I found twenty examples so named.

Black, unlike white, has comparatively far less of what Francis Crick in *The Astonishing Hypothesis* calls "pop-out." Crick speaks of the "spotlight" of visual attention regarding the matter of human perception. "Outside the spotlight, information is processed less, or differently or not at all." In relation to what the Hungarian psychologist Bela Julesz calls "preattentive processing," boundaried objects—and colors—are targets, as it were. According to Monet, Cézanne habitually kept a black hat and white handkerchief next to a model in order to ascertain, to fix, to examine the two poles between which to establish his "values." Although white can be considered a highly "salient" color, black with its remorseless absorption, assimilating all wavelengths, utterly engorging light, lacks such definition. Any radiation that strikes a "black hole," for example, is utterly absorbed, never to reappear. "A material that absorbs all light that falls on it is black, which is how this particular beast received its ominous name," write Robert Hazen and James Trefil in *Science Matters.* You could say that the color black is an "unattended" event, as it were, with no "fixation point." It detargets a visual place by its very nature, blots things out, becomes the ultimate camouflage. It is, as a distractor, the color of grimness and good-night. The high dark fog in San Diego is called *El velo de la luz,* the veil that hides the light. F.D.R. had the metal parts of his leg braces ("ten pounds of steel," he once pointed out) painted deep black at the ankles, so as to escape detection against his black socks and shoes. "Gobos" (or "flats," "niggers" or "flags") are those large black cloth shades used on Hollywood sets to block out unwanted light from the camera lens in order to avoid halation and other undesirable effects. Black by definition scumbles objects.

Where is it half the time when we *can* discern it? Isn't rude, unforgiving black, impossibly covert like midnight and airport macadam and prelapsarian ooze, merely a spreading brainless giant without shape or contour? Contour, remember, almost always changes a color's tone. A square centimeter of blue, Matisse argued, is not the same as a square meter of the same blue. Beyond that even, the extent of the area changes the tone, as well. And isn't black in its fat merciless gravitation almost by definition arealess? Without boundaries, at least without easily perceptible boundaries, black can be comfortless for that. If it doesn't threaten us, it can make us feel uneasy. Purple, which comes between blue and ultraviolet, resembles black in this. Although we accept that ultraviolet exists, there is little evidence of it in our daily lives. (The best evidence we have is sunburns and cataracts, neither of which are close to purple.) Black is bottomless, autogyromotive and indirigible. Given Spinoza's observation that everything longs to endure in its being, doesn't black, more than any other struggling tinct, show an unpardoning tendency to be its own archetype, traveling, not like night, but with a kind of deep and unspellable horror reaching, stretching out, gathering, by way of everything from the monstrositous depth of children's formless nightmares to the gruesome hood-black anonymity of an executioner's reality, very like bony Death's harvesting hand?

I wonder, does black invoke what might be called "enemy-memory"? Or is black *itself* the enemy-memory? The witches on the back fence? The wreck into which we dive? Didn't Italo Calvino warn us, "The eye does not see things but images of things that mean other things"?

We tend to go wild in lunar light, in dark light, in the grip of the "night mysterious," as the song lyric goes. As Sky Masterson (Marlon Brando) tells Sarah Brown (Jean Simmons) in the film of the Broadway musical *Guys & Dolls,* "Sarah, I know the nighttime. I live in it. It does funny things to you." The question we pose of night, when we do not recoil from it, recalls for me certain lines from "Night Voices," a passionately personal poem which the young German pastor Dietrich Bonhoeffer wrote in 1943, two years before he was hanged by the Nazis in the Flossenburg concentration camp:

> *I sink myself into the depths of the dark.*
> *You night, full of outrage and evil,*
> *Make yourself known to me!*
> *Why and for how long will you try our patience?*
> *A deep and long silence;*
> *Then I hear the night bend down to me:*
> *"I am not dark; only guilt is dark!"*
>
> (TRANSLATED BY KEITH R. CRIM)

As a color, black goes in more than several directions. It is the color of Saturn; the number 8—if for Pythagoras numbers have designs, why can't they have colors?—and symbolizes in China the North, yin, winter, water, as well as the tortoise among the Four Spiritually Endowed Animals. Ek Xib Chac, the western spirit of the Mayan rain-god, Chac, was black. In the Kabbala, black carries a value of understanding, while black in heraldry stands for prudence and wisdom. In the world of alchemy it is the color of fermentation. To ancient Egyptians, black symbolized rebirth and resurrection. Many Native American tribes who held the color black to be a powerful talisman wore it as war paint in battle and for feathers, because it made the warrior invulnerable. It is the fathomless color of everything from Nazi parachutes to Hernando's Hideaway, "where all you see are silhouettes," to the famous lunar eclipse on August 27, 413 B.C., which contributed to the terrible defeat of the Athenians (soothsayers, seeing the portent, advised delay) at the hands of the Spartans under Gylippus. What metaphor of need or hope or aspiration cannot be constructed of the ongoing paradox that black attracts the sun? The whole idea recapitulates the entire historical phenomenon of opposites: of the Beauty and the Beast, of Venus and Vulcan, of Plus and Minus, of Innocence and Guilt, of Death and Transfiguration. Noctiluca, "she who shines by night," wonderful paradox, is a classical synonym for Diana. Among some of the wilder, more extravagant and overingenious schemes presented over time to deal with the threat of dangerous, destructive glaciers, such as blowing them up, towing them, etc., someone once seriously suggested painting them solid black so that they would melt under the hot sun!

Although no two color blacks are alike—some would argue that one can almost always find a subtle and misleading gradualness of tone in whatever two examples are set side by side—as a basic color black seems, more often than not, invariable, solid, like no other, *la verità effetuale della cosa,* the nature of fact, true, although it has as many adjectives as it has hues—jet, inky, ebony, coal, swart, pitch, smudge, livid, sloe, raven, sombre, charcoal, sooty, sable and crow, among others. Things get smutched, darkened, scorched, besmirched in a thousand ways. (Common black pigments like ivory, bone, lamp, vine and drop black all basically consist of carbon obtained by burning various materials.) It is a color that reminds me in its many odd morphs of what photographer Diane Arbus chose to call freaks, "the quiet minorities," for its hues seem never the same, seem never alike, and in their enigmatic somberness, like freaks, having passed their trials by fire—black is *the end*—are, as Arbus once said of her odd subjects, often ogled by people pleading for their own to be postponed. Isn't it strange that if you're "in the black," you are doing well, but if your "future looks black," things are bad? Its profundity is its mystery. The way of what the depth of black in going beyond deepness hides of, as well as defines in, the color reminds me of what Martin Heidegger once said of Carl Orff's musical language, *"Die Sprache der Sprache zur Sprache zu bringen,"* that it gives voice to the language of language. The color is an irrational and complicated achromatic, a tetrical, heat-eating, merciless, unforgiving and obdurate color, jayhawking you in a hundred ways, and in certain riddling guises it often reminds me of Frank Sinatra's "It Never Entered My Mind," a song Ol' Blue Eyes sings quite brilliantly but which, filled with sharps and flats and atonal glissandi, constantly strikes me, an amateur, mind you, as almost impossible to sing. There are many shades and faded grades in the parade of black, very like the turbid and half-turbid sounds found in Japanese writing and pronunciation.

It is not commonly compared to song, however. The spoken word sounds like a gunshot. *Blak!* As a pronounced word it has the sudden finality of a beheading. *Blak!* What a convinced declaration is made, for example, in Rouault's black line! Or Beckmann's! Or de Kooning's! Henri Rousseau did not want lines. He sought to make a line happen, as in nature, by arranging the delicate contrast between contingent colors. Art, it may be argued, like personality, like character, like human behavior, is fractal—its contours cannot be mapped. Who first conjured the color black, however, sharing with Robert Frost, who frequently wrote of the dark, the stormy "inner weather" within us, surely insisted fences made good neighbors.

What is of particular interest is that Frost, a poet often highly pessimistic and more than well acquainted with the night, also believed that blackness had to be faced. Remember in his poem "The Night Light" how he chides a woman who while she sleeps burns a lamp to drive back darkness, declaring, "Good gloom on her was thrown away"?

The origins of the word black (ME *blak*, OE *blāec*, ON *blakkr*) go back to *flamma* (flame), and *flagrare* (L, to blaze up), words having to do with fire, flame, things that have been burned—compare *blush, bleak, blind, flare* and *flicker*—and is ultimately formed from the Indo-European *bhleg*, to burn with black soot or to burn black with soot. There are several Anglo-Saxon and Early English words for black or darkness: *piesternesse* (darkness), *blāeqimm* (jet) and *blakaz* (black). We find "blake" in *The Ancren Riwle*, or "Rule of Nuns," ca. 1210, and in *King Horn*, before A.D. 1210 ("He wipede bat blake of his swere"). A couplet from *The Story of Havelock the Dane*, an Anglo-Saxon tale, before A.D. 1300, goes as follows:

> *In a poke, ful and blac,*
> *Sone he caste him on his bac*

But do we in fact get our English word from sound symbolism or mispronunciation? Different meanings, amazingly enough, have derived from the very same original word by way of a sequence of semantic shifts and in the process ironically have moved in the opposite direction, as is evident in Old English in which *blāec* is "black." But the word *blac*, with no other phonetic difference than that of a vowel, actually once denoted, according to Anglo-Saxon scholars W. W. Skeat, Rev. Richard Morris and T. Wedgwood, what we now think of as its opposite. The original meaning of *black* is "pale," "colorless," "blank" or "white." Is this not astonishing? The word *black* (Anglo-Saxon *blac, blāec*), which is fundamentally the same as the old German *blach*—a word now only to be found in two or three compounds, e.g., *Blachfeld*, a level field—originally meant level, bare and by extension bare of color. According to William S. Walsh's *Handy-Book of Literary Curi-*

osities, the nasalized form of black is blank, a word which originally signified bare, and was used in the sense of white specifically and logically because white is (apparently) bare of color. In Anglo-Saxon we read, *"Se mona mid his blacan lēohte"*—the moon with her pale light. An old poet praises the beauty of *"blac hleor ides"*—the pale-cheeked girl or woman. *Blac* in *Beowulf* means "bright," "brilliant." In the great hall, Beowulf sees Grendel's mère for the first time by the bright firelight—*"fȳr-lēoht zeseah, blācne lēoman"* (l. 1516). The Old English infinitive *blǣcan* means not "to blacken" but rather "to bleach." Our words *bleak* and *bleach*—is this not passing strange?—are from the same root.

1995

Foucault once said that an essay is a vehicle. By his own admission, his was a method of exploratory questions rather than a full-fledged theory of opinion. Let us suppose that Lydia Davis, who has heard of Foucault, yet who still considers herself a storyteller, and whose writings have been anthologized as poems and essays and even dramatic monologues, has ridden her stories sometimes so far that their metaphors have evolved into memories, anecdotes transformed into arguments. "I never think quite the same thing," said Foucault, in an interview, before he died, "because for me my books are experiences, and an experience is something that one comes out of transformed." Even today, in Greece, where philosophy was born, modern-day travelers still ride a transit system that is known to all commuters as the *Metaphora*.

LYDIA DAVIS

Foucault and Pencil

Sat down to read Foucault with pencil in hand. Knocked over glass of water onto waiting-room floor. Put down Foucault and pencil, mopped up water, refilled glass. Sat down to read Foucault with pencil in hand. Stopped to write in notebook. Took up Foucault with pencil in hand. Counselor beckoned from doorway. Put away Foucault and pencil as well as notebook and pen. Sat with counselor discussing situation fraught with conflict taking form of many heated arguments. Counselor pointed to danger, raised red flag. Left counselor, went to subway. Sat in subway car, took out Foucault and pencil but did not read, thought instead about situation fraught with conflict, red flag, recent argument concerning travel: argument itself became form of travel, each sentence carrying arguers on to next sentence, next sentence on to next, and in the end, arguers were not where they had started, were also tired from traveling and spending so long face-to-face in each other's company. After several stations on subway thinking about argument, stopped thinking and opened Foucault. Found Foucault, in French, hard to understand. Short sentences easier to understand than long ones. Certain long ones understandable part by part, but so long, forgot beginning before reaching end. Went back to beginning, understood beginning, read on, and again forgot beginning before reaching end. Read on without going back and without understanding, without remembering, and without learning, pencil idle in hand. Came to sentence that was clear, made pencil mark in margin. Mark indicated understanding, indicated forward progress in book. Lifted eyes from Foucault, looked at other passengers. Took out notebook and pen to make note about passengers, made accidental mark with pencil in margin of Foucault, put down notebook, erased mark. Returned thoughts to argument. Argument not only like vehicle, carried arguers forward, but also like plant, grew like

hedge, surrounding arguers at first thinly, some light coming through, then
more thickly, keeping light out, or darkening light. By argument's end, arguers could not leave hedge, could not leave each other, and light was dim.
Thought of question to ask about argument, took out notebook and pen
and wrote down. Put away notebook and returned to Foucault. Understood more clearly at which points Foucault harder to understand and at
which points easier: harder to understand when sentence was long and
noun identifying subject of sentence was left back at beginning, replaced
by male or female pronoun, when forgot what noun pronoun replaced and
had only pronoun for company traveling through sentence. Sometimes
pronoun then giving way in mid-sentence to new noun, new noun in turn
replaced by new pronoun which then continued on to end of sentence.
Also harder to understand when subject of sentence was noun like thought,
absence, law; easier to understand when subject was noun like beach, wave,
sand, sanatorium, pension, door, hallway, or civil servant. Before and after
sentence about sand, civil servant, or pension, however, came sentence
about attraction, neglect, emptiness, absence, or law, so parts of book understood were separated by parts not understood. Put down Foucault and
pencil, took out notebook and made note of what was now at least understood about lack of understanding reading Foucault, looked up at other
passengers, thought again about argument, made note of same question
about argument as before though with stress on different word.

1996

"Follow the river and you will get to the sea." "A fence between makes love more keen." "Make hay while the sun
shines." "The water that bears the boat is the same that swallows it up." "Few have luck; all have death." Linguists believe
that the aphorism was one of the earliest literary forms—the
residue of complex thoughts filtered down to an easily digestible metaphor. By the second millennium B.C., in ancient
kingdoms like Sumer in the Middle East, aphorisms began
appearing together in anthologies—collections of the sayings
that were gathered and copied for noblemen, priests, and
kings. But not long after these groupings of aphorisms appeared, the lists soon started to be catalogued by theme:
"Honesty"; "Family Life"; "Death"; etc. When read together,
the collections of aphorisms could now be said to make a
general argument on their common themes. Imagine their effect together as that of a thesis, a treatise on the given theme,
and eventually from here, out of the seeds of editing and of
collage, it is easy to imagine the form germinating into longer,
more complex, more sustained and sophisticated essayings.
The Hebrew wisdom of *Ecclesiastes* is essentially a collection
of aphorisms. As is Heraclitus' philosophy, Ben Franklin's
Almanac, and Lao Tzu's pastoral religious musings. At some
point, these extended aphorisms eventually crossed the border into essay terrain, as in the elegant, gossipy diaries of Sei
Shōnagon, for example, or Anne Bradstreet's letters, or
Kafka's notebooks, Pound's criticism, or even in the unique

use of bumper stickers as a modern aphoristic form in David Shield's ingenious essay "Life Story." But, in this particular late-century North American year, there are 294 million souls now living on the continent, each with a story it wants desperately to tell. This, *Publishers Weekly* announces, is the year of the memoir. And Frank McCourt's *Angela's Ashes* and Michael Ryan's *Secret Life* and Katherine Harrison's *The Kiss* are being published to prove it. The aphorism, in this year, is the last thing on our mind.

DAVID SHIELDS

Life Story

First things first.

You're only young once, but you can be immature forever. I may grow old, but I'll never grow up. Too fast to love, too young to die. Life's a beach.

Not all men are fools; some are single. 100% Single. I'm not playing hard to get; I am hard to get. I love being exactly who I am.

Heaven doesn't want me and Hell's afraid I'll take over. I'm the person your mother warned you about. Ex-girlfriend in trunk. Don't laugh; your girlfriend might be in here.

Girls wanted, all positions, will train. Playgirl on board. Party girl on board. Sexy blonde on board. Not all dumbs are blonde. Never underestimate the power of redheads. Yes, I am a movie star. 2QT4U. A4NQT. No ugly chicks. No fat chicks. I may be fat, but you're ugly and I can diet. Nobody is ugly after 2 A.M.

Party on board. Mass confusion on board. I brake for bong water. Jerk off and smoke up. Elvis died for your sins. Screw guilt. I'm Elvis; kiss me.

Ten and a half inches on board. Built to last. You can't take it with you, but I'll let you hold it for a while.

Be kind to animals—kiss a rugby player. Ballroom dancers do it with rhythm. Railroaders love to couple up. Roofers are always on top. Pilots slip it in.

Love sucks and then you die. Gravity's a lie; life sucks. Life's a bitch; you marry one, then you die. Life's a bitch and so am I. Beyond bitch.

Down on your knees, bitch. Sex is only dirty when you do it right. Liquor up front—poker in the rear. Smile; it's the second-best thing you can do with your lips. I haven't had sex for so long I forget who gets tied up. I'm looking for love but will settle for sex. Bad boys have bad toys. Sticks and stones may break my bones, but whips and chains excite me. Live fast; love hard; die with your mask on.

So many men, so little time. Expensive but worth it. If you're rich, I'm single. Richer is better. Shopaholic on board. Born to shop. I'd rather be shopping at Nordstrom. Born to be pampered. A woman's place is the mall. When the going gets tough, the tough go shopping. Consume and die. He who dies with the most toys wins. She who dies with the most jewels wins. Die, yuppie scum.

This vehicle not purchased with drug money. Hugs are better than drugs. You are loved.

Expectant mother on board. Baby on board. Family on board. I love my kids. Precious cargo on board. Are we having fun yet? Baby on fire. No child in car. Grandchild in back.

I fight poverty; I work. I owe, I owe, it's off to work I go. It sure makes the day long when you get to work on time. Money talks; mine only knows how to say good-bye. What do you mean I can't pay off my Visa with my MasterCard?

How's my driving? Call 1-800-545-8601. If this vehicle is being driven recklessly, please call 1-800-EAT-SHIT. Don't drink and drive—you might hit a bump and spill your drink.

My other car is a horse. Thoroughbreds always get there first. Horse lovers are stable people. My other car is a boat. My other car is a Rolls-Royce. My Mercedes is in the shop today. Unemployed? Hungry? Eat your foreign car. My other car is a 747. My ex-wife's car is a broom. I think my car has PMS. My other car is a piece of shit, too. Do not wash—this car is undergoing a scientific dirt test. Don't laugh; it's paid for. If this car were a horse, I'd have to shoot it. If I go any faster, I'll burn out my hamsters. I may be slow, but I'm ahead of you. I also drive a Titleist. Pedal downhill.

Shit happens. I love your wife. Megashit happens. I'm single again. Wife and dog missing—reward for dog. The more people I meet, the more I like my cat. Nobody on board. Sober 'n' crazy. Do it sober. Drive smart; drive sober.

No more Mr. Nice Guy. Lost your cat? Try looking under my tires. I love my German shepherd. Never mind the dog—beware of owner. Don't fence me in. Don't tell me what kind of day to have. Don't tailgate or I'll flush. Eat shit and die. My kid beat up your honor student. Abort your inner child. I don't care who you are, what you're driving, who's on board, who you love, where you'd rather be, or what you'd rather be doing.

Not so close—I hardly know you. Watch my rear end, not hers. You hit it—you buy it. Hands off. No radio. No condo/No MBA/No BMW. You toucha my car—I breaka your face. Protected by Smith & Wesson. Warning: This car is protected by a large sheet of cardboard.

LUV2HNT. Gun control is being able to hit your target. Hunters make better lovers: they go deeper into the bush—they shoot more often—and they eat what they shoot.

Yes, as a matter of fact, I do own the whole damn road. Get in, sit down, shut up, and hold on. I don't drive fast; I just fly low. If you don't like the way I drive, stay off the sidewalk. I'm polluting the atmosphere. Can't do 55.

I may be growing old, but I refuse to grow up. Get even: live long enough to become a problem to your kids. We're out spending our children's inheritance.

Life is pretty dry without a boat. I'd rather be sailing. A man's place is on his boat. Everyone must believe in something; I believe I'll go canoeing. Who cares!

Eat dessert first; life is uncertain. Why be normal?

Don't follow me; I'm lost, too. Wherever you are, be there. No matter where you go, there you are. Bloom where you are planted.

Easy does it. Keep it simple, stupid. I'm 4 Clean Air. Go fly a kite. No matter—never mind. UFOs are real. Of all the things I've lost, I miss my mind the most. I brake for unicorns.

Choose death.

1997

In this year, NASA lands on Mars. Scotland clones a sheep. A cult of 39 kills itself in San Diego, preparing to board a spaceship that awaits them behind a comet. In this year from Chicago, a quirky local radio show called *This American Life* broadcasts internationally for the first time to instant cheer. In this year, America's best documentary filmmaker, Errol Morris, releases *Fast, Cheap & Out of Control,* his best documentary yet. And in this year when fiction writer David Foster Wallace turns his fact-obsessed attention to the Illinois State Fair, he proves, once again, that the world around us sometimes is more interesting than those within us.

David Foster Wallace

Ticket to the Fair

August 5, 1993, Interstate 55, Westbound, 8:00 A.M.

Today is Press Day at the Illinois State Fair in Springfield, and I'm supposed to be at the fairgrounds by 9:00 A.M. to get my credentials. I imagine
credentials to be a small white card in the band of a fedora. I've never been
considered press before. My real interest in credentials is getting into rides
and shows for free. I'm fresh in from the East Coast, for an East Coast
magazine. Why exactly they're interested in the Illinois State Fair remains
unclear to me. I suspect that every so often editors at East Coast magazines
slap their foreheads and remember that about 90 percent of the United
States lies between the coasts, and figure they'll engage somebody to do
pith-helmeted anthropological reporting on something rural and heart-
landish. I think they asked me to do this because I grew up here, just a
couple hours' drive from downstate Springfield. I never did go to the state
fair, though—I pretty much topped out at the county-fair level. Actually, I
haven't been back to Illinois for a long time, and can't say I've missed it.

The heat is all too familiar. In August it takes hours for the dawn fog to
burn off. The air is like wet wool. Eight A.M. is too early to justify turning
on the car's AC. The sun is a blotch in a sky that isn't so much cloudy as
opaque. The corn starts just past the breakdown lanes and goes right to the
sky's hem. August corn in Illinois is as tall as a tall man. With all the advances in fertilization, it's now knee-high by June 1. Locusts chirr in every
field, a brassy electric sound that Dopplers oddly inside the speeding car.
Corn, corn, soybeans, corn, exit ramp, corn, and every few miles an out-
post way off on a reach in the distance—house, tree with tire swing, barn,
satellite dish. Grain silos are the only skyline. A fog hangs just over the

345

fields. It is over eighty degrees and climbing with the sun. It'll be over ninety degrees by 10:00 A.M. There's that tightening quality to the air, like it's drawing itself in and down for a siege. The interstate is dull and pale. Occasional other cars look ghostly, their drivers' faces humidity-stunned.

9:00 A.M.

It's still a week before the fair, and there's something surreal about the emptiness of parking facilities so huge and complex that they have their own map. The parts of the fairgrounds that I can see are half-permanent structures and half tents and displays in various stages of erection, giving the whole thing the look of somebody half-dressed for a really important date.

9:05 A.M.

The man processing print-press credentials has a mustache and short-sleeve knit shirt. In line before me are newshounds from *Today's Agriculture,* the *Decatur Herald & Review, Illinois Crafts Newsletter, 4-H News,* and *Livestock Weekly.* Credentials are just a laminated mug shot with a gator clip for your pocket. Not a fedora in the house. Two older ladies behind me from a local horticulture organ engage me in shoptalk. One lady is the unofficial historian of the Illinois State Fair: she gives slide shows on the fair at nursing homes and Rotary lunches. She begins to emit historical data at a great rate—the fair started in 1853; there was a fair during the Civil War but not during WWII, and not in 1893, because Chicago was hosting the World's Columbian Exposition; the governor has failed to cut the ribbon personally on opening day only twice; etc. It occurs to me that I ought to have brought a notebook. I'm also the only person in the room in a T-shirt. It is a fluorescent-lit cafeteria in something called the Illinois Building Senior Center, uncooled. The local TV crews have their equipment spread out on tables and are lounging against walls. They all have mustaches and short-sleeve knit shirts. In fact, the only other males in the room without mustaches and golf shirts are the local TV reporters, four of them, all in suits. They are sleek, sweatless, deeply blue-eyed. They stand together up by the dais, which has a podium and a flag and a banner reading "Give Us a Whirl"—this year's theme. Middle-management types enter. A squelch of feedback on a loudspeaker brings the official Press Welcome & Briefing to order. It's dull. The words "excited," "proud," and "opportunity" are used repeatedly. Ms. Illinois County Fairs, tiara bolted to the tallest coiffure I've ever seen (bun atop bun, multiple layers, a ziggurat of hair), is proudly excited to have the opportunity to present two corporate guys, sweating freely in suits, who report the excited pride of McDonald's and Wal-Mart to have the opportunity to be this year's corporate sponsors.

9:50 A.M.

Under way at 4 mph on the Press Tour, on a kind of flatboat with wheels and a lengthwise bench so queerly high that everybody's feet dangle. The tractor pulling us has signs that say "ethanol" and "agripowered." I'm particularly keen to see the carnies setting up the rides in the fairgrounds' "Happy Hollow," but we head first to the corporate and political tents. Most every tent is still setting up. Workmen crawl over structural frames. We wave at them; they wave back; it's absurd: we're only going 4 mph. One tent says "Corn: Touching Our Lives Every Day." There are massive many-hued tents courtesy of McDonald's, Miller Genuine Draft, Morton Commercial Structures Corp., the Land of Lincoln Soybean Association ("Look Where Soybeans Go!"), Pekin Energy Corp. ("Proud of Our Sophisticated Computer-Controlled Processing Technology"), Illinois Pork Producers, the John Birch Society. Two tents that say "Republican" and "Democrat." Other, smaller tents for various Illinois officeholders. It is well up in the nineties and the sky is the color of old jeans.

We go over a system of crests to Farm Expo—twelve acres of wicked-looking needle-toothed harrows, tractors, seeders, harvesters. Then back around the rear of the big permanent Artisans' Building, Illinois Building Senior Center, Expo Center, passing tantalizingly close to Happy Hollow, where half-assembled rides stand in giant arcs and rays and shirtless guys with tattoos and wrenches slouch around them, fairly oozing menace and human interest, but on at a crawl up a blacktop path to the livestock buildings. By this time, most of the press is off the tram and walking in order to escape the tour's PA speaker, which is tinny and brutal. Horse Complex. Cattle Complex. Swine Barn. Sheep Barn. Poultry Building and Goat Barn. These are all long brick barracks open down both sides of their length. Some contain stalls; others have pens divided into squares with aluminum rails. Inside, they're gray cement, dim and yeasty, huge fans overhead, workers in overalls and waders hosing everything down. No animals yet, but the smells still hang from last year—horses' odors sharp, cows' rich, sheep's oily, swine's unspeakable. No idea what the Poultry Building smelled like, because I couldn't bring myself to go in. Traumatically pecked once, as a child, at the Champaign County Fair, I have a long-standing phobic thing about poultry.

The ethanol tractor's exhaust is literally flatulent-smelling as we crawl out past the Grandstand, where later there will be evening concerts and harness and auto racing—"World's Fastest One-Mile Dirt Track"—and head for something called the Help Me Grow tent, to interface with the state's First Lady, Brenda Edgar. The first sign of the Help Me Grow area is the nauseous bright red of Ronald McDonald's hair. He's capering around a small plastic playground area under candy-stripe tenting. Though the fair is ostensibly closed, troupes of kids mysteriously appear and engage in rather rehearsed-looking play as we approach. Two of the kids are black, the first black people I've seen anywhere on the grounds. No parents in view. The governor's wife stands surrounded by flinty-eyed aides. Ronald pretends to fall down. The press forms into a ring. There are several state troopers in khaki and tan, streaming sweat under their Nelson Eddy hats. Mrs. Edgar is cool and groomed and pretty in a lacquered way. She's of the female age that's always suffixed with "-ish." Her tragic flaw is her voice, which sounds almost heliated. The Help Me Grow program, when you decoct the rhetoric, is basically a statewide crisis line for over-the-edge parents to call and get talked out of beating up their kids. The number of calls Mrs. Edgar says the line has fielded just this year is both de- and impressive. Shiny pamphlets are distributed. Ronald McDonald, voice slurry and makeup cottage-cheesish in the heat, cues the kids to come over for some low-rent sleight of hand and Socratic banter. Lacking a real journalist's killer instinct, I've been jostled way to the back, and my view is obscured by the towering hair of Ms. Illinois County Fairs, whose function here is unclear. I don't want to asperse, but Ronald McDonald sounds like he's under the influence of something more than fresh country air. I drift away under the tent. All the toys and plastic playground equipment have signs that say "Courtesy of" and then a corporate name. A lot of the photographers in the ring have dusty green safari vests, and they sit cross-legged in the sun, getting low-angle shots of Mrs. Edgar. There are no tough questions from the media. The tram's tractor is putting out a steady sweatsock shape of blue-green exhaust. I notice that the grass under the Help Me Grow tent is different—pine-green and prickly-looking. Solid investigative bent-over journalism reveals that it is artificial. A huge mat of plastic artificial grass has been spread over the knoll's real grass, under the tent. I have my first moment of complete East Coast cynicism: a quick look under the edge of the fake-grass mat reveals the real grass underneath, flattened and already yellowing.

August 13, 9:25 A.M.

Official opening. Ceremony, introductions, verbiage. Big brass shears, for cutting the ribbon across the main gate. It is cloudless and dry, but forehead-tighteningly hot. Noon will be a kiln. No anthropologist worth his pith helmet would be without the shrewd counsel of a colorful local, and I've lured a Native Companion here for the day with the promise of free admission, unlimited corn dogs, and various shiny trinkets. Knit-shirt press and rabid early fairgoers are massed from the gate all the way out to Springfield's Sangamon Avenue, where homeowners with plastic flags invite you to park on their front lawn for five dollars. We stand near the back. I gather that "Little Jim" Edgar, the governor, isn't much respected by the press. Governor Edgar is maybe fifty and greyhound-thin, with steel glasses and hair that looks carved out of feldspar. He radiates sincerity, though. After the hacks introduce him, he speaks sanely and, I think, well. He invites everybody to get in there and have a really good time and to revel in watching everybody else also having a good time—a kind of reflexive exercise in civics. The press corps seems unmoved.

But this fair, the idea and now the reality of it, does seem to have something uniquely to do with state-as-community, a grand-scale togetherness. And it is not just the claustrophobic mash of people waiting to get inside. The fair occupies space, and there's no shortage of empty space in downstate Illinois. The fairgrounds take up 300-plus acres on the north side of Springfield, a depressed capital of 109,000 where you can't spit without hitting a Lincoln-site plaque. The fair spreads itself out, and visually so. The main gate is on a rise, and through the two sagged halves of ribbon you get a specular vantage on the whole thing—virgin and sun-glittered, even the tents looking freshly painted. It seems garish and endless and aggressively special. Kids are having little epileptic fits all around us, frenzied with a need to take in everything at once. I suspect that part of the self-conscious community thing here has to do with space. Rural Midwesterners live surrounded by unpopulated land, marooned in a space whose emptiness is both physical and spiritual. It is not just people you get lonely for. You're alienated from the very space around you, for here the land is not an environment but a commodity. The land is basically a factory. You live in the same factory you work in. You spend an enormous amount of time with the land, but you're still alienated from it in some way. I theorize to Native Companion (who worked detasseling summer corn with me in high school) that the state fair's animating thesis involves some kind of structured, decorated interval of communion with both neighbor and space—the sheer *fact* of the land is to be celebrated here, its yields ogled and its stock groomed and paraded. A special vacation from alienation, a chance, for a moment, to love what real life out here can't let you love. Native Companion gives me a look, then rummages for her cigarette lighter, quite a bit more interested in that.

10:40 A.M.

The livestock venues are at full occupancy animalwise, but we seem to be the only fairgoing tourists from the ceremony who've dashed right over to tour them. You can tell which barns are for which animals with your eyes closed. The horses are in their own individual stalls, with half-height doors and owners and grooms on stools by the doors, a lot of them dozing. The horses stand in hay. Billy Ray Cyrus plays loudly on some stableboy's boom box. The horses have tight hides and apple-sized eyes that are set on the sides of their heads, like fish. I've rarely been this close to fine livestock. The horses' faces are long and somehow suggestive of coffins. The racers are lanky, velvet over bone. The draft and show horses are mammoth and spotlessly groomed, and more or less odorless: the acrid smell in here is just the horses' pee. All their muscles are beautiful; the hides enhance them. They make farty noises when they sigh, heads hanging over the short doors. They're not for petting, though. When you come close they flatten their ears and show big teeth. The grooms laugh to themselves as we jump back. These are special competitive horses, with intricately bred highstrung artistic temperaments. I wish I'd brought carrots. Animals can be bought, emotionally. Stall after stall of horses. Standard horse-type colors. They eat the same hay they stand in. Occasional feedbags look like gas masks. A sudden clattering spray-sound like somebody hosing down siding turns out to be a glossy dun stallion peeing. He's at the back of his stall getting combed, and the door is wide open. The stream of pee is an inch in diameter and throws up dust and hay and it looks like even chips of wood from the floor. A stallion is a male horse. We hunker down and have a took upward, and suddenly for the first time I understand a certain expression describing certain human males, an expression I'd heard but never quite understood till now.

You can hear the cows all the way from the Horse Complex. The cow stalls are all doorless and open to view. I don't guess a cow presents much of an escape risk. They are white-spotted dun or black, or else white with big continents of dun or black. They have no lips and their tongues are wide. Their eyes roll and they have huge nostrils, gaping and wet and pink or black. Cow manure smells wonderful—warm and herbal and blameless— but cows themselves stink in a rich biotic way, rather like a wet boot. Some of the owners are scrubbing down their entries for the upcoming beef show over at the Coliseum (so says my detailed media guide). These cows stand immobilized in webs of canvas straps inside a steel frame while ag-professionals scrub them down with a hose-and-brush thing that also oozes soap. The cows do not like this one bit. One cow, whose face is eerily reminiscent of Winston Churchill's, trembles and shudders and makes the frame clank, lowing, its eyes rolling up almost to the whites. Native Companion and I cringe and make soft appalled noises. The cow's lowing starts other cows lowing, or maybe they just see what they're in for. The cow's legs keep half-buckling, and the owner kicks at them. White mucus hangs from its snout. Other ominous drippings and gushings from elsewhere. The cow almost tips the frame over, and the owner punches her in the ribs.

Swine Barn. Swine have fur! I never thought of swine as having fur. I've actually never been up very close to swine, for olfactory reasons. A lot of the swine in here are show hogs, a breed called Poland China, their thin fur a kind of white crewcut over pink skin. A lot of the swine are down on their sides, stuporous and throbbing in the barn's heat. The awake ones grunt. They stand and lie on very clean large-curd sawdust in low-fenced pens. A couple of barrows are eating both the sawdust and their own excrement. Again, we're the only tourists here. A bullhorn on a wall announces

that the Junior Pygmy Goat judging is under way over at the Goat Barn. A
lot of these swine are frankly huge—say a third the size of a Volkswagen.
Every once in a while you hear about farmers getting mauled or killed by
swine. No teeth in view here, though their hoofs are cloven and pink and
obscene. I'm not sure whether they're called hoofs or feet on swine. Rural
Midwesterners learn in second grade that there's no such word as "hooves."
Some of the swine have large fans blowing in front of their pens, and
twelve ceiling fans roar, but it is still hellish in here. Pig smell is both vomity and excremental, like some hideous digestive disorder on a grand scale.
Maybe a cholera ward would come close. The swineherds and owners have
on rubber boots nothing like the L. L. Bean boots worn on the East Coast.
Some of the standing swine commune through the bars of their pens,
snouts almost touching. The sleeping swine thrash in dreams, their legs
working. Unless they're in distress, swine grunt at a low constant pitch. It is
a pleasant sound.

But now one butterscotch-colored swine is screaming. Distressed swine
scream. The sound is both human and inhuman enough to make your hair
stand. The professional swinemen ignore the pig, but we fuss on over,
Native Companion making concerned baby-talk sounds until I shush her.
The distressed pig's sides are heaving; it is sitting up with its front legs quivering, screaming horribly. This pig's keeper is nowhere in sight. A small sign
on its pen says it is a Hampshire. It is having respiratory trouble, clearly: I'm
guessing it inhaled either sawdust or excrement. Its front legs now buckle,
so it is on its side, spasming. Whenever it can get enough breath it screams.
It's unendurable, but none of the ag-professionals comes vaulting over the
pens to administer aid. Native Companion and I wring our hands with
sympathy. We both make plangent little noises at the pig. Native Companion tells me to go get somebody instead of standing there with my thumb
up my butt. I feel enormous stress—the nauseous smell, impotent sympathy, plus we're behind schedule. We are currently missing the Junior Pygmy
Goats, Philatelic Judging at the Expo Building, a 4-H Dog Show at Club
Mickey D's, the semifinals of the Midwest Arm-Wrestling Championships,
a Ladies Camping Seminar, and the opening rounds of the Speed Casting
Tournament. A swineherd kicks her Poland China sow awake so she can
add more sawdust to its pen; Native Companion utters a pained sound.
There are clearly only two animal-rights advocates in this Swine Barn. We
both can observe a kind of sullen, callous expertise in the demeanor of the

ag-pros. Prime example of spiritual-alienation-from-land-as-commodity, I posit. Except why take all the trouble to breed and care for and train a special animal and bring it to the Illinois State Fair if you don't care anything about it?

Then it occurs to me that I had bacon yesterday and am even now looking forward to my first corn dog of the fair. I'm standing here wringing my hands over a distressed swine and then I'm going to go pound down a corn dog. This is connected to my reluctance to charge over to a swine pro and demand emergency resuscitative care for this agonized Hampshire. I can sort of picture the look the farmer would give me.

Not that it's profound, but I'm struck, amid the pig's screams and wheezes, by the fact that these agricultural pros do not see their stock as pets or friends. They are just in the agribusiness of weight and meat. They are unconnected, even at the fair's self-consciously special occasion of connection. And why not?—even at the fair their products continue to drool and smell and scream, and the work goes on. I can imagine what they think of us, cooing at the swine: we fairgoers don't have to deal with the business of breeding and feeding our meat; our meat simply materializes at the corn-dog stand, allowing us to separate our healthy appetites from fur and screams and rolling eyes. We tourists get to indulge our tender animal-rights feelings with our tummies full of bacon. I don't know how keen these sullen farmers' sense of irony is, but mine's been honed East Coast keen, and I feel like a bit of an ass in the Swine Barn.

11:50 A.M.

Since Native Companion was lured here for the day by the promise of free access to high-velocity rides, we make a quick descent into Happy Hollow. Most of the rides aren't even twirling hellishly yet. Guys with ratchet wrenches are still cranking away, assembling the Ring of Fire. The Giant Gondola Wheel is only half-built, and its seat-draped lower half resembles a hideous molary grin. It is over 100 degrees in the sun, easy.

Happy Hollow's dirt midway is flanked by carnival-game booths and ticket booths and rides. There's a merry-go-round and a couple of tame kiddie rides, but most of the rides look like genuine Near-Death Experiences. The Hollow seems to be open only technically, and the ticket booths are unmanned, though little heartbreaking jets of AC air are blowing out through the money slots in the booths' glass. Attendance is sparse, and I notice that none of the ag-pro or farm people are anywhere in sight down here. A lot of the carnies slouch and slump in the shade of awnings. Every one of them seems to chain-smoke. The Tilt-a-Whirl operator has got his boots up on his control panel reading a motorcycle-and-naked-girl magazine while guys attach enormous rubber hoses to the ride's guts. We sidle over for a chat. The operator is twenty-four and from Bee Branch, Arkansas, and has an earring and a huge tattoo of a flaming skull on his triceps. He's far more interested in chatting with Native Companion than with me. He's been at this gig five years, touring with this one here same company here. Couldn't rightly say if he liked it or not. Broke in on the Toss-a-Quarter-Onto-the-Plates game and got, like, transferred over to the Tilt-a-Whirl in '91. He smokes Marlboro 100's but wears a cap that says "Winston."

All the carny game barkers have headset microphones; some are saying "Testing" and reciting their pitch lines in tentative warm-up ways. A lot of the pitches seem frankly sexual: You got to get it up to get it in. Take it out and lay 'er down, only a dollar. Make it stand up. Two dollars, five chances. Make it stand up. Rows of stuffed animals hang by their feet in the booths like game put out to cure. It smells like machine grease and hair tonic down here, and there's already a spoiled, garbagy smell. The media guide says Happy Hollow is contracted to "one of the largest owners of amusement attractions in the country," one Blomsness-Thebault Enterprises, of Crystal Lake, Illinois, near Chicago. But the carnies are all from the middle South—Tennessee, Arkansas, Oklahoma. They are visibly unimpressed by the press credentials clipped to my shirt. They tend to look at Native Companion like she's food, which she ignores. I lose four dollars trying to "get it up and in," tossing miniature basketballs into angled baskets in such a way that they don't bounce out. The game's barker can toss them behind his back and get them to stay, but he's right up next to the baskets. My shots carom out from eight feet away; the straw baskets look soft, but their bottoms make a suspicious steely sound when hit.

It's so hot that we move in quick vectors between areas of shade. I'm reluctant to go shirtless because there'd be no way to display my credentials. We zigzag gradually westward. One of the fully assembled rides near the Hollow's west end is something called the Zipper. It's riderless as we approach, but in furious motion, a kind of Ferris wheel on amphetamines.

Individual caged cars are hinged to spin on their own axes as they go around in a tight vertical ellipse. The machine looks less like a Zipper than the head of a chain saw. It sounds like a shimmying V-12 engine, and it is something I'd run a mile in tight shoes to avoid riding.

Native Companion starts clapping and hopping, though. The operator at the controls sees her and shouts down to git on over and git some, if she's a mind. He claims they want to test it somehow. He's elbowing a colleague next to him in a way I don't much care for. We have no tickets, I point out, and none of the cash-for-ticket booths are manned. "Ain't no sweat off my balls," the operator says without looking at me. The operator's colleague conducts Native Companion up the waffled-steel steps and straps her into a cage, upping a thumb at the operator, who pulls a lever. She starts to ascend. Pathetic little fingers appear in the cage's mesh. The Zipper's operator is ageless and burnt-brown and has a mustache waxed to wicked points like a steer's horns, rolling a Drum cigarette with one hand as he nudges levers upward and the ellipse of cars speeds up and the individual cars themselves start to spin on their hinges. Native Companion is a blur of color inside her cage, but operator and colleague (whose jeans have worked down his hips to the point that the top of his butt-crack is visible) watch studiously as Native Companion's spinning car and the clanking empty cars circle the ellipse once a second. I can barely watch. The Zipper is the color of unbrushed teeth, with big scabs of rust. The operator and colleague sit on a little steel deck before a panel of black-knobbed levers. The colleague spits Skoal into a can he holds and tells the operator, "Well then take her up to eight then you pussy." The Zipper begins to whine and the thing to spin so fast that a detached car would surely be hurled into orbit. The colleague has a small American flag folded into a bandanna around his head. The empty cars shudder and clank as they whirl and spin. One long scream, wobbled by changes in vector, is coming from Native Companion's cage, which is going around and around on its hinges while a shape inside tumbles like stuff in a clothes dryer. My neurological makeup (extremely sensitive: carsick, airsick, heightsick) makes just watching this an act of great personal courage. The scream goes on and on; it is nothing like a swine's. Then the operator stops the ride abruptly with her car at the top, so she's hanging upside down inside the cage. I call up—is she okay? The response is a strange high-pitched noise. I see the two carnies gazing upward very intently, shading their eyes. The operator is stroking his mustache contemplatively. The cage's inversion has made Native Companion's dress fall up. They're ogling her nethers, obviously.

Now the operator is joggling the choke lever so the Zipper stutters back and forth, forward and backward, making Native Companion's top car spin around and around on its hinges. His colleague's T-shirt has a stoned Ninja Turtle on it, toking on a joint. There's a distended A-sharp scream from the whirling car, as if Native Companion is being slow-roasted. I summon saliva to step in and really say something stern, but at this point they start bringing her down. The operator is deft at his panel; the car's descent is almost fluffy. His hands on the levers are a kind of parody of tender care. The descent takes forever—ominous silence from Native Companion's car. The two carnies are laughing and slapping their knee. I clear my throat twice. Native Companion's car descends, stops. Jiggles of movement in the car, then the door's latch slowly turns. I expect whatever husk of a person emerges from the car to be hunched and sheet-white, dribbling fluids.

Instead she bounds out. "That was fucking *great!* Joo *see* that? Son of a bitch spun that car *sixteen times,* did you see?" This woman is native Midwestern, from my hometown. My prom date a dozen years ago. Her color is high. Her dress looks like the world's worst case of static cling. She's still got her *chewing gum* in, for God's sake. She turns to the carnies: "You sons bitches, that was fucking *great.*" The colleague is half-draped over the operator; they're roaring with laughter. Native Companion has her hands on her hips, but she's grinning. Am I the only one who's in touch with the sexual-harassment element in this whole episode? She takes the steel stairs several at a time and starts up the hillside toward the food booths. Behind us the operator calls out, 'They don't call me King of the Zipper for nuthin', sweet thang!"

She snorts and calls back over her shoulder, "Oh, *you.*"

I'm having a hard time keeping up. "Did you hear that?" I ask her.

"Jesus I thought I bought it for sure, that was so great. Assholes. But did you *see* that one spin up top at the end, though?"

"Did you hear that Zipper King comment?" I protest. She has her hand around my elbow and is helping me up the hillside's slick grass. "Did you sense something kind of sexual-harassmentish going on through that whole sick little exercise?"

"Oh for fuck's sake, it was fun—son of a bitch spun that car *sixteen times.*"

"They were looking up your *dress*. You couldn't see them, maybe. They hung you upside down at a great height and made your dress fall up and ogled you. They shaded their eyes and commented to each other."

"Oh for Christ's sake."

I slip a bit and she catches my arm. "So this doesn't bother you? As a Midwesterner, you're unbothered? Or did you just not have a sense of what was going on?"

"So if I noticed or didn't, why does it have to be *my* deal? What, because there's assholes in the world I don't get to ride the Zipper?"

"This is potentially key," I say. "This may be just the sort of regional eroto-political contrast the East Coast magazine is keen for. The core value informing a kind of eroto-willed political stoicism on your part is your prototypically Midwestern appreciation of fun—"

"Buy me some pork skins, you dipshit."

"—whereas on the East Coast, eroto-political indignation *is* the fun. In New York a woman who'd been hung upside down and ogled would get a whole lot of other women together and there'd be this frenzy of eroto-political indignation. They'd confront the guy. File an injunction. The management would find themselves litigating—violation of a woman's right to non-harassed fun. I'm telling you. Personal and political fun merge somewhere just east of Cleveland, for women."

Native Companion kills a mosquito without looking. "And they all take Prozac and stick their finger down their throat too out there. They ought to try just climbing on and spinning and saying, 'Fuck 'em.' That's pretty much all you can do with assholes."

12:35 P.M.

Lunchtime. The fairgrounds are a Saint Vitus' dance of blacktop footpaths, the axons and dendrites of mass spectation, connecting buildings and barns and corporate tents. Each path is flanked, pretty much along its whole length, by booths hawking food, and I realize that there's a sort of digestive subtheme running all through the fair. In a way, we're all here to be swallowed up. The main gate's maw admits us, and tightly packed slow masses move peristaltically along complex systems of branching paths, engage in complex cash-and-energy transfers at the villi alongside the paths, and are finally, both filled and depleted, expelled out of exits designed for heavy-flow expulsion. And then, of course, the food itself. There are tall Kaopectate-colored shacks that sell Illinois Dairy Council milk shakes for an off-the-scale $2.50—though they're mind-bendingly good milk shakes, silky and so thick they don't even insult your intelligence with a straw or spoon, giving you instead a kind of plastic trowel. There are uncountable pork options—Paulie's Pork Out, The Pork Patio, Freshfried Pork Skins, The Pork Avenue Cafe. The Pork Avenue Cafe is a "100 Percent All-Pork Establishment," says its loudspeaker. No way I'm eating any pork after this morning's swine stress, anyway. And it is at least ninety-five degrees in the shade, and due east of Livestock the breeze is, shall we say, fragrant. But food is being bought and ingested at an incredible clip all up and down the path. Everyone's packed in, eating and walking, moving slowly, twenty abreast, sweating, shoulders rubbing, the air spicy with armpits and Coppertone, cheek to jowl, a peripatetic feeding frenzy. Fifteen percent of the female fairgoers here have their hair in curlers. Forty percent are clinically fat. By the way, Midwestern fat people have no compunction about wearing shorts or halter tops. The food booths are ubiquitous, and each one has a line before it. Zipper or no, Native Companion is *"storved,"* she says, "to *daith.*" She puts on a parodic hick accent whenever I use a term like "peripatetic."

There are Lemon Shake-Ups, Ice Cold Melon Man booths, Citrus Push-Ups, and Hawaiian Shaved Ice you can suck the syrup out of and then crunch the ice. But a lot of what's getting bought and gobbled is not hot-weather food at all: bright-yellow popcorn that stinks of salt; onion rings as big as leis; Poco Peños Stuffed Jalapeño Peppers; Zorba's Gyros, shiny fried chicken; Bert's Burritos—"Big As You're [sic] Head"; hot Italian beef; hot New York City beef; Jojo's Quick Fried Doughnuts; pizza by the shingle-sized slice; and chitlins and crab Rangoon and Polish sausage. There are towering plates of "Curl Fries," which are pubic-hair-shaped and make people's fingers shine in the sun. Cheez-Dip hot dogs. Pony pups. Hot fritters. Philly steak. Ribeye BBQ Corral. Joanie's Original 1/2-lb. Burgers booth's sign says "2 Choices—Rare or Mooin'." I can't believe people eat this stuff in this kind of heat. There's the green reek of fried tomatoes. The sky is cloudless and galvanized, and the sun fairly pulses. The noise of deep fryers forms a grisly sound-carpet all up and down the paths. The crowd moves at one slow pace, eating, densely packed between the rows of booths. The Original 1-lb. Butterfly Pork Chop booth has a sign: "Pork: The Other White Meat"—the only discernible arm wave to the health-conscious. This is the Midwest: no nachos, no chili, no Evian, nothing Cajun. But holy mackerel, are there sweets: fried dough, black walnut taffy, fiddlesticks, hot Crackerjack. Caramel apples for a felonious $1.50. Angel's Breath, known also as Dentist's Delight. There's All-Butter Fudge, Rice Krispie–squarish things called Krakkles. Angel Hair cotton candy. There are funnel cakes: cake batter quick-fried to a tornadic spiral and rolled in sugared butter. Another artery clogger: elephant ears, an album-sized expanse of oil-fried dough slathered with butter and cinnamon-sugar—cinnamon toast from hell. No one is in line for ears except the morbidly obese.

1:10 P.M.

"Here we've got as balanced in dimension a heifer as any you'll see today. A high-volume heifer, but also solid on mass. Good to look at in terms of rib length to depth. Depth of forerib. Notice the depth of flank on the front quarter. We'd like to see maybe perhaps a little more muscle mass on the rear flank. Still, an outstanding heifer."

We're in the Jr. Livestock Center. The ring of cows moves around the perimeter of the dirt circle, each led by an ag-family kid. The "Jr." apparently refers to the owners, not the animals. Each cow's kid holds a long poker with a right-angled tooth at its end and prods the cow into the center of the ring to move in a tighter circle. The beef-show official is dressed just like the kids in the ring—dark new stiff jeans, check shirt, bandanna around neck. On him it doesn't look goofy. Plus he's got a stunning white cowboy hat. While Ms. Illinois Beef Queen presides from a dais decked with flowers sent over from the horticulture show, the official stands in the arena itself, his legs apart and his thumbs in his belt, 100 percent man, radiating livestock savvy. "Okay this next heifer, a lot of depth of rib but a little tighter in the fore flank. A bit tighter-flanked, if you will, from the standpoint of capacity."

The owners—farm kids, deep-rural kids from back-of-beyond counties like Piatt, Moultrie, Vermilion, all here because they're county-fair winners—are earnest, nervous, pride-puffed. Dressed rurally up. Straw-colored crewcuts. High number of freckles per capita. Kids remarkable for a kind of classic Rockwellian USA averageness, the products of balanced diets,

vigorous daily exertion, and solid GOP upbringings. The Jr. Livestock
Center bleachers are half-full, and it is all ag-people, parents mostly, many
with video cameras. Cowhide vests and ornate dress-boots and simply amazing hats. Illinois farmers are rural and inarticulate, but they are not poor.
Just the amount of revolving credit you need to capitalize a hundred-acre
operation—seed and herbicides, heavy equipment and crop insurance—
makes a lot of them millionaires on paper. Media dirges notwithstanding,
banks are no more keen to foreclose on Midwestern farms than they are on
Third World nations; they're in that deeply. Nobody here wears sunglasses;
everyone's in long pants and tanned in an earth-tone, all-business way. And
if the fair's ag-pros are also stout, it is in a harder, squarer, somehow more
earned way than the tourists on the paths outside. The fathers in the
bleachers have bushy brows and simply enormous thumbs, I notice. Native
Companion keeps making growly throat noises about the beef official.
The Jr. Livestock Center is cool and dim and spicy with livestock. The atmosphere is good-natured but serious. Nobody's eating any booth-food,
and nobody's carrying the fair's complimentary "Governor Edgar" shopping bags.

"An excellent heifer from a profile standpoint."

"Here we have a low-volume heifer, but with exceptional mass in the
rear quarter."

I can't tell whose cow is winning.

"Certainly the most extreme heifer out here in terms of frame to depth."

Some of the cows look drugged. Maybe they're just superbly trained.
You can imagine these farm kids getting up so early they can see their
breath and leading their cows in practice circles under the cold stars, then
having to do their chores. I feel good in here. The cows all have colored ribbons on their tails. They are shampooed and mild-eyed and lovely, inconti-
nence notwithstanding. They're also assets. The ag-lady beside us says her
family's operation will "realize" perhaps $2,500 for the Hereford in the
Winners Auction coming up. Illinois farmers call their farms "operations,"
rarely "farms" and never "spreads." The lady says $2,500 is "maybe about
around half" what the ag-family has spent on the heifer's breeding and
care. "We do this for pride," she says. This is more like it—pride, care, self-
less expense. The little boy's chest puffs out as the official tips his blinding
hat. Farm spirit. Oneness with crop and stock. The ag-lady says that the of-

ficial is a beef buyer for a major Peoria packing plant and that the bidders in the upcoming auction (five brown suits and three string ties on the dais) are from McDonald's, Burger King, White Castle, etc. Meaning that the mild-eyed winners have been sedulously judged as meat. The ag-lady has a particular bone to pick with McDonald's, " 'cause they always come in and overbid high on the champions and don't care about nothing else. Mess up the pricing." Her husband confirms they got "screwed back to front" on last year's bidding.

3:00 P.M.

We hurtle here and there. Paid attendance today is 100,000-plus. A scum of clouds cuts the heat, but I'm on my third shirt. Society horse show at Coliseum. Wheat-weaving demonstration in Hobbies, Arts & Crafts Building. Peonies like supernovas in the horticulture tent. I have no time. I'm getting a sort of visual-overload headache. Native Companion is also stressed. And we're not the only tourists with this pinched glazed hurry-up look—there are just too damn many things to experience. Arm-wrestling finals where bald men fart audibly with effort. Drum and bugle competition in Miller Beer tent. Corn-fed girls in overalls cut off at the pockets. Everyone's very excited at everything. Tottery Ronald McD. is working the crowd at Club Mickey D's 3-on-3 Hoops. Three of the six basketball players are black, the first I've seen since Mrs. Edgar's hired kids. Pygmy Goat Show at Goat Barn. Native Companion has zinc oxide on her nose. I'm sure we'll miss something.

4:05 P.M.

We're about 100 yards shy of the Poultry Building when I break down. I've been a rock about the prospect of poultry all day, but now my nerve goes. I can't go in there. *Listen* to the thousands of sharp squawking beaks in there, I say. Native Companion not unkindly offers to hold my hand, talk me through it. It is 100 degrees and I have pygmy-goat shit on my shoe and am almost crying with fear and embarrassment. I have to sit down on a green bench to collect myself. The noise of the Poultry Building is horrifying. I think this is what insanity must sound like. No wonder madmen clutch their heads. There's a thin stink. Bits of feather float. I hunch on the bench. We're high on a ridge overlooking the carnival rides. When I was eight, at the Champaign County Fair, I was pecked without provocation, flown at and pecked by a renegade fowl, savagely, just under the right eye.

Sitting on the bench, I watch the carnies way below. They mix with no one, never seem to leave Happy Hollow. Late tonight, I'll watch them drop flaps to turn their booths into tents. They'll smoke cheap dope and drink peppermint schnapps and pee out onto the midway's dirt. I guess they're the gypsies of the rural United States—itinerant, insular, swarthy, unclean, not to be trusted. You are in no way drawn to them. They all have the same blank hard eyes as people in the bathrooms of East Coast bus terminals. They want your money and maybe to look up your skirt; beyond that you're just blocking the view. Next week they'll dismantle and pack and haul up to the Wisconsin State Fair, where they'll never set foot off the midway they pee on.

While I'm watching from the bench, an old withered man in an Illinois Poultry Association cap careers past on one of those weird three-wheeled carts, like a turbocharged wheelchair, and runs neatly over my sneaker. This ends up being my one unassisted interview of the day, and it's brief. The man keeps revving his cart's engine like a biker. *"Traish,"* he calls the carnies. "Lowlifes." He gestures down at the twirling rides. "Wouldn't let my own kids go off down there on a goddamn bet." He raises pullets down near Olney. He has something in his cheek. "Steal you blind. Drug-addicted and such. Swindle you nekked them games. Traish. Me, I ever year we drive up, I carry my wallet like this here." He points to his hip. His wallet's on a big steel clip attached to a wire on his belt; the whole thing looks vaguely electrified. Q: "But do they want to? Your kids? Hit the Hollow?" He spits brownly. *"Hail* no. We all come for the shows." He means the livestock competitions. "See some folks, talk stock. Drink a beer. Work all year round raising 'em for show birds. It's for pride. And to see folks. Shows're over Tuesday, why, we go on home." He looks like a bird himself. His face is mostly nose, his skin loose and pebbly like poultry's. His eyes are the color of denim. "Rest of this here's for city people." Spits. He means Springfield, Decatur, Normal. "Walk around, stand in line, eat junk, buy soovneers. Give their wallet to the traish. Don't even know there's folks come here to work up here." He gestures up at the barns, then spits again, leaning way out over the cart to do it. "We come up to work, see some folks. Drink a beer. Bring our own goddamn food. Mother packs a hamper. Hail, what we'd want to go on down there for? No folks we know down there." He laughs. Asks my name. "It is good to see folks," he says before leaving me and peeling out in his chair, heading for the chicken din. "We all stayin' up to the *mo*tel. Watch your wallet, boy."

August 14, 6:00 A.M.

The dawn is foggy. The sky looks like soap. It rained in brutal sheets last night, damaged tents, tore up corn near my motel. Midwestern thunderstorms are real Old Testament temple clutchers: Richter-scale thunder, big zigzags of cartoon lightning. Happy Hollow is a bog as I walk along the midway, passing an enfilade of snores from the booths and tents. Native Companion went home last night. My sneakers are already soaked. Someone behind the flaps of the Shoot-2D-Ducks-With-an-Air-Rifle booth is having a wicked coughing fit, punctuated with obscenities. Distant sounds of garbage Dumpsters being emptied. The Blomsness-Thebault management trailer has a blinky electric burglar alarm on it. The goddamn roosters in the Poultry Building are at it already. Thunder-mutters way off east over Indiana. The trees shudder and shed drops in the breeze. The paths are empty, eerie, shiny with rain.

6:20 A.M.

Sheep Barn. I am looking at legions of sleeping sheep. I am the only waking human in here. It is cool and quiet. Sheep excrement has an evil vomity edge to it, but olfactorily it is not too bad in here. One or two sheep are upright but silent. No fewer than four ag-pros are also in the pens, sleeping right up next to their sheep, about which the less speculation the better as far as I'm concerned. The roof in here is leaky and most of the straw is sopping. In here are yearling ewes, brood ewes, ewe lambs, fall lambs. There are signs on every pen. We've got Corriedales, Hampshires, Dorset Horns, Columbias. You could get a Ph.D. just in sheep, from the looks of it. Rambouillets, Oxfords, Suffolks, Shropshires, Cheviots, Southdowns. Outside again, undulating ghosts of fog on the fairground paths. Everything set up but no one about. A creepy air of hasty abandonment.

8:20 A.M.

Press room, fourth floor, Illinois Building. I'm the only credentialed member of the press without a little plywood cubbyhole for mail and press releases. Two guys from an ag-newspaper are trying to hook a fax machine up to a rotary-phone jack. A state-fair PR guy arrives for the daily press briefing. We have coffee and unidentifiable muffinish things, compliments of Wal-Mart. This afternoon's highlights: Midwest Truck and Tractor Pull, the "Bill Oldani 100" U.S.A.C. auto race. Tonight's Grandstand show is to be the poor old doddering Beach Boys, who I suspect now must make their entire living from state fairs. The special guest is America, another poor old doddering group. The PR guy cannot give away all his free press passes to the concert. I learn that I missed some law-and-order dramatics yesterday: two Zipper-riding minors were detained last night when a vial of crack fell from the pocket of one of them and direct-hit a state trooper alertly eating a Lemon Push-Up on the midway below. Also reported: a rape or date rape in Parking Lot 6, assorted buncos and D&D's. Two reporters also vomited on from great heights in two separate incidents under two separate Near-Death-Experience rides, trying to cover the Hollow.

8:40 A.M.

A Macy's-float-sized inflatable Ronald, seated and eerily Buddha-like, presides over the Club Mickey D's tent. A family is having their picture taken in front of the inflatable Ronald, arranging their little kids in a careful pose.

8:42 A.M.

Fourth trip to the bathroom in three hours. Elimination can be a dicey undertaking here. The fair has scores of Midwest Pottyhouse-brand portable toilets—man-sized plastic huts, somewhat reminiscent of Parisian *pissoirs,* each with its own undulating shroud of flies, and your standard heavy-use no-flush outhouse smell—and I for one would rather succumb to a rupture than use a Pottyhouse, though the lines for them are long and cheery. The only real rest rooms are in the big exhibit buildings. The Coliseum's is like a grade-school boys' room, especially the long communal urinal, a kind of huge porcelain trough. Performance anxieties and other fears abound here, with upwards of twenty guys flanking and facing one another, each with his unit out. The highlight is watching Midwestern ag-guys struggle with suspenders and overall straps as they exit the stalls.

9:30 A.M.

I'm once again at the capacious McDonald's tent, at the edge, the titanic inflatable clown presiding. There's a fair-sized crowd in the basketball bleachers at one side and rows of folding chairs on another. It's the Illinois State Jr. Baton-Twirling Finals. A metal loudspeaker begins to emit disco, and little girls pour into the tent from all directions, gamboling and twirling in vivid costumes. In the stands, video cameras come out by the score, and I can tell it's pretty much just me and a thousand parents.

The baroque classes and divisions, both team and solo, go from age three(!) to sixteen, with epithetic signifier—the four-year-olds compose the Sugar'N'Spice division, and so on. I'm in a chair up front behind the competition's judges, introduced as "varsity twirlers" from (oddly) the University of Kansas. They are four frosted blondes who smile a lot and blow huge grape bubbles.

The twirler squads are all from different towns. Mount Vernon and Kankakee seem especially rich in twirlers. The twirlers' spandex costumes, differently colored for each team, are paint-tight and brief in the legs. The coaches are grim, tan, lithe-looking women, clearly twirlers once, on the far side of their glory now and very serious-looking, each with a clipboard and whistle. The teams go into choreographed routines, each routine with a title and a designated disco or show tune, full of compulsory baton-twirling maneuvers with highly technical names. A mother next to me is tracking scores on what looks almost like an astrology chart, and is in no mood to explain anything to a novice baton watcher.

The routines are wildly complex, and the loudspeaker's play-by-play is mostly in code. All I can determine for sure is that I've bumbled into what has to be the most spectator-hazardous event at the fair. Missed batons go all over, whistling wickedly. The three-, four-, and five-year-olds aren't that dangerous, though they do spend most of their time picking up dropped batons and trying to hustle back into place—the parents of especially fumble-prone twirlers howl in fury from the stands while the coaches chew gum grimly. But the smaller girls don't really have the arm strength to endanger anybody, although one judge takes a Sugar'N'Spice's baton across the bridge of the nose and has to be helped from the tent.

But when the sevens and eights hit the floor for a series of "Armed Service medleys" (spandex with epaulets and officers' caps and batons over shoulders like M16's), errant batons start pinwheeling into the ceiling, tent's sides, and crowd, all with real force. I myself duck several times. A man just down the row takes one in the solar plexus and falls out of his metal chair with a horrid crash. The batons are embossed "Regulation Length" on the shaft and have white rubber stoppers on each end, but it is that hard dry kind of rubber, and the batons themselves aren't light. I don't think it's an accident that police nightsticks are also called service batons.

Physically, even within same-age teams, there are marked incongruities in size and development. One nine-year-old is several heads taller than another, and they're trying to do a complex back-and-forth duet thing with just one baton, which ends up taking out a bulb in one of the tent's steel hanging lamps, showering part of the stands with glass. A lot of the younger twirlers look either anorexic or gravely ill. There are no fat baton twirlers.

A team of ten-year-olds in the Gingersnap class have little cotton bunny tails on their costume bottoms and rigid papier-mâché ears, and they can do some serious twirling. A squad of eleven-year-olds from Towanda does an involved routine in tribute to Operation Desert Storm. To most of the acts there's either a cutesy ultrafeminine aspect or a stern butch military one, with little in between. Starting with the twelve-year-olds—one team in black spandex that looks like cheesecake leotards—there is, I'm afraid, a frank sexuality that begins to get uncomfortable. Oddly, it's the cutesy feminine performances that result in the serious audience casualties. A dad standing up near the top of the stands with a Toshiba video camera to his eye takes a tomahawking baton directly in the groin and falls over on somebody eating a funnel cake, and they take out good bits of several rows below them, and there's an extended halt to the action, during which I decamp. As I clear the last row of chairs yet another baton comes *wharp-wharping* cruelly right over my shoulder, caroming viciously off big Ronald's inflated thigh.

11:05 A.M.

The Expo Building, a huge enclosed mall-like thing, AC'd down to eighty degrees, with a gray cement floor and a hardwood mezzanine overhead. Every interior inch is given over to commerce of a special and lurid sort. Just inside the big east entrance, a man with a headset mike is slicing up a block of wood and then a tomato, standing on a box in a booth that says "SharpKut," hawking these spin-offs of Ginsu knives, "As Seen on TV." Next door is a booth offering personalized pet-ID tags. Another for the infamous mail-order-advertised Clapper, which turns on appliances automatically at the sound of two hands clapping (but also at the sound of a cough, sneeze, or sniff, I discover; *caveat emptor*). There's booth after booth, each with an audience whose credulity seems sincere. A large percentage of the booths show signs of hasty assembly and say "As Seen on TV" in bright brave colors. The salesmen all stand on raised platforms; all have headset mikes and rich neutral media voices.

The Copper Kettle All-Butter Fudge booth does a brisk air-conditioned business. There's something called a Full Immersion Body Fat Analysis for $8.50. A certain CompuVac, Inc., offers a $1.50 Computerized Personality Analysis. Its booth's computer panel is tall and full of blinking lights and reel-to-reel tapes, like an old bad sci-fi-film computer. My own Personality Analysis, a slip of paper that protrudes like a tongue from a red-lit slot, says, "Your Boldness of Nature Is Ofset [sic] with the Fear of Taking Risk." There's a booth that offers clock faces superimposed on varnished photorealist paintings of Christ, John Wayne, Marilyn Monroe. There's a Computerized Posture Evaluation booth. A lot of the headsetted vendors are about my age or younger. Something overscrubbed about them suggests a Bible-college background. It is just cool enough in here for a sweat-soaked shirt to get clammy. One vendor recites a pitch for Ms. Suzanne Somers's Thighmaster while a woman in a leotard demonstrates the product, lying on her side on the fiberboard counter. I'm in the Expo Building almost two hours, and every time I look up the poor woman's still at it with the Thighmaster. Most of the vendors won't answer questions and give me beady looks when I stand there making notes. But the Thighmaster lady, cheerful, friendly, violently cross-eyed, informs me she gets an hour off for lunch at 2:00 P.M., then goes another eight hours to closing at 11:00 P.M. I say her thighs must be pretty darn well Mastered by now, and her leg sounds like a banister when she raps her knuckle against it. We both have a laugh, until her vendor asks me to scram.

Booth after booth. A Xanadu of chintzola. Obscure non-stick cookware. "Eye Glasses Cleaned Free." A booth with anti-cellulite sponges. Dippin' Dots futuristic ice cream. A woman with Velcro straps on her sneakers gets fountain-pen ink out of a linen tablecloth with a Chapsticky-looking spot remover whose banner says "As Seen on TV's 'Amazing Discoveries,'" a late-night infomercial I'm kind of a fan of. A booth that for $9.95 will take a photo and superimpose your face on either an FBI Wanted poster or a *Penthouse* cover. An "MIA—Bring Them Home!" booth staffed by women playing Go Fish. An anti-abortion booth called Lifesavers, that lures you over with little candies. Sand art. Shredded-ribbon art. A booth for "Latest Advance! Rotary Nose Hair Clippers" whose other sign reads (I kid you not), "Do Not Pull Hair From Nose, May Cause Fatal Infection." Two different booths for collectible sports-star cards, "Top Ranked Investment of the Nineties." And tucked way back on one curve of the mezzanine's ellipse—*yes*—black velvet paintings, including—*yes*—several of Elvis in pensive poses.

Also on display is the expo's second economy—the populist evangelism of the rural Midwest. It is not your cash they want but to "Make a Difference in Your Life." And they make no bones about it. A Church of God booth offers a Computerized Bible Quiz. Its computer is CompuVacish in appearance. I go eighteen for twenty on the quiz and am invited behind a chamois curtain for a "person-to-person faith exploration," which no thanks. The conventional vendors get along fine with the Baptists and Jews for Jesus who operate booths right near them. They all laugh and banter back and forth. The SharpKut guy sends all the vegetables he's microsliced over to the Lifesavers booth, where they put them out with the candy. The scariest spiritual booth is right up near the west exit, where something called Covenant Faith Triumphant Church has a big hanging banner that asks, "What Is the ONE Man Made Thing Now in Heaven?" and I stop to ponder, which with charismatics is death, because a heavy-browed woman is out around the booth's counter like a shot and into my personal space. She says, "Give up? Give up do you?" She's looking at me very intensely, but there's something about her gaze: it is like she's looking *at* my eyes rather than *in* them. "What one manmade thing?" I ask. She puts a finger to her palm and makes screwing motions. Signifying coitus? I don't say "coitus" out loud, though. "Not but one thing," she says. "The holes in Christ's palms," screwing her finger in. Except isn't it pretty well known that Roman crucifees were nailed at the wrists, since palm-flesh won't support weight? But now I've been drawn into the dialogue, going so far as to let her take my arm and pull me toward the booth's counter. "Lookee here for a second now," she says. She has both hands around my arm. A Midwestern child of humanist academics gets trained early on to avoid these weird-eyed eager rural Christians who accost your space, to say "Not interested" at the front door and "No thanks" to mimeoed pamphlets, to look right through streetcorner missionaries like they were stemming for change. But the woman drags me toward the Covenant Faith counter, where a fine oak box rests, a sign propped on it: "Where Will YOU Be When YOU Look Like THIS?" "Take a look-see in here," the woman says. The box has a hole in its top. I peek. Inside the box is a human skull. I'm pretty sure it's plastic. The interior lighting is tricky, but I'm pretty sure the skull isn't genuine. I haven't inhaled for several minutes. The woman is looking at the side of my face. "Are you *sure?* is the question," she says. I manage to make my straightening-up motion lead right into a backing-away motion. "Are you a hundred percent *sure?*" Overhead, on the mezzanine, the Thighmaster lady is still at it, smiling cross-eyed into space.

1:36 P.M.

I'm on a teetery stool watching the Illinois Prairie Cloggers competition in a structure called the Twilight Ballroom that's packed with ag-folks and well over 100 degrees. I'd nipped in here only to get a bottle of soda pop on my way to the Truck and Tractor Pull. By now the pull's got to be nearly over, and in half an hour the big U.S.A.C. dirt-track auto race starts. But I cannot tear myself away from the scene in here. I'd imagined goony Jed Clampett types in tattered hats and hobnail boots, a-stompin' and a-whoopin', etc. I guess clogging, Scotch-Irish in origin and the dance of choice in Appalachia, did used to involve actual clogs and boots and slow stomps. But clogging has now miscegenated with square dancing and honky-tonk boogie to become a kind of intricately synchronized, absolutely kick-ass country tap dance.

There are teams from Pekin, Le Roy, Rantoul, Cairo, Morton. They each do three numbers. The music is up-tempo country or dance-pop.

Each team has anywhere from four to ten dancers. Few of the women are under thirty-five, fewer still under 175 pounds. They're country mothers, red-cheeked gals with bad dye jobs and big pretty legs. They wear western-wear tops and midiskirts with multiple ruffled slips underneath; and every once in a while they grab handfuls of cloth and flip the skirts up like can-can dancers. When they do this they either yip or whoop, as the spirit moves them. The men all have thinning hair and cheesy rural faces, and their skinny legs are rubberized blurs. The men's western shirts have piping on the chest and shoulders. The teams are all color-coordinated—blue and white, black and red. The white shoes all the dancers wear look like golf shoes with metal taps clamped on.

Their numbers are to everything from Waylon and Tammy to Aretha, Miami Sound Machine, Neil Diamond's "America." The routines have some standard tap-dance moves—sweep, flare, chorus-line kicking. But it is fast and sustained and choreographed down to the last wrist-flick. And square dancing's genes can be seen in the upright, square-shouldered postures on the floor, and there's a kind of florally enfolding tendency to the choreography, some of which uses high-speed promenades. But it is methedrine-paced and exhausting to watch because your own feet move; and it is erotic in a way that makes MTV look lame. The cloggers' feet are too fast to be seen, really, but they all tap out the exact same rhythm. A typical routine is something like: *ta*tatata*ta*tatata*tatata*. The variations around the basic rhythm are baroque. When they kick or spin, the two-beat absence of tap complexifies the pattern.

The audience is packed in right to the edge of the portable hardwood flooring. The teams are mostly married couples. The men are either rail thin or have big hanging guts. A couple of the men on a blue-and-white team are great fluid Astaire-like dancers, but mostly it is the women who compel. The men have constant smiles, but the women look orgasmic; they're the really serious ones, transported. Their yips and whoops are involuntary, pure exclamation. They are arousing. The audience claps savvily on the backbeat and whoops when the women do. It is almost all folks from the ag and livestock shows—the flannel shirts, khaki pants, seed caps and freckles. The spectators are soaked in sweat and extremely happy. I think this is the ag-community's special treat, a chance here to cut loose a little while their animals sleep in the heat. The transactions between cloggers and crowd seem synecdochic of the fair as a whole: a culture talking to itself, presenting credentials for its own inspection, bean farmers and herbicide brokers and 4-H sponsors and people who drive pickup trucks because they really need them. They eat non-fair food from insulated hampers and drink beer and pop and stomp in perfect time and put their hands on neighbors' shoulders to shout in their ears while the cloggers whirl and fling sweat on the crowd.

There are no black people in the Twilight Ballroom, and the awakened looks on the younger ag-kids' faces have this astonished aspect, like they didn't realize their race could dance like this. Three married couples from Rantoul, wearing full western bodysuits the color of raw coal, weave an incredible filigree of high-speed tap around Aretha's "R-E-S-P-E-C-T," and there's no hint of racial irony in the room; the song has been made this people's own, emphatically. This Nineties version of clogging does have something sort of pugnaciously white about it, a kind of performative nose-thumbing at M. C. Hammer. There's an atmosphere in the room— not racist, but aggressively *white*. It's hard to describe—the atmosphere is the same at a lot of rural Midwest events. It is not like a black person who came in would be ill treated; it's more like it would just never occur to a black person to come here.

I can barely hold the tablet still to scribble journalistic impressions, the floor is rumbling under so many boots and sneakers. The record player is old-fashioned, the loudspeakers are shitty, and it sounds fantastic. Two of the dancing Rantoul wives are fat, but with great legs. Who could practice this kind of tapping as much as they must and stay fat? I think maybe rural Midwestern women are just congenitally big. But these people clogging get *down*. And they do it as a troupe, a collective, with none of the narcissistic look-at-me grandstanding of great dancers in rock clubs. They hold hands and whirl each other around and in and out, tapping like mad, their torsos upright and almost formal, as if only incidentally attached to the blur of legs below. It goes on and on. I'm rooted to my stool. Each team seems the best yet. In the crowd's other side across the floor I can see the old poultry farmer, he of the carny hatred and electrified wallet. He's still got his poultry cap on, making a megaphone of his hands to whoop with the women, leaning way forward in his geriatric scooter, body bobbing like he's stomping in time, while his little cowboy boots stay clamped in their stays.

4:36 P.M.

Trying to hurry to the Grandstand, eating a corn dog cooked in 100 percent soybean oil. I can hear the hornety engines of the U.S.A.C. 100 race. A huge plume of track dust hangs over the Grandstand. Tinny burble of excited PA announcer. The corn dog tastes strongly of soybean oil, which itself tastes like corn oil that's been strained through an old gym towel. Tickets for the race are an obscene $13.50. Baton twirling is *still* under way in Club Mickey D's tent. A band called Captain Rat & the Blind Rivets is playing at Lincoln Stage, and as I pass I can see dancers in there. They look jagged and arrhythmic and blank, bored in that hip young East Coast way, facing in instead of out, not touching their partners. The people not dancing don't even look at them, and after the clogging the whole thing looks unspeakably numb and lonely.

4:45 P.M.

The official name of the race is the William "Wild Bill" Oldani Memorial 100 Sprint Car Race of the Valvoline-U.S.A.C. Silver Crown Series. The Grandstand seats 9,800 and is packed. The noise is beyond belief. The race is nearly over: the electric sign on the infield says "LAP 92." The leader is number 26, except his black-and-green Skoal car is in the middle of the pack. Apparently he's lapped people. The crowd is mostly men, very tan, smoking, 70 percent with mustaches and billed caps with automotive associations. Most of them wear earplugs; the ones in the real know wear thick airline-worker noise-filter headsets. The seventeen-page program is almost impenetrable. There are either forty-nine or fifty cars, called either Pro Dirt or Silver Crown, and they're basically go-carts from hell, with a soapbox-derby chassis and huge dragster tires, gleaming tangles of pipes and spoilers jutting out all over, and unabashedly phallic bulges up front. The program says these models are what they used to race at Indy in the 1950s. The cars' cockpits are open and webbed in straps and roll bars; the drivers wear helmets the same color as their cars, with white masks on their faces to keep out the choking dust. The cars come in all hues. Most look to be sponsored by either Skoal or Marlboro. Pit crews in surgical white lean out into the track and flash obscure commands written on little chalkboards.

The infield is clotted with trailers and tow trucks and officials' stands and electric signs. Women in skimpy tops stand on some of the trailers, seeming very partisan.

I can barely take my hands off my ears long enough to turn the program's pages. The cars sound almost like jets—that insectile scream—but with a diesely, lawn-mowerish component you can feel in your skull. The seating is on just one side of the Grandstand, on the straightaway, and when the mass of cars passes it's unendurable: your very skeleton hurts from the noise, and your ears are still belling when they come around again. The cars go like mad bats on the straightaways and then shift down for the tight turns, their rear tires wobbling in the dirt. Certain cars pass other cars, and some people cheer when they do. Down at the bottom of the section a little boy held up by his father is rigid, facing away from the track, his hands clamped over his ears so hard his elbows stick way out, and his face is a rictus of pain when they pass. The little boy and I sort of rictus at each other. A fine dirty dust hangs in the air and coats everything, including tongues. Then all of a sudden binoculars come out and everyone stands as there's some sort of screeching slide and crash on a far turn, all the way across the infield; and firemen in slickers and hats go racing out there in full-sized fire trucks, and the PA voice's pitch goes way up but is still incomprehensible, and a man with those airline earmuffs in the officials' stand leans out and flails at the air with a bright-yellow flag, and the go-carts throttle down to autobahn speed, and the pace car, a Trans Am, comes out and leads them around, and everybody stands, and I stand too. It is impossible to see anything but a swizzle stick of smoke above the far turn, and the engine noise is endurable and the PA silent, and the relative quiet hangs there while we all wait for news; and I look around at all the faces below the raised binoculars, but it's not at all clear what we're hoping for.

5:30 P.M.

Ten-minute line for a chocolate milk shake. Oily blacktop stink on heated paths. I ask a little boy to describe the taste of his funnel cake, and he runs away. My ears are still mossily ringing—everything sounds car-phonish. Display of a 17.6-lb. zucchini squash outside the Agri-Industries Pavilion. One big zucchini, all right. In the Coliseum, the only historical evidence of the tractor pulls is huge ideograms of tire tracks, mounds of scored dirt, dark patches of tobacco juice, smells of burnt rubber and oil. Nearby is a bus on display from the city of Peoria's All-Ethanol Bus System; it is painted to resemble a huge ear of corn.

6:00 P.M.

Back again at the seemingly inescapable Club Mickey D's. The tent is now set up for Illinois Golden Gloves Boxing. Out on the floor is a square of four boxing rings. The rings are made out of clothesline and poles anchored by cement-filled tires, one ring per age division: Sixteens, Fourteens, Twelves, Tens(!). Here's another unhyped but riveting spectacle. If you want to see genuine violence, go check out a Golden Gloves tourney. None of your adult pros' silky footwork or Rope-a-Dope defenses here. Here human asses are thoroughly kicked in what are essentially playground brawls with white-tipped gloves and brain-shaped head guards. The combatants' tank tops say things like "Peoria Jr. Boxing" and "Elgin Fight Club." The rings' corners have stools for the kids to sit on and get worked over by their teams' coaches. The coaches are clearly dads: florid, blue-jawed, bull-necked, flinty-eyed men who oversee sanctioned brawls. Now a fighter's mouth guard goes flying out of the Fourteens' ring, end over end, trailing strings of spit, and the crowd around that ring howls. In the Sixteens' ring is a local Springfield kid, Darrell Hall, against a slim fluid Latino, Sullivano, from Joliet. Hall outweighs Sullivano by a good twenty pounds. Hall also looks like every kid who ever beat me up in high school, right down to the wispy mustache and upper lip's cruel twist. The crowd around the Sixteens' ring is all his friends—guys with muscle shirts and gym shorts and gelled hair, girls in cutoff overalls and complex systems of barrettes. There are repeated shouts of "Kick his *ass,* Darrell!" The Latino sticks and moves. Somebody in this tent is smoking a joint, I can smell. The Sixteens can actually box. The ceiling's lights are bare bulbs in steel cones, hanging cockeyed from a day of batons. Everybody here pours sweat. The reincarnation of every high-school cheerleader I ever pined for is in the Sixteens' crowd. The girls cry out and frame their faces with their hands when Darrell gets hit. I do not know why cutoff overall shorts have evaded the East Coast's fashion ken; they are devastating. The fight in

Fourteens is stopped for a moment to let the ref wipe a gout of blood from one kid's glove. Sullivano glides and jabs, orbiting Hall. Hall is implacable, a hunched and feral fighter, boring in. Air explodes through his nose when he lands a blow. He keeps trying to back the Latino against the clothesline. People cool themselves with wood-handled fans from the Democratic Party. Big hairy mosquitoes work the crowd. The refs keep slapping at their necks. The rain has been heavy, and the mosquitoes are the bad kind, field-bred and rapacious. I can also see the Tens from this vantage, a vicious free-for-all between two tiny kids whose head guards make their skulls look too big for their bodies. Neither ten-year-old has any interest in defense. Their shoes' toes touch as they windmill at each other, scoring at will. Scary dads chew gum in their corners. One kid's mouth guard keeps falling out. Now the Sixteens' crowd explodes as their loutish Hall catches Sullivano with an uppercut that puts him on his bottom. Sullivano gamely rises, but his knees wobble and he won't face the ref. Hall raises both arms and faces the crowd, disclosing a missing incisor. The girls betray their cheerleading backgrounds by clapping and jumping up and down at the same time. Hall shakes his gloves at the ceiling as several girls call his name, and you can feel it in the air's very ions: Darrell Hall is going to get laid before the night's over.

The digital thermometer in the Ronald-Buddha's left hand reads ninety-three degrees at 6:30 P.M. Behind him, big ominous scoop-of-coffee-ice-cream clouds are massing at the western horizon, but the sun's still above them and very much a force. People's shadows on the paths are getting pointy. It's the part of the day when little kids cry from what their parents naïvely call exhaustion. Cicadas chirr in the grass by the tent. The ten-year-olds stand toe to toe and whale the living shit out of each other. It is the sort of savage mutual beating you see in black-and-white films of old-time fights. Their ring now has the largest crowd. The fight will be all but impossible to score. But then it is over in an instant at the second intermission, when one of the little boys, sitting on his stool, being whispered to by a dad with tattooed forearms, suddenly throws up. Prodigiously. For no apparent reason. Maybe a stomach punch recollected in tranquillity. It is kind of surreal. Vomit flies all over. Kids in the crowd go "Eeeyuuu." The sick fighter starts to cry. His scary coach and the ref wipe him down and help him from the ring, not ungently. His opponent, watching, tentatively puts up his arms.

7:30 P.M.

So the old heave-ho is the last thing I see at Golden Gloves Boxing and then the first thing I see at Happy Hollow, right at sunset. Standing on the midway looking up at the Ring of Fire—a set of flame-colored train cars sent around and around the inside of a 100-foot neon hoop, the operator stalling the train at the top and hanging the patrons upside down, jack-knifed over their seat belts, with loose change and eye-glasses raining down—looking up, I witness a thick coil of vomit arc from a car; it describes a 100-foot spiral and lands with a meaty splat between two young girls, who look from the ground to each other with expressions of slapstick horror. And when the flame train finally brakes at the ramp, a mortified-looking little kid wobbles off, damp and pale, staggering over toward a Lemon Shake-Up stand.

This is my last day at the fair, and I've put off a real survey of the Near-Death Experiences until my last hour. I want to get everything catalogued before the sun sets. I've already had some distant looks at the nighttime Hollow and have an idea that being down here in the dark, amid all this rotating neon and the mechanical clowns and plunging machinery's roar and jagged screams and barkers' pitches and high-volume rock, would be like the depiction of a bum acid trip in a bad Sixties movie. It strikes me hardest in the Hollow that I'm not spiritually Midwestern anymore, and no longer young—I do not like crowds, screams, amplified noise, or heat. I'll endure them if I have to, but they're sure not my idea of a magic community-interval. The crowds in the Hollow, though—mostly high-school couples, local toughs, and kids in single-sex packs, as the demographics of the fair shift to prime time—seem radically happy, vivid, somehow awakened, sponges for sensuous data, not bombarded by the stimuli but feeding on it. It is the first time I've felt really lonely at the fair.

Nor do I understand why some people will pay money to be careened and suspended and dropped and whipped back and forth at high speeds and hung upside down until somebody vomits. It seems to me like paying to be in a traffic accident. I do not get it; never have. It's not a regional or cultural thing. I think it's a matter of neurological makeup. The world divides into those who like the managed induction of terror and those who don't. I do not find terror exciting. I find it terrifying.

And Happy Hollow, I discover, offers nothing if not managed terror.

And not one but two Tilt-a-Whirls. An experience called Wipe Out straps riders into fixed seats on a big lit disc that spins with a wobble like a coin that won't lie down. The Pirate Ship puts forty folks in a plastic galley and swings it in a pendulous arc until they're facing straight up and then down. The carny operating the Pirate Ship is made to wear an eye patch and parrot and hook, on the tip of which hook burns an impaled Marlboro. The operator of the Funhouse is slumped in a plastic control booth that reeks of sinsemilla.

The 104-foot Giant Gondola Wheel is a staid old Ferris wheel that puts you facing your seatmate in a kind of steel teacup. Its rotation is stately, but the cars at the top look like little lit thimbles, and you can hear thin female screams from up there as their dates grab the teacups' sides and joggle.

The lines are the longest for the really serious Near-Death Experiences: Ring of Fire, the Zipper, Hi Roller—which runs a high-speed train around the inside of an ellipse that is itself spinning at right angles to the train's motion. The crowds are dense and reek of bug repellent. Boys in Chicago Cubs shirts clutch their dates as they walk. There's something intensely *public* about young Midwestern couples. The girls have tall hair and bee-stung lips, and their eye makeup runs in the heat and gives them a vampirish aspect. The overt sexuality of high-school girls is not just a coastal thing. The Amour Express sends another little train at 60-plus mph around a topologically wobbled ring, half of which is enclosed in a fiberglass tunnel with neon hearts and arrows. A fallen packet of Trojans lies near the row of Lucite cubes in which slack-jawed cranes try to pick up jewelry.

It seems journalistically irresponsible to try to describe the Hollow's rides without experiencing at least one firsthand. The Kiddie Kopter is a carousel of miniature Sikorsky prototypes rotating at a sane and dignified clip. The propellers on each helicopter rotate as well. My copter is a bit snug, admittedly, even with my knees drawn up to my chest. I get kicked off the ride, though, when the whole machine's tilt reveals that I weigh quite a bit more than the maximum 100 pounds; and I have to say that both the little kids on the ride and the carny in charge were unnecessarily snide about the whole thing. Each ride has its own PA speaker with its own discharge of adrenalizing rock; the Kiddie Kopter's speaker is playing George Michael's "I Want Your Sex." The late-day Hollow itself is an enormous sonic mash from which different sounds take turns protruding—

mostly whistles, sirens, calliopes, heavy-metal tunes, human screams hard to distinguish from recorded screams.

Both the Thunderboltz and the Octopus hurl free-spinning modular cars around a topologically complex plane; the Thunderboltz's sides reveal further evidence of gastric distress. Then there's the Gravitron, basically a centrifuge—an enclosed, top-shaped structure inside which is a rubberized chamber that spins so fast you're mashed against the wall like a fly on a windshield. A small boy stands on one foot tugging the Gravitron operator's khaki sleeve, crying that he lost a shoe in there. The best description of the carnies' tan is that they're somehow *sinisterly* tanned. I notice that many of them have the low brow and prognathous jaw one associates with fetal alcohol syndrome. The carny operating the Scooter—bumper cars that are fast, savage, underinsulated, a sure trip to the chiropractor—has been slumped in the same position in the same chair every time I've seen him, staring past the frantic cars and tearing up used ride-tickets with the vacant intensity of someone on a locked ward. I lean casually against his platform's railing so that my credentials dangle and ask him in a neighborly way how he keeps from going out of his freaking mind with the boredom of his job. He turns his head very slowly, revealing a severe facial tic: "The fuck you talkin' 'bout?"

The same two carnies as before are at the Zipper's controls, in the exact same clothes, looking up into the full cars and elbowing each other. The midway smells of machine oil and fried food, smoke and Cutter repellent and mall-bought adolescent perfume and ripe trash in the bee-swarmed cans. The very Nearest-to-Death ride looks to be the Kamikaze, way down at the western end by the Zyklon roller coaster. Its neon sign has a skull with a headband and says "Kamikaze." It is a 70-foot pillar of white-painted iron with two 50-foot hammer-shaped arms hanging down, one on either side. The cars are at the ends of the arms, twelve-seaters enclosed in clear plastic. The two arms swing ferociously around, as in 360 degrees, vertically, and in opposite directions, so that twice on every rotation it looks like your car is going to get smashed up against the other car, and you can see faces in the other car hurtling toward you, gray with fear and squishy with G's. An eight-ticket, four-dollar waking nightmare.

Then I find the worst one. It wasn't even here yesterday. The Sky Coaster stands regally aloof at the Hollow's far western edge, just past the Uphill-Bowling-for-Dinnerware game, in a kind of grotto formed by trailers and dismantled machinery. It is a 175-foot construction crane, one of the really big mothers, with a tank's traction belts instead of wheels, a canary-yellow cab, and a long proboscis of black steel, towering, canted upward at maybe 70 degrees. This is half the Sky Coaster. The other half is a 100-foot tower assembly of cross-hatched iron that's been erected about two football fields to the north of the crane. There's a folding table in front of the clothesline cordoning off the crane, and a line of people at the table. The woman taking their money is fiftyish and a compelling advertisement for sunscreen. Behind her on a vivid blue tarp are two meaty blond guys in Sky Coaster T-shirts helping the next customer strap himself into what looks like a combination straitjacket and utility belt, bristling with hooks and clips. From here the noise of the Hollow behind is both deafening and muffled. My media guide, sweated into the shape of my butt pocket, says, "If you thought bungee jumping was a thrill, wait until you soar high above the Fairgrounds on Sky Coaster. The rider is fastened securely into a full-body harness that hoists them [sic] onto a tower and releases them to swing in a pendulum-like motion while taking in a spectacular view of the Fairgrounds below." The signs at the folding table are more telling: "$40.00. AMEX Visa MC. No Refunds. No Stopping Half Way Up." The two guys are leading the customer up the stairs of a rolling platform maybe ten feet high. One guy is at each elbow, and I realize they're helping hold the customer up. Who would pay $40 for an experience requiring you to be held up as you walk toward it? There's also something off about the customer, odd. He's wearing tinted aviator glasses. No one in the rural Midwest wears aviator glasses, tinted or otherwise. Then I see what it really is. He's wearing $400 Banfi loafers. Without socks. This guy, now lying prone on the platform below the crane, is *from the East Coast.* He's a ringer. I almost want to shout it. A woman is on the blue tarp, already in harness, wobbly kneed, waiting her turn. A steel cable descends from the tip of the crane's proboscis, on its end a fist-sized clip. Another cable leads from the crane's cab to the tower, up through ring-tipped pitons all up the tower's side, and over a pulley at its top, another big clip on the end. One of the guys waves the tower's cable down and brings it over to the platform. The clips of both cables are attached to the back of the East Coast guy's harness, fastened and locked. The guy is trying to look around behind him to see what-all's attached as the two big blonds leave the platform. Another blond man in the yellow cab throws a lever, and the tower's cable pulls tight in the grass and up the tower's side and down. The crane's cable stays slack as the guy is lifted into the air by the tower's cable. The harness covers his shorts and top, so he looks babe-naked as he rises. The one cable sings with tension as the East Coaster is pulled slowly to the top of the tower. He's still stomach-down, limbs wriggling. At a certain height he starts to look like livestock in a sling. You can tell he's trying to swallow until his face gets too small to see. Finally he's all the way up at the top of the tower, his ass against the pulley, trying not to writhe.

I can barely take notes. They cruelly leave him up there a while, slung, a smile of slack cable between him and the crane's tip. I am constructing a mental list of the personal violations I would undergo before I'd let anyone haul me ass-first to a great height and swing me like high-altitude beef. One of the blond guys has a bullhorn and he's playing to the crowd's suspense, calling up to the slung East Coaster: "Are. You. *Ready*." The East Coaster's response noises are more bovine than human. His tinted aviator glasses hang askew from just one ear; he doesn't bother to fix them. I can see what's going to happen. They're going to throw a lever and detach the tower-cable's clip, and the man in sockless Banfis will free-fall for what will seem forever, until the slack of the crane's cable is taken up and the line goes taut behind him and swings him way out over the grounds to the south, his upward arc almost as high as the crane's tip, and then back, and then forth, the man prone at the arc's bottom and seeming to stand on ei-ther side, swinging back and forth against a rare-meat sunset. And just as the cab man reaches for his lever and everyone inhales, I lose my nerve and disappear into the crowd.

9:15 P.M.

Walking aimlessly. Seas of fairgoing flesh, plodding, elbowing, looking, still eating. They stand placidly in long lines. No East Coast games of Beat the Crowd. Midwesterners lack a certain public cunning. No one gets im-patient. Don't the fairgoers mind the crowds, lines, noise? But the state fair is deliberately about the crowds and jostle, the noise and overload of sight and event. At last an overarching theory blooms inside my head: mega-lopolitan East Coasters' summer treats and breaks are literally "getaways," flights-from—from crowds, noise, heat, dirt, the stress of too many sen-sory choices. Hence the ecstatic escapes to glassy lakes, mountains, cabins, hikes in silent woods. Getting away from it all. They see more than enough stimulating people and sights Monday through Friday, thank you, stand in enough lines, elbow enough crowds. Neon skylines. Grotesques on public transport. Spectacles at every urban corner practically grab you by the lapels, commanding attention. The East Coast existential treat is escape from confines and stimuli—quiet, rustic vistas that hold still, turn inward, turn away. Not so in the rural Midwest. Here you're pretty much away all the time. The land is big here—board-game flat, horizons in every direction. See how much farther apart the homes are, how broad the yards: compare with New York or Boston or Philly. Here a seat to yourself on all public transport, parks the size of airports, rush hour a three-beat pause at a stop sign. And the farms themselves are huge, silent, vacant: you can't see your neighbor. Thus the urge physically to commune, melt, become part of a crowd. To see something besides land and grass and corn and cable TV and your wife's face. Hence the sacredness out here of spectacle, public event: high-school football, Little League, parades, bingo, market day, fair. All very big deals, very deep down. Something in a Midwesterner sort of *actuates,* deep down, at a public event. The faces in the sea of faces are like the faces of children released from their rooms. Governor Edgar's state-spirit rhetoric at the ribbon-cutting rings true. The real spectacle that draws us here is us.

1998

When writers primarily known as poets use in their work forms of prose, the prose is primarily considered poetry. For example: *Bells in Winter; Human Wishes; Notes for Echo Lake.* In these works, as in many recent others, stanzas more closely resemble paragraphs, lines are extended to the length of sentences. What is the formal difference between prose and poetry if there are no lines being broken in either? If there is no meter employed in either? In Italy *stanza* means "a room." In Spain *stanza* means "a shelter." In France, where Wayne Koestenbaum imagines his subject, *stanza* can be used to describe "a stance"—a way of carrying oneself.

WAYNE KOESTENBAUM

Darling's Prick

"... I only wish I could have you in my arms, so I could
hold you and squeeze you tight. Remember the things we
used to do together. Try to recognize the dotted lines. And
kiss it. A thousand big kisses, sweetheart, from
                                    Your Darling."
The dotted line that Darling refers to is the outline of his
prick. I once saw a pimp who had a hard-on while writing
to his girl place his heavy cock on the paper and trace its
contours. I would like that line to portray Darling.
                                    Fresnes Prison, 1942

JEAN GENET, OUR LADY OF THE FLOWERS,
TRANS. BERNARD FRECHTMAN

I am not interested in the prick per se. I am interested in prose.

I want to dispense with mediation, including the mediation of the "I."

At the end of Jean Genet's novel, a writer puts his heavy cock on the
paper and traces its contours. He would like the line to portray Darling.
But the line won't necessarily do the writer's bidding.

I want the prick, but also it is my prick that tells me what I want. So the
prick announces hunger but also advertises a system of hungers.

I don't want to write "about" the prick, I want to write the prick.

Which doesn't mean I like pricks. In fact I am rather indifferent to them.

To want to place the prick on the page is to deplore mediation and abstraction. The "I" here is a writer speaking up impatiently and dogmati-
cally on behalf of other prisoners of representation.

Pornographic pictures don't do the trick. Nor do explicit descriptions.

I don't want pictures of sex. I don't want sex. I want writing.

Often of course I want sex and often of course I want pictures but more regularly I want writing.

The "I" here is the paradigmatic pornographer whose aesthetic I am trying to limn and justify.

It is difficult to understand the aesthetic of the pornographer, which is incidentally the aesthetic of the consumer of fiction and the casual movie-goer and the eater.

A person is sitting in a Cineplex Odeon putting popcorn in his or her mouth.

A person is playing a video game.

A person is filling out a questionnaire.

A person is waiting at a bus stop, listening to rainfall.

A person is watching a ceiling fan rotate.

A person on a beach towel opens a novel about the presidential primaries.

A person eats corn flakes while reading the box.

A person writes a sentence. The sentence is neither good nor bad, but poses its subject and predicate in the ordinary fashion.

Maybe you, too, are sick of mediation, of words that get in the way of what you want to say.

Assume there is a state of mind called "wanting to say," a desire that precedes words. The point is to stick as closely as possible to the desire, and not get lost in the words. Unless, of course, you desire words.

How convenient, how ultimate, if instead of the clutter of words we could have things.

I don't have enough words; I want more of them. And I want their emergence to be clean and genital.

I want what I read to have the clarity of a spotlit body.

I suppose some pornographers have the option of sleeping with their subjects.

I suppose some writers have already experienced what they write about.

I suppose that if I say I want to put my heavy prick on the page and trace its outline, then I have the option of letting you assume I possess a prick and that you and I agree on what a prick is.

And if I don't possess a prick, if I possess something else, and I put that something else on the page, then you have to figure out what that something else is.

How do you know if you desire the something else? I will have to draw its outline very precisely, so you can decide if its outline matches the other possessions you have desired.

If I am typing, then I can't put my prick or my something else on the page. I can only put fingers on the keys.

The outline drawn around the prick, on the page, encloses blank space. The reader must hypothesize a prick inside the dotted lines.

The beautiful part is the hypothesis, not the prick.

Darling's prick is long dead—incinerated or decomposed. Other pricks have taken Darling's place. All are the same. One after another. But the outline of Darling's prick has original poignance.

I once saw a pimp place his heavy cock on the paper. He was writing to his girl.

The pimp was my teacher. The pimp practiced mimesis.

I followed suit. I put my cock on the paper, too.

Most poetry is pornographic, since I define poetry as language that envies the scene it is describing. Poetry is words watching and wanting to approach the objects it renders.

By *Darling's prick* I mean the thing you press on the page when you write a love letter or describe a scene you want to join. By *Darling's prick* I mean the urge to be more present in the scene of composition.

Sometimes word and thing are indistinguishable. I don't know whether to advocate this indistinguishability. Instead, more modestly, I want to point to it.

To say: sometimes flesh (I don't know what else to call it) is present in the act of writing—or sometimes flesh wishes to present itself.

The writer draws a dotted line around the inappropriately thrust forward presence. Let's not call this presence a "self." Genet calls it, in shorthand, a prick. You could as easily call it a buttock cheek, a nipple, a nose.

It depends what turns you on.

All I ask is to be alive.

I don't expect miracles.

Gertrude Stein is the most pornographic writer I know.

Her language exemplifies a presence of the "thing" where the reader does not expect it, a presence of the uncalled-for.

Stein's language puts forward embarrassment: *you didn't expect this.*

I think about Gertrude Stein when I contemplate my desire to write pornographically—the wish to put forward the subjects of my regard, rather than words describing those subjects.

A dull word to describe this practice is *performance.* Dull, because expected.

And I don't want to put forward anything expected.

I suppose a prick is expected. It is a usual subject.

Let us say that you are throwing a costume party. Someone comes dressed as Roy Cohn. Also, the real Roy Cohn comes to the party. Confusion ensues. The real Roy Cohn has not put on a mask. He has decided to come as himself. So there are two Roy Cohns at the ball.

Writing is a masquerade party. You must come dressed as someone plausible.

If I am already Roy Cohn, I must think up a different disguise to put over my Roy Cohn face.

Darling's prick—not mine, not Genet's—is at stake here.

Darling is the life you want, when you read; the life you read toward.

The outline of Darling's prick posits the simplicity of an urtext.

One way to look at sexuality: it is the image bank you plunder while you have sex or while you wait to have sex. Once you are done having sex, the image bank is closed, defunct. Until the next time.

Another way to look at sexuality: it is the image bank you use all the time. It is the modus operandi of your motility.

Usually I think of sexuality as a matter of acceleration and deceleration. Instead I should think of it as how and why I think.

I should consider sex to be the art of making propositions. I should reverence the beauty of argument.

I have put forward a few new ideas today.

Class dismissed.

Class resumed.

I like simple sentences because they are rude and clean. They are sexual because naked. I have practiced a sexuality of the baroque but I will now commence a sexuality of the unembellished.

This class is taking place in the field of the contemporary Anglophone sentence.

Darling's prick has made paragraphs newly interesting.

If you stick forward your body every time you speak, then you are often sticking forward your body.

Genitals and writing have the same imaginary intensity. They are both put forward.

Darling's prick on the paper is a metaphor or replacement for the real prick.

Real pricks are necessary yet overrated. Imaginary pricks go farther.

Styles are simple or styles are complex. Children's literature is simple. Pornography is simple.

Children's literature and pornography concretely denote what the reader might wish.

I quickly outgrew children's literature, which is why I have returned, at this advanced age, to practicing it.

It isn't coy to put my heavy prick on the page. And yet it is the height of indirection.

I am interested in sentences, paragraphs, poetry, pornography, ecstasy, exhibitionism, privacy, love, representation, enigma.

When I trace a desire, I try to follow its outline as closely as possible.

I try not to impose a foreign form on its shape.

I adhere to the perimeters of imaginary anatomy.

I hate going backwards.

The "I" here is not the writer but an exemplary intelligence, prick-shaped, operating on your heart. The "I" here is a person deliberately putting forward identical shapes.

Again and again the same shape.

So you might as well get used to being accosted by what you have already seen.

Portrayal is very silent, as are sentences.

Here you see portrayed a pornography of the sentence. It is childish, exhibitionistic. It is slow and quick.

It demands that you kiss it.

Pornography is an industry but the pornography of the sentence (Darling's prick) is nonprofit.

Each sentence is a suppository.

That's how we write in the porn industry. That's how we write in Hollywood. That's how we write in the genre fiction factory. That's how we write in the academy.

Slow and quick.

Darling has a hard-on; that's why he writes.

That's why he stops writing.

Why represent, if you can kiss the cock's contours?

That is exactly why he writes. That is exactly the logic of the desire to portray.

I film your speech because I want to make your desire clear.

If you watch this videotaped documentary film of yourself speaking, you might discover how to speak more effectively, which might help you make money.

If you watch this film of yourself going door to door trying to sell bad Bibles, you might become a more effective salesperson.

Would you like to buy a fake creed?

Would you like to buy a botched gospel?

May I offer you a farcical crucifixion?

Class dismissed.

1999

Some history: The word *prose* came into English by way of the Latin *prosus,* the Vulgate's paired-down simplification of *prorsus,* itself the contracted form of *proversus,* "to move forward," as in Cicero's *prosa oratio,* "speech going straight ahead without turns." Notice, however, that this Latin root of *prose* has in it the root for *verse.* It comes from the Greek word *verso,* the little mechanism on a plow that allowed a farmer to turn a furrow—or, in terms of literature, a line. In Latin, *verso* became *versus* and its verb form *vertere,* meaning "to turn," hence the English *vertex, vertigo,* and even the word *conversant* ("one capable of spinning an interesting tale"). In other words, when a line in poetry bumps up against whatever it is that a line bumps up against—death, confusion, the other, unknowns, a rough and rooty patch of impenetrable earth—the line gets to turn around, start over, make as many running charges at its subject as it wants. An essay, on the other hand, defined by the arbitrary margins of a page, cannot cut itself short, cannot go back to start. If, as Bacon noted, an essay only exists once we have something to say and we say it, what do we call those fields left half-plowed by some essayists?

CAROLE MASO

The Intercession of Saints

Saints hold a tambourine, a lily, a pomegranate, a flame, a red book, a plum.

A chalice of seawater. The world's last music. A fire in a stone bowl. A starling. A globe.

Their longing makes a burning sound. Their most precious blood tolls.

A dulcimer. An egg. A basket of plums. A plume of smoke.

The saints marvel. They love nothing more than a miracle or two: the child's small hand in mine, milk flowing from an open vein, or the covenant made anew each day.

Saints sing like ships sing. Like fog. Like the phases of the moon. Like a mantle of blue. A rhapsody. Saints sing.

They believe in the new covenant of the replaced blood.

A perched village on a platter. A tiny basilica. A ruby casting its jewel tone. Bone ash. Marrow. Cup of mysterious universe.

The temptation to believe is great.

The heart swings like a pendulum toward and then away from God. Toward and then away. Nearer and then farther. The heart's proximities are two carrier pigeons. Are the message they carry. A logic of wings. A philosophy of light.

Saints with rakes are out harvesting bone marrow while we speak.

Their pure health. Their faith like crazy.

The weight of their sweat more precious than gold.

The saints say: *one conquers the temptations of the world through pain.*

Saint Agatha under her veil of sorrows. Holding the last handfuls of hair in her hands.

The anesthesia is like dusk: soft, hot, blue, misty. They float through so beautifully now, cradling their symbols.

A scale, a spade, a goose.

The saints in their infinite sweetness renounce the world.

Dancing saints have a lilting charm.

Who could not love Saint Theresa doing her frenzied wedding dance?

She sang like a bird.

Falling into a collapsed time.

Saints hold a head, a sonnet, a tongue. A lily, a pomegranate, an apple, a plum.

Above the crucified Christ a swan and its young.

Saint Francis in his holy hovel.

The Madonna with five angels.

Madame holding a chalice of seawater.

The angel holding Matthew's inkwell.

Novice saints hold a fragment of flame in their hair.

Saints hold keys, fish, small ships, a rooster, a stone.

Saints hold.

Your body is a heart, an angel flagellated, a wheel, a flame, and darkness.

They visit the hospital in a kind of solidarity. They fall and swoon. They carry little vessels of bone and hope.

Saints sun-bake in the God-light. *The job of the soul is to suffer.*

Saints hold the flame whole in their perfect hands. Saints can.

I wish I were a bird with a crimson head.
A garden.
His mother's hair.

The saints hold a staff, a lamb, a feather, the bambino. Or clutch a small bird.

I thought the two weeks of apparitions had ended. The *frisson* of weeping angels, the thorns in a cup, the ladle of white blood soup, the violations at the grave.

As if the halo were being scissored off, as if the light were being sliced, as if you could take that away from an angel or a person just like that—with a blade.

Voices come, they die away.

You were more precious than song.

They saints carry their regrets. Their 7.5 pound unborn babies each, their condolences.

Saints suffer down the page. They fall like roses. Pale birds.

On the last rung of the ladder in the Seventh House of the Apocalypse.

The saints pierce themselves on swastikas. Smuggle children to the borders. Move to the ends of earthly pain.

Saint Catherine of Siena: *one tries not enough.*

Saints suffer their way.

In the anesthesia called twilight the saints attempt to defeat time.

Filing by one by one:

Saint Hippolytus torn by horses.
Saint Helena dreaming of the Cross, the coat of nails, the road.
Saint John the Baptist and his attributes: a lamb, wings and a honey pot.
Saint Rose of Lima, too beautiful.
Saint Wenceslaus still trudging through the bitterly cold night carrying logs
     for a poor man's fire. His footprints in the snow.
Saint Martha with a ladle and keys and a broom.
Saint Hildegarde, pop star, with five hits on the charts.
Saint Apollonia holding a tooth in a pair of pincers.

The hermits and scholars sit quietly in intensive care thinking and brooding. Saint Giles, one of the 14 Holy Helpers holding a chamber pot. Saint Sebastian like a fountain.

Saint Christopher has a rakish charm with his river and flowing staff and arrows and dog's head.

What's up with the dog's head?

Saints look on bewildered by the weapons of mass destruction.

The dream too often, during sex, or when contemplating God, is the dream of annihilation.

Saint Ava in ecstasy.

Trance

After pain a floating feeling comes.

From the open chest in the operating theater: birds fly. Soul goes off.

Look closely at the child holding a small bouquet of violets—a sweet offering to the now sutured chest. Taking the heart out. Putting it back in.

Burning. The river is burning. The children are burning.

Saints smolder.

Saints lay their bodies down in front of tanks. War has a boyish charm: Desert Fox, Desert Storm. The saints sigh.

The body turned into a torch. A lantern. A bell.

The heart out.

The saints say *one day paradise.* They put on their moody Houdini suits and wait.

The saints say.

7 Saints stand in the 7 Churches of the Apocalypse.

Deciding to fast, refusing all food, until the killing stops, they recite the 404 verses.

Tiny parachutes on the Normandy coast. The heart back in.

A rain of roses.

World's end.

A fever of roses.

A love letter laced in Anthrax.

I wish my hand might touch the fire between the letters of the alphabet. I wish I could translate God's reticence.

For seven months she held the child under her heart.

The ocean is a cistern overflowed with tears. The world does not beat.

Some saints I'm told smell like roses after their death.

A chalice of heartbreak, a peace offering, a forest of semaphores. A ball of fire, a lion, a cloak split in half.

The heart like a metronome swings.

We're a little lost. In the semiotics. And not a graduate student in sight.

Not to worry, the saints hold their compass rose.

Saint Francis throws himself onto a bed of thorns to quell desire. Such sad and useless heroics.

The desolate heights. Heat and light.

One day you are walking to the university where you teach, you happen to look up, and what—what is it you see—in that one instant—your death unfolds as if on a paper scroll—you lift your hand—the light shines through . . .

The light shines through you.

The world is not a trinket or an oyster or an ornament.

And you fall into time while the angels watch.

Ava Klein, you fall into time—

As when you were pregnant and you watched its explicit work on you.

Never had you felt the workings of time—just time—so dramatically.

The saints reiterate *life is unbearable without suffering.*

OK, OK.

See how the infant in utero already waves to a distant horizon.

Complicity with the dark. Complicity with the light. That saints look up and hum.

I hear the last light in the sky. *Wish I may—wish I might—*

I wish I were bells.

Have the wish I wish tonight.

The saints whisper sweet nothings. Make no promises. This no nonsense brand of saint can really grate.

There were many things that nothing could cure.

Not prayer, not song, not alcohol, not chemotherapy—certainly not.

The saints whisper sweet nothings in my ear.

I wish I were bells, something plangent and beautiful and able to modulate the dark—sing God's silences.

In the hush of the lung, in the shadow the T cell casts, you, solitary saint sing a perfect nocturne.

The long bones of illness, her tuning fork.

I wish I were a field of wheat.

Blood and light collected in a chalice.

Lovingly she takes the shroud and places it at my feet.

Music for a too late afternoon.

Anatole, saved from drowning.

Francesco weeps. He loves Italian saints. Saint Chiara. Saint Francis of Assisi,

Who hurls himself one more time onto a rosebush—seedlings sprouting wherever the drops of blood fall.

Francesco loves him best of all. He reads from *The Book of Saints*:

"Paintings depict Francis with and without a dog's head (it was believed that he begged the Lord to make him ugly as a dog to escape the attention of women), carrying Jesus as a child and surrounded by two prostitutes (sometimes envisioned as sexy mermaids)."

The adoration of the saint.

Their relics gleam. Luminous in agony—brilliant at it. Locked as they are away in sarcophagi, reliquaries, under glass—for a thousand lira they light up like July.

I wish I were a 6 stringed instrument.

Or locked away in the chambers of the heart. Saint Valentine in bondage.

Or the head off.

Wishing for sleep I see Aunt Sophie at the ditch, barefoot and pregnant and begging.

Sophie, at the mouth of the world—a latter day saint.

Saints fly like falling stars.

Saints sail in hot air balloons rescuing the doomed. *Hey Sophie, we're up here!* They lend a hand.

High above the troubled world.

Blood and light collected in a chalice. *Live* they whisper.

Saints burn in extremis.

Saints whiz by fueled by adoration, in the day, in the night. Intoxicating, don't you think?

Yes I do.

The intensity of saints.

There's no real cure for it.

The pure oxygen.

Wings burn. They burn.

Desire one more time hurls Saint Francis into thorns.

Snow works I'm told. *Oh right.*

Saints emit an eerie light. Roses open.

The five wounds of the crucified Christ on mortified flesh bloom. *Stigmata*—a kind of board game they like to play those saints.

Saints hold very nice looking tarts in their hands. The key to a perfect crust is ice water.

Saints hold a mandolin. A quill. An apple. A small bird.

Witness Saint Agnes and her lamb offering her maidenhead to God.

Saint Anthony of Padua and the presentation of the Host to the Mule. That's a good one.

Saint Catherine of Genoa recites the Treatise on Purgatory.

Saint Jerome in the desert. A fire in a stone bowl. The arc of blood. A dove at his throat. An angel in red.

Some saints carry bunches of bananas on their heads to feed the poor.

Saints at the soup kitchen. Saints at the cinema. Saints in every imaginable place.

In Firenze Francesco, the angel holds a scroll over the sleeper's head revealing the dream to us. Not even the solitude of dreams anymore.

In Siena, meanwhile

Saint Catherine undoes the collar and lets the head drop onto her lap after the chop—good God! When the cadaver was taken away she says, my soul rested in such delicious peace and I rejoiced so in the perfume of that blood that I did not wish them to take away that thing that lay upon my clothes.

That's just how saints are.

Her favorite words were *fire* and *blood.*

What is the head doing off?

She used a stone for a pillow.

She was known to go into the *Capella dela Volte* where many Sienese watched the host go flying from the hand of the priest directly into her mouth.

She was cut up by the Romans.

Her head ensconced in a golden reliquary.

Brain scan.

The Venetians have a foot.

An earthquake in Assisi. Saint Francis crumbling.

Saints sigh *this world.* The women swoon for their doozy bridegroom.

They carry bouquets of bloodroot and bleeding heart and trillium. That's nice.

Under the weeping willow saints play.

Dulcimer. Bone ash. Sparrow.

In their blood they carry bits of the true cross splintered.

Bone marrow transplant.

Saint Rose waves at the vanishing point.

At the melting point.

At the place the blood freezes, saints say *let it bleed.*

The saints wait patiently.

They forge virginity certificates.

They idolize their bleary bridegroom. They practice *I do* and *I will,* as if they needed to. Weeping and fever become them. They wait for Him with the patience of, well, you know.

Saints in ecstasy say strange things.

The saints carry blankets for all night international flights.

They sing the *Stabat Mater Dolorosa* so beautifully. In a wounded way.

The saints carry little nuclear winters under tiny glass domes. They keep us safe they say.

They pray over the hazardous wastes.

The saints trudge up the mountain, the saints trudge down. (Concern for the cat, the pot still simmering, the clothes on their backs, etc.)

They carry an ocean of sorrow in their cupped hands.

They carry the *fin-de-siècle* on their backs.

Children are jumping.

They carry the origin of tears.

Amniotic, last, most perfect night.

Children are flying.

Cupping a chalice of seawater.

God wades through the tears of the saints to his next destination.

Joan burns. She burns.

Through the smoke of the saints.

And the seraphs.

With the patience of a saint you wait, Francesco, as if with perfect attention you might change the course of what will be.

Cats moving in and out—scanning the place for available saints.

You've got a crazy faith.

God wades through a universe of tears.

The sleeping children float in the safety of Saint Lucy's blue pupil.

Three women dreaming next to water recall how at just the sight of the angel's wing . . . The infinitesimal world taking shape in their gaze.

Carrying so much hope.

A rain of roses will fall at my death. Saint Therese.

I wish I could decipher your silence.

They cradle the head.

A blue ghost in the bones.

The human skin remembers everything. Everything. So the child in surgery becomes a saint his whole life.

Open heart. There is always hope, the saints say.

And the saints carry wedding cakes and twelve wedding rings.

There is always love they whisper through the cobalt light.

The saints in blue with rakes in otherworldly loneliness.

Pluck ashes from the filling mouth.

The saints smuggle children with forged passports to the border.

The saints understand it is almost time, but not yet.

Roses to the border.

The saints know ashes.

Mend us with fire.

Their longing makes a burning sound.

Those crazy saints! They have sheepish charm.

In anesthesia's twilight.

They whisper *How beautiful are the feet.*

Mother, it certainly does seem—the blood begins to sing.

cup bearer

orbit

soul

The seven sleepers . . .

Saints cast a lovely light.

2000

I think essayists write for the sake of preservation; in order to find solutions to problems, in order to remain intellectually, emotionally, or spiritually awake amidst the full rumbling fury of the world. "An essay that becomes a lyric," Plutarch once wrote, presumably about his own formally wayward work, "is an essay that has killed itself." A prose line can stave off this death for as long as the seams of its syntax hold. And when they fail to hold, a run-on can seem less a sloppy piece of grammar than a desperate act to stay alive.

Monument

A small war had ended. Like all wars, it was terrible. Things which had stood in existence were now vanished. I had come back because I had survived and survivors come back, there is nothing else left for them to do. I had been on long travels connected to the war, and I had been to the centerpiece of the war, that acre of conflagration. And now I was sitting on a park bench, watching ducks land and take off from a pond. They too had survived, though I had no way of knowing if they were the same ducks from before the war or if they were the offspring of ducks who had died in the war. It was a warm day in the capital and people were walking without coats, dazed by the warmth, which was not the heat of war, which had engulfed them, but the warmth of expansion, in which would grow the idea of a memorial to the war, which had ended, and of which I was a veteran architect. I knew I would be called upon for my ideas in regards to this memorial and I had entered the park aimlessly, trying to escape my ideas, as I had been to the centerpiece, that acre of conflagration, and from there the only skill that returned was escapement, any others died with those who possessed them. I was dining with friends that evening, for the restaurants and theatres and shops had reopened, the capital was like a great tablecloth being shaken in midair so that life could be smoothed and reset and go on, and I had in my mind a longing to eat, and to afterwards order my favorite dessert, cherries jubilee, which would be made to flame and set in the center of the table, and I had in my mind the idea of submitting to the committee a drawing of an enormous plate of cherries, perpetually burning, to be set in the center of the park, as a memorial to the war, that acre of conflagration. And perhaps also in my mind was the hope that such a ridiculous idea would of course be ignored and as a result I would be left in peace, the one thing I desired, even beyond cherries. And I could see the committee, after abandoning my idea, remaining in their seats fighting over the designs of others, far into the after-hours of the work day, their struggles never seeming to end, and then I wanted to submit an idea of themselves as a memorial for the war, the con-ference table on an island in the middle of the pond, though at least some of them would have to be willing to die in the enactment. And then I saw on the ground an unnamed insect in its solitary existence, making its laborious way through tough blades of grass that threatened its route, and using a stick that lay nearby I drew a circle around the animal—if you can call him that—and at once what had been but a moment of middling drama became a the-atre of conflict, for as the insect continued to fumble lopsided in circles it seemed to me that his efforts had increased, not only by my interest in them, but by the addition of a perimeter which he now seemed intent on escaping. I looked up then, and what happened next I cannot describe without a con-siderable loss of words: I saw a drinking fountain. It had not suddenly ap-peared, it must have always been there, it must have been there as I walked past it and sat down on the bench, it must have been there yesterday, and during the war, and in the afternoons before the war. It was a plain gunmetal drinking fountain, of the old sort, a basin on a pedestal, and it stood there, an ordinary object that had become an unspeakable gift, a wonder of civi-lization, and I had an overwhelming desire to see if it worked, I stood up then and approached it timidly, as I would a woman, I bent low and put my hand on its handle and my mouth hovered over its spigot—I wanted to kiss it, I was going to kiss it—and I remembered with a horrible shock that in ris-ing from the bench I had stepped on and killed the insect, I could hear again its death under my left foot, though this did not deter me from finishing my kiss, and as the water came forth with a low bubbling at first and finally an arch that reached my mouth, I began to devise a secret route out of the park that would keep me occupied for some time, when I looked up, holding the miraculous water in my mouth, and saw the ducks in mid-flight, their wings shedding water drops which returned to the pond, and remembered in amazement that I could swallow, and I did, then a bit of arcane knowledge returned to me from an idle moment of reading spent years ago, before the war: that a speculum is not only an instrument regarded by most with hor-ror, as well as an ancient mirror, and a medieval compendium of all knowl-edge, but a patch of color on the lower wing segments of most ducks and some other birds. Thus I was able, in serenest peace, to make my way back to my garret and design the memorial which was not elected and never built, but remained for me an end to the war that had ended.

2 0 0 1

Worldwide last year we celebrated the arrival of a new millennium, even though it was not a new millennium and everyone worldwide knew it. John McPhee won a Pulitzer Prize last year for a collection of essays that were first collected separately and published long ago. But, so what? His book is not another history of the Civil War years; it is not a collection of criticism of work in other genres; it is not a sad memoir of someone's stubbed toe. It is, as described by one critic, "a collection of essays that reminds us all what a collection of essays is capable of." In that year, young essayists everywhere were taking heart. This year they are publishing books that act like the essays they grew up reading but that look like something else. An essay in lines, for example, is not an entirely wacky thing now. Nor is the concept of a found essay, or one employing stage directions, or metatext, or several genres at once.

THALIA FIELD

A ∴ I

I occupy this comfortable chair in your office and you stare at me. We are not speaking to one another, so you've called this uncomfortable time *silence.*

A cat wanders around your legs.

I rushed here and made it on time to the door, stood outside and turned up late. Now I find it funny you should have produced this thoughtless word. A cat falls from a bookshelf and lands on its feet.

A cat collects itself to jump. A pleasure to watch. A relief to see a creature inhabiting itself comfortably.

I have heard that staring is a predator's first weapon.

A big bang, one first cell, a tiny clue, a kernel of truth, an unrevealed fact that puts all of me in perspective. Your job is to espy and co-author that spot. From beyond the horizon a searchlight seems sourceless and impossible to deflect.

I will keep pointing out the cat. That specific cat, I don't know its name. How easily it slips from the room.

A foghorn intrudes and the lighthouse beam cuts through a marsh. The probing light keeps night ships wary of land—aware of land as an obstacle or a destination.

I am not speaking to you but if you could get beyond that, there is much to celebrate. Minutes have passed. Invisible kicks to the pendulum compensate for the effects of air resistance.

An eye grows accustomed so that vision takes shape in a dark room, though it's been said that the shapes emerge. A basket of plastic flowers looks perfect on your desk.

I count on the fact that in another thirty minutes this episode will end and I'll walk back onto a street where nobody is speaking to me, and yet I would never call it silent.

A girl strolls through a bustling market, walking alone from fence to fence, around the backs of benches, wandering without stalling.

I see another basket, empty of plastic flowers.

A job, what a job—to connect so many carelessly scattered spots. The spread of seeds, the search for new stars. The whole entanglement of sowing and harvest is utterly for the birds—which is why birds are such menaces to the farmers. And big scarecrows guard the broken earth. And swarms of bats suck the night clear of insects.

I mean, the bats hear exactly where we are.

A girl, in your book, is never alone. So I must be the third person here. The girl in an open-air market speaks to no one, as she was taught to do by a protective parent, or by experience. And so she is silent, and so you'd say she and I are identical. Eden is a small town on most maps and yet people pretend not to know it, only allude to it as the first place, the justifiable cause of where we are today.

I won't pick up the looks you flick onto the rug between us. This may be "the most silent you've ever seen me," but your seeing has become suspect since you've made a career out of it. *How many times do you see her? Oh, I see her twice a week.*

A moth saw a flame and thought what it saw was its heart and it said, "What is my heart doing over there, away from me?" And believing that it could not be whole without an organ it had never even used, the moth dove toward it, hoping to reabsorb it in open surgery, but instead there was a sound as empty as a lit match extinguished on water, and in an instant the heart that had stood away from the moth became the central unimagined ecstasy the moth couldn't live without.

I fear that there is no such thing as being naked.

A hood has practical use. A veil. The eyelid is a very sensual place to be kissed. A kiss here, no matter how delicate, shocks the eyeball underneath which doesn't yet think of itself as a physical sphere able to be touched. And the brain doesn't know how this touch feels, there is no word for it. A hood hides a spot in every culture. In some, the concealing is worshipped, in some undone—and you can't tell which—yet you want desperately to find it.

I may squirm with a pleasure I didn't know I had, that you can show me, that is really your pleasure.

A hand skims back and forth causing small ripples in an ocean of bath water.

I won't emerge. The Polaroid wasn't loaded so all that develops is the feeling of panic as we discover that the candids are lost: *"We would have lived life differently had we known the dumb thing was empty!"* A girl is approached by a stranger at the market. He will ask her if she's lost, not where she's going.

A cat pushes his way into the room. He rubs against the couch, and then my knees and then yours, joining us with his attention.

I try and forget how tightly sealed the window is as I focus on the street scene through it, as I focus on squeezing the air from the bottom of my lungs.

A girl searches an open-air market for something to buy with the change in her pocket. Her slow consideration of everything takes on the rhythm of water spilling across a table, growing as vastly clear as sunlight on a blank wall.

I'm going to ask the question at the end of our time, as your hand reaches for the door, "Is that cat alive or dead?"

A hat flies up and a girl loses it in the blinding hole, the sun. It spills on the concrete and she steps off the sidewalk to pick the hat up, looking to see if anyone saw her. An amateur astronomer kneels at the base of his telescope as the glow from a fifteen-million-year-old supernova slowly appears to him.

I feel my cheeks burn as if they might peel off and fly toward the window, striking against it, a terrifying wet bird.

A girl sniffs the gyros from a full block away, remembering the salty oil and the soft wings of meat, desiring them as she approaches the colorful banners. A girl picks her way through the stalls, searching for ways to spend her money. She thought she would buy a scarf, but she has become hungry.

I guess you could say I've brought this situation on myself; sitting here is no different than paying for a parking space when I don't own a car. We don't spend money on words when we put them to waste, so why spend it on the choice not to use them?

A network TV movie languishing unmade, you might say.

I could sell the rights if I could simply tell the story. The relief on your face whenever I toss up a detail! The tastiest ones I have robbed from half-strangers, their open mouths like velvet sacks to pull back before you, leaving a pile of glittering rock sugar, jewels, what you believe is the rarest vein of my soul visible across a table. They sparkle in your eyes and you tackle them efficiently and with style. Suddenly crime seems to pay. Confession is the climax of the seduction. So you can lean back and uncross your legs, looking as relaxed as you'd like me to.

"A" sounds like "I" when spoken.

I sort of wish you'd tap that pencil. But that sort of gesture, at some point in your training, has been labeled unprofessional.

A third ring.

I stare at you. The phone rings a fourth time and the answering machine sucks the sound into its plastic body where on turning tape a voice discharges.

A voice is calling you—

I know you want to press the button, lean in, soak up the wet sweet words. However, owing to your professionalism, you can only shoot glances at the clock.

A strategy has prevailed as in all battles; the power of mundanity.

                                                    "So how was your
                                                    weekend?"

I know what you mean. I know the story you want—there's that pleasure in driving too fast that in speaking would slow way down and vanish, the motion rolling to a stop with the force of friction if I would try to describe what happened.

A spot like that can't be looked into. A place on the map, a motel for fossils that slip out at night and skulk along the cooled sidewalks, leaning back flat against painted wood, familiar patterns of bones casting Sanskrit shadows.

I know that between any two people in conversation resides the potential to give birth to the world. But could it begin with two like us, sitting in comfortable chairs, not speaking? Who would the epic infant look like, me or you? The fantasy of stealing my mother's baby enters my mind. If this is transference, may I ask you to remove your clothing?

A payment of money for this is ridiculous.

"I surveyed the ceiling of my prison . . . It was the painted figure of Time as he is commonly represented, save that, in lieu of a scythe, he held what, at a casual glance, I supposed to be the picture of a pendulum." You twist the watch around your wrist as though time might gain momentum—you try again to throw me something: a swath of speech so solid we can both see it, but which, falling, covers more.

"You took care of
yourself I hope."

A cat like yours is a Schrödinger's cat, sealed up in an office where someone's disintegration provides a 50–50 chance of its death. *Take care of her,* says the mobster to the hit man, winking verbally. At the end of an hour the lid will be lifted to see the results.

I've never seen you this way. Darkness and a hushed room are alike when you walk into them. A night sky and a silent god have a lot in common.

An irresponsible look brews in your eyes.

I may repeat stories about *a girl* in so many different forms you think you're encountering a life. Maybe you think it's *my* life? Always assume that nothing relates. A girl, the invention of plastic, amateur cosmologists, "I," "you," pieces of paper, my chair, it's just a combination that continues until a stopping place is reached and the time is up, frame busted, and then it continues despite us. The cat sits alive, dead, or whatever it is, just inside the door pulling its claws.

A girl once went to confession and said, *I have never spoken truthfully about myself* to a priest whose eyes widened as he nodded in that fascinating way.

I know you need me to start speaking up before I become dangerous.

A parade of lives roams the street, sealed out. Silent, and yet you don't seem concerned about them.

I lean forward and think we shouldn't see each other any more. I might say I spent the weekend idling outside a motel in an upstate town. Then you would ask me why I came back, and I would think why I was idling. I found an open place and I watched it come into view. A raw motel. A car parked suddenly. A place of clothing. An entrance. If I named my sins they would become obligations. On my back finally opened sideways on a brown bedspread I thought pleasantly of nothing while I gave pleasure with my tongue.

A billboard comes down piece by piece. You thought you heard me say something? A wall, a line, a galaxy, or the flesh of our heads stand between us. Where you see a barrier, there is a place of opportunity.

I do flatter you with a look now and then, which you grab up eagerly like undeserved flowers. In one flower you could hear a thousand words, but you can't read minds, you've often said, trying to keep my gaze from falling back to the window, which of course I let it do.

A room in which walls, ceiling, and floor are totally bare behaves to sound in the same way it would to light if it were lined with mirrors. When two people communicate, their brains begin to mirror each other and the boundaries between them dissolve.

I wonder what it is about darkness that makes us sure we can't move safely through it. Something about bumping into things with our bodies first. That the touch might be painful, erotic, before we understand it.

A pair of cats rushes in—entangled—a live cat and a dead cat screeching and hissing, baring excruciating flashes of claw. The display brings you to your feet and you chase them away.

"I cautiously moved forward, with my arms extended, and my eyes straining from their sockets, in the hope of catching some faint ray of light." As I get older I lie in fewer words.

A bat, trapped in a house where people are screaming and swatting at it, swoops and narrowly misses them and every silver portrait on the mantel. Around the room it banks and plummets until as it hears the plate-glass window and turns to avoid it, the bat realizes what it hears is always where it heads and wonders, "What is my future doing over there, away from me?" Terrified it won't live to see a future free from the blaring echo of its mind always already in front of it, the bat dives toward the glass, silencing it with constant attention.

I drove through fog on my way north and the headlights made even the tiniest particles of air blaze. I could see best when I turned the lights off completely.

A girl laughed out loud leaving the confession booth where behind the wooden panel the priest had grown angrier, shaking the whole box with outrage as minutes passed and the girl would neither speak nor leave. *Make her do one thing or the other,* he prayed to God.

I think *window* several times. In the mind, words are heard bone-dry without the benefit of breath.

A billboard rises across the dusty sunset, saying something about buying or driving a new car. In the image I step into a mini-mart for cigarettes and on the way out I spot another billboard where I'm enjoying a good smoke. At night up north I practiced echo-locating off unfamiliar ears.

At first your questions—like flashlights toward Orion—vanished into the paradox of the dark night sky: an infinite universe filled infinitely with stars should make any line of sight eventually hit a star in the sky, strike a word, a memory. This being so, and there being infinite lines of sight, why is the night sky dark and not a screen of burning light?

Edgar Allan Poe thought about this and concluded that time was on his side. The farther into space he looked the further back in time he saw—back to where stories first formed in fiery spit and crashing density—and he realized that even if he couldn't travel the past, he could simply wait and it would come to him. "The only mode therefore . . . in which we could comprehend the voids which our telescopes find in innumerable directions, would be by supposing the distance of the invisible background so immense that no ray from it has yet been able to reach us at all."

And the thing I'm counting on is that time is on my side too; that I can sit here for long enough for you to run that clock down and admit a certain defeat with the envelope I'll hand you with your fee. In many ways, we are as gothic as the thick illogical spaces between stars, between good ideas, between motel rooms. For different reasons we may both be right: I am making myself crazy.

A car pulls up outside your building and begins honking.

I traveled alone in a real metal vehicle, the touch of the vinyl, the invitation of familiar music to a foot, a certain weight collecting, bearing down on a pedal connected to a machine I can neither understand nor fix. And yet I accelerated too. The sky was brewing a dark drink as I idled outside the motor lodge.

A girl lost her change and so tries to retrace where she's been, kneeling in the dirt between tables and legs. The temporary booths sway in the heavy breeze, bent nails slide from the soft wood as the tarping whips off. A girl studies faces for the one who has taken her money. So much for the open-air, for the kindness of improvised spaces.

I know you are only a fading echo of Poe and that I, unable to form a counter theory to his, stubbornly occupy a losing position. For you too have faith that at the horizon of what you can see lies *the creation,* awaiting revelation, eventually emerging for your inspection. The farther the light travels, the harder the words come, the more they reflect the original state of things. Numerous but feeble rays whispering the inchoate talking cure of the big bang. Admit it, in my silence you think you see the possibility of everything there is to know about me. A dictionary left on this leather chair when I go would serve you equally in conjuring me up. I refer to this when I say,

"I'm thinking of stopping . . ."

A better Poe might have spoken about the universe that moves away from itself at all times, that perhaps has no center, that at all points surges in every direction so the future and the past are only as strong as fences of human hair, catching sparks in the ether.

"I counted the rushing vibrations of the steel! Inch by inch, line by line . . ."

A false distinction lies between music and the noise of garbage cans pulled along pavement.

I know in the city the sky at night isn't dark at all, and that's one reason this dialogue may never have been possible. When the lights were out and I lay across the brown bedspread, the face that leaned down and touched mine was as empty as a window.

"How long have you felt
this way?"

A whole nest of possibilities falls between us and yet you try to save only the already dead. I understand why you look at me the way you do: a boarded up window painted on it; understanding someone is the most irrational contract there is.

I prefer the cat which is now a messy melange of live and dead cats.

A girl runs through the market with the scarf she stole as the booths collapsed. When she reaches an alley where nobody can see her she runs her hands out to the full length of the fabric, folding it around her head.

I feel a constriction in my chest. What can I say to get you to open the window? That kind of transparency is suffocating.

A girl travels in the city unrecognized. Her youth and her face now covered in soft blue printed cotton. She was irrepressible when I first saw her, she is even lighter now.

I am really the criminal you won't say I am. In instance after instance, I kill you. And each procession I hear of myself is a funeral. The hill is muddy, silence surrounds your coffin, and because you are dead, even the patter of the dirt as it touches you is like affection you can't feel. Too bad you have to die in here. Some of me is very sorry and wants to disrupt the killing spree. Some of me wants to torture you because you make it so easy. Some of me is the guard on duty who looks blithely the other way and later denies the whole affair. I am all the murderers who served their silence up cold; can you tell I'm looking at you now—

A vacuum of agreement is between us.

I reach across the two feet of space and lift the window without asking. There is no reverberation as I let the impatient rustle of traffic into this "silent" room.

A sound made in the open air travels away, and for the most part doesn't return.

I hear the street like a reprieve. I am so aware of all the noise outside I can barely look at you. And how is it that you don't know my mind is as loud as your staring at my hands—now that they are refusing to fidget as they have in the past. In the stillness of my hands you suddenly think you hear something.

A star once discovered is given a name. New words come into the language as technology changes, as people change. Still, there are light waves you do not see which go into your mind undetected. There are sounds that flow up through your feet from where I've pushed the earth and it's pushed you back.

I pay you money so that we may share this kind of history.

A car runs smoothly when the teeth of one gear enter and leave the spaces of another.

I read that on the witness stand, the murderer's father appeared guiltier than his son when asked about their Sunday dinners or why he suspected nothing.

A girl looks up through the buildings sensing someone staring. Into the fisheye of a giant telescope on a planet as distant as a pleasant sound, she thumbs her nose and shakes a motor from her tongue. *I know exactly where I am,* she is prepared to say to any gloved hand that stops her.

I can't think of a more sublime torture than a subpoena.

A girl races now, away from her shadow. She dashed past me on the way in here, and I stood for several minutes outside your door, hoping to eventually emerge as her, or at least running that quickly.

I know an instant before it happens that this time is suddenly over.

"Oh!"

A startled noise as the hour jumps to your eyes like a cat to your lap and you turn almost sheepish, raise yourself from the chair. Nervously you indicate the clock, your watch, the door, even the answering machine as though you fear I might linger eternally. You want me to see that every-thing in the room has conspired to elapse. Yet that is all I ever wanted. That, and this intimate look.

2002

And should a thesis crack open and spill its feelings all out—

BRIAN LENNON

Sleep

At first things collide, collude, drive you along. Only later do they begin to "fall apart." You move in a kind of trance, the blind trust that day after day brings somehow usable experience, and that even if you are only waiting, something is bound to happen that will clarify just what was all along at stake. But it is a privilege to speak of one's experience as though it were unique, not quotidian, not irreducibly ordinary. In complex moments when my window frames an indigo dawn, or the lunch-hour inferno, or a sunset of profound silhouettes, nothing can be further from the truth. The pageantry of Broadway furnishes proof: fistfights, arguments, embraces, self-conscious posturing of all kinds; the way people walk or set their mouths when they feel threatened, or angry; favor and petition flickering on faces. Those silhouettes. "Blank windows gargle signals through the roar" (Crane).

Under the ground of the self, too, there is a system: lanterns and signs, spelling out something. What? Regret, ambition, hope, despair; wreckage and splintering and boredom. And other, happier, more wholesome modes and tropes. For the others, mnemonics constructs a composite, surface image: heart's photograph. In this picture, boxy yellow taxis glide serenely through the midday autumn mist; a theater marquee, right center, is missing letters; yellow light floods through the glass doors onto the pavement. A figure stands there, pondering. The marquee is pitched just slightly over her head. The film is entitled *Sleep*.

The mystery of lives, recursively in how many waves, a near-infinity of ghosts: concentration of the City. In the hour between 3 and 4 A.M., when it breathes in an equilibrium of surge and repose, you can hear something like the footsteps of the dead—

Attempting the conception of a diagram of one's own life. Key information might be represented as on the map of an old city, with its center, its concentric rings. Here and there might be marked—with pins, or flags—the homes of friends and lovers, the place of one's birth, schools one attended; this map would, presumably, link up with others, representing the essence of one's life, the vitals of its location, and perhaps its flow—much as one might, from the précis of a book, construct a chart of the arguments.

"I" sits looking out over the street. It is noisy and brightly lit. "I" watches traffic accidents during the day, brawls outside Cannon's at night. From the chair at my desk "I" looks down a thoroughfare—Upper Broadway—that vanishes, foreshortened, as yellow taxis stream into points of light.

An ambulance turns into side streets, disappears, emerges—lost?—then, almost calmly, grinds over the median: one front wheel dangling, trailing shards. A figure gets out, looks doubtfully around, throws up its hands, sits on a trash can, lights a cigarette. It is snowing. The figure throws up its hands again. *You* are passing—dressed in black; quickly turning white.

Perhaps the city, always erasing and being erased, renders the notion of "origin" absurd; and yet there is a sanctity that sticks to *place,* as we know when we recall the apartments and restaurants, the park benches and public telephones, long since claimed by others, that once were accessories of our own—

Fire is there or it is not there. Look! my child-brother said slicing his finger through the candle flame, It doesn't hurt.—But surely there is a word for that moment when a fire log, beneath its bark, has become one immanent ember, winking like a City or a circuit board; for that moment when you know only the desire, no, the *need* to *stir it up*. What is on fire, you ask yourself, staring into that waiting. What is that moment. What is the word?

2003

If in this year we were to follow traditional literary definitions, I suppose nonfiction writers would still technically have to be considered the godparents of everything *not* poetry, *not* fiction, *not* drama, *not* song: all the black and white data that make the world tick—all the map legends, political speeches, history textbooks, precepts, slogans, mottos, columns, committee-meeting minutes, sea captains' logs, celebrity memoirs, teenage diaries, philosophies, obituaries, forecasts, postcards . . . a genre, in other words, that would be defined by fact. And yet despite the obvious abundance of documentation in nonfiction, some of the literature in this genre challenges that very presumption of fact; the very character, in other words, of what "nonfiction" means. The lyric essay, as some have called the form, asks what happens when an essay begins to behave less like an essay and more like a poem. What happens when an essayist starts imagining things, making things up, filling in blank spaces, or—worse yet—leaving the blanks blank? What happens when statistics, reportage, and observation in an essay are abandoned for image, emotion, expressive transformation? In this year, as we continue to wade slowly through the start of a new century, our anxiety, either real or imagined, needles us over the crest of the rest of what's left. The afterward of postmodernism waits for us there. There are now questions being asked of facts that were never questions before. What, we ask, is a fact these days? What's a lie, for that matter? What constitutes an "essay," a "story," a "poem"? What, even, is "experience"? In the words of Wallace Stevens, we have to find what will suffice. For years writers have been responding to this slippage of facts in a variety of ways—from the fragmentary forms of LANGUAGE poetry that try to mimic this loss, to the narrative-driven attempts by novelists and memorists to smooth over the gaps. But the lyric essay takes another approach. The lyric essay inherits from the principal strands of nonfiction the makings of its own hybrid version of the form. It takes the subjectivity of the personal essay and the objectivity of the public essay, and conflates them into a literary form that relies on both art and fact, on imagination and observation, rumination and argumentation, human faith and human perception. What the lyric essay inherits from the public essay is a fact-hungry pursuit of solutions to problems, while from the personal essay what it takes is a wide-eyed dallying in the heat of predicaments. The result of this ironic parentage is that lyric essays seek answers, yet seldom seem to find them. They may arise out of a public essay that never manages to prove its case, or may emerge from the stalk of a personal essay to sprout out and meet "the other." They may start out as travelogues that forget where they are, or begin as prose poems that refuse quick conclusions. They may originate as lines that resist being broken, or full-bodied paragraphs that start slimming down. They are unconventional essays, hybrids that perch on the fence between the willed and the felt. Facts, in these essays, are not clear-cut things. What is a lyric essay? It's an oxymoron: an essay that's also a lyric; a kind of logic that wants to sing; an argument that has no chance of proving anything.

JENNY BOULLY

The Body

---

1   It was the particular feel of him that made me want to go back: everything that is said is said underneath, where, if it does matter, to acknowledge it is to let on to your embarrassment. *That I love you makes me want to run and hide.*

2   It is not the story I know or the story that you tell me that matters; it is what I already know, what I don't want to hear you say. Let it exist this way, concealed; let me always be embarrassed, knowing that you know that I know but pretend not to know.

---

3   One thing the great poet confessed before biting into her doughnut: a good poem writes itself as if it doesn't care—never let on that within this finite space, your whole being is heavy with a need to emote infinitely.

4   I never uttered that loose word; I only said, "I opened my legs and let him."

5   It wasn't that the ice-cream man came everyday; he came whenever the child heard his music.

6   I *Corinthians* 13:5 "Doth not behave itself unseemly, seeketh not her own, is not easily provoked, thinketh no evil"; 13:7 "Beareth all things, believeth all things, hopeth all things, endureth all things"; 13:11 "When I was a child, I spake as a child, I understood as a child, I thought as a child: but when I became a woman, I put away childish things"; 13:12 "For now we see through a glass, darkly; but then face to face: now I know in part; but then shall I know even as also I am known." Given these passages, it is easy for the reader to infer that the protagonist, aside from despising her pubic hair, also believed that she was being watched and thus began her odd behavior of hiding and casting her voice into a void.

7   The visit to the circus is of particular import if one considers this passage from a letter written to the man whom she regarded as her guardian angel (to whom she also dedicated a great number of poems). Dated in her 23rd year, the author writes:

> . . . I told Lousine that I was terrified of clowns, no, not just childishly afraid like being afraid of the dark, but really, really fearful, like starting-your-period-for-the-first-time scared. Anyhow, she looked at me serious-like and made me promise in that strong Armenian-Brooklyn way of hers that I would never reveal this to anyone because anyone could be an enemy. She made me swear up and down and on graves and holy books and the needle in the eye and all sorts of crazy shit that drove me insane. I can't help but think now that something bad is waiting to happen and that there's this little man staring at me from between the fence slats. I can see his little eyeball sometimes, showing up in the various holes in my apartment. But you know what scares me the most? It's that clown in Antony and Cleopatra who says to Cleopatra, "You must not think I am so simple but I know the devil himself will not eat a woman. I know that a woman is a dish for the gods, if the devil dress her not. But truly, these same whoreson devils do the gods great harm in their women; for in every ten that they make, the devils mar five." So you see, Andy, I have been seriously stressed. Am I marred? Eric says he cannot love me now and that I have a dark side he is afraid of . . .

8   One thing the great poet would never confess was that afterwards, she took me into the back room and slapped me for loving her.

9   The confessions denoted here are lies, as it would be senseless to list my true regrets. The true regrets are indexed under the subject heading "BUT EVERYONE DIES LIKE THIS," found at the end of the text.

10   Given this information, the definition of "footnote" is of particular interest to the overall understanding of "bedlam." Consider, for instance, this denotation: *n.2. Something related to but of lesser importance than a larger work or occurrence.*

11   Although the text implies a great flood here, know this is seen through a child's eyes, and here she actually played in sprinklers while loving Heraclitus: "A lifetime [or eternity] is a child playing, playing checkers; the kingdom belongs to a child" (Hippolytus, *Refutation* 9.9.4 = 22B52).

12   See also De Sica's *Bicycle Thief;* thus the leitmotif of this body: *What will I have found in the end if I am seeking as if I am seeking one thing in particular?*

13   The last time I saw the great poet, I brought her strawberries, hoping she would ask me to bed. Instead, she only suggested that I touch how soft her fuzzy pink sweater was. I broke down crying as soon as I made my confession. I told her that I had written a bad poem, that in the space between me and him, I emoted, through speech and touch, too much and I made it known that I was willing to emote infinitely; the poem was so bad, he left. I was hoping that the great poet would kiss me then, but instead, she slapped me again and forbade me from telling anyone that I was her student. I left her, and I never told her that I was on my hands and knees, picking those berries for her.

14   It should be understood that Heraclitus also lost a bicycle. In *Miscellanies* (2.17.4 = 22B18), Clement of Alexandria quotes Heraclitus as saying, "Unless he hopes for the unhoped for, he will not find it, since it is not to be hunted out and is impassable."

_____

15   Ms. Boully must have been confused, as it was actually _____,
not _____, who uttered "_____
_____ " and thus became such a symbolic figure
in her youth. However, critic and playwright Lucia Del Vecchio (who is
known to transcribe some of her dialogue directly from audiocassettes she
and Boully recorded during their undergraduate years) argues that Boully
was well-acquainted in _____. As this is a suspicious oversight, Del
Vecchio cites evidence from a recorded conversation where Boully argues
_____
_____.

16   It was the suspicion that he was reconstructed and retold from ethereal
ponderings occurring in some heaven or other that made me want to sleep
next to him.

17   Although the narrative is rich with detail and historical accounts, the
author is blatantly supplying false information. For example, the peaches
were not rotten and there were no flies or rain for that matter. The man she
claims to have kissed never existed, or rather, the man existed; however, she
never kissed him, and because she never kissed him, she could only go on
living by deluding herself into believing that he never existed.

---

18   The illustration also represents various states of being. The student of
art should be particularly cautious of interpreting such depictions without
proper background training, as it is often easy to confuse source light with
light from another world, as in movies when it is easy to confuse internal
sound with external sound.[a] Sometimes, the artist, as does the director,
plays tricks for symbolic purposes.[b]

> [a] In cinematic terms, "actual sound" refers to sound which comes
> from a visible or identifiable source[*] within the film. "Commenta-
> tive sound" is sound which does not come from an identifiable
> source within the film but is added for dramatic effect.[**]

> [b] See footnote 1.

>> [*] By "identifiable source" it is meant that there exists a pre-
>> supposition, an understanding that an opposing "unidenti-
>> fiable source" exists.

>> [**] By "commentative sound" it is meant that there exists a
>> presupposition, an understanding of a "commentator" who
>> is thereby executing the "commentary."

19   But in those days, I thought that by believing in magic and miracles, by believing hard enough, harder than anyone on earth, I would be made witness to the sublime. And so, what I was doing on the rooftop was praying. I was praying for the gift of flight, for the black umbrella and the hidden angels to aid me.

20   ". . . for a child—if one allows the awareness of such entities as guardian angels to be true, then the child MUST, as it is contingent, allow for evil to be real as well. For the sublime world of the good and miraculous necessitates the dark, scary walk down the hall each night . . ."

21   Besides the obvious lost marbles or stolen purse or misplaced lottery
ticket, the theme of loss preoccupied her even in sleep. The following is
from a dream dated in the author's 33rd year:

> (But then, I remembered in my dream that this was only a dream
> and that when you lose something in a dream, when you wake up,
> you realize it's still there. Of course, the reverse is true as well, as
> when I dreamt I had silver eyes and wings, but upon waking up,
> upon looking into the mirror, I discovered brown eyes, no wings.
> So, in my dream, I woke up from my dream in my dream, thereby
> correcting the situation on my own.

> This reminds me of Kafka's *Trial,* in a passage deleted by the au-
> thor: ". . . it is really remarkable that when you wake up in the
> morning you nearly always find everything in exactly the same place
> as the evening before.")

22   Ezra Pound: Questing and passive. . . . / "Ah, poor Jenny's case" . . .

23   After my sister and I stared at the magazine, we were, the both of us, afraid to part our legs or even to pee. For months, we were inseparable in the bathroom, but then we became brave and decided to look for our holes, and if the spider did in fact come out we would kill it.

24   It is odd that she chose not to record this particular dream about E. in her log, but instead made loose notes in her journal and later wrote in a letter to Andy:

> ". . . he died again. This time, I refused to accept his death because I could still communicate with him and so I asked him if he had, of late, been walking on water or on air, and he answered 'neither.' I only began to cry at his funeral, and the mourners, they didn't know that it was I who made them; it was I who glued the dragonflies to the scene and said, 'You must read his stories.' I woke because in my dream, I had been crying too profusely. I slept again and this time, I dreamt the dream of his resurrection: he arrived in my mailbox wrapped in his fiction and covered with butterflies. I ran around, shouting, 'He's not dead!' But he is, you see. The dream wants to tell me that he is dead *to me*. The dream wants to inform me not to be fooled by pretty packages, that in matters of correspondence, the body is tragically absent."

---

25   Never assume that the actors are "sticking to the script." It is recommended that students engaged in cinema studies consult the original scripts and make notes of alterations. Sometimes the director orders last-minute changes. Sometimes too, when one speaks, it is never as one had intended. The student should take note and reconcile the irony that exists between "what should have been"c and "what is."d

> c ". . . .when you see him you will be glad; you will love him . . . and he will never forsake you. This is the meaning of the dream." (G.)*
>
> d "Although I should go in sorrow and in pain, with sighing and with weeping, still I must go." (G.)*
>
> > * This particular footnote is imagined as being elucidated by a future editor.

---

26   *Genesis* 37:5.2 "And J. dreamed a dream, and she told it to her brethren: and they hated her yet the more." 37:8.222 "And they hated her yet the more for her dreams, and for her words." 37:20.7519 "Come now therefore, and let us slay her, and cast her into some pit, and we will say, Some evil beast hath devoured her: and we shall see what will become of her dreams." 40:8.4iiixvc5yktg/89.:3lbπ∞ "And they said unto her, You have dreamed a dream, and there is no interpreter of it."

27   "I wish he would have said 'in language there are only distances.' I've discovered, while watching butterflies mate, that time and metaphor, tragically, are contingent upon each other. For the non-sentient being, there is no time (only eternity). The experience of time translates itself into language, and language translates itself into distance which translates itself into longing, which is the realization of time. Yes, ironically, it seems as if I've only discovered that Sassure was correct. All the same, how sad and strange that I, Jenny Boully, should be the sign of a signifier or the signifier of a sign, moreover, the sign of a signifier searching for the signified."

28   This was corrected in the second edition by the author. In the original, she wrote: "Prayer is merely a hopeful form of apostrophe."

---

29   I was the lonely tripod. I was the empty cup of tea left behind.

30   The particular nursery rhyme was "Stopping the Swing":

    Die, pussy, die,
    Shut your little eye;
    When you wake,
    Find a cake—
    Die, pussy, die.

---

31   Hamlet must have slept in a similar bed, for in Act II, Scene ii, he says, "O God, I could be bounded in a nutshell, and count myself a king of infinite space—were it not that I have bad dreams."

.

32   The cartographer, in this case, purposely placed the "X" in an obvious, yet incorrect location. The treasure actually rested towards the northeastern edge of the dark wood, 967 paces over the creek away from the side door of the mill house, past 240 cow flops, over 90 large rocks, in the grove of the 540 lilac blossoms where 473 bumble bees seek whatever it is they seek in the air where 1,601[e] pebbles were tossed.

  [e] The future editor should take great care in discerning the significance of these specific numbers.

---

33   In the prop room, she found the collection of butterflies, fossilized bones, her mother's hairbrush, bedsheets belonging to a past love, an earring she lost when she was ten, and a box containing letters which X would compose to her until her death.

34   *Ibid.*, p. xliv.

35   In this case, it was not the *deus ex machina* who was responsible, but rather a certain type of *zeitgeist*.

36   It was after this incident that the leaves began eavesdropping.

---

37   In the original production, Boully was positioned stage center, the vase contained lilacs, not violets, the hills spread out like fallen pears, and _____ was originally cast to play the role of _____ who, in the original production, entered on the cue of broken glass to ask if she would _____ him. The addition of black curtains, which replaced the billowing, transparent ones, was made in the year _____. Del Vecchio contends this is indicative of Boully's growing apprehension of _____. The change in the set design was intended to symbolize the changes made in the dialogue, as _____ would no longer be asking if she would _____ him, but if she was okay with just _____ing him.

38   Not the celestial body, but the cleaning agent, which was commonly used to scrub toilets and dislodge mildew from cracks and crevices.

---

39   July 8, 1976.

40   The fact that she named her imaginary child Zeno should be considered along with the following excerpts. The last time she saw X, they met in New York on her birthday. She wrote on a series of postcards to Andy, and these are given in the order in which they arrived in his mailbox:

> (POSTCARD 4): "Therefore, place does not exist." But he was mistaken, Andy, terribly mistaken. Moving through these streets, flying away from E. time and time again, measuring "out my life with coffee spoons," I harbor a sure sense always of always existing in the plane of "here" while E. is always "there," always "elsewhere." I miss you. I wish I were not here, and I remain, as ever, yours, etc., JB

> (POSTCARD 2): of hotel sheets. I am already envying them their placement of ornaments on Christmas trees and their china and silver sets. At my age, a woman should be wary of having children. Zeno of Elea is known to have said, "If place exists, where is it? For everything that exists is in a place. Therefore, place is in a place."

> (POSTCARD 1): My dearest Andy, today, I turned 36 and summertime in NY is no longer pink candlelight. My eyes carry the crumbling veins of autumn leaves, and E., who is 40, has just confessed to asking a 20 yr old to marry him, to which she replied yes and that this must be the last of our time together as lovers who can share no secrets anyhow under cover

> (POSTCARD 3): This goes on to infinity.

41   It is futile for the student engaged in cinema studies to write a paper on any aspect of film without first explicating the significance of the fortune teller's answer to Antonio when he inquires again about his stolen bicycle. She says to him, "Either you find it now or you never will."

42   Or whatever the translation might be. _____'s dictionary gives: *to long for something (despite one's logical reasoning which intuits there is nothing to be gained in expectation of its fulfillment)*. As a noun, however, a source and reason for this longing is posited in the very definition.

43   Recall that sometimes the world *is* violet and amass with wanderers, and a woman in white, long sought, appears innocent, as if in a pin-up in which anticipation and promise grope one another.

---

44   *John* 20:9 "For as yet they knew not the scripture, that he must rise
again from the dead": 20:11.6.10.99 "But she stood without at the sepulchre
weeping: and as she wept, she stooped down, and *looked* into the sepulchre,"[f] 20:13 "And they say unto her, Woman, why weepest thou? She saith
unto them, Because they have taken away my Lord, and I know not where
they have laid him": 20:14.21401 "And when she had thus said, she turned
herself back, and saw _____ standing, and knew not that it was
_____." 20:15.33333 . . . "_____ saith unto her, Woman,
why weepest thou? whom seekest thou?"

    [f] Not a sepulchre, but an envelope; not an envelope, but a door; not
a door, but a fire escape.[*]

        [*]The inclusion of this note was deemed necessary by the ed-
itor, lest false surmises[†] lead to injuries.

            [†] "And there is a third nature, which is space and is
eternal, and admits not of destruction and provides a
home for all created things, and is apprehended,
when all sense is absent, by a kind of spurious reason, and is hardly real—which we, beholding as in a
dream, say of all existence that it must of necessity
be in some place and occupy a space, but that what is
neither in heaven nor in earth has no existence. Of
these and other things of the same kind, relating to
the true and waking reality of nature, we have only
this dreamlike sense, and we are unable to cast off
sleep and determine the truth about them" (52*b-c*).

45   Because the weather and landscape were forever shifting and birds
gave birth to new birds that birthed new birds *ad infinitum*, this passage is,
historically, inaccurate. The main argument, however, remains unaffected.

46   When the protagonist happens upon the crime scene, when she stumbles into the prop room, when she reads the work of the great poet, and
most importantly, when she holds the letter up to the sun to read between
the lines, the author is supplying examples of *dramatic irony*.[g]

> [g] "Dramatic irony usually refers to a situation in a play wherein a
> character, whose knowledge is limited, says, does, or encounters
> something of greater significance than she knows" (*Ibid.*, p. 29).

47   For types of drama, see: *absurd, literature of the; atmosphere; chronicle
plays; commedia dell'arte; comedy; comedy of humours; drama of sensibility;
epic theater; expressionism; folk drama; heroic drama; masque; melodrama;
miracle plays, morality plays, and interludes; mummer's play; pantomime and
dumb show; pastoral; problem play; satire; sentimental comedy; tragedy; tragi-
comedy.*

48   ". . . for spectators at a circus to find themselves suddenly beholding a
greater and more horrific show than they had paid for" (*Ibid.*, p. 30).

---

49   Besides the need to act out various life-or-death scenarios, children of every culture engage in a variation of some type of game of *hide-and-go-seek*.

50   Lacan: ". . . _____ is both an obstacle to remembering, and a making present of the closure of the _____, which is the act of missing the right meeting just at the right moment."

51   Gilgamesh also lost a bicycle: "Gilgamesh, where are you hurrying to? You will never find that life for which you are looking" . . . "I found a sign and I have lost it."

52   "Because of the finitude of this type of travel, one should pack lightly, as words have different connotations according to different witnesses, as all people do not hear the same note of music at the same time, nor do events that appear simultaneous visually seem to be audibly simultaneous.
      "Light and prayer also have finite speeds, so we never see an instantaneous snapshot of eternity. The flight of light is so swift that within a single lifetime we obtain effectively an instantaneous snapshot, but this is certainly not the case astronomically. We see the moon as it was just over a second ago, and the sun as it was about 8 min. ago. At the same time, we see the stars by light that departed from them years ago, and the other galaxies as they were millions of lifetimes in the past. We do not observe the world about us at an instant in time, but rather we see different possible lives about us as different events in spacetime.
      "Relatively moving observers do not even agree on the order of events . . ." (Ibid., p 523).

---

53   Despite all his expertise in mimicry, the movie director could not put
_____ back together again; moreover, he could not properly render
the realism of the crime scene: notice the microphone dangling in the
upper-left corner of the frame, the blood which appeared before the kill,
the lipstick on the antagonist's left cheek when the protagonist clearly
kissed him on his right, the visible strings of all the flying things, the wax
and Popsicle sticks comprising the wings, the letter read before the envelope was unsealed, the death certificate found and forged before the death,
the cicadas leaving their ghosts on fences and vines, the appearance of butterflies before the splitting of cocoons, the outline of the body drawn in
chalk before the collapse of the victim, the ill-timed street lights, the collection, in the detective's book of clues, of evidence before the crime was even
committed, and the supposedly random appearance of the man in the fedora offering flowers when, in the previous scene, he had discarded them in
the river.

54   "Audiences have, for decades, been entranced by her films; however,
when she made a cameo appearance (falling from the sky in the manner of
Icarus), ironically, the audience, as well as film critics, failed to take notice."

---

55   "You will never find the life for which you are searching."

56   Except, perhaps, for poets and prostitutes.

57   That he gave her this particular flower as opposed to that particular flower, that he presented it to her in such and such a way, that the cows' behavior was odd indeed and cow flops were unavoidable, that although it was a pleasant day, the chilly night air moved slyly in, and that they disagreed about the shade of the dusk sky should not fool the casual reader into believing that the scene was set in such and such a way at random and without purpose. After all, in the editing room, the editor often wields greater power than the director.

58

59   Although the argument is convincing and its logic flawless, we must keep in mind that during this stage, the author also professed to having been in a deep coma and taking to walking and talking in her sleep.

60   "But a trace in the strict sense disturbs the order of the world. It occurs by overprinting. Its original signifyingness is sketched out in, for example, the fingerprints left by someone who wanted to wipe away his traces and commit a perfect crime."

61   Joseph Campbell: "It is the realm that we enter in sleep. We carry it within ourselves forever. All the ogres and secret helpers of our nursery are there, all the magic of childhood."

62   See also Federico Fellini's *8 1/2,* paying close attention to the meaning of *Asa Nisa Masa.* Perhaps if our protagonist had access to the right words, she could have navigated through the painting, which, in the dark each night, revealed itself as a passage.

63   Read the onset of menstruation along with the following: "a little brook, the redness of which still makes me shudder…which the sinful women share among them" (Dante, *Inferno*).

64   "It is getting so dark that I can scarcely go on writing; and my brush is all worn out. Yet I should like to add a few things before I end." (Sei Shōnagon, *The Pillow Book*).

---

65   The following is a found fragment addressed to the great poet, dated
two years after the death of the great poet:

> ". . . It was my cunt, too—not the velvet one, of course, but the
> center one with the hanged man attached to it. That same summer,
> my sister and I turned detective and held the spy glass over the ants
> and discovered they were busy planning hoaxes. Everything I do, I
> do because I know I am dying. My most favorite of things are opti-
> cal illusions. We don't become senile or 'lose our minds,' it's just
> that as we get older, we have more to think of in less time—we must
> think of more in a compressed amount of time. I think I know now
> what you've tried to teach me, that poetry is an instant, an instant in
> which transcendence is achieved, where a miracle occurs and all of
> one's knowledge, experiences, memories, etc. are obliterated into
> awe. Is anything I say real? And by real, I mean *sincere*—or is every-
> thing an attempt to have love? I know now why the line breaks: it is
> because something dies, and elsewhere, is born again . . ."

---

66   Filmmaker Lousine Shamamian suggests that the fade out leaving the sound of snapping twigs is meant to imply that the protagonist grew weary of impersonating herself.

67   ". . .all women secretly desire to be sacrifices; they long to be the 'chosen one.'"

68   The introduction of the third person occurred in the year 19__. The director placed him stage left, right by the oldest of willow trees where Boully was sitting, contemplating the river. However, in order to create the right level of surprise on Boully's part, the director kept this character hidden until opening night; the result was the most convincing of performances in that Boully was totally out of character.

69   Emmanuel Levinas: ". . .the whole weight of being can be resolved into a play of inwardness and stand on the brink of illusion, so rigorous is the adequation [sic]. The apparition of being is possibly but appearance. The shadow is taken for a prey; the prey is let loose for the shadow" (*The Trace of the Other*).

70   "As in the dark month, the month of shadows, so without him there is no light . . . O _____, this was the meaning of your dream."

71   "You had better go inside; it's getting dark."

72   If Hamlet was indeed sleeping in a similar bed, then Vladimir Na-
bokov was bounded in a nutshell similar to Hamlet's. The following excerpt
from *Speak, Memory,* written in E.'s handwriting, was pasted into one of her
journals: "I have to make a rapid inventory of the universe, just as a man in a
dream tries to condone the absurdity of his position by making sure he is
dreaming. I have to have all space and all time participate in my emotion, in
my mortal love, so that the edge of its mortality is taken off, thus helping me
to fight the utter degradation, ridicule, and horror of having developed an
infinity of sensation and thought within a finite existence."

73   After the author's death, it was Tristram who went through her various papers and came across the many folders labeled "footnotes." It wasn't
until years later, when he was curious as to which papers the footnotes cor-
responded that Tristram discovered that the "footnotes" were actually daily
journals of the author's dreams. Del Vecchio recalls a later audiocassette
recording with the author saying, "I have it all worked out. I write down
my dreams because I understand them once symbols become written.
They're all so sexually charged and I almost always feel ugly in them; they're
embarrassing and filthy. But I have it all worked out. No one will know.
I've relabeled everything in my study, including my books—you think
you're getting Shakespeare, but really, it's astrophysics and cosmology or
you open Hesse and you actually get Kierkegaard. I'm not so off am I? But
really, I must confess . . ." Del Vecchio, in her words, says, "And then she
started going on and on about this Robert Kelly[h] guy."

> [h] The following excerpt from Robert Kelly's "Edmund Wilson on
> Alfred de Musset: The Dream" was pasted above the author's vari-
> ous beds in the various places she lived: "Dreams themselves are
> footnotes. But not footnotes to life. Some other transactions they
> are so busy annotating all night long."

---

74   The mastermind of this roller coaster, in an interview, confessed that the goal of his work is to replicate a ride where participants are scared out of their minds, yet feel the comforting presence of someone there, riding along and watching over them.

75   The future editor should note here the fault of the present editor for selecting the photographs from the wrong box. Photograph 34 is unthinkable in that she never had children; photograph 12 is also bogus because in any event, the engagement ring is on the wrong finger; photograph 56 is dated three years before her birth; photograph 108 shows her happy; as she never looked anyone in the eye, photograph 9 must be compiled from one of the other possible lives, because she wouldn't ever think of looking a camera lens in the eye; this goes on to infinity.

76   This situation also contains *cosmic irony* or *irony of fate*: "some Fate with a grim sense of humor seems cruelly to trick a man" (*Ibid.*, p. 30) & "God, or destiny, or the process of the universe, is represented as though deliberately manipulating events so as to lead the protagonist to false hopes, only to frustrate and mock them."

77 Often, she heard her father whistling, beckoning her home and she would run, abandoning whatever game she had been playing in a neighbor's house or yard somewhere, and her father would be calmly sitting, wanting nothing in particular, saying he had not whistled, that she must have heard this out of some sort of homesickness.

78 The essence behind the curtain, i.e., the stage, is composed of the yearning to determine what may be seen and what will remain unseen. This should be understood in the definition of "staging."

78 The reason why she chose green for the final act may be given in this passage from her dream log:

> . . . I was in bed with [illegible]. We were in the old house, in the room with the red carpet. We were afraid because there were people outside who wished to shoot us. I turned and asked him, "From where do you think they'll start shooting? I'm so afraid." We went out to the living area. There were others there. Outside, a girl dressed in black was by the sliding glass doors, writing in her memo book. "Close the curtains!" I heard someone say. I heard someone say no, that they were afraid. The curtains were the same green curtains from my childhood, and so I moved forth to close them because I, more than anyone, would know just how to do so. But I backed off when I thought of the possibility of being killed . . .

78.999 . . . *Translator's Note*—This sentence in the original is obviously meant to illustrate the fault of which it speaks. It does so by the use of a construction very common in the original,‡ but happily unknown in translation;§ however, the fault itself still exists nonetheless, though in different form.

‡ *original* as in *this life.*

§ *translation* as in *the next.*

Things To Do Today

1. thaw the wounded

2. carry the portraits out into the sea and rest them upon the breaking wave

3. destroy the capital with picturesque caress

4. mention the inexplicably famous

5. dredge the lightest bunches (ASAP!)

6. burn the symbols as soon as bone starts to become apparent in them

7. decrease the drama to the point of gesture, phrase, a weathered and weathering yard

8. descend upon the living sound of propriety

9. gather the weight of not having said and place it upon the prettiest graves

10. organize and dispense an imperceptible *the*

11. perfect the ground

12. motion at the shore (as if familiar with the families there)

13. restore hunger analogies to the feast scene which has no before and no after

14. demand to see the sleep that has not been earned

15. motivate the habitually sick

16. sing the lack of anticipation upon which we are most certainly impaled

17. recall Mother

18. disconnect the vaguer images from one another and from the way in which we get on with it

19. determine the cause of the cause

20. facilitate the ways of children

21. earn what is needed for remaining beneath the sky

22. set the famous criminals free

23. force the unmonied nudes into view (and so, into wealth/evaporation)

24. urge the animals to retract themselves, their lack of standard grammar

25. rouse the allegedly unpregnant from their unfathomable slumber

26. make the beautiful go to work

27. distract the keepers of the calendar and, when they are distracted, detach and destroy their unforgivable hobbies

28. people the pin-prick this evening alone makes in the atrophied muscle of common sense

29. grope and ogle the money machine

30. make a list of things to do in case of consenting adults

31. profit from the simple inability of a given body to own the breath it absently rides toward its own concept

32. get the fuck out (i.e., get to fuck)

33. develop humble obsessive donors

34. locate the words with which the deaf-mutes are never done thinking

35. mass-murder the animals with overly smooth minds

36. place a hand upon the brand-new gash in each picture—not to stop the bleeding but to know it is true

37. prepare the eyes for the oncoming absence of voices

38. nibble at the warm stone of what has been

39. mourn the continuing success of the Snack Area

40. indict the misleading absence of spontaneity following each and every serious injury

41. understand nothing but the trap in which these many fine bones are inextricably lodged

42. produce a striking likeness of any one unproductive moment

43. be mindful of the ring-card-girl-pose in oneself and in others, and be ready to make the difference a fateful myth

44. listen to the involuntary gatherers wishing for an impossible poverty

45. bless the bait-shop employees who remain unopposed to an on-going radical renovation of the idea of what is to be caught

46. collide with the hidden zoo and act surprised by the amount of unnecessary sleep hidden therein

47. picture the dirty dull scissors at work in the seeming

48. refuse to pay the suggested amount

49. tremble with the hunger of cameras fixed upon a spot incapable of becoming predestined

50. oversleep

51. distribute faulty prevention devices

52. establish eligibility for the death penalty

53. clarify a morning posture

54. sing of eyes freezing, thighs giving birth, what have you

55. overestimate the degree to which the new scene, the scene that is just now being written, is fixed

56. overestimate the degree to which the new scene, the scene that is just now being written, is broken

57. lament those who are already on the way

58. postpone, for as long as possible, moving in to the sentence that is never not under construction

59. insist on the sad waste at the heart of all honest work

60. bury the elderly in the laughter which heals each instance of prayer

61. require the intellectuals to attend indoor night-time drug-taking picnics

62. complain about the way the various escalating dangers seem to conspire

63. nudge the drowsy lumberjack

64. adhere to the faint golden grunt (even when it dips into where it comes from, where it can't go)

65. use the definite article to make a broth

66. confine the untoward

67. polish the pre-birth emotion until it does not shine

68. mourn the health of the debonair

69. drudge the nowsy mumblejack

70. control the urge to farm

71. suck the body part of an other until there is a new feeling of closeness

72. offer help to the dying

73. embarrass that which abstracts itself from the secretly intentional clash of heads

74. endure the baby-sitting which knows no names

75. rehabilitate the truth tellers

76. devalue the circus tender

77. practice saying something

78. scrape the forgotten music from the great stadiums it accidentally built and failed to keep up

79. try to fluster the bulk of language with the idea of buried faces

80. discontinue the breadth of the applicable horizon

81. lance and drain the churches

82. define the deceased

83. derive the trajectory of absolution

84. attack the display

85. let yourself "go"

86. pray for the institution of a consistently glancing blow

87. mimic the open area

88. elaborate the impasse from which each orgasm seems to shrink

89. look for what's left of the portraits on the shore

90. post signs indicating relevant battlefields

91. expose the most casual technology in the world to the logic of its various fictional aftermaths

92. make the faithful look at us

93. weep new syllables

—Joe Wenderoth

Acknowledgments

Foremost among those to be acknowledged are the writers whose essays appear in here, each of whom was generous with his or her fee requests. Also among the acknowledged are the publishing companies that own the essays here, each of which cooperated with speed and fairness and even a little cheer. Acknowledged, too, is Fred Courtright of the Permissions Company, who offered free advice, and the people of Graywolf Press, who have faith in this little genre, and all my former students, who showed the essay some love. And finally to be acknowledged is you, you who are reading this sometime in the future—very near or very far—with thanks for keeping the essay alive.

"Captivity" reprinted from *First Indian on the Moon* copyright 1993 by Sherman Alexie, by permission of Hanging Loose Press.

"The Theory and Practice of Postmodernism: A Manifesto" by David Antin was previously published in *Conjunctions*. Reprinted by permission of the author.

"The Body" by Jenny Boully was previously published in *Seneca Review*. Reprinted by permission of the author.

"Kinds of Water" from *Plainwater* by Anne Carson, copyright 1995 by Anne Carson. Used by permission of Alfred A. Knopf, a division of Random House, Inc.

"Erato   Love Poetry" by Theresa Hak Kyung Cha. Scanned and reprinted by permission of the Regents of the University of California and the University of California, Berkeley Art Museum.

"And" by Guy Davenport, from *A Table of Green Fields,* copyright 1993 by Guy Davenport. Reprinted by permission of New Directions Publishing Corp.

"Foucault and Pencil" from *Almost No Memory* by Lydia Davis. Copyright 1997 by Lydia Davis. Reprinted by permission of Farrar, Straus & Giroux, LLC.

"The White Album" reprinted from *The White Album* by Joan Didion. Copyright 1979 by Joan Didion. Reprinted by permission of Farrar, Straus & Giroux, LLC.

"Total Eclipse" from *Teaching a Stone to Talk: Expeditions and Encounters* by Annie Dillard, copyright 1982 by Annie Dillard. Reprinted by permission of Harper-Collins Publishers Inc.

"A ∴ I" by Thalia Field, from *Point and Line,* copyright 2000 by Thalia Field. Reprinted by permission of New Directions Publishing Corp.

"Delft" from *Great Topics of the World.* Reprinted by permission of David R. Godine, Publisher, Inc. Copyright 1994 by Albert Goldbarth.

"Red Shoes" from *The Eros of Everyday Life* by Susan Griffin, copyright 1995 by Susan Griffin. Used by permission of Doubleday, a division of Random House, Inc.

"Girl" from *At the Bottom of the River* by Jamaica Kincaid. Copyright 1983 by Jamaica Kincaid. Reprinted by permission of Farrar, Straus & Giroux, LLC.

"Darling's Prick" from *Cleavage: Essays on Sex, Stars & Aesthetics* by Wayne Koestenbaum, copyright 2000 by Wayne Koestenbaum. Used by permission of Ballantine Books, a division of Random House, Inc.

"Sleep" copyright 2002 by Brian Lennon. Reprinted from *City: An Essay* with the permission of the University of Georgia Press, Athens, Georgia.

"The Raven" reprinted from *Desert Notes* by permission of Sterling Lord Literistic, Inc. Copyright 1976 by Barry Holstun Lopez.

"The Intercession of the Saints" by Carole Maso was previously published in *Conjunctions.* Reprinted by permission of the author.

"Country Cooking from Central France: Roast Boned Stuffed Shoulder of Lamb *(Farce Double)*" by Harry Mathews reprinted from *The Way Home* (Atlas Press: London) with the permission of the author.

"The Search for Marvin Gardens" from *Pieces of the Frame* by John McPhee. Copyright 1975 by John McPhee. Reprinted by permission of Farrar, Straus & Giroux, LLC.

". . . and nobody objected" copyright 1997 by Paul Metcalf. Reprinted from *Collected Works: Volume Three, 1987–1997* with the permission of Coffee House Press, Minneapolis, Minnesota.

"Notes Toward a History of Scaffolding" by Susan Mitchell was previously published in *Provincetown Arts.* Reprinted by permission of the author.

"Oil" by Fabio Morabito reprinted from *The Toolbox* with the permission of Bloomsbury Publishing. Translated by Geoff Hargreaves.

"Monument" by Mary Ruefle was previously published in *Seneca Review*. Reprinted by permission of the author.

"Life Story" by David Shields reprinted from *Remote* with the permission of the author.

"The Marionette Theater" by David Silk reprinted from *William the Wonder-Kid* with the permission of Sheep Meadow Press.

"Unguided Tour" copyright 1978 by Susan Sontag. Originally published in *I, Etcetera*. Reprinted with the permission of The Wylie Agency.

"Black" by Alexander Theroux was previously published in *Conjunctions*. Reprinted by permission of the author.

"Needs" by George Trow, copyright by George Trow. Originally published in *The New Yorker*. Reprinted by permission of the author.

"Ticket to the Fair" reprinted from *A Supposedly Fun Thing I'll Never Do Again* by David Foster Wallace. Copyright 1997 by David Foster Wallace. By permission of Little, Brown and Company, Inc.

"The Dream of India" by Eliot Weinberger, from *Works on Paper*, copyright 1980, 1981, 1982, 1983, 1984, 1985, 1986 by Eliot Weinberger. Reprinted by permission of New Directions Publishing Corp.

"Things To Do Today" by Joe Wenderoth was previously published in *Seneca Review*. Reprinted from *It Is If I Speak* with the permission of Wesleyan University Press.

"May Morning" from *Above the River: The Complete Poems* by James Wright. Copyright 1990 by Anne Wright.

A Note About the Title

By "Next" is meant those essays that will be inspired by these. By "American," of course, I mean not the nation. And by "Essay," I mean a verb.

A Note About the Editor

John D'Agata is the author of *Halls of Fame*.

A Note About the Typography

The text of these essays has been set in Adobe Garamond, a typeface drawn by Robert Slimbach and based on type cut by Claude Garamond in the sixteenth century.

Book design by Wendy Holdman.
Typesetting by Stanton Publication Services, Inc., St. Paul, Minnesota.
Manufactured by Friesens on acid-free paper.

Graywolf Press is a not-for-profit, independent press. The books we publish include poetry, literary fiction, essays, and cultural criticism. We are less interested in best-sellers than in talented writers who display a freshness of voice coupled with a distinct vision. We believe these are the very qualities essential to shape a vital and diverse culture.

Thankfully, many of our readers feel the same way. They have shown this through their desire to buy books by Graywolf writers; they have told us this themselves through their e-mail notes and at author events; and they have reinforced their commitment by contributing financial support, in small amounts and in large amounts, and joining the "Friends of Graywolf."

If you enjoyed this book and wish to learn more about Graywolf Press, we invite you to ask your bookseller or librarian about further Graywolf titles; or to contact us for a free catalog; or to visit our award-winning web site that features information about our forthcoming books.

We would also like to invite you to consider joining the hundreds of individuals who are already "Friends of Graywolf" by contributing to our membership program. Individual donations of any size are significant to us: they tell us that you believe that the kind of publishing we do *matters*. Our web site gives you many more details about the benefits you will enjoy as a "Friend of Graywolf"; but if you do not have online access, we urge you to contact us for a copy of our membership brochure.

www.graywolfpress.org

Graywolf Press
2402 University Avenue, Suite 203
Saint Paul, MN 55114
Phone: (651) 641-0077
Fax: (651) 641-0036
E-mail: wolves@graywolfpress.org